JUSTICE

DICKENSON TITLES OF RELATED INTEREST

Problems of Moral Philosophy: An Introduction, Second Edition
edited by Paul W. Taylor

Reason and Responsibility: Readings in Some Basic Problems of Philosophy, Third Edition
edited by Joel Feinberg

Philosophy of Law
edited by Joel Feinberg and Hyman Gross

The Logic of Grammar
edited by Donald Davidson and Gilbert H. Harman

Philosophical Problems of Causation
edited by Tom L. Beauchamp

Individual Conduct and Social Norms
by Rolf Sartorius

Freedom and Authority: An Introduction to Social and Political Philosophy
edited by Thomas Schwartz

Principles of Ethics: An Introduction
by Paul W. Taylor

Man in Conflict: Traditions in Social and Political Thought
by Louis I. Katzner

Metaphysics: An Introduction
by Keith Campbell

Understanding Moral Philosophy
edited by James Rachels

Morality in the Modern World
edited by Lawrence Habermehl

A Preface to Philosophy
by Mark Woodhouse

A Guide Through the Theory of Knowledge
by Adam Morton

Moral Philosophy: Classic Texts and Contemporary Problems
edited by Joel Feinberg and Henry West

Contemporary Issues in Bioethics
edited by Tom L. Beauchamp and LeRoy Walters

JUSTICE

SELECTED READINGS

edited by
Joel Feinberg
and
Hyman Gross

DICKENSON PUBLISHING COMPANY, INC., ENCINO, CALIFORNIA,
AND BELMONT, CALIFORNIA

ISBN: 0-8221-0201-3
Library of Congress Catalog Card Number: 76–52736

Printed in the United States of America
Printing (last digit): 9 8 7 6 5 4 3 2 1

Cover by Jill Casty

CONTENTS

THE DICKENSON SERIES IN PHILOSOPHY

Philosophy, said Aristotle, begins in wonder—wonder at the phenomenon of self-awareness, wonder at the infinitude of time, wonder that there should be anything at all. Wonder in turn gives rise to a kind of natural puzzlement: How can mind and body interact? How is it possible that there can be free will in a world governed by natural laws? How can moral judgments be shown to be true?

Philosophical perplexity about such things is a familiar and unavoidable phenomenon. College students who have experienced it and taken it seriously are, in a way, philosophers already, well before they come in contact with the theories and arguments of specialists. The good philosophy teacher, therefore, will not present his subject as some esoteric discipline unrelated to ordinary interests. Instead he will appeal directly to the concerns that already agitate the student, the same concerns that agitated Socrates and his companions and serious thinkers ever since.

It is impossible to be a good teacher of philosophy, however, without being a genuine philosopher oneself. Authors in the Dickenson Series in Philosophy are no exceptions to this rule. In many cases their textbooks are original studies of problems and systems of philosophy, with their own views boldly expressed and defended with argument. Their books are at once contributions to philosophy itself and models of original thinking to emulate and criticize.

That equally competent philosophers often disagree with one another is a fact to be exploited, not concealed. Dickenson anthologies bring together essays by authors of widely differing outlook. This diversity is compounded by juxtaposition, wherever possible, of classical essays with leading contemporary materials. The student who is shopping for a world outlook of his own has a large and representative selection to choose among, and the chronological arrangements, as well as the editor's introduction, can often give him a sense of historical development. Some Dickenson anthologies treat a single group of interconnected problems. Others are broader, dealing with a whole branch of philosophy, or representative problems from various branches of philosophy. In both types of collections, essays with opposed views on precisely the same questions are included to illustrate the argumentative give and take which is the lifeblood of philosophy.

Joel Feinberg
Series Editor

PREFACE

The appearance early in 1975 of our book, *Philosophy of Law,* prompted the suggestion from many quarters that each part be published separately in paperback form for readers with a more limited range of interests. In this volume we act once again on the suggestion, and add to the selections on justice which appear in that volume further essays and cases which show more fully the many faces of justice in our legal system. We have included work that presents and eases important difficulties in the very concept of justice. At the same time we have endeavored through other selections to present leading issues of injustice and public policy that are urgent social problems to be addressed by lawyers and philosophers.

Joel Feinberg
Hyman Gross

J U S T I C E

INTRODUCTION

One of the very oldest conceptions of justice, which must be close to the original seed of the modern concept, derives from pre-Socratic Greek cosmology and its picture of a morally ordered universe in which everything has its assigned place, or natural role. Justice *(dike)* consisted of everything staying in that assigned place, and not usurping the place of another thereby throwing the whole system out of kilter. Elements of this early notion survive in Plato's theory of justice as a virtue both of men and of states. Social justice, according to Plato, exists when every man performs the function for which he is best fitted by nature (his own proper business) and does not infringe upon the natural role of another. A corollary of this principle is that the rulers of the state should be those best fitted by their natures to rule; hence democracy, or rule by everybody, is inherently unjust.

The reason why men live in political communities in the first place, Plato argues in *The Republic,* is that no mere individual is self-sufficient. For all of us to satisfy our needs, we must divide up our labors, with each person performing the task for which he is best fitted by his natural aptitudes. Instead of every man being his own carpenter, toolmaker, farmer, tailor, soldier, and policeman, each man can work at the one thing he does best, while enjoying the benefits of the full-time labors of other specialists. The principle of cooperation by means of the specialization of labor explains what social organization is *for,* and why it should exist. There is justice in a society when everyone does his proper work: when square pegs are in square holes; when no talent is wasted or misused; when those who are naturally fit to rule do rule, and those who are naturally fit to obey, do obey. The sole criterion, then, for justice in assigning positions in society is *fitness for a function.* This in turn is best promoted, according to Plato, by fair educational and testing procedures that give each child, regardless of his race, or sex, or the social rank of his parents, an equal opportunity to rise to his appropriate slot in the social hierarchy.

EQUAL TREATMENT

Aristotle, in the famous discussion of the virtue of justice which leads off this section, shares Plato's view that only the best should rule and Plato's disdain for perfect equality in the distribution of political burdens and benefits. His analysis of justice, however, is more subtle and more faithful to complexities in the concept's multifaceted employment. He acknowledges at the start that the word for justice is ambiguous, referring both to the whole of social virtue ("virtue in relation to our neighbor") and to one specific type of social virtue. The wider or generic concept Aristotle calls "universal justice"; the narrower he calls "particular justice." Unlike Plato in the *Republic,* Aristotle's chief concern is with the particular virtue that is only a part, not the whole, of social virtue. He does say of universal justice, however, that it coincides with conformity to *law.* What he apparently means by this is that the positive law of the state *should* aim at the enforcement of the social virtues (including not only "particular justice" but also benevolence, charity, fidelity, and so on), and that insofar as a given legal code does support social virtue, violation of "universal justice" will at the same time be violation of positive law.

Particular justice, as Aristotle understands it, is the same as *fairness.* The Greek word for fairness in Aristotle's time also meant *equality.* Thus, Aristotle's initial contention is that there are two concepts of justice: lawfulness and equality. Particular justice (fairness), he tells us, is of two kinds: *distributive and rectificatory justice.* His conviction that most fair distributions are unequal, held at a time when "just" meant or strongly suggested "equal," drove him (as Gregory Vlastos has put it) to "linguistic acrobatics." [1] Distributive justice, he argued ingeniously, does not consist in absolute equality (that is, perfectly equal shares for all those among whom something is to be distributed) but rather a proportionate equality, which is to say an equality of ratios. What justice requires, he insists, is that equal cases be treated alike (equally), and that unequal cases be treated unalike (unequally) in direct proportion to the differences (inequalities) between them, so that between any two persons the ratio between their shares ($S_1 : S_2$) should equal the ratio between their qualifying characteristics ($C_1 : C_2$).

Aristotle concedes that people disagree over which characteristics of persons should be taken into account in assessing their equality or the degree of their inequality, but all parties to these disagreements (except extreme democrats who insist upon absolute equality) employ tacitly the notion of proportionate equality. However "merit" is conceived, for example, those for whom it would be the sole criterion in awarding shares would give one person twice as large a share of some benefit as they would to any other person deemed only half as meritorious. The common object of these distributors, even when they disagree over what merit is, will be to divide shares into a ratio (2 : 1) equal to the ratio of the merits of the two persons (2 : 1). Such distributions are sometimes necessarily impressionistic (how can one person's value be seen to be exactly one half another's?), but when the criterion of merit is exactly definable, and the shares themselves can be measured in terms of money, the calculations can sometimes achieve a mathematical precision. Aristotle sometimes seems to have in mind, for example, "the distribution of profits between partners in proportion to what each has put into the business." [2] Such contributions ("merits" in an extended, but properly Aristotelian, sense) as capital, time, and labor are readily measurable.

Since any two persons will be unequal in some respects and equal in others, Aristotle's theory of distributive justice is incomplete until he tells us which personal characteristics are *relevant* factors to be considered in the balancing of ratios. Various criteria of relevance have been proposed by writers of different schools. Some have held that A's share should be to B's share as A's ability is to B's ability, or as A's moral virtue is to B's, or as A's labor is to B's, and so on. All the above maxims could be said to specify different forms of "merit," so that a *meritarian* theorist would be one who held that the only personal characteristics relevant to a just distribution of goods are such forms of personal "merit." Aristotle was undoubtedly a meritarian in this broad sense. Meritarian social philosophers then can disagree among themselves over which forms of merit are relevant and over criteria for assessing a given form of merit, or they might hold that some forms of merit are relevant to some types of distribution, and other merits to other types. A nonmeritarian theory would be one which found exclusive relevance in personal characteristics (for example, needs) that are in no sense "merits," and of course mixed theories too are possible. Even a "democratic" or "equalitarian" theory, one which is wholly nonmeritarian, might plausibly be said to employ tacitly Aristotle's *analysis* of distributive justice as proportionate equality, while rejecting of course Aristotle's suggested criteria of relevance. Even a perfect equalitarian presumably would wish to endorse such maxims as: A's share should be to B's share as A's needs are to B's needs, or as A's "infinite human worth" is to B's "infinite human worth" (that is, the same). It seems likely, therefore, that all complete theories of social justice must contain maxims specifying relevant characteristics, and that all of them presuppose Aristotle's formal analysis of distributive justice as proportionate equality between shares and relevant characteristics.

Distributive justice applies to statesmen distributing honors, rewards, public property (as, for example, land in a new Athenian or Macedonian colony), public assistance to the needy, or to divisions of corporate profits or inheritances. Aristotle does not discuss the distribution of burdens such as taxation and military service, but his principle of proportionate equality presumably applies to them too. The second kind of particular justice, *rectificatory justice,* applies to private transactions or business deals in which some unfair advantage or undeserved harm has occurred and one party sues for a "remedy." (Aristotle's phrase for rectificatory justice is sometimes translated as "remedial," as well as "corrective" or "compensatory" justice). A judge then must assess the damages and order one party to make a payment to the other. These cases, Aristotle says, are of two kinds. In one type the harm to the plaintiff results from a transaction in which he voluntarily participated: buying, selling, loaning, pledging, depositing, hiring out, and the like. The law governing these cases corresponds roughly to our law of contracts. In the other type of case, the harm to the plaintiff results from a "transaction" in which he involuntarily participates as a victim from the start: fraud, theft, adultery, assault, imprisonment, or homicide. The law governing these cases, when the aim is to correct an unfairness by compensating a victim for his loss or injury, corresponds roughly to our law of torts.

Rectificatory justice, too, essentially involves the notion of equality. Its aim, Aristotle says, is to redress the "inequality" that results when one person profits unfairly at the expense of another. If A steals one hundred dollars from B, for example, he becomes one hundred dollars better off, an amount that is exactly equal to the amount by which B becomes worse off. The "equality" between A and B was their starting position before the "transaction," and that equality is restored by an order that requires A to pay to B exactly one hundred dollars. It is well to notice that rectificatory justice, as Aristotle understands it, does not apply to the criminal law at all. If there is a justice in punishing A for his peculation beyond the penalty that merely restores the *status quo ante,* that must be justice of a different kind. Retributive justice, as such, does not receive a thorough discussion in Aristotle, and does not even receive a separate rubric in his classification of the types of justice.

Neither does Aristotle's analysis of rectificatory justice appear to be an adequate guide through the complexities of the law of torts. More than the restoration of equality by a simple arithmetical formula, at any rate, is involved in all but the simplest cases in deliberations aiming at the determination of compensatory damages. Suppose A's wrongful act makes him $500 better off and B (the plaintiff) $200 worse off? What if A's malevolence or spitefulness toward B is so great that he is willing to undergo a loss for himself in order to inflict one on B? Suppose, in that example, that A's malicious act costs himself $500 and inflicts only a $100 loss on B. Or suppose, what is admittedly somewhat fanciful, that A's wrongful act actually creates a $100 windfall for wholly innocent B while earning himself $1,000. It will tax the student reader's ingenuity (in itself a good thing) to apply Aristotle's simple formulas for "arithmetical progression" to these hypothetical cases.

Some parts of Aristotle's discussion are primarily of antiquarian interest. His sketchy account in Chapter 5, for example, of "Justice in Exchange" is one of the earliest discussions on record of economic justice. Several other sections of his treatment of justice are important both for their intrinsic interest and their historical influence. Chapter 7 on "Natural and Legal Justice," for instance, is a classical source for the long and still vital tradition of natural law, and the theory of Equity in Chapter 10 (to be discussed below) has had a direct effect on the development of legal institutions that is still felt. In addition to the distinctions between natural and legal justice and between equity and law, there is still another important distinction that Aristotle was the first to treat with great subtlety: that between the just or unjust *quality* of an act and the just or unjust *effect* of an act on others. Injustice is always a violation of someone's rights or deserts, but such an effect can be brought about involuntarily, in which case the action that produced it cannot be unjust in itself, for normally to ascribe an unjust act to a person is to blame him, and involuntary acts are not blameworthy. Moreover, there are occasions, unhappily, in which a person can be fully justified in voluntarily producing an unjust effect on another: when that effect, for example, is the least evil result the actor could produce in the circumstances. *A* may be justified in violating *B*'s rights instead of *C*'s and *D*'s when there is no third alternative open to him, but that justification does not cancel the injustice done to *B*. In that case, we can say that *B* was unjustly *treated* although *A*'s act resulting in that effect was not an instance of unjust *behavior*. For an act to have an unjust quality (whatever its effects) it must be, objectively speaking, the wrong thing to do in the circumstances, unexcused and unjustified, voluntarily undertaken, and deliberately chosen by an unrushed actor who is well aware of the alternatives open to him. Other parties can be injured by unforeseeable accidents (mere mishaps), foreseeable accidents (blunders), by voluntary acts done in a fit of anger *(akrasia),* or by deliberate choice. Only in the last case is there unjust behavior, although there is blameworthiness of other kinds (negligence and hot-tempered impetuousness) in blunders and in angry violence, too.

Equity, Aristotle tells us in Chapter 10, is "a correction of law where it is defective owing to its universality." Richard A. Wasserstrom, in the second essay in this section, criticizes Aristotle's view that the character of law as "universal" *necessarily* leads to injustices in some individual cases. It is always possible in theory, Wasserstrom argues, to reformulate universal laws so that they contain exceptive clauses excluding hardship cases from the scope of their application. In practice, however, this might lead to an unworkable proliferation of very precise rules, each applying to very few cases. Aristotle's account of equity then is an overstatement, but one which suggests to Wasserstrom some important theses about the role of general rules in a just legal system. Wasserstrom's essay is a chapter drawn from his important book, *The Judicial Decision.* His primary concern in that chapter is to evaluate the group of theories about proper courtroom decision procedures which hold that cases can and should be decided "by direct appeal to justice or equity rather than by legal rules," and that the best decision, in some if not all kinds of cases, is the one based on unique features of the particular case before the court. In his vindication of the function of rules, Wasserstrom criticizes not only Aristotle, but also Jerome Frank, for whom rules have little relevance to just decision-making, and Roscoe Pound, who restricts their relevance to a relatively narrow class of cases. (The reader should notice that Wasserstrom, in the chapter included here, like Aristotle, seems to have "controversies between litigants" in civil cases, and not criminal trials, primarily in mind).

The essay by the distinguished contemporary moral philosopher, William K. Frankena, is mainly about distributive justice. Like most other writers, Frankena begins by accepting Aristotle's formal principle of justice, that relevantly similar cases should be treated similarly, but Frankena devotes more attention than Aristotle did to the selection of a material principle of distribution. He agrees with Aristotle that the essence of distributive injustice is arbitrary discrimination between relevantly similar cases, but disagrees over which characteristics are relevantly similar and which discriminations are arbitrary, aligning himself with Aristotle's old adversaries, the equalitarian democrats. The "foundational principle of social justice," Frankena concludes, is that the benefits and burdens of social life should be distributed not with the primary aim of rewarding "merit," but rather to ensure that "everyone has an equal chance of achieving the best life he is capable of." Frankena's recommendations have a direct bearing on the philosophy of law, constituting an ultimate criterion for assessing the justice of laws that affect distributions.

NONCOMPARATIVE JUSTICE

Justice as the equal treatment of relevantly similar cases is indeed the concept whose application is at issue in some of our more difficult public controversies, from proposed tax exemptions and school financing schemes to proposals for rectifying racial and sexual discrimination. As Joel Feinberg points out, however, not all applications of the concept of justice require comparisons of various individuals or groups. When we make critical judgments, assign grades, or impose punishments, for example, justice requires not merely that we treat different persons equally (if that at all), but rather that we compare "each in turn with an objective standard and judge each (as we say) 'on his merits.' " The sorts of fair treatment that do not in the very nature of the case require that we compare people with one another are governed by standards of what Feinberg calls "noncomparative justice." The particular species of the noncomparative genus that he finds most interesting (and neglected by other writers) he calls "the justice of judgments," a notion expressed in everyday discourse when it is said that one person's opinion about another doesn't "do him justice," or "is not fair to him." Feinberg attempts a detailed analysis of judgmental injustice, and in his final section relates that analysis to problems in the law of defamation.

JUSTICE AND SOCIAL UTILITY

Some of the most important contributions to the theory of justice, especially in Great Britain, have been made by writers in the utilitarian moral tradition. In the eighteenth century, David Hume argued that all rules of justice (thinking primarily of rules pertaining to contracts and property) "owe their origin and existence to that utility which results to the public from their strict and regular observance." [3] Hume admitted that there may sometimes be negative social utility in a particular observance of a rule of justice. For example, restoring a fortune to a miser or a seditious bigot is just, but socially harmful. "But however single acts of justice may be contrary either to public or private interest, 'tis certain that the *whole plan or scheme* is highly conducive, or indeed absolutely requisite to the support of society and the wellbeing of every individual." [4] Hume, in short, is a rule-utilitarian, not an act-utilitarian.

There is some doubt whether John Stuart Mill, the next essayist presented, would make conductibility to the common good the standard of right conduct applying directly to *single acts,* or make it the standard of *good rules* applying to the products of the legislature's work or to the determination of the sound rules of natural morality. The balance of reasons, however, as J. O. Urmson has shown convincingly,[5] favors the interpretation of Mill as a rule-utilitarian whose view is a further elaboration of Hume's. Mill's theory is interesting primarily for the way it accounts for the "distinguishing character of justice" and the way he *argues* that justice is derived from utility rather than being an underivative independent principle in its own right.

What distinguishes injustice from other types of wrongdoing, according to Mill, is that injustice must always be injustice *to* someone or other, the violation of the rights or deserts of some "assignable" person who is thereby entitled to feel aggrieved and righteously indignant on his own behalf. Duties of justice, therefore, are only one subclass of moral duties generally. If I fail to discharge my moral obligation to be generous, or beneficent, I do wrong, but there is no determinate person who can complain of being personally wronged by my omission, for "no one has a moral right to our generosity or beneficence." But it is clearly otherwise when I renege on a promise, a vow, or a loan; when as an authority, I treat my friends or relations more leniently or generously than others; when as a teacher, I give a low grade to an excellent student who deserves better; when as a legislator, I help create a statute that arbitrarily discriminates against a whole class of persons; or when as policeman or judge, I enforce the law irregularly or unequally among those to whom it explicitly applies. In all these cases, valid moral claims have been ignored or rejected, and the claimants have at least "a right to complain," and at most, a right to rectification, restitution, or even retribution.

That the standard of justice is independent of social utility is usually supported by an attempt to show that social utility as an ultimate moral principle would in some circumstances justify acts, rules, or practices that are patently unjust. Mill does very little to defend utilitarianism against this charge, which has been debated so thoroughly by twentieth century philosophers. Instead, he takes the offensive as a utilitarian, attacking what he calls "the alternative view of justice as independent of utility, a standard *per se,* which the mind can recognize by simple introspection of itself." The argument is simple enough. If there is an autonomous sense of justice limiting the dictates of utility and guiding us to the right moral decision where utility would lead us astray, how are we to understand "why the internal oracle is so ambiguous?" When people leave off calculating utilities to voice instead their sense of justice, there is nothing but controversy, with no rational resolution of differences possible. "In fact, justice is not some one rule, principle or maxim, but many, which do not always coincide in their dictates, and in choosing between which, one is guided either by some extraneous standard [such as social utility] or by his own personal predilections."

Mill then provides numerous persuasive examples of the conflict between plausible maxims of justice that apply to controversies over punishment, distribution of wealth, and taxation. In each instance justice seems to have "two sides to it." Mill turns from these controversies in bewilderment, concluding that each of the opposed maxims "from its own point of view is unanswerable, and any choice between them on grounds of justice must be perfectly arbitrary. Social utility alone can decide the preference."

Mill's argument is hardly decisive. A defender of "the alternative theory of justice" might well reply: The contention that justice is a principle independent of, and sometimes in conflict with, utility does not imply that the dictates of justice are always perfectly clear and unambiguous, or that there is even one supreme principle of justice harmonizing all the conflicting maxims. That the method of determining justice is distinct from the method of calculating social utility does not imply that one is simple and the other difficult, or even that one has necessary priority over the other. It means simply what it says: that the one is distinct from, and irreducible to, the other.

Moreover, Mill's opponent might argue, the method of utility involves just as many complexities and difficulties as the method of justice. One might even speak of distinct and rival "maxims" of utility. What promotes the greatest good may help the smallest number and what helps the largest number may promote the smallest net good. What creates the most happiness may entail the most blissful ignorance as by-product, and what promotes knowledge may increase despair; and yet both happiness and knowledge are presumably components of "utility." And which should the utilitarian choose when he must choose between irreconcilable goods of separate groups or separate individuals, or when a net gain in pleasure and knowledge is balanced against a net loss in virtue and equality, or when intense pleasure of short duration is the alternative to mild pleasure of long duration? This *tu quoque,* while also undecisive, has considerable punch.

JUSTICE AND FAIRNESS

Philosophers often distinguish between the fairness or unfairness of procedures and the justice or injustice of outcomes. Sometimes the labels "procedural" and "substantive" justice are used to mark the distinction, and the student should be wary of confusing these technical terms with the phrases "formal" and "material" which are used to mark the quite different distinction between the "formal" requirement that similar cases be treated similarly, and "material" interpretations of that requirement that provide criteria for the relevance of differences. (To compound the terminological confusion, Brian Barry uses the term "equity," which as we have seen already has the Aristotelian sense of "modification of general rules to meet special situations," [6] to refer to the basic "formal" requirement that rules should treat like cases alike).

The selection from Barry presupposes the discussion in an earlier part of his important book, *Political Argument,* in which he classifies the various contexts in which the notions of fair procedure and just outcome have application. These contexts all involve the employment of techniques for settling conflicts of wants or opinions. Barry calls these "social decision procedures," and lists the following seven types:

1. *Combat.* The issue is settled directly by force.
2. *Discussion on Merits.* The parties argue the rights and wrongs of the conflict and seek agreement by appealing to jointly accepted standards, ideals, or rules.
3. *Bargaining.* "One party offers another either some advantage or the removal of the threat of disadvantage in return for the other party's performing some specific action." [7] The rights and wrongs of the conflict, or the merits of the opposed positions, are not considered.
4. *Voting* (where more than two parties are involved).
5. *Chance* (for example, by flipping a coin or drawing straws).
6. *Contest* (for example, foot races, boxing matches) for settling the question of which contestant is "best at" some activity requiring skill.
7. *Authoritative Determination.* The issue is settled by the judgment of a party (or parties) whose authority to do so, under the governing rules, is recognized by the disputants, for example, an administrative tribunal, a judge or jury, a labor arbitrator.

A decision procedure (excepting combat, a special case) may itself be fair or unfair, and even a fair procedure may be applied fairly or unfairly in a given case. Taking each type of procedure in turn, Barry tells us what fair application consists in, and what further is required as "background fairness." In the case of authoritative determination, the application of a specified procedure can be appraised as fair or unfair in a distinctively legalistic way (Barry calls this "legal justice"), namely, by determining whether rules requiring certain decisions in cases of a specified kind have been adhered to.

Barry then asks why procedural fairness should be valued as an important thing. He advances both utilitarian and equalitarian considerations (he calls these "aggregative" and "distributive," respectively) for taking "legal justice" seriously. Similarly, in respect to procedural and background fairness, he finds their justifications in their conduciveness to "some more general consideration," namely, their tendency to produce just results. Thus Barry concludes that "the value of [procedural] fairness is subordinate to that of justice," and finds in the opposite view an element of irrational "rule worship."

John Rawls also attaches importance to the distinction between justice (of results) and fairness (of procedures), but as his title, "Justice as Fairness" indicates, fairness is given a certain methodological priority. But that is not to say that Rawls is in serious disagreement with Barry. His essay (the germ of his monumental study, *A Theory of Justice*) is addressed to somewhat different questions. Rawls is almost exclusively concerned with the justice of political, social, and economic institutions, as opposed to the justice of individual actions, persons, or policies. "The primary subject of justice," he wrote in *A Theory of Justice,* "is the basic structure of society." [8] Those basic institutions are just, Rawls maintains, that accord with the principles of justice that would be adopted by reasonable and normally self-interested persons employing an ideally fair selection procedure. Rawls describes that procedure and derives from it two basic principles of justice. These principles, and the method of their derivation, constitute the major alternative to utilitarianism among recent general theories of justice.

Rawls places great weight upon a purported duty of fair play. It requires those who accept the benefits of a social practice to follow the rules when in turn the rules require something of them. In his widely regarded book *Anarchy, State and Utopia,* Robert Nozick challenges assumptions upon which Rawls' theory of justice rests, and among the most important of these challenges is his criticism of the asserted duty of fair play. In the first of the selections from his book presented here, Nozick first argues that not all obligations need be enforceable, and so even assuming that a principle of fairness creates an obligation to abide by rules that is binding on those who take the benefits that the rules make possible, that obligation may not be enforceable. This would mean that an obligation which was in principle a just obligation might be a source of injustice if enforced. Nozick then proceeds to question the principle of fairness itself, arguing that a person who accepted and enjoyed certain benefits might nevertheless not be obligated in turn to participate according to the rules.

DISTRIBUTIVE JUSTICE

Contemporary concerns about justice most often reflect dissatisfaction with the way the good things of life are distributed among members of society, as well as among the more and the less affluent societies that compose the community of nations in the modern world. The problem of global injustice has special complications of its own; but just distribution within a society of wealth and of opportunities to enjoy what self-interested people normally want is a matter of constant public concern. It is no wonder then that contemporary philosophers, such as Rawls and Nozick, who interest themselves in a comprehensive theory of just distribution should enjoy the widest possible audience and be thought to have done work of fundamental importance for sound public policy.

In the second excerpt from his book *Anarchy, State, and Utopia,* Professor Nozick presents a view of just distribution that is critical of the usual model. Instead of looking at the way things stand at any given time and asking whether such a distribution is just, we are urged by Nozick to consider the history of how things come to be as they are. If possession by those who have is a result of proper transactions of acquisition and transfer, the distribution among them is just, for they are entitled to what they have. Such a conception stands in sharp contrast to what Nozick calls "patterned" principles of distribution. When according to a scheme of distribution a person is to receive more because there is some reason for him to receive it, there are at work principles of distribution aiming at some pattern of distribution as its end. Under such a conception, distribution at any given time is unjust to the extent that it does not accord with the pattern. But liberty has a subversive effect on patterned distribution, says Nozick, and he illustrates this by means of his widely noted "Wilt Chamberlain" example. The point is captured in the author's memorable phrase when he observes that a socialist society "would have to forbid capitalist acts between consenting adults."

In the second half of the chapter from which this selection is taken, Nozick goes on to criticize Rawls' theory of distributive justice which is sharply at odds with his own. The essentials of Rawls' view are presented with much illumination by Professor T. M. Scanlon in the selection titled "Distributive Justice and the Difference Principle". In his book *A Theory of Justice* Rawls is concerned with a just distribution of burdens and benefits among members of society, or more exactly, with the operating principles whose effect in society is to determine this distribution. Only distributions that are the result of just principles are themselves just, and according to Rawls, social and economic inequalities are to be arranged so that at any given time they benefit most those who are least advantaged. This fundamental principle of distributive justice Rawls refers to as the Difference Principle. It requires, upon pain of being unjust, that society be so organized as to constantly redistribute to lessen relative disadvantage among its members, and with the organization maximizing the expectations of those who are worst off. Such a scheme of organization is for Rawls a *fair* one. But it would seem to be an objectionable interference with liberty for Nozick, since in spite of the fact that distribution at any given time is the outcome of property transactions that are deemed proper, the very fact that some members of society are in a position of disadvantage relative to others would put in question as in some measure unjust the position of relative advantage that those others enjoy. The more fundamental conflict between Nozick's and Rawls' conceptions of fairness which were contrasted earlier once again seems important at this point. Is it unfair to require in the interest of justice that there be redistribution to overcome the effects of inequalities which those who lose by redistribution are not responsible for, or are all members of society in fairness obliged to remedy the effects of inequalities? The reader will wish to consider especially the relative merits of a conception of just distribution that makes reference only to how things are distributed now, and the alternative conception that makes reference to how it came to be that things are distributed as they are.

RACIAL AND SEXUAL DISCRIMINATION

Invidiously discriminatory treatment in the distribution of benefits (including opportunities) and burdens is the essential feature of what Aristotle called "distributive injustice." In the United States grossly discriminatory rules and practices have only recently begun to crumble, and for the first time in centuries there is hope that the ideal of equal opportunity will one day be fulfilled. To expect the effects of racial and sexual discrimination to vanish overnight with the abrogation of ancient rules, however, would be exceedingly naive. Many reformers, in fact, have been urging that the elimination of discriminatory practices is not enough, and that a kind of "reverse discrimination," especially in the allocation of educational and professional opportunities for such groups as blacks and women, is required by social justice. Louis Katzner, in his penetrating article, subjects this claim to close philosophical analysis, and concludes with a statement of four conditions which must be satisfied if reverse discrimination is to be justified. It is an interesting apparent consequence of Katzner's view that, while reverse discrimination in favor of blacks might in some circumstances be justified, reverse discrimination in favor of (all) women would likely not pass Katzner's test.

Universities now practice reverse discrimination not only in their hiring practices but in their admissions policies as well. Though many of the same arguments are offered to justify favoring members of designated groups at both the student and faculty level, in defending race-conscious admissions greater stress is placed on long-term benefits that are expected to result when there is more extensive and better education for those groups that have been in a position of educational disadvantage in the past. The Constitutional principle of equal protection under the law for all citizens, which is the fountainhead of legal objection to discrimination, appeared as though it might exhibit an internal contradiction when tested by *DeFunis v. Odegaard.* In that case a white applicant to the University of Washington Law School had been rejected, although his college grades and test scores were such that he would have been admitted had he been black or a member of certain other specially designated ethnic groups. The Supreme Court of the state of Washington upheld his rejection. In the earlier case of *Sweatt v. Painter* the Supreme Court of the United States had dealt with the rejection of a black applicant to the University of Texas Law School pursuant to a state law that restricted admission to whites. The Court found this discrimination offensive to the equal protection guarantee of the Constitution. Almost 25 years later the Court had before it the appeal of DeFunis from the Washington Supreme Court decision, but the Court side-stepped the question since the school had previously admitted DeFunis after the decision of the trial court in his favor. However, in a dissenting opinion Justice Douglas argued that the Court should have addressed the merits and vindicated DeFunis' claim. In his essay *The DeFunis Case: The Right to Go to Law School,* Ronald Dworkin takes up the difficult issues that sharply divided thoughtful and morally sensitive lawyers no less than ordinary citizens. He examines the complex strands of argument on both sides and concludes that the admissions policy in question is justifiable under morally enlightened principles of equal protection. Further cases may be expected to confront the issues which are analyzed in this selection.

Arbitrary differences in the law's treatment of various defined classes of the population is firmly prohibited by the "equal protection" clause of the Fourteenth Amendment, and (indirectly) by the "due process" clause of the Fifth Amendment. More and more, women have been relying on these constitutional grounds to secure judicial overruling of statutes that discriminate against them. In *Reed v. Reed,* included in this section, the United States Supreme Court in a unanimous opinion written by Mr. Chief Justice Burger argues that while it is constitutionally permissible for legislation to distinguish among classes, this must be done in a "reasonable, not arbitrary" way, and "not on the basis of criteria wholly unrelated to the objective of the statute." The language becomes explicitly Aristotelian when the court declares all statutes to be unconstitutional which command "dissimilar treatment for men and women who are . . . similarly situated."

In *Frontiero v. Richardson,* a somewhat more complicated case, another statute which made sex the basis of differences in the assignment of legal rights and duties was overturned, this time on the ground that the Fifth Amendment forbids discrimination that is "so unjustifiable as to be violative of due process." The Court's opinion in *Frontiero* declares that sex is a "suspect classification," that is, one whose moral or constitutional relevance is "inherently suspect," and therefore properly "subjected to close judicial scrutiny." Sexual distinctions in the law, in other words, are *prima facie* unjust, and will be declared unconstitutional unless "close judicial scrutiny" uncovers some general causal connection between sex difference and other traits that clearly are relevant to some valid legislative purpose, (presumably) like the strengthening of national security or the protection of individual privacy. Careful notice should be given to four points about the principles applied in the *Reed* and *Frontiero* decisions.

1. Like the Aristotelian "formal principle" that relevantly like cases should be treated in like ways, the Equal Protection clause of the Fourteenth Amendment also needs supplementation by criteria of the relevance or nonarbitrariness of differences between classes of persons.

2. Sex *as such* is not a relevant or nonarbitrary difference. Thus, statutory classifications whose *whole basis* is "the sex of the individuals involved" are "inherently invidious," and proscribed by the Equal Protection clause.

3. The causal connection between sex difference and traits that *are* relevant must be *perfectly* general. It is not sufficient that *most* males have greater physical strength or greater business experience than *most* females. Only if these connections were exceptionless and necessary would a statute permit sex to be a ground, say, for job qualifications, for example combat duty in the armed forces or administration of a decedent's estate. Otherwise, as Mr. Justice Brennan put it in *Frontiero,* "statutory distinctions between the sexes [would] often have the effect of invidiously relegating the entire class of females to inferior legal status without regard to the actual capabilities of its individual members."

4. Valid legislative purposes to which discrimination between the sexes might be reasonably related do not include "mere administrative convenience," though administrative convenience in the conduct of a war, say, might be so related to national security as to justify sexual distinctions in the assignment of combat duty; and *another* constitutional protection, for example, that said to be provided by the Constitution to personal privacy, might justify sexual distinctions in the rules permitting use of public rest rooms.

Despite the trend represented by the *Reed* and *Frontiero* decisions, most feminists are not content to rest the moral claim to equality on the Fourteenth Amendment, and have advocated instead an Equal Rights Amendment to the United States Constitution specifying that "Equality of rights under the law shall not be denied or abridged by the United States or by any State on account of sex." The proposed amendment, which would have the effect of making sex a suspect classification in line with the *Frontiero* opinion, was quickly approved by the Congress, but by June, 1973, it had run into fierce resistance in many state legislatures. Seldom has a controversial public issue been so ensnared in philosophical subtleties! The new equality often would make sexual difference an invalid ground for different legal classifications, but would that necessarily lead to bisexual rest rooms, female combat troops, the invalidating of statutes creating sex crimes or of those specifying the amount of weight a woman could be required to lift on a job? Even if the answers to these and similar questions are affirmative, would that necessarily be a bad thing? Leading constitutional scholars have differed in their approaches to these partly philosophical problems, and at the time of printing, the fate of the Equal Rights Amendment is still in doubt. No current public issue better illustrates the common concerns of philosophers and lawmakers.

WHO SHALL LIVE AND WHO SHALL DIE

There are no more poignant problems of justice than those of determining who shall be killed when some must die if any in the group are to live, and determining who shall be rescued when not everyone in a group can be saved. From ancient times philosophers, lawyers, and theologians have wrestled with problems of these sorts raised by actual and hypothetical tales of drowning swimmers clutching at floating planks, overcrowded lifeboats, plagues and famines from which some but not all can be saved, soldiers sacrificed to save their comrades in arms, and desperate shipwrecked sailors or trapped cave explorers who can be saved from starvation only by a resort to cannibalism. Modern technology, especially medical technology, has increased rather than diminished the number of occasions for such "tragic choices." Thousands of sick persons, for example, can be saved only by an organ transplant or an artificial substitute for a human organ, but the supply of such exotic life-saving resources is far short of the demand.

Perhaps as many as thirty or forty thousand persons die of kidney failure in the United States each year. In the early 1960's artificial kidney machines were developed which, by "washing the blood" of a patient connected to one at regular intervals, could save his life and even permit him, within limits, to work and live a normal life during the periods when he is not attached to the machine. By 1964, however, fewer than three hundred persons in the country had access to these machines, and most of them were chosen from hundreds of applicants by hospital selection committees composed of doctors and community leaders applying their own standards of utility and/or justice. In 1973 Congress amended the Social Security Act to provide Medicare funds to persons under sixty-five who are in need of artificial dialysis. By 1976 Medicare was paying almost 80 percent of the cost for artificial dialysis, and individual states most of the rest. More than 16,000 people in the United States were receiving regular dialysis from complex machines at a cost of almost a half a billion dollars a year. All of these lives would otherwise have been lost.

Selection committees for renal dialysis machines, then, no longer exist, and the questions of justice they debated in the 1960's are now moot. But some of the articles written in the earlier period that were directed explicitly at the dialysis machine allocation problem are among the most astute yet produced about the moral dilemmas of the person who must decide who is to live and who is to die. Three of the best of these are included in this volume. The Note from the *Harvard Law Review* and the article by Paul Freund both advocate exclusive reliance on random lotteries and the principle (where applicable) of "first come, first serve," arguing that only randomness is consistent with the doctrine of the equality of human life. Nicholas Rescher, on the other hand, finds an irreducible diversity of kinds of reasons that can have relevance in life or death decisions. His essay suggests to hospital selection committees that they combine lotteries and various "social worth factors" in complex formulae for ranking candidates for survival.

NOTES

1. Gregory Vlastos, "Justice and Equality," in *Social Justice,* ed. Richard B. Brandt (Englewood Cliffs, N.J.: Prentice-Hall, Inc., 1962), p. 32.

2. W. D. Ross, *Aristotle* (London: Methuen & Co., 1949), p. 210.

3. David Hume, *An Enquiry Concerning the Principles of Morals* (LaSalle, Illinois: The Open Court Publishing Co., 1947), p. 20.

4. David Hume, *A Treatise of Human Nature* (Oxford: The Clarendon Press, 1888), p. 497.

5. J. O. Urmson, "The Moral Philosophy of J. S. Mill," *The Philosophical Quarterly,* Vol. 3 (1953), pp. 33–39.

6. Brian Barry, *Political Argument* (London: Routledge, Kegan Paul, 1965), p. 96.

7. *Ibid.,* p. 86.

8. John Rawls, *A Theory of Justice* (Cambridge, Mass.: Harvard University Press, 1971), p. 7.

ARISTOTLE

Justice*

JUSTICE: ITS SPHERE AND OUTER NATURE: IN WHAT SENSE IT IS A MEAN

THE JUST AS THE LAWFUL (UNIVERSAL JUSTICE) AND THE JUST AS THE FAIR AND EQUAL (PARTICULAR JUSTICE): THE FORMER CONSIDERED

1. With regard to justice and injustice we must consider (1) what kind of actions they are concerned with, (2) what sort of mean justice is, and (3) between what extremes the just act is intermediate. Our investigation shall follow the same course as the preceding discussions.

We see that all men mean by justice that kind of state of character which makes people disposed to do what is just and makes them act justly and wish for what is just; and similarly by injustice that state which makes them act unjustly and wish for what is unjust. Let us too, then, lay this down as a general basis. For the same is not true of the sciences and the faculties as of states of character. A faculty or a science which is one and the same is held to relate to contrary objects, but a state of character which is one of two contraries does *not* produce the contrary results; for example, as a result of health we do not do what is the opposite of healthy, but only what is healthy; for we say a man walks healthily, when he walks as a healthy man would.

Now often one contrary state is recognized from its contrary, and often states are recognized from the subjects that exhibit them; for (A) if good condition is known, bad condition also becomes known, and (B) good condition is known from the things that are in good condition, and they from it. If good condition is firmness of flesh, it is necessary both that bad condition should be flabbiness of flesh and that the wholesome should be that which causes firmness in flesh. And it follows for the most part that if one contrary is ambiguous the other also will be ambiguous; for example, that if 'just' is so, 'unjust' will be so too.

Now 'justice' and 'injustice' seem to be ambiguous, but because their different meanings approach near to one another the ambiguity escapes notice and is not obvious as it is, comparatively, when the meanings are far apart, for example, (for here the difference in outward form is great) as the ambiguity in the use of $\kappa\lambda\epsilon\iota\varsigma$ for the collarbone of an animal and for that with which we lock a door. Let us take as a starting-point, then, the various meanings of 'an unjust man'. Both the lawless man and the grasping and unfair man are thought to be unjust, so that evidently both the law-abiding and the fair man will be just. The just, then, is the lawful and the fair, the unjust the unlawful and the unfair.

Since the unjust man is grasping, he must be concerned with goods—not all goods, but those with which prosperity and adversity have to do, which taken absolutely are always good, but for a particular person are not always good. Now men pray for and pursue these things; but they should not, but should pray that the things that are good absolutely may also be good for them, and should choose the things that *are* good for them. The unjust man does not always choose the greater, but also the less—in the case of things bad absolutely; but because the lesser evil is itself thought to be in a sense good, and graspingness is directed at the good, therefore he is thought to be grasping. And he is unfair; for this contains and is common to both.

*Book V (complete) from *The Nicomachean Ethics,* translated by W. D. Ross, from *The Oxford Translation of Aristotle* edited by W. D. Ross, vol. 9 (1925). Reprinted by permission of The Clarendon Press, Oxford. Some footnotes have been deleted. The remainder have been renumbered.

Since the lawless man was seen to be unjust and the law-abiding man just, evidently all lawful acts are in a sense just acts; for the acts laid down by the legislative art are lawful, and each of these, we say, is just. Now the laws in their enactments on all subjects aim at the common advantage either of all or of the best or of those who hold power, or something of the sort; so that in one sense we call those acts just that tend to produce and preserve happiness and its components for the political society. And the law bids us do both the acts of a brave man (for example, not to desert our post nor take to flight nor throw away our arms), and those of a temperate man (for example, not to commit adultery nor to gratify one's lust), and those of a good-tempered man (for example, not to strike another nor to speak evil), and similarly with regard to the other virtues and forms of wickedness, commanding some acts and forbidding others; and the rightly-framed law does this rightly, and the hastily conceived one less well.

This form of justice, then, is complete virtue, but not absolutely, but in relation to our neighbour. And therefore justice is often thought to be the greatest of virtues, and 'neither evening nor morning star' is so wonderful; and proverbially 'in justice is every virtue comprehended'. And it is complete virtue in its fullest sense because it is the actual exercise of complete virtue. It is complete because he who possesses it can exercise his virtue not only in himself but towards his neighbour also; for many men can exercise virtue in their own affairs, but not in their relations to their neighbour. This is why the saying of Bias is thought to be true, that 'rule will show the man'; for a ruler is necessarily in relation to other men, and a member of a society. For this same reason justice, alone of the virtues, is thought to be 'another's good', because it is related to our neighbour; for it does what is advantageous to another, either a ruler or a co-partner. Now the worst man is he who exercises his wickedness both towards himself and towards his friends, and the best man is not he who exercises his virtue towards himself but he who exercises it towards another; for this is a difficult task. Justice in this sense, then, is not part of virtue but virtue entire, nor is the contrary injustice a part of vice but vice entire. What the difference is between virtue and justice in this sense is plain from what we have said; they are the same but their essence is not the same; what,

as a relation to one's neighbour, is justice is, as a certain kind of state without qualification, virtue.

THE JUST AS THE FAIR AND EQUAL: DIVIDED INTO DISTRIBUTIVE AND RECTIFICATORY JUSTICE

2. But at all events what we are investigating is the justice which is a *part* of virtue; for there is a justice of this kind, as we maintain. Similarly it is with injustice in the particular sense that we are concerned.

That there is such a thing is indicated by the fact that while the man who exhibits in action the other forms of wickedness acts wrongly indeed, but not graspingly (for example, the man who throws away his shield through cowardice or speaks harshly through bad temper or fails to help a friend with money through meanness), when a man acts graspingly he often exhibits none of these vices—no, nor all together, but certainly wickedness of some kind (for we blame him) and injustice. There is, then, another kind of injustice which is a part of injustice in the wide sense, and a use of the word 'unjust' which answers to a part of what is unjust in the wide sense of 'contrary to the law'. Again, if one man commits adultery for the sake of gain and makes money by it, while another does so at the bidding of appetite though he loses money and is penalized for it, the latter would be held to be self-indulgent rather than grasping, but the former is unjust, but not self-indulgent; evidently, therefore, he is unjust by reason of his making gain by his act. Again, all other unjust acts are ascribed invariably to some particular kind of wickedness, for example, adultery to self-indulgence, the desertion of a comrade in battle to cowardice, physical violence to anger; but if a man makes gain, his action is ascribed to no form of wickedness but injustice. Evidently, therefore, there is apart from injustice in the wide sense another, 'particular', injustice which shares the name and nature of the first, because its definition falls within the same genus; for the significance of both consists in a relation to one's neighbour, but the one is concerned with honour or money or safety—or that which includes all these, if we had a single name for it—and its motive is the pleasure that arises from gain; while the other is concerned with all the objects with which the good man is concerned.

It is clear, then, that there is more than one kind of justice, and that there is one which is distinct from virtue entire; we must try to grasp its genus and differentia.

The unjust has been divided into the unlawful and the unfair, and the just into the lawful and the fair. To the unlawful answers the aforementioned sense of injustice. But since the unfair and the unlawful are not the same, but are different as a part is from its whole (for all that is unfair is unlawful, but not all that is unlawful is unfair), the unjust and injustice in the sense of the unfair are not the same as but different from the former kind, as part from whole; for injustice in this sense is a part of injustice in the wide sense, and similarly justice in the one sense of justice in the other. Therefore we must speak also about particular justice and particular injustice, and similarly about the just and the unjust. The justice, then, which answers to the whole of virtue, and the corresponding injustice, one being the exercise of virtue as a whole, and the other that of vice as a whole, towards one's neighbour, we may leave on one side. And how the meanings of 'just' and 'unjust' which answer to these are to be distinguished is evident; for practically the majority of the acts commanded by the law are those which are prescribed from the point of view of virtue taken as a whole; for the law bids us practise every virtue and forbids us to practise any vice. And the things that tend to produce virtue taken as a whole are those of the acts prescribed by the law which have been prescribed with a view to education for the common good. But with regard to the education of the individual as such, which makes him without qualification a good *man*, we must determine later whether this is the function of the political art or of another; for perhaps it is not the same to be a good man and a good citizen of any state taken at random.

Of particular justice and that which is just in the corresponding sense, (A) one kind is that which is manifested in distributions of honour or money or the other things that fall to be divided among those who have a share in the constitution (for in these it is possible for one man to have a share either unequal or equal to that of another), and (B) one is that which plays a rectifying part in transactions between man and man. Of this there are two divisions; of transactions (1) some are voluntary and (2) others involuntary—voluntary such transactions as sale, purchase, loan for consumption, pledging, loan for use, depositing, letting (they are called voluntary because the *origin* of these transactions is voluntary), while of the involuntary (*a*) some are clandestine, such as theft, adultery, poisoning, procuring, enticement of slaves, assassination, false witness, and (*b*) others are violent, such as assault, imprisonment, murder, robbery with violence, mutilation, abuse, insult.

DISTRIBUTIVE JUSTICE, IN ACCORDANCE WITH GEOMETRICAL PROPORTION

3. (A) We have shown that both the unjust man and the unjust act are unfair or unequal; now it is clear that there is also an intermediate between the two unequals involved in either case. And this is the equal; for in any kind of action in which there is a more and a less there is also what is equal. If, then, the unjust is unequal, the just is equal, as all men suppose it to be, even apart from argument. And since the equal is intermediate, the just will be an intermediate. Now equality implies at least two things. The just, then, must be both intermediate and equal and relative (for example, for certain persons). And *qua* intermediate it must be between certain things (which are respectively greater and less); *qua* equal, it involves *two* things; *qua* just, it is for certain people. The just, therefore, involves at least four terms; for the persons for whom it is in fact just are two, and the things in which it is manifested, the objects distributed, are two. And the same equality will exist between the persons and between the things concerned; for as the latter—the things concerned—are related, so are the former; if they are not equal, they will not have what is equal, but this is the origin of quarrels and complaints—when either equals have and are awarded unequal shares, or unequals equal shares. Further, this is plain from the fact that awards should be 'according to merit'; for all men agree that what is just in distribution must be according to merit in some sense, though they do not all specify the same sort of merit, but democrats identify it with the status of freemen, supporters of oligarchy with wealth (or with noble birth), and supporters of aristocracy with excellence.

The just, then, is a species of the proportionate

(proportion being not a property only of the kind of number which consists of abstract units, but of number in general). For proportion is equality of ratios, and involves four terms at least (that discrete proportion involves four terms is plain, but so does continuous proportion, for it uses one term as two and mentions it twice; for example, 'as the line A is to the line B, so is the line B to the line C'; the line B, then, has been mentioned twice, so that if the line B be assumed twice, the proportional terms will be four); and the just, too, involves at least four terms, and the ratio between one pair is the same as that between the other pair; for there is a similar distinction between the persons and between the things. As the term A, then, is to B, so will C be to D, and therefore, *alternando,* as A is to C, B will be to D. Therefore also the whole is in the same ratio to the whole;[1] and this coupling the distribution effects, and, if the terms are so combined, effects justly. The conjunction, then, of the term A with C and of B with D is what is just in distribution,[2] and this species of the just is intermediate, and the unjust is what violates the proportion; for the proportional is intermediate, and the just is proportional. (Mathematicians call this kind of proportion geometrical; for it is in geometrical proportion that it follows that the whole is to the whole as either part is to the corresponding part.) This proportion is not continuous; for we cannot get a single term standing for a person and a thing.

This, then, is what the just is—the proportional; the unjust is what violates the proportion. Hence one term becomes too great, the other too small, as indeed happens in practice; for the man who acts unjustly has too much, and the man who is unjustly treated too little, of what is good. In the case of evil the reverse is true; for the lesser evil is reckoned a good in comparison with the greater evil, since the lesser evil is rather to be chosen than the greater, and what is worthy of choice is good, and what is worthier of choice a greater good.

This, then, is one species of the just.

RECTIFICATORY JUSTICE, IN ACCORDANCE WITH ARITHMETICAL PROGRESSION

4. (B) The remaining one is the rectificatory, which arises in connexion with transactions both voluntary and involuntary. This form of the just has a different specific character from the former. For the justice which distributes common possessions is always in accordance with the kind of proportion mentioned above (for in the case also in which the distribution is made from the common funds of a partnership it will be according to the same ratio which the funds put into the business by the partners bear to one another); and the injustice opposed to this kind of justice is that which violates the proportion. But the justice in transactions between man and man is a sort of equality indeed, and the injustice a sort of inequality; not according to that kind of proportion, however, but according to arithmetical proportion. For it makes no difference whether a good man has defrauded a bad man or a bad man a good one, nor whether it is a good or a bad man that has committed adultery; the law looks only to the distinctive character of the injury, and treats the parties as equal, if one is in the wrong and the other is being wronged, and if one inflicted injury and the other has received it. Therefore, this kind of injustice being an inequality, the judge tries to equalize it; for in the case also in which one has received and the other has inflicted a wound, or one has slain and the other been slain, the suffering and the action have been unequally distributed; but the judge tries to equalize things by means of the penalty, taking away from the gain of the assailant. For the term 'gain' is applied generally to such cases—even if it be not a term appropriate to certain cases, for example, to the person who inflicts a wound—and 'loss' to the sufferer; at all events when the suffering has been estimated, the one is called loss and the other gain. Therefore the equal is intermediate between the greater and the less, but the gain and the loss are respectively greater and less in contrary ways; more of the good and less of the evil are gain, and the contrary is loss; intermediate between them is, as we saw, the equal, which we say is just; therefore corrective justice will be the intermediate between loss and gain. This is why, when people dispute, they take refuge in the judge; and to go to the judge is to go to justice; for the nature of the judge is to be a sort of animate justice; and they seek the judge as an intermediate, and in some states they call judges mediators, on the assumption that if they get what is intermediate they will get what is just.

The just, then, is an intermediate, since the judge is so. Now the judge restores equality; it is as though there were a line divided into unequal parts, and he took away that by which the greater segment exceeds the half, and added it to the smaller segment. And when the whole has been equally divided, then they say they have 'their own'—that is, when they have got what is equal. The equal is intermediate between the greater and the lesser line according to arithmetical proportion. It is for this reason also that it is called just (δίκαιον), because it is a division into two equal parts (δίχα), just as if one were to call it δίχαιον; and the judge (δικαστής) is one who bisects (διχαστής). For when something is subtracted from one of two equals and added to the other, the other is in excess by these two; since if what was taken from the one had not been added to the other, the latter would have been in excess by one only. It therefore exceeds the intermediate by one, and the intermediate exceeds by one that from which something was taken. By this, then, we shall recognize both what we must subtract from that which has more, and what we must add to that which has less; we must add to the latter that by which the intermediate exceeds it, and subtract from the greatest that by which it exceeds the intermediate. Let the lines AA', BB', CC' be equal to one another; from the line AA' let the segment AE have been subtracted, and to the line CC' let the segment CD[1] have been added, so that the whole line DCC' exceeds the line EA' by the segment CD and the segment CF; therefore it exceeds the line BB' by the segment CD.

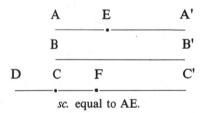

sc. equal to AE.

These names, both loss and gain, have come from voluntary exchange; for to have more than one's own is called gaining, and to have less than one's original share is called losing, for example, in buying and selling and in all other matters in which the law has left people free to make their own terms; but when they get neither more nor less but just what belongs to themselves, they say that they have their own and that they neither lose nor gain.

Therefore the just is intermediate between a sort of gain and a sort of loss, to wit, those which are involuntary;[3] it consists in having an equal amount before and after the transaction.

JUSTICE IN EXCHANGE,
RECIPROCITY IN ACCORDANCE
WITH PROPORTION

5. Some think that *reciprocity* is without qualification just, as the Pythagoreans said; for they defined justice without qualification as reciprocity. Now 'reciprocity' fits neither distributive nor rectificatory justice—yet people *want* even the justice of Rhadamanthus to mean this:

Should a man suffer what he did, right justice would be done.

—for in many cases reciprocity and rectificatory justice are not in accord; for example, (1) if an official has inflicted a wound, he should not be wounded in return, and if someone has wounded an official, he ought not to be wounded only but punished in addition. Further (2) there is a great difference between a voluntary and an involuntary act. But in associations for exchange this sort of justice does hold men together—reciprocity in accordance with a proportion and not on the basis of precisely equal return. For it is by proportionate requital that the city holds together. Men seek to return either evil for evil—and if they cannot do so, think their position mere slavery—or good for good—and if they cannot do so there is no exchange, but it is by exchange that they hold together. This is why they give a prominent place to the temple of the Graces—to promote the requital of services; for this is characteristic of grace—we should serve in return one who has shown grace to us, and should another time take the initiative in showing it.

Now proportionate return is secured by cross-conjunction.[4] Let A be a builder, B a shoemaker, C a house, D a shoe. The builder, then, must get from the shoemaker the latter's work, and must himself give him in return his own. If, then, first there is proportionate equality of goods, and then reciprocal action takes place, the result we mention will be effected. If not, the bargain is not equal, and does not hold; for there is nothing to prevent the work of the one being better than that of the other; they must therefore be equated. (And this is true of the other arts also; for they would have been destroyed if what the patient suffered had not been just what the agent did, and of the same amount and kind.) For it is not two doctors that associate for exchange, but a doctor and a farmer, or in general people who are different and unequal; but these must be equated. This is why all things that are exchanged must be somehow comparable. It is for this end that money has been introduced, and it becomes in a sense an intermediate; for it measures all things, and therefore the excess and the defect—how many shoes are equal to a house or to a given amount of food. The number of shoes exchanged for a house [or for a given amount of food] must therefore correspond to the ratio of builder to shoemaker. For if this be not so, there will be no exchange and no intercourse. And this proportion will not be effected unless the goods are somehow equal. All goods must therefore be measured by some one thing, as we said before. Now this unit is in truth demand, which holds all things together (for if men did not need one another's goods at all, or did not need them equally, there would be either no exchange or not the same exchange); but money has become by convention a sort of representative of demand; and this is why it has the name 'money' (νόμισμα) —because it exists not by nature but by law (νόμος) and it is in our power to change it and make it useless. There will, then, be reciprocity when the terms have been equated so that as farmer is to shoemaker, the amount of the shoemaker's work is to that of the farmer's work for which it exchanges. But we must not bring them into a figure of proportion when they have already exchanged (otherwise one extreme will have both excesses), but when they still have their own goods. Thus they are equals and associates just because this equality can be effected in their case. Let A be a farmer, C food, B a shoemaker, D his product equated to C. If it had not been possible for reciprocity to be thus effected, there would have been no association of the parties. That demand holds things together as a single unit is shown by the fact that when men do not need one another, that is, when neither needs the other or one does not need the other, they do not exchange, as we do when someone wants what one has oneself, for example, when people

permit the exportation of corn in exchange for wine. This equation therefore must be established. And for the future exchange—that if we do not need a thing now we shall have it if ever we do need it—money is as it were our surety; for it must be possible for us to get what we want by bringing the money. Now the same thing happens to money itself as to goods—it is not always worth the same; yet it tends to be steadier. This is why all goods must have a price set on them for then there will always be exchange, and if so, association of man with man. Money, then, acting as a measure, makes goods commensurate and equates them; for neither would there have been association if there were not exchange, nor exchange if there were not equality, nor equality if there were not commensurability. Now in truth it is impossible that things differing so much should become commensurate, but with reference to demand they may become so sufficiently. There must, then, be a unit, and that fixed by agreement (for which reason it is called money); for it is this that makes all things commensurate, since all things are measured by money. Let A be a house, B ten minae, C a bed. A is half of B, if the house is worth five minae or equal to them; the bed, C, is a tenth of B; it is plain, then, how many beds are equal to a house, to wit, five. That exchange took place thus before there was money is plain; for it makes no difference whether it is five beds that exchange for a house, or the money value of five beds.

We have now defined the unjust and the just. These having been marked off from each other, it is plain that just action is intermediate between acting unjustly and being unjustly treated; for the one is to have too much and the other to have too little. Justice is a kind of mean, but not in the same way as the other virtues, but because it relates to an intermediate amount, while injustice relates to the extremes. And justice is that in virtue of which the just man is said to be a doer, by choice, of that which is just, and one who will distribute either between himself and another or between two others not so as to give more of what is desirable to himself and less to his neighbour (and conversely with what is harmful), but so as to give what is equal in accordance with proportion; and similarly in distributing between two other persons. Injustice on the other hand is similarly related to the unjust, which is excess and defect, contrary to proportion, of the useful or hurtful. For which reason injustice is excess and defect, to wit, because it is productive of excess and defect—in one's own case excess of what is in its own nature useful and defect of what is hurtful, while in the case of others it is a whole like what it is in one's own case, but proportion may be violated in either direction. In the unjust act to have too little is to be unjustly treated; to have too much is to act unjustly.

Let this be taken as our account of the nature of justice and injustice, and similarly of the just and the unjust in general.

POLITICAL JUSTICE AND ANALOGOUS KINDS OF JUSTICE

6. Since acting unjustly does not necessarily imply being unjust, we must ask what sort of unjust acts imply that the doer is unjust with respect to each type of injustice, for example, a thief, an adulterer, or a brigand. Surely the answer does not turn on the difference between these types. For a man might even lie with a woman knowing who she was, but the origin of his act might be not deliberate choice but passion. He acts unjustly, then, but is not unjust; for example, a man is not a thief, yet he stole, nor an adulterer, yet he committed adultery; and similarly in all other cases.

Now we have previously stated how the reciprocal is related to the just, but we must not forget that what we are looking for is not only what is just without qualification but also political justice. This is found among men who share their life with a view to self-sufficiency, men who are free and either proportionately or arithmetically equal, so that between those who do not fulfil this condition there is no political justice but justice in a special sense and by analogy. For justice exists only between men whose mutual relations are governed by law; and law exists for men between whom there is injustice; for legal justice is the discrimination of the just and the unjust. And between men between whom injustice is done there is also unjust action (though there is not injustice between all between whom there is unjust action), and this is assigning too much to oneself of things good in themselves and too little of things evil in themselves. This is why we do not allow a *man* to rule, but *rational principle*, because a man behaves thus in his own interests and becomes a tyrant. The magistrate on the other hand is the guardian of justice, and, if of justice, then of equality also. And since he is assumed to have no more than his share, if he is just (for he does not assign to himself more of what is good in itself, unless such a share is proportional to his merits—so that it is for others that he labours, and it is for this reason that men, as we stated previously, say that justice is 'another's good'), therefore a reward must be given him, and this is honour and privilege; but those for whom such things are not enough become tyrants.

The justice of a master and that of a father are not the same as the justice of citizens, though they are like it; for there can be no injustice in the unqualified sense towards things that are one's own, but a man's chattel,[5] and his child until it reaches a certain age and sets up for itself, are as it were part of himself, and no one chooses to hurt himself (for which reason there can be no injustice towards oneself). Therefore the justice or injustice of citizens is not manifested in these relations; for it was as we saw according to law, and between people naturally subject to law, and these as we saw are people who have an equal share in ruling and being ruled. Hence justice can more truly be manifested towards a wife than towards children and chattels, for the former is household justice; but even this is different from political justice.

NATURAL AND LEGAL JUSTICE

7. Of political justice part is natural, part legal, —natural, that which everywhere has the same force and does not exist by people's thinking this or that; legal, that which is originally indifferent, but when it has been laid down is not indifferent, for example, that a prisoner's ransom shall be a mina, or that a goat and not two sheep shall be sacrificed, and again all the laws that are passed for particular cases, for example, that sacrifice shall be made in honour of Brasidas, and the provisions of decrees. Now some think that all justice is of this sort, because that which is by nature is unchangeable and has everywhere the same force (as fire burns both here and in Persia), while they see change in the things recognized as just. This, however, is not true in this unqualified way, but is true in a sense; or rather, with the gods it is perhaps not true at all, while with us there is something that is just even by nature, yet all of it is changeable; but still some is by nature, some

not by nature. It is evident which sort of thing, among things capable of being otherwise, is by nature; and which is not but is legal and conventional, assuming that both are equally changeable. And in all other things the same distinction will apply; by nature the right hand is stronger, yet it is possible that all men should come to be ambidextrous. The things which are just by virtue of convention and expediency are like measures; for wine and corn measures are not everywhere equal, but larger in wholesale and smaller in retail markets. Similarly, the things which are just not by nature but by human enactment are not everywhere the same, since constitutions also are not the same, though there is but one which is everywhere by nature the best.

Of things just and lawful each is related as the universal to its particulars; for the things that are done are many, but of *them* each is one, since it is universal.

There is a difference between the act of injustice and what is unjust, and between the act of justice and what is just; for a thing is unjust by nature or by enactment; and this very thing, when it has been done, is an act of injustice, but before it is done is not yet that but is unjust. So, too, with an act of justice (though the general term is rather 'just action', and 'act of justice' is applied to the correction of the act of injustice).

Each of these must later be examined separately with regard to the nature and number of its species and the nature of the things with which it is concerned.

JUSTICE: ITS INNER NATURE AS INVOLVING CHOICE

THE SCALE OF DEGREES OF WRONGDOING

8. Acts just and unjust being as we have described them, a man acts unjustly or justly whenever he does such acts voluntarily; when involuntarily, he acts neither unjustly nor justly except in an incidental way; for he does things which happen to be just or unjust. Whether an act is or is not one of injustice (or of justice) is determined by its voluntariness or involuntariness; for when it is voluntary it is blamed, and at the same time is then an act of injustice; so that there will be things that are unjust but not yet acts of injustice, if voluntariness be not present as well. By the

voluntary I mean, as has been said before, any of the things in a man's own power which he does with knowledge, that is, not in ignorance either of the person acted on or of the instrument used or of the end that will be attained (for example, whom he is striking, with what, and to what end), each such act being done not incidentally nor under compulsion (for example, if A takes B's hand and therewith strikes C, B does not act voluntarily; for the act was not in his own power). The person struck may be the striker's father, and the striker may know that it is a man or one of the persons present, but not know that it is his father; a similar distinction may be made in the case of the end, and with regard to the whole action. Therefore that which is done in ignorance, or though not done in ignorance is not in the agent's power, or is done under compulsion, is involuntary (for many natural processes, even, we knowingly both perform and experience, none of which is either voluntary or involuntary; for example, growing old or dying). But in the case of unjust and just acts alike the injustice or justice may be only incidental; for a man might return a deposit unwillingly and from fear, and then he must not be said either to do what is just or to act justly, except in an incidental way. Similarly the man who under compulsion and unwillingly fails to return the deposit must be said to act unjustly, and to do what is unjust, only incidentally. Of voluntary acts we do some by choice, others not by choice; by choice those which we do after deliberation, not by choice those which we do without previous deliberation. Thus there are three kinds of injury in transactions between man and man; those done in ignorance are mistakes when the person acted on, the act, the instrument, or the end that will be attained is other than the agent supposed; the agent thought either that he was not hitting any one or that he was not hitting with this missile or not hitting this person or to this end, but a result followed other than that which he thought likely (for example, he threw not with intent to wound but only to prick), or the person hit or the missile was other than he supposed. Now when (1) the injury takes place contrary to reasonable expectation, it is *misadventure*. When (2) it is not contrary to reasonable expectation, but does not imply vice, it is a *mistake* (for a man makes a mistake when the fault originates in him, but is the victim of accident when the origin lies outside him). When (3) he acts with knowledge but not after deliberation, it is an *act of injustice*—for example, the acts due to anger or to other passions necessary or natural to man; for when men do such harmful and mistaken acts they act unjustly, and the acts are acts of injustice, but this does not imply that the doers are unjust or wicked; for the injury is not due to vice. But when (4) a man acts from choice, he is an *unjust man* and a vicious man.

Hence acts proceeding from anger are rightly judged not to be done of malice aforethought; for it is not the man who acts in anger but he who enraged him that starts the mischief. Again, the matter in dispute is not whether the thing happened or not, but its justice; for it is apparent injustice that occasions rage. For they do not dispute about the occurrence of the act—as in commercial transactions where one of the two parties *must* be vicious[6]—unless they do so owing to forgetfulness; but, agreeing about the fact, they dispute on which side justice lies (whereas a man who has deliberately injured another cannot help knowing that he has done so), so that one thinks he is being treated unjustly and the other disagrees.

But if a man harms another by choice, he acts unjustly; and *these* are the acts of injustice which imply that the doer is an unjust man, provided that the act violates proportion or equality. Similarly, a man *is just* when he acts justly by choice; but he *acts justly* if he merely acts voluntarily.

Of involuntary acts some are excusable, others not. For the mistakes which men make not only in ignorance but also from ignorance are excusable, while those which men do not from ignorance but (though they do them *in* ignorance) owing to a passion which is neither natural nor such as man is liable to, are not excusable.

Can a man be voluntarily treated unjustly? Is it the distributor or the recipient that is guilty of injustice in distribution? Justice is not so easy as it might seem, because it is not a way of acting but an inner disposition

9. Assuming that we have sufficiently defined the suffering and doing of injustice, it may be asked (1) whether the truth is expressed in Euripides' paradoxical words:

'I slew my mother, that's my tale in brief.'
'Were you both willing, or unwilling both?'

Is it truly possible to be willingly treated unjustly, or is all suffering of injustice on the contrary involuntary, as all unjust action is voluntary? And is all suffering of injustice of the latter kind or else all of the former, or is it sometimes voluntary, sometimes involuntary? So, too, with the case of being justly treated; all just action is voluntary, so that it is reasonable that there should be a similar opposition in either case—that both being unjustly and being justly treated should be either alike voluntary or alike involuntary. But it would be thought paradoxical even in the case of being justly treated, if it were always voluntary; for some are unwillingly treated justly. (2) One might raise this question also, whether everyone who has suffered what is unjust is being unjustly treated, or on the other hand it is with suffering as with acting. In action and in passivity alike it is possible for justice to be done incidentally, and similarly (it is plain) injustice; for to do what is unjust is not the same as to act unjustly, nor to suffer what is unjust as to be treated unjustly, and similarly in the case of acting justly and being justly treated; for it is impossible to be unjustly treated if the other does not act unjustly, or justly treated unless he acts justly. Now if to act unjustly is simply to harm someone voluntarily, and 'voluntarily' means 'knowing the person acted on, the instrument, and the manner of one's acting', and the incontinent man voluntarily harms himself, not only will he voluntarily be unjustly treated but it will be possible to treat oneself unjustly. (This also is one of the questions in doubt, whether a man can treat himself unjustly.) Again, a man may voluntarily, owing to incontinence, be harmed by another who acts voluntarily, so that it would be possible to be voluntarily treated unjustly. Or is our definition incorrect; must we to 'harming another, with knowledge both of the person acted on, of the instrument, and of the manner' add 'contrary to the wish of the person acted on'? Then a man may be voluntarily harmed and voluntarily suffer what is unjust, but no one is voluntarily treated unjustly; for no one wishes to be unjustly treated, not even the incontinent man. He acts contrary to his wish; for no one *wishes* for what he does not think to be good, but the incontinent man does *do* things that he does not think he ought to do. Again, one who gives what is his own, as Homer says Glaucus gave Diomede

Armour of gold for brazen, the price of a hundred
beeves for nine,

is not unjustly treated; for though to give is in his
power, to be unjustly treated is not, but there
must be someone to treat him unjustly. It is plain,
then, that being unjustly treated is not voluntary.

Of the questions we intended to discuss two
still remain for discussion; (3) whether it is the
man who has assigned to another more than his
share that acts unjustly, or he who has the excessive share, and (4) whether it is possible to treat
oneself unjustly. The questions are connected; for
if the former alternative is possible and the distributor acts unjustly and not the man who has
the excessive share, then if a man assigns more to
another than to himself, knowingly and voluntarily, he treats himself unjustly; which is what
modest people seem to do, since the virtuous man
tends to take less than his share. Or does this
statement too need qualification? For (a) he perhaps gets more than his share of some other good,
for example, of honour or of intrinsic nobility.
(b) The question is solved by applying the distinction we applied to unjust action, for he suffers
nothing contrary to his own wish, so that he is not
unjustly treated so far as this goes, but at most
only suffers harm.

It is plain too that the distributor acts unjustly,
but not always the man who has the excessive
share; for it is not he to whom injustice is done
that acts unjustly, but he to whom it appertains
to do the unjust act voluntarily, that is, the person
in whom lies the origin of the action, and this lies
in the distributor, not in the receiver. Again, since
the word 'do' is ambiguous, and there is a sense
in which lifeless things, or a hand, or a servant
who obeys an order, may be said to slay, he who
gets an excessive share does not act unjustly,
though he 'does' what is unjust.

Again, if the distributor gave his judgement in
ignorance, he does not act unjustly in respect of
legal justice, and his judgement is not unjust in
this sense, but in a sense it *is* unjust (for legal
justice and primordial justice are different); but if
with the knowledge he judged unjustly, he is himself aiming at an excessive share either of gratitude or of revenge. As much, then, as if he were
to share in the plunder, the man who has judged
unjustly for these reasons has got too much; the
fact that what he gets is different from what he

distributes makes no difference, for even if he
awards land with a view to sharing in the plunder
he gets not land but money.

Men think that acting unjustly is in their
power, and therefore that being just is easy. But
it is not; to lie with one's neighbour's wife, to
wound another, to deliver a bribe, is easy and in
our power, but to do these things as a result of a
certain state of character is neither easy nor in
our power. Similarly to know what is just and
what is unjust requires, men think, no great wisdom, because it is not hard to understand the
matters dealt with by the laws (though these are
not the things that are just, except incidentally);
but how actions must be done and distributions
effected in order to be just, to know *this* is a
greater achievement than knowing what is good
for the health; though even there, while it is easy
to know that honey, wine, hellebore, cautery, and
the use of the knife are so, to know how, to whom,
and when these should be applied with a view to
producing health, is no less an achievement than
that of being a physician. Again, for this very
reason[7] men think that acting unjustly is characteristic of the just man no less than of the unjust,
because he would be not less but even more capable of doing each of these unjust acts, for he could
lie with a woman or wound a neighbour; and the
brave man could throw away his shield and turn
to flight in this direction or in that. But to play
the coward or to act unjustly consists not in doing
these things, except incidentally, but in doing
them as the result of a certain state of character,
just as to practise medicine and healing consists
not in applying or not applying the knife, in using
or not using medicines, but in doing so in a certain way.

Just acts occur between people who participate
in things good in themselves and can have too
much or too little of them; for some beings (for
example, presumably the gods) cannot have too
much of them, and to others, those who are incur-
ably bad, not even the smallest share in them is
beneficial but all such goods are harmful, while to
others they are beneficial up to a point; therefore
justice is essentially something human.

EQUITY, A CORRECTIVE OF LEGAL JUSTICE

10. Our next subject is equity and the equitable
and their respective relations to justice and the

just. For on examination they appear to be neither absolutely the same nor generically different; and while we sometimes praise what is equitable and the equitable man, at other times, when we reason it out, it seems strange if the equitable, being something different from the just, is yet praiseworthy; for either the just or the equitable is not good, if they are different; or, if both are good, they are the same.

These, then, are pretty much the considerations that give rise to the problem about the equitable; they are all in a sense correct and not opposed to one another; for the equitable, though it is better than one kind of justice, yet is just, and it is not as being a different class of thing that it is better than the just. The same thing, then, is just and equitable, and while both are good the equitable is superior. What creates the problem is that the equitable is just, but not the legally just but a correction of legal justice. The reason is that all law is universal but about some things it is not possible to make a universal statement which shall be correct. In those cases, then, in which it is necessary to speak universally, but not possible to do so correctly, the law takes the usual case, though it is not ignorant of the possibility of error. And it is none the less correct; for the error is not in the law nor in the legislator but in the nature of the thing, since the matter of practical affairs is of this kind from the start. When the law speaks universally, then, and a case arises on it which is not covered by the universal statement, then it is right, where the legislator fails us and has erred by over-simplicity, to correct the omission—to say what the legislator himself would have said had he been present, and would have put into his law if he had known. Hence the equitable is just, and better than one kind of justice—not better than absolute justice, but better than the error that arises from the absoluteness of the statement. And this is the nature of the equitable, a correction of law where it is defective owing to its universality. In fact this is the reason why all things are not determined by law, to wit, that about some things it is impossible to lay down a law, so that a decree is needed. For when the thing is indefinite the rule also is indefinite, like the leaden rule used in making the Lesbian moulding; the rule adapts itself to the shape of the stone and is not rigid, and so too the decree is adapted to the facts.

It is plain, then, what the equitable is, and that it is just and is better than one kind of justice. It is evident also from this who the equitable man is; the man who chooses and does such acts, and is no stickler for his rights in a bad sense but tends to take less than his share though he has the law on his side, is equitable, and this state of character is equity, which is a sort of justice and not a different state of character.

CAN A MAN TREAT HIMSELF UNJUSTLY?

11. Whether a man can treat himself unjustly or not, is evident from what has been said. For (a) one class of just acts are those acts in accordance with any virtue which are prescribed by the law, for example, the law does not expressly permit suicide, and what it does not expressly permit it forbids. Again, when a man in violation of the law harms another (otherwise than in retaliation) voluntarily, he acts unjustly, and a voluntary agent is one who knows both the person he is affecting by his action and the instrument he is using; and he who through anger voluntarily stabs himself does this contrary to the right rule of life, and this the law does not allow; therefore he is acting unjustly. But towards whom? Surely towards the state, not towards himself. For he suffers voluntarily, but no one is voluntarily treated unjustly. This is also the reason why the state punishes; a certain loss of civil rights attaches to the man who destroys himself, on the ground that he is treating the state unjustly.

Further, (b) in that sense of 'acting unjustly' in which the man who 'acts unjustly' is unjust only and not bad all round, it is not possible to treat oneself unjustly (this is different from the former sense; the unjust man in one sense of the term is wicked in a particularized way just as the coward is, not in the sense of being wicked all round, so that his 'unjust act' does not manifest wickedness in general). For (i) that would imply the possibility of the same thing's having been subtracted from and added to the same thing at the same time; but this is impossible—the just and the unjust always involve more than one person. Further; (ii) unjust action is voluntary and done by choice, and *takes the initiative* (for the man who because he has suffered does the same in return is not thought to act unjustly); but if a man harms himself he suffers and does the same things *at the same time.* Further, (iii) if a man could treat himself unjustly, he could be voluntarily treated unjustly. Besides, (iv) no one acts unjustly without committing particular acts of injustice; but no one can commit adultery with his own wife or housebreaking on his own house or theft on his own property.

In general, the question 'Can a man treat himself unjustly?' is solved also by the distinction we applied to the question 'Can a man be voluntarily treated unjustly?'

(It is evident too that both are bad, being unjustly treated and acting unjustly; for the one means having less and the other having more than the intermediate amount, which plays the part here that the healthy does in the medical art, and the good condition does in the art of bodily training. But still acting unjustly is the worse, for it involves vice and is blameworthy—involves vice which is either of the complete and unqualified kind or almost so (we must admit the latter alternative, because not all voluntary unjust action implies injustice as a state of character), while being unjustly treated does not involve vice and injustice in oneself. In itself, then, being unjustly treated is less bad, but there is nothing to prevent its being incidentally a greater evil. But theory cares nothing for this; it calls pleurisy a more serious mischief than a stumble; yet the latter may become incidentally the more serious, if the fall due to it leads to your being taken prisoner or put to death by the enemy.)

Metaphorically and in virtue of a certain resemblance there is a justice, not indeed between a man and himself, but between certain parts of him; yet not every kind of justice but that of master and servant or that of husband and wife. For these are the ratios in which the part of the soul that has a rational principle stands to the irrational part; and it is with a view to these parts that people also think a man can be unjust to himself, to wit, because these parts are liable to suffer something contrary to their respective desires; there is therefore thought to be a mutual justice between them as between ruler and ruled.

Let this be taken as our account of justice and the other, that is, the other moral, virtues.

NOTES

1. Person A + thing C to person B + thing D.
2. The problem of distributive justice is to divide the distributable honour or reward into parts which are to one another as are the merits of the persons who are to participate. If

A (first person): B (second person) :: C (first portion) : D (second portion),

then (*alternando*) A : C :: B : D,

and therefore (*componendo*) A + C : B + D :: A : B.

In other words the position established answers to the relative merits of the parties.

3. that is, for the loser.
4. The working of 'proportionate reciprocity' is not very clearly described by Aristotle, but seems to be as follows. A and B are workers in different trades, and will normally be of different degrees of 'worth'. Their products, therefore, will also have unequal worth, that is (though Aristotle does not expressly reduce the question to one of time) if A = nB, C (what A makes, say, in an hour) will be worth n times as much as D (what B makes in an hour). A fair exchange will then take place if A gets nD and B gets 1 C; that is if A gives what it takes him an hour to make, in exchange for what it takes B n hours to make.
5. that is, his slave.
6. The plaintiff, if he brings a false accusation; the defendant, if he denies a true one.
7. that is, that stated in 11. 4 f., that acting unjustly is in our own power.

RICHARD A. WASSERSTROM

Equity*

THE CASE FOR AN EQUITABLE DECISION PROCEDURE

A decision procedure based upon precedent, it can be argued, is an anachronism if not an absurdity. For despite the possible benefits of certainty and efficiency that might accrue from its operation, it stands ultimately for the proposition that legal rules are to be applied to particular cases simply because they are the extant legal rules. Even the most uncritical examination of the function of a legal system reveals, however, that rules should never be applied in this manner. Courts of law obviously are created to dispense justice in the cases that come before them for adjudication. The most desirable procedure, therefore, is one that seeks to ensure that all cases and controversies will be decided justly.

Were society so organized that conflicts never arose, the argument might continue, were there never "pathological cases," a legal system might well be a superfluous societal institution. But problems do arise, conflicting interests require accommodation, and as a result of acts both intentional and unintentional, parties find themselves in situations that call for the aid of some disinterested third party before whom they can place their problems and by whose authority compromise and resolution can be effected.

In a society such as ours, the legal system is called upon to resolve a multiplicity of problems and to settle innumerable controversies. It is also its function to ensure that certain standards are given effect in the deliberative dealings of man with man. The judiciary is entrusted with a delicate but almost boundless power over the lives of those persons who have been accused of transgressions against the community; it is also given the authority to decide what shall be done in those cases in which the parties have quite inadvertently worked themselves into a position from which voluntary extrication is impossible. These situations may all involve considerations of the greatest import to the litigants; they all surely demand that the judiciary function in such a way that each case is justly decided.

For this reason it is unnecessary, so the argument continues, for there to be positive, mechanically applied rules of law within the legal system. Not only is it unnecessary, but it is also undesirable. Rules of law are superfluous because it is the justice of the result that counts. Rules of law are undesirable because of the danger that they may be mechanically applied without regard for the justice in the case. The problems with which a judiciary is forced to deal, and the matters with which it should concern itself, lend themselves far better to a direct consideration of the merits of each particular case than to the sterile, unfeeling application of extant laws. Opposed, therefore, to the theory that justice requires the application of fixed rules of law to particular cases is the notion that justice means the "natural," "individualistic," or "discretionary" adjudication of each case as it arises.

This is the position that must now be examined: the view that it is both possible and desirable for cases to be decided by an appeal to considerations of justice or equity rather than by reference to legal rules.

The concept that forms the basis of this decision procedure has enjoyed a long life under a variety of names—"equity," "discretion," "natural justice," "good conscience," "fairness," and "righteousness" are all epithets that have been applied to it. This position, moreover, is one that

*Chapter 5 (complete) of *The Judicial Decision: Toward a Theory of Legal Justification,* by Richard A. Wasserstrom (Stanford, California: Stanford University Press, 1961). Reprinted by permission of the publishers, Stanford University Press, and by permission of the author. © 1961 by the Board of Trustees of the Leland Stanford Junior University.

at first sight is quite attractive, and that has at times been widely accepted and advocated. For it seems to insist from the outset that the legal system must perform precisely those duties for which it most obviously exists.

Proponents of an equitable decision procedure, as we shall see, have been both ambiguous and unspecific in directing their approval toward a process of equitable justification. But there is one characteristic about which they appear to be in accord. In all equitable procedures of justification, the necessary and sufficient justification for any particular decision consists in the fact that the decision is the *most just for the particular case.* That the decision may be deducible from some legal rule is irrelevant; that the decision in itself is just for the case is alone significant.

Examples of what have been considered systems in which justice has been administered by means of an equitable decision process are highly diverse. Roscoe Pound, for instance, suggests the example of Oriental justice. In his discussion of this "lawless" kind of judicial administration, Pound refers to Kipling's description of the court of the Oriental sovereign.

By the custom of the East, any man or woman having a complaint to make, or an enemy against whom to be avenged, has the right of speaking face to face with the king at the daily public audience. . . . The privilege of open speech is of course exercised at certain personal risk. The king may be pleased and raise the speaker to honour for that very bluntness of speech which three minutes later brings a too imitative petitioner to the edge of the ever-ready blade.[1]

Another example offered by Pound, and one much more familiar to the Occidental way of life, is martial law. For here, too, controversies are solved not by an appeal to laws as such, but rather by the direct intervention and application of the general's authority. "Martial law is regulated by no known or established system or code of laws, as it is over and above all of them. The commander is the legislator, judge and executioner."[2]

Somehow, both examples miss the main feature of the procedure of equitable adjudication. They are, admittedly, systems in which particular cases are not decided by an appeal to rules of law. But they are also clearly systems in which there is no emphasis upon the desirability of effecting justice between the parties. They impose no re-

quirement that he who pronounces decisions should attempt to do justice. They guarantee only that decisions will be made. The general theory of "natural justice" may have many serious weaknesses, but it surely sets a higher ideal of adjudication than this.

There is, however, one example that embodies many of the characteristics of such a procedure, namely, the system of equitable adjudication, which has played so conspicuous and so controversial a part in the history of Anglo-American law. As a historical proposition it is doubtless incorrect to consider the equity courts as a complete, self-contained institution for the administration of justice. It is surely more accurate to regard the function performed by the equity courts as only one of the several functions that the Anglo-American judicial system has in fact fulfilled.[3] Reference to the courts of equity is useful, nevertheless, because many of the adherents of a decision procedure based upon "doing justice in the particular case" have pointed to the equity courts as exemplifying the kind of procedure that is desirable. And it is a fruitful example, too, because the equity courts have at times spoken of this procedure in an equally approving manner. Thus, although to do so is to be false to the historical meaning or function of the courts of equity, I shall refer to procedures which share this characteristic as "equitable" procedures of justification.

Descriptions of an equitable decision procedure abound in the literature of judicial opinions; typical are the two that follow.

One of the most salutary principles of chancery jurisprudence is that it, strictly speaking, has no immutable rules. It lights its own pathway; it blazes its own trail; it paves its own highway; it is an appeal to the conscience of the chancellor. It had its origin in the breast of the king, who upon complaint of one of the king's subjects who found he had no plain, adequate, and complete remedy at law, appealed to his king, who thereupon instructed an ecclesiastic, the keeper of the king's conscience, to make an investigation, and regardless of the narrow and technical rules of law, mete out equal and exact justice. The Lord Chancellor became the head of these ecclesiastical or chancery courts, and thus the jurisdiction of courts of equity rests upon the fundamental principles of right and fair dealing; its creed is justice between man and man.

A court of equity acts only when and as conscience commands, and if the conduct of the plaintiff be offensive to the dictates of natural justice . . . he will be held remediless. . . . A court of equity has been said to be the forum of conscience, and an appeal directed to it is an appeal to the moral sense of the judge. In a proper case, the court acts upon the conscience of the defendant and compels him to do that which is just and right.[4]

Commentators have furnished (although not always with approval) comparable characterizations. John Pomeroy, for example, speaks of one possible concept of equity—he finds it undesirable—as being that theory which asserts that judges have the power

and even the duty resting upon them—to decide every case according to a high standard of morality and abstract right; that is, the power and duty of the judge to do justice to the individual parties in each case. This conception of equity was known to the Roman jurists, and was described by the phrase, *Arbitrium boni viri,* which may be freely translated as the decision upon the facts and circumstances of a case which would be made by a man of intelligence and of high moral principles . . .

Charles Phelps provides a comparable characterization:

By juridical equity is meant a systematic appeal for relief from a cramped administration of defective laws to the disciplined conscience of a competent magistrate, applying to the special circumstances of defined and limited cases the principles of natural justice, controlled in a measure as much by consideration of public policy as by established precedent and by positive provisions of law.

In describing the ideal function of the judge, Jerome Frank gives a clearly commendatory statement of the same position.

The judge, at his best, is an arbitrator, a "sound man" who strives to do justice to the parties by exercising a wise discretion with reference to the peculiar circumstances of the case. He does not merely "find" or invent some generalized rule which he "applies" to the facts presented to him. He does "equity" in the sense in which Aristotle—when thinking most clearly—described it. . . . The arbitral function is the central fact in the administration of justice.

And Julius Stone provides a more neutral account:

In the last resort what he prescribed was a dictate of his, the Chancellor's, conscience—or at least the King's conscience secreted in the Chancellor's breast.

Although much rhetoric invoking the divine law and universal justice is to be found, equity jurisdiction was based essentially on the appeal to the particular reason or conscience of the King and his Chancellor. Again this jurisdiction was not pursued, ostensibly at any rate, by promulgating rules binding on all men. At first, both in theory and practice, it was enforced by an appeal to the particular defendant's conscience, he being if necessary detained so as to permit his conscience to operate. . . . The main difference between the Chancellor and the natural lawyer was that the former refrained from formulating in advance the assumptions on which he proceeded.[5]

The espousal of a decision procedure which ensures that justice will be done in every case is certainly commendable. Like the commitments to goodness, truth, beauty, and motherhood, devotion to justice is self-evidently praiseworthy. But to insist that justice ought to be done is not to tell us how it can be, and unfortunately, the advocates of an equitable decision procedure have not carried the task of specification very far. They seem rather to have assumed that once the goal of doing justice in the particular case has been postulated, the way in which this goal is to be realized becomes obvious. They have not indicated the nature of the specific decision procedure according to which such justice is best attained.

It would, however, be unfair to assert that nothing in the way of substantive methodology or argumentation has been offered to clarify the form and content of an equitable decision procedure. It has been argued, for example, that there are *certain features* of legal rules and particular cases that make it inappropriate to decide cases by an appeal to legal rules. Concomitantly, many have insisted that for this reason a nonrational, nondeductive method of justification should be employed. Intuition rather than reason, it is urged, should be the means by which *justification* is effected.* It should be noted, however, that

*Throughout this chapter the word "intuition" is used in a special sense, one that admittedly is broader than ordinary philosophical usage. For I employ "intuition" to denote any process by which truth or correctness is *directly apprehended.* In this sense it includes both intuition in the more usual philosophic sense and also such things as *emotional apprehension.* In other words, I do not distinguish between an epistemology based upon an intuition of justice and one based upon knowledge directly acquired by the "sense of justice" or the "sense of injustice." There may be differences between the two approaches, but for my purposes they can be treated as being essentially similar.

reliance upon a nonrational methodology is not characteristic of all equitable procedures, although an appeal to intuition is present in most.

This chapter deals in detail with only two of the above general claims: (1) that the intuition of justice should be the essential attribute of an equitable decision procedure; and (2) that the nature of particular cases and of legal rules makes the application of legal rules to these cases undesirable . . .

As it is usually presented, the first of these claims—that an intuitive approach ought to be employed—is difficult to discuss and evaluate, for the requirement is in itself far from unambiguous, and the proponents of this procedure have provided little in the way of elucidation. Consequently, this chapter is primarily an attempt to explicate various procedures, all of which might be considered intuitive in nature. There are, more specifically, at least two distinct decision procedures that could be called "intuitive procedures" and that must be delineated and analyzed in turn. I cannot confidently assert that either of these procedures has in fact been advocated by anyone. I can only suggest that the description of these variant processes probably includes most or all of the more specific procedures that proponents of the intuitive approach have had in mind.

The first of these intuitive procedures rests upon what I shall call the theory of *particular justice*. In its simplest and most extreme form, it is the view that there is some particular feature or set of features in every case that makes it both possible and desirable to determine directly the justice or injustice of the decision in the instant controversy. The justification of any decision results from a particular intuition that reveals the decision to be just for this particular case. The second decision procedure can be characterized as a modified version of the theory of particular justice. Its basic premise is that some cases, but not all, are to be justified by an appeal to the relevant legal rule and that some cases, but not all, are to be justified by an intuition of the justness of the decision.

The modified version has itself commonly assumed one of two forms. The first of these forms, here termed the *bifurcation theory of justice*, holds that *all* members of *some* classes of cases coming before the legal system for adjudication cannot be properly decided by appealing to the relevant legal rule. The theory holds, too, that intuition must be used for those classes of cases for which rules are inappropriate.

The second form of the modified version, here termed the *Aristotelian theory of equity*, insists that *some* members of *all* classes of cases coming before the legal system for adjudication cannot be properly decided by appeal to the relevant legal rule.

A third, rather different, equitable decision procedure is delineated (but not evaluated) in this chapter. This nonintuitive procedure stipulates that a decision is justifiable if and only if it best takes into account the interests of the litigants before the court. It says nothing about intuition being the criterion for justifying a decision, and it says nothing about the kinds of cases for which this justification ought to be conclusive. It requires only that such things as the satisfactions, pleasure, needs, and aspirations of the two litigants be accorded exclusive consideration in the justification of any decision.

Besides attempting to specify more precisely the nature of these various procedures, this chapter will examine the theoretical assumptions upon which they rest, and assess the degree to which some of them would in fact succeed in realizing the goal of consistently just decisions.

THE THEORY OF PARTICULAR JUSTICE

As we have noted, the advocates of an equitable decision procedure have failed to specify the way in which such a procedure should operate. It is uncertain, therefore, whether anyone has ever urged the desirability of a decision procedure based upon the theory of particular justice. Cryptic statements, which could be interpreted as adopting such a position and as prescribing its implementation, can be located. Oliphant, for example, in a passage cited earlier observed that "courts are dominantly coerced, not by the essays of their predecessors but by a surer thing—*by an intuition of fitness of solution to problem.*"[6] Judge Joseph Hutcheson, Jr., was insistent that the crucial moment in the judicial decision process occurred at the moment when the judge was witness to that "intuitive sense of what is right or wrong for that cause."[7] And Jerome Frank has offered a similar assessment. The judge should have the utmost latitude, Frank insists, if he is to effect real justice between the parties. The judge can and should respond to the unique aspects of each case that comes before him. For it is this "power to individualize and to legislate judically [which] is of the very essence of [his] function."[8]

At a minimum the theory of particular justice as here presented is not inconsistent with these and comparable suggestions. For the theory insists that any judicial decision has been properly justified if and only if the decision has been directly perceived to be the just decision for the particular case. An appeal to a legal rule, a moral principle, or a future consequence is both inconclusive and unresponsive. The justice-creating features of the case are just in and of themselves. Once they are known by direct intuition, inquiry about justification is at an end. Until the features of the case are so grasped by intuition, all other investigation is futile.

It should be evident that what is *not* at issue is whether intuition can or should *suggest* to the judge what decision ought to be rendered. What is *not* relevant is the question of to what degree decisions are initially "hit upon" by intuition. (Or, in other words, what is *not* at issue is the question of discovery.) Rather, the theory of particular justice, as here interpreted, insists that a procedure of justification ought to be employed in which the fact that a judge has had an intuition of some kind is a conclusive justification for making that intuition the binding decision of the case. If a judge has intuited that a particular decision is the just one for this case, then the fact that this intuition was present is what makes the decision justifiable. Whether the judge suddenly "sees" *the decision* which ought to be given or intuits *that a certain decision* ought to be rendered, it is the intuition which provides the justification for the decision.

The significant features of this theory of justification emerge most clearly from an examination of what could count as a valid justification for any particular legal decision. The following imaginary dialogue between a judge and a questioner is admittedly not the kind of justification that any court has ever given for a decision. But if the language of some of the proponents of equity is to be taken seriously, it does indicate accurately the attributes that a procedure based strictly upon intuitions of particular justice would possess. The following discourse is one between a judge who has decided a case in a certain way and

a questioner who is seeking to ascertain the justification for the judge's decision.

Q: "On what grounds do you justify your decision in this case?"

J: "The justification for this decision rests upon the fact that I have intuited this result to be the best possible one for this case."

Q: "Oh, you mean that there is some general moral principle which requires that a case involving this kind of fact situation be decided in this way?"

J: "No, I mean simply that this decision is just because I have intuited it to be just for this case."

Q: "But how can I decide whether or not you have intuited correctly?"

J: "Just look at all the facts of this case. Doesn't it seem obvious to you that this is the only just result? Look again and perhaps you will have the same intuition."

Q: "But if I cannot have an intuition of any kind, or if I have a contrary one, then is there nothing else you can tell me in order to persuade me of the justifiability of your decision?"

J: "That is correct. I know that the decision is just, and so does everyone else with the same intuition."

Q: "I suppose it would be fair to say, at least, that you would decide other cases of this kind in the same way?"

J: "No. I cannot commit myself, a priori, to a conclusion of what would be just in any other case. I have to have all of the facts of each particular case before me before I can properly intuit what would be truly just for that case. I can only discover what is the just decision for any case as that case is actually presented for adjudication."

Assuming that this caricature of any actual judicial justification is true to the essential features of the procedure of particular justice, there are several grounds upon which the desirability of such a justificatory procedure may be doubted. The first of these relates to eliminating the probability of bias or prejudice in the judicial decision process.

In Chapter 4 it was assumed that the legal system ought to be free from the biases, partialities, and like peculiarities of the judges who render decisions. It was concluded in that chapter that the precedential decision procedure was a partially ineffective means by which to realize that end. A stronger objection can be made to the efficacy of the theory of particular justice in this respect. Roscoe Pound has put the point this way:

Scientific law is a reasoned body of principles for the administration of justice, and its antithesis is a system of enforcing magisterial caprice, however honest, and however much disguised under the name of justice or equity or natural law. . . . Law is scientific in order to eliminate so far as may be the personal equation in judicial administration, to preclude corruption and to limit the dangerous possibilities of magisterial ignorance.[9]

The sentiments expressed by Pound are admirable; but they require further amplification if it is to be shown that the theory of particular justice does not succeed in eliminating this "personal equation."

For the purposes of this inquiry, the assertion that certain procedures are more conducive than others to the achievement of impartiality can be understood to be either an accurate empirical observation or a defensible normative hypothesis. Those procedures, moreover, which can best achieve that end must have at least three characteristics. First, under such procedures there should be certain independent criteria by which the one who makes a decision can evaluate the conclusion reached or the course of action decided upon. This requirement ensures, among other things, that the proponent of any plan of behavior must first persuade himself on "external" grounds of the desirability of his proposal. The second, and perhaps a more significant, requirement is that the justification for any proposal should be submitted to and should be able to withstand public examination. For the prerequisite of publicity provides what has consistently proved to be the most effective means by which the enthusiasms of the advocate and the visions of the would-be seer can be measured against the less personal and more sober and disinterested wisdom of the community. To require that the grounds of a decision be made public is to insist that an avenue of independent verification and criticism be kept open. The third requirement, which is closely related to the first two, stipulates that *all* the grounds or reasons for the decision be both revealed and evaluated. It insists that the processes of argumentation, justification, and enlightened persuasion not be prematurely cut

short. It demands that the process of justification continue until the "ultimate" premise upon which any decision stands and from which it draws its claim for acceptability is fully revealed. For it is only after this point has been reached that it is legitimate—if it is ever legitimate—to conclude that grounds for intelligent discussion no longer in fact exist. To urge that these requirements be present is to insist that men be *rational* —in the best sense of the word—so that the conclusions they have reached may be as accurate as possible, and the conduct undertaken as beneficial as possible.

The central role that rational inquiry and justification should play in the law has been nicely indicated in an essay by John Dewey, entitled "Logical Method and Law."

Courts not only reach decisions; they expound them, and the exposition must state justifying reasons. . . . Exposition implies that a definitive solution is reached, that the situation is now determinate with respect to its legal implication. Its purpose is to set forth grounds for the decision reached so that it will not appear as an arbitrary dictum, and so that it will indicate a rule for dealing with similar cases in the future. It is highly probable that the need of justifying to others conclusions reached and decisions made has been the chief cause of the origin and development of logical operations in the precise sense; of abstraction, generalization, regard for consistency of implications. It is quite conceivable that if no one had ever had to account to others for his decisions, logical operations would never have developed, but men would use exclusively methods of inarticulate intuition and impression, feeling; so that only after considerable experience in accounting for their decisions to others who demanded a reason, or exculpation, and were not satisfied till they got it, did men begin to give an account to themselves of the process of reaching a conclusion in a justified way. However this may be, it is certain that in judicial decisions the only alternative to arbitrary dicta, accepted by the parties to a controversy only because of the authority or prestige of the judge, is a rational statement which formulates grounds and exposes connecting or logical links.[10]

A procedure founded upon intuitions of particular just decisions does not meet these conditions. Intuitions are essentially private affairs. They are difficult to obtain; they are even harder to repeat and thereby verify. The evidence for the correctness of the conclusion reached and advanced must consist in the testimony of the "intuitor" that he has had the proper intuition. Unless one has had a comparable intuition, the word of the "intuitor" must be taken both for the fact that he has had the vision and for the fact that he has interpreted its commands faithfully. The course of human history has revealed the desirability of imposing far more stringent requirements than this in other areas of consequence; it seems strange, therefore, to argue that an institution so vital as the legal system ought to settle for so little.

This is of course not to suggest that what is needed before a good legal system is possible is an "escape from the prison house of the body" into a realm of abstract, nonsensual existences. The requirement that decisions be justifiable on rational grounds imposes no such demand. What is insisted upon, however, is that intuitions, especially if of particular decisions, should not constitute the kind of *ground* which justifies a legal decision. Since they are perforce private in nature, dependence upon them precludes any external evaluation of the judicial command. Being in essence nonrational, they can only blur the divide between fantasy and fact, between wish and ideal. Certainly it may be true that even the rational life, in this sense of the term, has not proved as conducive to happiness and freedom from conflict as some have supposed. But it is just as certainly true that the number and magnitude of undesirable actions performed under the banner of private truth and personal revelation is infinitely greater. It is surely a commonplace to observe that so long as there are men there will be judges who think they have had infallible intuitions of particular justice. But again it is also true that reliance upon the intuitive faculty as the ideal criterion of justification can only be deemed an unwise, ill-conceived, and indefensible normative position.

A related point deserves some mention, if not discussion. It was seen in Chapter 4 that the possibility of antecedent prediction of judicial consequences was a significant and desirable attribute for a legal system to possess. This goal, too, seems singularly unattainable by the kind of intuitive theory of justification presented here. If the judge is to adjudicate cases on the basis of what is just *in the particular case,* and solely in the light of the uniqueness of that case, then three things follow:

first, the task of classification becomes increasingly difficult, if not impossible; second, because the *particularity* of the situation is what is crucial, past decisions are, *ex hypothesi,* extremely unreliable guides for future judicial action; and third, to the extent to which intuitions are apt to be peculiar to a particular judge, the path of adjudication is rendered still more wavering and unpredictable.

It could be argued that the justice-making conditions of particular cases need not be different in every case. But if this is so, it is hard to see why proponents of the theory of particular justice insist that it is the *unique* factors of each case that are truly significant. It is also possible to argue that independent verification might be achievable because other people can have the same intuition of particular justice and thereby test the original conclusion's correctness. But if so, then the empirical thesis upon which this claim rests ought to be demonstrated quite convincingly before it is accepted—particularly in the light of the extensive historical evidence to the contrary.

The failure of the theory of particular justice to provide a means by which a decision can be tested on rational grounds, or sufficient legal data from which rational inferences about the future can successfully be made, constitutes one of the more serious limitations upon the possible value of such a theory of justification. Equally important is the previously postulated inherent unreliability of particular intuitions. If the theory of equity implies the acceptance of a procedure such as this (and of course it need not), there are, it is submitted, reasons more than sufficient to justify its rejection.

MODIFIED THEORIES OF PARTICULAR JUSTICE

That all decisions ought to be fully justified solely by an intuition of the justice of the decision is admittedly an extreme position. It is perhaps inaccurate even to attribute its advocacy to any particular legal philosopher. But there are two restricted or modified versions of the theory of particular justice which have been quite explicitly formulated and widely accepted. On the one hand, the *bifurcation theory of justice,* urged most consistently by Roscoe Pound, insists that there is a fundamental distinction between two kinds of cases, namely those which relate to matters of property and contract, and those which involve conflicts of human conduct and enterprises. The former class of cases should, Pound insists, be decided by appeal to rule; the latter class by appeal to intuition. The *Aristotelian theory of equity,* on the other hand, holds that legal rules ought to be used to decide cases of all kinds, but that within every class of cases there are some particular cases to which legal rules are *necessarily* inapplicable.

Both theories raise two questions: (1) Why should rules of the form of ordinary legal rules not be used to decide all cases coming before the courts for adjudication? and (2) How should those cases which should not be decided by appeal to legal rules be decided? Because neither Pound nor Aristotle has provided a convincing argument in support of the dichotomies proposed, the first question will be the focal point of the discussion. The theories are studied essentially for the arguments offered in support of the thesis that at least some cases ought to be decided by appeal to something other than the relevant legal rule which has been or which could be formulated. However, to the extent to which they suggest a different way in which cases of this kind ought to be decided, these procedures are also analyzed.

THE BIFURCATION THEORY OF JUSTICE

The clearest and most complete statement of the bifurcation theory is found in a lengthy article by Pound, entitled "The Theory of Judicial Decision." Here, relying heavily upon his own interpretation of Henri Bergson's metaphysics, Pound proposes that cases involving contract and property rights be decided by rules and abstract conceptions. And he proposes that cases which are concerned with human conduct ought to be dealt with intuitively.

We should not be ashamed, Pound insists, to admit that intuition should play the decisive role in the adjudication of cases involving human life.

Bergson tells us that intelligence, which frames and applies rules, is more adapted to the inorganic, while intuition is more adapted to life. In the same way rules of law and legal conceptions which are applied mechanically are more adapted to property and to business transactions; standards where application

proceeds upon intuition are more adapted to human conduct and to the conduct of enterprises. Bergson tells us that what characterizes intelligence as opposed to instinct is "its power of grasping the general element in a situation and relating it to past situations." But, he points out, this power is acquired by loss of "that perfect mastery of a special situation in which instinct rules." Standards applied intuitively by court or jury or administrative officer, are devised for situations in which we are compelled to take circumstances into account; for classes of cases in which each case is to a large degree unique. For such cases we must rely on the common sense of the common man as to common things and the trained common sense of the expert as to uncommon things. Nor may this common sense be put in the form of a syllogism. To make use once more of Bergson's discussion of intelligence and instinct, the machine works by repetition; "its use is mechanical and because it works by repetition there is no individuality in its products." The method of intelligence is admirably adapted to the law of property and to commercial law, where one fee simple is like every other and no individuality of judicial product is called for as between one promissory note and another. On the other hand, in the handwrought product the specialized skill of the workman, depending upon familiar acquaintance with particular objects, gives us something infinitely more subtle than can be expressed in rules. In the administration of justice some situations call for the product of hands not of machines. Where the call is for individuality in the product of the legal mill—for example, where we are applying law to human conduct and to the conduct of enterprises—we resort to standards and to intuitive application.[11]

The foundation offered by Pound for the bifurcation of cases is this: One fee simple or one promissory note is like every other one of the same class. Consequently, each can be treated like every other. Any case involving human conduct is essentially different from every other one. Consequently, each must be treated intuitively on its own merits and peculiar facts.[12] The dichotomy, when based upon this rationale, is untenable. In order to demonstrate wherein lies the fallacy of Pound's argument and in order to be certain that he is not being misinterpreted, an acceptable example of each of the two kinds of cases must first be given.

Examples of the first kind of case are plentiful. I assume that Pound would accept the following as an illustration of the kind of property or contract case that should be adjudicated mechanically or conceptually. *A,* the owner of Blackacre in fee simple, has leased Blackacre to *B* for one year for a yearly rental of $5,000. At the end of the year, despite *A's* insistent pleas, *B* fails to vacate the premises and remains in possession of Blackacre after the expiration date of the lease. *A* sues *B* for $5,000, claiming that since *B* "held over" beyond the time of the original rental period, *A* can treat *B* as a tenant for another term —in this case one year—and recover the rental for that term.

I am not so confident that I can locate a clear-cut example of the second kind of case. I think, however, that Pound would agree that the following exemplifies the type of case that manifestly called for intuitive adjudication because it had circumstances which required individualized treatment.

On July 8, 1916, Harvey Hynes, a lad of sixteen, swam with two companions from the Manhattan to the Bronx side of the Harlem river or United States Ship Canal, a navigable stream. Along the Bronx side of the river was the right of way of the defendant, the New York Central railroad, which operated its trains at that point by high tension wires, strung on poles and crossarms. Projecting from the defendant's bulkhead above the waters of the river was a plank or springboard from which the boys of the neighborhood used to dive. One end of the board had been placed under a rock on the defendant's land, and nails had been driven at its point of contact with the bulkhead. . . . For more than five years swimmers had used it as a diving board without protest or obstruction.

On this day Hynes and his companions climbed on top of the bulkhead intending to leap into the water. One of them made the plunge in safety. Hynes followed to the front of the springboard, and stood poised for his dive. At that moment a crossarm with electric wires fell from the defendant's pole. The wires struck the diver, flung him from the shattered board, and plunged him to his death below. His mother, suing as administratrix, brings this action for her damages.[13]

Assuming that Pound would accept these as typical of the two kinds of cases distinguished, he might argue by way of clarification that they should be so distinguished on the following grounds. In the case between *A* and *B* there was a perfectly valid written lease between the parties, under which *B* was only entitled to the premises for one year. By refusing to vacate by the termination date of the lease, *B* became a "holdover"

tenant. A holdover in this case is no different from a holdover in any other case. Consequently, *B's* rights should be no different from any other holdover tenant's and *A* should, therefore, be able to recover the rental for the entire term.

The case of poor Harvey Hynes is essentially different. All sorts of imponderables are present in such a case, and because they are imponderables, they cannot be clearly specified. Although only approximations of the nature of *this* case, the fact that Harvey was a poor city boy who had nowhere else to swim, the fact that he and his friends had been swimming there for years, the fact that the defendant was a wealthy railroad, and the fact that it probably knew the boys had been swimming there, all go to make this particular case the kind that should not be decided by the mechanical application of the rules of trespasser-landowner liability.

When stated in this fashion, Pound's bifurcation has ostensive persuasiveness. The comparison of one lease with another lease, one can argue, does not reveal any significant differences between them; the respective positions of Harvey Hynes and the New York Central Railroad, when put in the particular context of Harvey's death, seem to make a special case. The persuasiveness of the dichotomy lies not in any substantial difference between two kinds of cases, however, but rather in the way in which the two cases are described. The superficiality of the supposed essential distinction can be demonstrated most dramatically by reporting the two cases at issue in a quite different fashion. Instead of merely announcing that there was a properly executed lease between two unnamed persons—two letters —*A* and *B,* the so-called "property" kind of case can be described in the following manner. The lessee, Herter by name, admits that he was to vacate the lessor's dwelling house on May 1, 1895. But on May 1, 1895, Herter's mother, who lived in the house with him, was afflicted with a disease which

confined her to her bed so that it would have endangered her life to take her from the house; that for that reason, and no other, of which the plaintiff [lessor] had full knowledge and notice, the defendants were obliged to and did occupy a small portion of the premises until May 15th; that all their property, furniture and belongings and their family were removed from the premises, and every part thereof, on May 1, 1895, except from the sick room in which their mother was confined, and that they were forbidden by the physician in charge to remove her until May 15th, when she was at once removed.[14]

In the same manner, the *Hynes* case can be presented in an impersonal fashion: *A,* a trespasser upon *B's* land, was killed when an electric wire, necessary to the operation of *B's* business, fell from its point of attachment and struck the trespasser. The trespasser's estate sues the landowner, *B,* for damages.

The point of these two restatements is simply this. It seems just as plausible to argue that one trespass is like any other trespass as it does to argue that one lease is like any other lease. If one looks only to the "transaction" and not to the parties to the transaction, a "mechanical" application of rule to transaction seems precisely as sensible in the one case as in the other. Conversely, if one looks to the "special circumstances" of a case, just as many special circumstances may constitute a property case as a tort case.

The conclusion is not that "special circumstances" ought never to be taken into account, nor that all cases ought to be decided "mechanically." Rather, it is simply that the differentiation of cases *on the grounds that all property cases are alike whereas all tort cases are different* cannot be intelligently sustained. There may indeed be good reasons for treating property and contract cases in one way, and cases like the *Hynes* case in a different way. Some of these reasons are discussed in the next chapters. But to assert that the realm of legal cases should be bifurcated for the reason given by Pound just does not make sense. If one should decide not to consider the special circumstances in property cases but to consider them in tort cases, then of course there will be a difference between the two kinds of cases. The fact remains, nevertheless, that special circumstances are present in any property case precisely to the same extent to which they are present in any other case that might require adjudication. A lease is no more and no less unique than a trespass. Circumstances can be taken into account just as sensibly in the one kind of case as in the other. If the two kinds of cases ought to be treated differently, it is not because there is any-

thing *inherently* different about either class. Thus, if the bifurcation is to be allowed to stand, some other substantiation must be forthcoming.

Similarly, there may be nothing objectionable in suggesting, as Pound does, that there are some cases which ought to be decided by an appeal to different kinds of rules than the rules used to justify other decisions. It is probably of considerable significance to observe that there are some kinds of cases that can best be decided by rules which themselves contain reference to some very general standard rather than to some more narrow set of conditions. This appears to be what Pound has in mind when he says:

> Frequently application of the legal precept, as found and interpreted, is intuitive. This is conspicuous when a court of equity judges of the conduct of a fiduciary, or exercises its discretion in enforcing specific performance, or passes upon a hard bargain, or where a court sitting without a jury determines a question of negligence. However repugnant to our nineteenth century notions it may be to think of anything anywhere in the judicial administration of justice as proceeding otherwise than on rule and logic, we cannot conceal from ourselves that in at least three respects the trained intuition of the judge does play an important rôle in the judicial process. One is in the selection of grounds of decision—in finding the legal materials that may be made both to furnish a legal ground of decision and to achieve justice in the concrete case. It is an everyday experience of those who study judicial decisions that the results are usually sound, whether the reasoning from which the results purport to flow is sound or not. The trained intuition of the judge continually leads him to right results for which he is puzzled to give unimpeachable legal reasons. Another place where the judge's intuition comes into play is in development of the grounds of decision, or interpretation. This is especially marked when it becomes necessary to apply the criterion of the intrinsic merit of the possible interpretations. A third is in application of the developed grounds of decision to the facts.[15]

Like so many discussions of the role of intuition, the above quotation is more than a little perplexing. Perhaps Pound is correct in suggesting that tort cases, for instance, are and ought to be decided by an appeal to a standard of reasonableness rather than by reference to particular rules which specify with greater precision what shall and shall not be reasonable conduct. (This is a matter which is discussed in greater detail in

Chapter 7.) But even if this is what Pound means, it does not follow that two different "kinds" of justification ought to be employed *because* there are two fundamentally different kinds of cases, for example, those which are essentially similar one to another and those which are inherently unique.

Furthermore, it is hard to understand what it means to say that the grounds of decision are and ought to be selected intuitively. If this means that the only justification which can be given for supporting a decision on a certain ground is that the judge intuited the ground to be appropriate for the decision, then the intuitive selection of grounds seems open to the same criticism made earlier of the intuitive selection of particular decisions. And in this connection it is even more difficult to comprehend how developed grounds are to be applied intuitively to facts. For if there is one place in which logic—in the narrow or formal sense—seems directly applicable, it is in the application of rules or grounds to the particular fact situations already described.

Again, if it is correct to say that there are cases in which a general standard, rather than a legal rule, ought to be appealed to, it does not follow that the appeal need be intuitive in nature. Even if there are cases in which the crucial question is one of whether conduct was reasonable or unreasonable, it is not obvious that this is the kind of question which cannot be answered "rationally." Pound's remarks are at least open to the interpretation that if a general standard is to be applied to conduct, the only thing which can be said about that conduct is that the activity was intuited to be reasonable or unreasonable. Yet it does seem that reasons of a nonintuitive kind can be given to support a view that conduct was or was not reasonable in the light of a particular standard. Indeed, it is difficult to understand what role the standard is to play in the process of justification if it is to be taken into account only intuitively.

And finally, if Pound is correct in asserting that judges have "reached the right results" even though they have given the wrong reasons, then he seems here to be suggesting that there are "right reasons" which could and should have been given. Now perhaps all he means by a right reason is an intuition of the correctness of the decision. But if he means something else, if he

means that there are other criteria by which the "rightness" of a decision can be evaluated, then it would seem that it is *these* criteria, rather than intuition, which ought to be explicated. The fact that courts have often given "wrong reasons" does not by itself imply that reasons ought not be given. And if it makes sense to talk about the "rightness" or "wrongness" of judicial decisions (in some nonintuitive sense), this would seem to imply that there are reasoned justifications that courts could and should have given for their decisions. It is these reasons that the courts should have given but did not give which ought to count as the proper justification for deciding a case in a certain fashion. And whatever it is that makes these reasons "good" ought to be made the criteria of justification. Thus, although there may be some purpose in retaining Pound's bifurcation, the justification for retaining it remains unstated. And although it may be useful to observe that some cases ought to be decided by appealing to a standard rather than a rule, this does not imply that intuition ought to be the criterion of either their correct selection or their application.

THE ARISTOTELIAN THEORY OF EQUITY

The acceptance of an argument like Pound's is not uncommon. Far more usual, however, is the recourse to an argument based upon the thesis that rules cannot properly be employed to decide *all* cases of any *class*. There will always be, it is insisted, *some* members of any class for which the application of the desirable legal rule is inappropriate. Legal rules simply cannot take an adequate account of all cases of any kind; some cases must be decided by a direct appeal to considerations of justice.

Such a view has been accepted quite uncritically by almost all commentators upon and philosophers of the law as well as by many courts.[16] The *locus classicus* of this position is Chapter 10, Book v, of the *Nicomachean Ethics;* in more recent sources, Aristotle's language is repeated with only a minimum of alteration. As stated by Aristotle and reiterated by subsequent philosophers, the justification for this hypothesis is, I submit, without substantial foundation. But deference to both its author and its widespread acceptance requires that the proposal be given careful consideration.

Aristotle begins by distinguishing between two kinds of justice: legal justice and some other form of justice with which equity is perhaps to be equated. This distinction is necessary because, says Aristotle, there is something about the generality of rules which makes it incorrect to identify completely justice with rules. The reason this is so

is that all law is universal but about some things it is not possible to make a universal statement which shall be correct. In those cases, then, in which it is necessary to speak universally, but not possible to do so correctly, the law takes the usual case, though it is not ignorant of the possibility of error. And it is none the less correct; for the error is not in the law nor in the legislator but in the nature of the thing, since the matter of practical affairs is of this kind from the start . . . Hence the equitable is the just, and better than one kind of justice—not better than absolute justice but better than the error that arises from the absoluteness of the statement. And this is the nature of the equitable, a correction of law where it is defective owing to its universality. In fact this is the reason why all things are not determined by law, to wit, that about some things it is impossible to lay down a law, so that a decree is needed.[17]

It should be evident that this passage reveals a reliance upon some of the theories and problems with which this analysis has already dealt. But Aristotle's statement also presents several new issues; in particular, these conditions under which a relevant rule ought not to be applied to a particular fact situation must be formulated and evaluated more precisely. There appear to be two possible interpretations of what Aristotle has in mind.

On the one hand, the passage might be construed to be merely putting forth the view that there will always be some cases that will not have been envisioned ahead of time by a legislator. This might be what Aristotle means when he says: "When the law speaks universally, then, and a case arises on it which is not covered by the universal statement, then it is right, where the legislator fails us and has erred by oversimplicity, to correct the omission—to say what the legislator himself would have said had he been present, and would have put into his law if he had known."[18] The Swiss Civil Code appears to follow Aristotle's advice here. "The Law must be applied in all cases which come within the letter or the spirit of any of its provisions. Where no provision is applicable, the judge shall decide according to existing Customary Law and, in default thereof, according to the rules which he would lay down if he had himself to act as legislator."[19] If, in other words, a case arises for which there is no relevant legal rule, then the judge clearly must look to something other than the set of positive rules for the justification for his decision.

For example, there is not at present any relevant law on the subject of drivers' licenses for interspace vehicles. The legislator—and here it is immaterial whether he be the legislator *qua* legislator or the judge *qua* legislator—would quite understandably not have enacted such a law simply because there does not, at present, appear to be any need to regulate such a class of occurrences. And there doubtless is a limitless number of classes of cases which at any given time cannot be foreseen and therefore legislated about simply because the existence of any of their members has not yet been envisioned.

On the other hand, it is also apparent that this is not the real import of Aristotle's point. On the contrary, the first passage quoted above rests on quite a different supposition. It seems to depend upon the premise, also crucial to Pound's bifurcation theory and to the theory of particular justice, that there are at least some situations that are *simply not amendable to general rules of any kind.* In at least three different places Aristotle comments on this point: "about some things it is not possible to make a universal statement which shall be correct"; "the error is not in the law nor in the legislator but in the nature of the thing"; "about some things it is impossible to lay down a law."

These passages, in turn, would once again appear to support two different interpretations. (1) Aristotle might mean that there are certain classes of acts or situations about which rules ought not to be laid down at all. The characteristics of some kinds of cases do not justifiably permit of that abstraction and classification necessary for the adjudication of particular cases by means of ordinary legal rules. Aristotle might, that is, be suggesting a theory very much like Pound's: There are fundamentally two different kinds of classes of cases.

(2) There is, however, another more plausible interpretation of these same statements. The passages appear to imply that for any given general rule which prescribes how any member of a class of cases is to be treated, there will always be some particular fact situation which is indisputably a member of that class of situations, but which nevertheless ought not to be treated in accordance with that law. This interpretation has been accepted by modern theorists as the explanation for the so-called hardship case.

In many of the hardship cases some characteristic of the individual claimant's situation which indicates weakness (but which is legally irrelevant in private law under the principle of "equality before the law") arouses sympathy for him or her: The widow who bought from the banker her deceased husband's worthless note, giving her valuable promise; the poor city youth who found his precarious recreation on the springboard projecting over the river from the wealthy railroad's right-of-way; the poor manual worker who loyally crippled himself for life in order to save his employer from injury; a veteran of a recent war, seeking a desperately needed home for his family and himself, [who] made a contract on Sunday for the purchase of a house.[20]

It is this second interpretation of Aristotle which calls for careful analysis.

The most troublesome feature of the theory centers about the claim that the fault lies not in the general laws. Aristotle does not appear to argue that the law was improperly or incorrectly formulated, that, in other words, the legislator failed to take into account certain factors which should have been considered. Nor does he rest his claim upon the premise that there are certain borderline cases in which classification is extremely difficult and in which, therefore, there is always the possibility that an unjust result will be reached because the case was not in fact properly a member of the class controlled by the rule. The problem, in short, is neither one of insufficient legislative competence nor one of incorrect judicial application. Rather, the claim appears to be that regardless of the care with which any law may be drafted, it is not possible that it can adequately take into account all relevant cases.

If the latter interpretation is correct, the theory is bewildering simply because it is so difficult to envision a substantiating example. While one can think, for example, of hundreds of cases in which an "unjust" result might be reached by applying a given rule to a case, one cannot think of a single instance in which a rule could not be formulated that would cover the instant case and all other cases of the same kind in such a way as to produce a just result in all cases. If Aristotle is saying merely that *for any given set of rules,* it will probably happen that some unjust results will occur when these rules are applied in all relevant instances, then the thesis is unobjectionable. But if something more is meant, if it is insisted that the continual revision of the rules would still not alleviate the problem, then the theory is less intelligible. For it seems always theoretically possible to formulate a rule whose classification would be sufficiently restrictive to exclude all cases in which an "unjust" result might be produced. Another way to make the same point is to observe that in theory to make an exception to a rule is simply to introduce two more restrictive rules in place of the original.

Reference to one of the "hardship cases" may help to clarify the issue. The case of Webb, the devoted employee, is typical.[21] Webb was at work on one of the upper floors of the Smith Company Lumber Mill. He was clearing the floor of scrap wood. The usual and accepted way of doing this was by dropping the wood down to the floor below. As he was just about to drop a 75-pound block of pine, Webb saw that his employer, J. Greely McGowin, was standing directly on the spot that would be hit by the block if it were to fall straight down. The only way by which Webb could prevent McGowin from being seriously injured was for him, Webb, to divert the block from its course of fall; and the only way he could reasonably do this was by falling to the ground with the block. This is precisely what he did. He saved McGowin from harm but only at the cost of inflicting serious injury upon himself. He was, in fact, badly crippled for the remainder of his life.

McGowin, understandably grateful, soon entered into an agreement with Webb whereby he promised to pay Webb $15 every two weeks for the remainder of Webb's life in gratitude for Webb's courageous act. McGowin did this up until the time of his death. His estate continued the payments for another three years and then stopped them even though Webb was still alive. The problem confronting the court when Webb brought suit to compel the estate to continue payment was this: There was a rule of long standing which held that a promise is binding upon the promisor if and only if it is given in exchange for services which have yet to be performed or for a promise to perform some act in the future. In other words, the fact that Webb acted with no prior request from McGowin, coupled with McGowin's subsequent promise to pay Webb for his past injuries, amounted to a mere "past" or "moral" consideration, the kind of consideration which could not support a legal action to enforce performance of that promise.

Let it be assumed that Webb ought to be able to enforce McGowin's agreement and that an unjust result would be reached if he were not allowed to do so. Let it also be agreed that to apply the extant rule to this case would produce an unjust result. To grant these two premises is still not to grant Aristotle's point. Why, if it is unjust not to give legal effect to this agreement, is this not a *kind* of case for which a rule could be formulated that would be capable of producing a just result if applied to all cases of this class? For example, a rule such as the following might be introduced: "Whenever an employee engaged in a proper course of conduct finds that the only way he can reasonably prevent serious injury to his employer is by injuring himself, and whenever a promise is made thereafter by the person saved from injury to pay that person for his injury, this promise is enforcible." It is difficult to find anything which *in theory* requires the inference that if this rule were to be applied to all members of the specified class, some unjust results would necessarily be produced. As will become evident in a moment, there may be weaknesses inherent in rules of this specificity; but the difficulties are practical rather than theoretical. The issue here is simply that there is nothing which *in principle* prevents a situation such as the one Webb found himself in from being treated as one of a definite class of situations. And if it can be treated as a member of one or more classes, then, again, there is nothing in principle that precludes the formulation of a rule which could produce just results when applied to every member of that class.

The plausibility of a view such as Aristotle's derives in part perhaps from a confusion between two different concepts—from the failure to distinguish what I shall call a law's *universality* from its *generality*. To say that a law is or should be *universal* is simply to assert that the law applies without exception to all the members of the class included within the scope of the law. To speak of the universality of law is to refer to that feature which renders the law applicable to every member of the specified class. A strong case can be made for the analytic truth of the proposition that all laws are universal in this sense.

The generality of a law is something quite different. To speak of a law's generality is to observe the degree to which the class which is governed by the law is discriminated from all other possible classes. The generality of a law is concerned, therefore, with the particular class which is named and controlled by the law; universality, on the other hand, is concerned with the way in which the law is to be applied to the members of the class. Universality is a formal characteristic; generality is a material one.

An adherence to this distinction permits more meaningful discussion of the Aristotelian thesis and its implications. For it becomes obvious that the most important problems it raises center about the generality rather than the universality of rules. That all laws should be universal seems evident; that all laws should be of *any particular* generality is far less certain. Two competing considerations are relevant to the question of what constitutes the desirable generality of ordinary rules of law.

First, if all rules of law were absolutely general, that is, if they dictated the same result for every member of the class consisting of all persons, the number of substantively unjust results would undoubtedly be very great. For as was observed above, it is only as the generality of the rule is "contracted" that the chance of just results in every case increases. As more conditions are placed upon membership in the class controlled by the rule, it becomes increasingly unlikely that an "exceptional" case will arise.

Second, and serving to support the contrary hypothesis that legal rules should "expand" their generality, is the consideration that as rules become too specific their utility *qua* rules diminishes. That is, although the proposed rule for the Webb type of situation may be sufficiently "narrow" so that injustices will not result, it is also so specific that it enables prediction of very few cases. The issue here is wholly analogous to one raised earlier. Rules are useful because they enable one to predict a legal result in advance. But if the rule applies only to a very limited class, if its generality is minimal, then knowledge of the rule does not permit the accurate prediction of many cases. Concomitantly, a minimal generality requires—if prediction is to be possible—a proliferation of rules. Because each rule controls only a small class, many rules are needed to take account of all cases. A mastery of the content of a great number of rules becomes a precondition of successful prediction.

Thus in a different context, Aristotle's position is not without significance. Theoretically, the thesis is untenable. Given an indefinitely large number of rules there is no reason why all cases could not be decided justly by means of an appeal to rules. But as a practical matter, rules cannot become too specific and still fulfill their most important function as rules. The number of rules cannot be multiplied indefinitely without creating a comparable impairment of function. Thus if the rules of a legal system are to be general enough to function properly as rules, there is good reason to suppose that they might not be able to take an adequate account of all cases controlled by the rules . . .

Before we leave the question of minimal generality one point deserves some mention. It has been argued by Patterson, among others, that the principle of "equality before the law" is at issue here; but it is difficult to see how the introduction of this principle clarifies or solves anything. For this principle, although doubtless commendable in the abstract, proves to have amazingly little content in concrete situations. What does it mean to say that people ought to be treated equally before the law? Does it mean that the only rules of law which are justifiable are those which apply indiscriminately to all persons? If so, then such a law is sufficiently rare as to be a curiosity. For almost every law, either explicitly or implicitly, makes exceptions for children, incompetents, sleepwalkers, and the like. In addition, almost all laws further circumscribe the class of persons who are to be treated in "equal" fashion by specifying the conditions that must be present before the law is to be applied. And here, too, very often these conditions include certain characteristics of possible litigants. For instance, there is generally one property law for good-faith purchasers and

another for purchasers with notice; there may be one set of constitutional protections for aliens and another for citizens.

If, on the other hand, the principle of equality before the law imposes a weaker requirement upon justifiable laws—the requirement alluded to earlier that there be some reason for making the distinction made by the law—then appeal to the principle is simply not very helpful in any a priori fashion. Perhaps, for example, there is no good reason for making a rule which expressly recognizes that class of employees who have aided their employer, been injured, and subsequently received a promise of compensation from their grateful employer. Perhaps on balance such a "specialized" classification would be undesirable. But saying this is something quite different from asserting simply that the principle of "equality before the law" is necessarily violated whenever such a classification is made. Unless one is prepared to assert that all classifications, except those which include all human beings without exception, are inherently undesirable, an appeal to the principle of "equality before the law" is not by itself a forceful or convincing criticism of some "less inclusive" law. What must be shown is not the presence of a more selective classification, but rather the undesirability of making this kind of classification in this kind of case.

This does not mean that laws which make distinctions between persons on the basis of race, religion, place of origin, and the like cannot in most circumstances be condemned. This does not mean that laws which treat "equals unequally" are less abhorrent now than before. But it does mean that there may always be good reasons for making certain kinds of distinctions among persons. And it does mean that it is more appropriate to criticize the reasons offered than just to appeal to the principle of "equality before the law." The fact that a law discriminates among persons does not make the law bad; the fact that the law discriminates badly does. A "bad" law should be shown to be "bad" on this latter ground.

NONINTUITIVE EQUITY

In the course of the discussion so far, an equitable procedure has been defined as one that holds an intuition of the justness of a decision to be the necessary and sufficient justification for deciding a case in a certain fashion. It should be apparent, however, that those who have opposed equity to precedent have not limited their proposals solely to a demand for intuitive adjudication. Instead, much of what has been written about the desirability of equity has been written in praise of a procedure of justification in which precedents are not followed *and* in which intuition plays no role. Thus, even if intuition should be rejected as a criterion of justification—either for all cases or only for some—it does not follow that some other form of equitable justification must thereby be dismissed as unsatisfactory. In the remainder of this chapter the character of a nonintuitive equitable procedure will be presented very briefly; in the succeeding chapters it will be evaluated in considerably greater detail.

As has already been observed, the concept of an equitable procedure of justification rests very largely upon the notion that the peculiar or unique facts of each case ought to be taken into express account and given primary significance in order to do justice in the particular case. And there is at least one distinctly nonintuitive equitable procedure that would do just that. This nonintuitive equitable procedure stipulates that the court should concentrate upon the facts of a particular case, and should, after a "rational" consideration of all the facts, decide the case in such a way that justice is done for the litigants. Here, the rule of decision would prescribe that a decision is justifiable if and only if it best takes into account the interests of the litigants who are currently before the court. A decision is not justifiable because it is intuited to be such, or because it accords with some precedent. Rather, it is justifiable because the consequences of that decision are found to be more desirable for the litigants than those of any other possible decision. The interests of the litigants are primary; the consequences to them of deciding the case in one way rather than another are alone relevant to the question of what shall be regarded as a justifiable decision. If the courts consistently focus their attention upon the ways in which the litigants themselves will be affected by various possible decisions, and if the courts justify their decisions accordingly, then, it might be argued, they will render more justifiable decisions than they would were they to employ any other procedure of justification. Thus, this kind of nonintuitive equity would be embodied in a procedure in which

courts justified their decisions solely on the basis of what decision would be best for the litigants.

A decision process such as this has considerable initial appeal. It does not seem to be open to the same criticisms which were made earlier of intuition as a criterion of justification. For under this form of an equitable procedure a judge could give perfectly good, independently verifiable reasons for deciding a case in a certain fashion. He could point to the way in which the decision would produce a minimum of discomfort and a maximum of satisfaction vis-à-vis the two litigants. He could receive evidence and analyze arguments that tended to show that one rather than another decision would be more justifiable on these grounds. Furthermore, such an equitable procedure would be free from many of the defects latent in a precedential procedure. Courts would not be bound by the errors of earlier procedure. They would be unhampered by tradition. They could meet each case as it came along and feel free to decide it and nothing more. This is, therefore, a procedure which surely requires careful study. And it may very well be the procedure which so many proponents of equitable adjudication have been implicitly suggesting all the time. Throughout the remainder of this work, I shall restrict the denotation of "equitable procedure" to a procedure which prescribes that cases ought to be decided in such a way as to bring about the best result as between the parties at present before the court. I shall assume that this is or can be a distinctly nonintuitive procedure.

At this juncture someone might object that, although the possibility of nonintuitive equitable procedures has been recognized, the discussion is still incomplete. For there is, the objection might continue, an additional and perhaps related theme which runs through almost all discussions of equity. It concerns the desirability of adjudicating either some or all cases by an appeal to moral rules or principles. Under this view, an equitable decision procedure is one which courts are instructed to take moral rules or standards expressly into account and to employ these rules, rather than legal rules, as the criteria by which to justify particular decisions. Such a procedure could also be nonintuitive since moral rules can, arguably, be applied in the same fashion in which any other rules are applied. And the procedure could be nonprecedential, since an appeal to moral rules, rather than to already existing legal rules, constitutes the justification for deciding a case in a certain fashion.

This suggestion that cases ought to be decided in accordance with moral rather than legal rules is surely to be found in many of the writings to which reference has already been made. As usually formulated, however, its precise meaning is unclear. More specifically, there are at least two questions which must be resolved before it can even be considered as a possible, independent program of legal justification.

First, the *role* that moral rules or standards are to play in the process of justification must be delineated more precisely. Are the moral principles to function in the same manner in which legal rules function in a precedential decision procedure? If so, they would serve directly as the justification for a particular decision. Or are they to function instead as the criterion by which to evaluate particular legal rules? If so, they would not be the ostensible justification for particular decisions, but rather would be the justification for using a particular legal rule as the justification for a particular decision.

And second, the differences, if any, between moral and legal rules or principles must be examined more closely. Are there any formal differences between the two that would make it possible to say of any rule that if it is clearly a moral rule then it cannot be a legal rule, or if it is clearly a legal rule then it cannot be a moral rule? If a rule is a moral rule, does it follow that it cannot function in a procedure of justification in the same fashion in which a legal rule would function? If there is no inherent difference between the two kinds of rule, then is the suggestion that cases ought to be decided by an appeal to moral rules any different from the proposal that cases ought to be justified by reference to "new" or "alterable" legal rules? Is the suggestion that courts ought to be "equitable" any different from the proposal that courts ought to be free to change existing legal rules? Until these questions are answered, the possible significance of this second kind of nonintuitive equitable procedure cannot be fully understood. And once these questions are answered, as the questions themselves suggest, it may turn out that this is not even a distinctly equitable procedure at all.

Because almost all discussions of equity do invoke reference to adjudication in accordance with moral rules, and because this in turn can mean any one of several things, the following chapter constitutes something of a digression—although a necessary one—from the course of the argument so far. For in recent years, moral philosophers have been concerned with certain issues that have considerable relevance to a resolution of some of the problems just raised. In particular, they have sought to concern themselves with the role that the principle of utility ought to play in the justification of individual moral acts or decisions. The controversy that has been engendered over this point and the solutions that have been proposed are particularly useful in that they furnish instructive analogies to the possible roles which moral rules or principles—such as, for example, the principle of utility—might play in a procedure of legal justification.

NOTES

1. Kipling, "The Ameer's Homily," quoted in Pound, "Justice According to Law," p. 697 n.
2. *In re* Egan, 5 Blatchford 319, 321 (1866), quoted in *ibid.*, p. 697.
3. Cf., for instance, Pound's thesis that there are two fundamental elements present in all mature legal systems, namely, the "legal" and the "discretionary." "Before the law we have justice without law; and after the law and during the evolution of law we still have it under the name of discretion, or natural justice, or equity and good conscience, as an antilegal element." Pound, "The Decadence of Equity," p. 20.
4. *Cobb v. Whitney,* 124 Okla. 188, 192 (1926); *Kenyon v. Weissberg,* 240 F. 536, 537 (1917).
5. Pomeroy, *A Treatise on Equity Jurisprudence,* pp. 46–47; Phelps, *Elements of Juridical Equity,* § 143; Frank, *Law and the Modern Mind,* p. 157; Stone, *The Province and Function of Law,* pp. 228–29.
6. Oliphant, "A Return to Stare Decisis," p. 159. Italics mine.
7. Hutcheson, "The Judgment Intuitive," p. 285. As is characteristic of one who adheres to an intuitive scheme of justification, Hutcheson resorts at times to rather mystical statements of approval. He announces, for example, that: "It is such judicial intuitions, and the opinions lighted and warmed by the feeling which produced them, that not only give justice in the cause, but like a great white way, make plain in the wilderness the way of the Lord for judicial feet to follow" (pp. 287–88).
8. Frank, p. 121. See also Gmelin, "Sociological Method," in *Science of Legal Method,* p. 100, where he seems to be proposing a similar view: "We need a vivid understanding of the facts, a sympathetic treatment of the human destinies that are passing before our eyes. We must strive to penetrate into the needs of the parties who come before the judge as patients come before the physician, so that we may not offer them the stone of bald reasoning but the bread of sympathetic relief."
9. Pound, "Mechanical Jurisprudence," p. 605.

10. Dewey, "Logical Method and Law," p. 24.

11. Pound, "The Theory of Judicial Decision," pp. 951–52.

12. Although giving a somewhat different justification for treating all contract and property cases in a manner different from tort and other analogous kinds of cases, Dickinson seems to adopt Pound's rationale at least in part. For he agrees with Pound that there is a field in which "every case involves a multitude of pertinent elements which vary in importance from case to case, [and therefore] it is practically impossible fairly to select any special factor or factors and apply them as criteria over the whole field. This is true of all ordinary matters of conduct not definitely directed, like business transactions, to the production of a legal result." Dickinson, *Administrative Justice and the Supremacy of Law*, pp. 145–46.

13. *Hynes v. New York Central RR. Co.*, 231 N.Y. 229, 231 (1921).

14. *Herter v. Mullen*, 159 N.Y. 28, 41–42 (1899).

15. Pound, "The Theory of Judicial Decision," p. 951.

16. Cf., for instance, Frank, pp. 118–19, and Patterson, *Jurisprudence*, p. 582. Cf. also Salmond, *Jurisprudence*, p. 83: "For the law lays down general principles, taking of necessity no account of the special circumstances of individual cases in which such generality may work injustice. . . . In all such cases, in order to avoid injustice, it may be considered needful to go beyond the law, or even contrary to the law, and to administer justice in accordance with the dictates of natural reason."
For a judicial expression of the same view see *Berkel v. Berwind-White Coal Mining Co.*, 220 Pa. 65 (1908): "The whole system of equity jurisprudence is founded on the theory that the law, by reason of its universality, is unable to do justice between the parties, and equity, not being bound by common-law forms and pleadings, has more elasticity and can better reach this end" (p. 75).
Ehrlich seems to make a still stronger assertion along the same lines: "It is certain that one need not expect better or juster results from such technical decisions than from free ones. Generally speaking, it is undoubtedly much easier to decide a definite case correctly than to establish an abstract rule universally applicable for all imaginable cases; and surely it can hardly be maintained seriously that such a rule will invariably result in the fairest decision, even in those cases which nobody had thought of when the rule was made." (Ehrlich, "Judicial Freedom of Decision," in *Science of Legal Method*, p. 63.)
The dichotomy, as set up by Ehrlich, appears convincing. The difficult problem, however, concerns the ways, if any, in which knowing that a definite case has been decided correctly differs from formulating and applying a rule for that kind of case. If a case cannot be decided correctly without laying down a rule, then the argument advanced by Ehrlich seems less attractive. See Chaps. 6 and 7, in which this point is explored in detail.

17. Aristotle, *Nicomachean Ethics*, 1137b, 12–29.

18. *Ibid.*, 20.

19. Swiss Civil Code, Article I. See also Cardozo, *The Nature of the Judicial Process*, pp. 142–43.

20. Patterson, p. 582.

21. *Webb v. McGowin*, 27 Ala. App. 82 (1935).

WILLIAM K. FRANKENA

Some Beliefs About Justice*

"Masters, give unto your servants that which is just and equal."

St. Paul, *Colossians,* 4:1.

The topic of this lecture is social justice, more specifically, distributive justice. One of the good things about this topic is that one does not have to be kind to it; one has only to be just. Having twice in the past sought to do it justice without success,[1] I now propose to try once more. If I fail to do it justice this time—and I am sure I shall —at least it will not be for lack of trying.

Now, as Aristotle points out, one can conceive of justice as covering the whole area of morality, of moral virtue, or at least of moral rightness; Plato, Kant, and, more recently, C. I. Lewis come close to conceiving it thus. But this seems to be distributing justice a little thin. As J. S. Mill says, we must distinguish between justice and "other obligations of morality" like "charity or beneficence."[2] Even if, like Lewis, we refuse to regard charity or beneficence as obligations of morality, we still cannot identify distributive justice with the whole requirement of the moral. For, as Aristotle also says, the justice we are investigating is only a part of virtue, as is shown by the fact that, if a man throws down his shield in battle, uses abusive language, refuses to assist a friend with money, or commits adultery, we accuse him, not of injustice (certainly not of distributive injustice), but of cowardice, bad temper, meanness, or profligacy.

"Well," it may be said at this point, "this is true of justice as ascribed to *individuals;* there are other things that morality requires of individuals besides justice. However, all that can be required of a *society* or *state* is that it be just—that it

distribute justly what it is within its power to distribute. That is, in the case of society or the state virtue equals justice, distributive justice." This view has a good deal of plausibility, but it raises the problems of the relation of justice to welfare and of welfare to the state, and we cannot discuss these here. Our concern now is with the question when a society or state is distributively just, not with the question whether this is all it should be.

I.

There is one principle of distributive justice on which there seems to be general agreement, namely, that like cases or individuals are to be dealt with in the same way or treated alike, or that similar cases are to be treated similarly. Chaim Perelman calls this the *formal* principle of justice.[3] Now, it does seem clear that an act of distributing is at least *prima facie* unjust if it involves treating differently, or discriminating between, individuals whose cases are similar in all important respects. If my case is substantially like yours but it is treated differently, one of us has grounds for crying that injustice has been done, as any child seems to see instinctively. In this sense, the formal principle of justice does formulate a *necessary* condition of the existence of distributive justice. For justice to exist there must be regularities or rules that are followed in the distribution of what is distributed. Yet a land may be without justice even if similar cases are always treated similarly, even if it always distributes according to rules which are known. A society may have and act without fail on rules, laws, and conventions, and yet be an epitome of injustice. It depends on what the rules and conventions are. In other words, rules, laws, and conventions may themselves be unjust or incorporate injustice. They all take the form, "Treat every case of kind

*The Lindley Lecture, 1966. Reprinted with permission of the author and the Department of Philosophy of the University of Kansas.

X in manner Y," as is required by the formal principle, but the manner specified may in fact be an unjust way of treating things of the kind in question.

Any set of rules that may prevail in a given society is a selection from among all possible rules. They classify people in terms of certain similarities and neglect others; they also neglect certain dissimilarities. They likewise select, from among the possible ways of treating people, certain ones, and they assign these ways of treatment to the different classes they define. But human beings are alike and unlike in all sorts of respects. Not all of their similarities and differences are important or even relevant to the question how they are to be treated, and not just any manner of treatment may be assigned to just any class of cases. Consistency is a requirement of justice, not merely "a hobgoblin of little minds"; but it is not enough, it is not the whole of justice.

In other words, the formal principle of justice does not give us a *sufficient* condition for the existence of justice. As Perelman insists,[4] we must also have some *material* principles of distribution, principles that tell us something more about the content of our rules, more about the similarities and differences that are to be regarded as relevant, more about what Jesus called the measures with which we are to mete and be measured to. This is what we must look for. I shall, however, not seek to give a complete and systematic account of the material principles of justice. I shall limit my discussion almost entirely to a review of some views about the nature of the most *basic* material principle of justice, and to a defense of one of them.

It is sometimes said that, while the formal principle of justice is certain but empty, any material principle must be arbitrary and uncertain. We must choose one, if we are to have any system of justice at all, but our choice cannot have any rational basis, since equally valid reasons can be given for choosing another.[5] I shall not try to take this metaethical position by frontal attack, but, instead, will seek to bypass it by offering, not indeed a "proof" of any material principle of distributive justice, but what Mill calls "considerations determining the intellect to give its assent" to one view of justice and to withhold it from others.[6] That is, I shall simply try to give a rational case for one principle and against others. Af-

ter all, as someone once said, the best way to answer a man who says there are no giraffes is to show him one. The only trouble about that is that one may be caught by a skeptical lion while looking for a giraffe, like the drunk who saw double and tried to climb the wrong tree.

II.

Aristotle's discussion of distributive justice in the *Ethics* and *Politics* will serve as a useful basis for our inquiry.[7] Following his lead we may say that the typical case of distributive justice involves (1) at least two persons, A and B, (2) something to be distributed, P, (3) some basis of distribution, Q, and (4) a geometrical proportion or ratio such that

$$\frac{\text{A's share of P}}{\text{B's share of P}} = \frac{\text{A's share of Q}}{\text{B's share of Q}}$$

Then a society is distributively just or has distributive justice in so far as it distributes P among its members in proportion to their shares of Q. Not all theories of distributive justice accept this model quite literally, as we shall see, but we can nevertheless use it in order to state the problems involved and the main ways in which they may be answered. Clearly, there are two questions:

(a) What is P? That is, what is to be distributed?
(b) What is Q? What is to be taken as the basis of distribution?

Different theories about the material principles of distributive justice give different answers to these two questions, especially to the second.

Actually, P, or what is to be distributed, may be almost anything, and will vary from context to context; but on all theories of social justice it will consist primarily of such things as offices, privileges, tasks, tax burdens, powers, goods, educational opportunities, vocational opportunities, and the conditions of happiness or of the good life. As for Q, or the basis of distribution, one might, of course, have different theories about the nature of Q depending on what P is; for example, if it is musical instruments that are to be distributed one might take musical aptitude or taste as a basis of distribution, but if it is college credits and grades one might, and presumably should, take performance in college courses as a basis.

Even so, we want to know—and this is our main problem—what the most *basic* Q is, if there is one, on the basis of which such P's as have been mentioned are to be distributed.

In his discussion of this question Aristotle indicates that there have been three main theories of social justice: the oligarchical, the aristocratic, and the democratic theories. They agree about what P is: offices, powers, honors, external goods, etcetera; what they differ about is Q, the basis of distribution. The oligarchical theory says that Q is wealth or property, that is, that P is to be distributed to people in proportion to their wealth; the aristocratic theory holds that Q is merit, that is, that P is to be distributed in accordance with merit; and the democratic theory, as Aristotle conceives of it, claims that Q is simply the fact of free birth and that P is to be distributed equally among those who are born free, but, of course, he was making allowance for slavery, and a contemporary democrat would prefer to say that Q is simply the fact of being human.

Revising Aristotle's scheme somewhat, we may classify theories of distributive justice as follows: (1) Inequalitarian theories hold that P is to be distributed in proportion to some Q which people have in different amounts, degrees, or forms, that is, in proportion to some feature in which people are unequal. They are of three sorts: (a) the oligarchical theory, (b) the meritarian or aristocratic theory, (c) other inequalitarian theories, for example, those that identify Q with blood, sex, color, height, or native intelligence. (2) Equalitarian or democratic theories hold that basically P is to be distributed equally. They are of two kinds:[8] (a) Substantive equalitarianism holds that P is to be distributed in proportion to Q; and it identifies Q with some feature in which all men are alike or equal. It is hard to give a good example of such a theory because it is hard to find any feature in which all men are alike and equal. That is one reason why this kind of equalitarianism finds it so difficult to answer the argument that men are not equal since there is no Q, no property, which they all have in the same amount and form. For example, they all have reason, but they have it in different degrees. They all have color, presumably in the same degree, but they have it in different forms. One might reply that all men are alike or equal in being men or in being human, but it is very difficult to make out just what property "being human" is, or whether it is

a property at all, let alone one which everyone has in the same degree and form. (b) Procedural equalitarianism agrees with inequalitarianism in denying that there is any Q which all men have in the same degree and form. But it still maintains a basically equalitarian view of distributive justice. To do this it gives up the Aristotelian model which holds that P is to be distributed in accordance with some Q. There is, it maintains, no Q of the kind required. It therefore regards equalitarianism as a "procedural" principle: Treat people equally unless and until there is a justification for treating them unequally. This is a procedural principle because it says, not that men are equal in a certain respect and therefore should be treated equally, but only that unequal treatment must be justified or defended, whereas equality of treatment needs no justification.

Before going on, I should like to say something here about the question, "Are Men Equal?" All equalitarians answer "Yes" to this in some sense, and all inequalitarians "No." But we must notice that the question has two senses, a factual sense and a normative one. In the factual sense it asks, "Is there any respect in which all men are in fact equal, any Q which they all have in the same degree and form?" In the normative sense it asks something very different, namely, "*Ought* all men to be treated as equals?" Thus there are really two distinct questions, though this is not always noticed. The real issue between equalitarians and inequalitarians is over the normative question whether all men ought to be treated equally; it is to this question that the former must say "Yes" and the latter "No." But the inequalitarians always say "No" to the factual question too, and, in fact, they rest their negative answer to the normative question at least in part on a negative answer to the factual one; they argue that men should be treated differently because they are different. Equalitarians, on the other hand, though they all say "Yes" to the normative questions, may say either "Yes" or "No" to the factual one. Substantive equalitarians say "Yes," and procedural equalitarians say "No." These points are very important to keep in mind in any discussion of distributive justice.

III.

Let us now proceed to a discussion of inequalitarian theories of the basic material principle of distributive justice. The oligarchical theory is perhaps not often espoused in so many words, but it does appear to be acted on to a considerable extent in practice, and, in any case, it is a very instructive theory to study. It maintains, it will be remembered, that the Q in proportion to which P is to be distributed is wealth, material possessions. It takes quite literally at least the first part of the saying of Jesus,

> For whosoever hath, to him shall be given,
> and he shall have more abundance; but
> whosoever hath not, from him shall be taken
> away, even that he hath.[9]

But, with all due respect for Jesus' real meaning, it seems reasonable to say that the oligarchical way of favoring the haves over the have nots is a very paradigm of injustice. Such a theory of distributive justice seems to be mistaken in principle, and it is important to see why. It is mistaken, it seems to me, for this reason: because the Q which it takes as a basis for distribution is itself something that is distributed by human actions and social institutions, and hence something that may itself be or have been distributed justly or unjustly, namely wealth or property. If this point is well taken, then we may argue quite generally that no theory is acceptable which offers as its *basic* principle of distribution the principle that P is to be distributed in proportion to some Q whose distribution is itself dependent on human action and social policy, for example, wealth, power, or social position. It also follows that even the democratic theory, as Aristotle understood it, is mistaken; for its Q was "free birth," and this, in the sense in which the Greeks took it, was something socially determined, not something one had either by nature or by one's own efforts.

It should be added that, in any case, already possessed wealth is plausible as a basis for distributing other things only if it is a reliable index of the presence of some other Q which is more reasonably taken as a basis of distribution, for example, ability, intelligence, or merit. This is shown by the fact that the defenders of oligarchy have usually argued that the possession of wealth actually is an index of something more fundamental, when they have bothered to give any argument at all.

Putting off the meritarian or aristocratic theory for a moment, let us look at inequalitarian views of our third sort, those taking as a basis for distri-bution such Q's as blood, sex, color, height, or native intelligence. These views are right in not choosing as the fundamental basis of distribution anything that is directly distributable by man or society. Instead they take as the basis of distribution some Q whose presence is due to nature (though, indirectly, through eugenics, man can do something even about the distribution of color, etcetera). It seems apparent, however, that this too is a mistake. For it is reasonable to claim that the use of blood, color, height, etcetera, as a fundamental basis of distribution is also unjust in itself. It is fair enough to use them as a basis of distribution in certain contexts, for example, as for basis for distributing costumes or parts in plays. But to take any of them as the most basic Q for the distribution of opportunities, offices, etcetera, is as unjust as taking wealth as one's basic Q, though for a different reason. The reason (the main reason, not the only one) in this case, I think, is that, if we take color, height, etcetera, as a basis for distributing P, then we are basing our distribution on a feature which discriminates [among] between individuals but which the individual has done and can do nothing about; we are treating people differently in ways that profoundly effect their lives because of differences for which they have no responsibility.

The most plausible of the natural Q's just mentioned to take as a basis of distribution is native intelligence. Even native intelligence (to be distinguished here from developed intelligence) will not do, however, as our ultimate basis of distribution, though it is certainly in a better case than height or color of skin. For it is something that can be adequately detected and gauged only in the course of some kind of program of education, formal or informal, so that its use as a basis of distribution presupposes a prior equal distribution of the opportunities for such an education.

In any case, we may also say that blood, sex, color, height, etcetera, cannot reasonably be taken as important bases of distribution unless they serve as reliable signs of some Q, like ability or merit, which is more justly employed as a touchstone for the treatment of individuals. This gain is shown by the fact that when proponents of racial discrimination and slavery have given arguments at all, they have often argued precisely that these features may be taken as signs of such more acceptable Q's.

We have mentioned merit as clearly a more acceptable Q than acquired features like wealth on the one hand or natural ones like color on the other. Shall we then use merit as our most fundamental basis of distribution? That we should is the position of the aristocrats or meritarians, including Aristotle himself and, more recently, Sir David Ross. What do they mean by "merit?" Aristotle meant excellence or virtue, and he distinguished two kinds of excellences or virtues: intellectual ones and moral ones; Sir David, however, means by "merit" simply moral virtue.[10] We may therefore understand the meritarians to hold that, basically at any rate, P is to be distributed to people in proportion to their degree of excellence, intellectual, moral, or both. What shall we say of this conception of social justice?

It certainly has a good deal of plausibility. In particular, its Q does not suffer from the defects of those of the other two kinds of inequalitarianism. For merit or excellence is not something distributed (differentially) by nature without any help from the individual, as color, blood, and height are; nor is it something that can be distributed justly or unjustly by man or his social institutions, as wealth is. Only the potentialities for excellence can be provided by nature, and only the opportunities and accessories for it can be provided by society; excellence or merit itself must be achieved or won by individuals themselves. It looks, therefore, as if merit may be just the Q we are looking for. Nevertheless, I am convinced that it will not do either. I tried to show this once or twice before but now suspect that the argument I then used is fallacious.[11] There is, however, another argument which I hope is better. This argument is that merit cannot be the *basic* Q in matters of distributive justice, since a recognition of merit as the basis of distribution is justified only if every individual has an equal chance of achieving all the merit he is capable of (and it cannot simply be assumed that they have had this chance). If the individuals competing for P have not had an equal chance to achieve all the merit they are capable of, then merit is not a fair basis for distributing shares of P among them. If this is so, then, before merit can reasonably be adopted as a ground of distribution, there must first be a prior *equal* distribution of the conditions for achieving merit, at least so far as this is within the power of human society. This is where

such things as equality of opportunity, equality before the law, and equality of access to the means of education come into the picture. In other words, recognition of merit as a criterion of distribution is reasonable only against the background of a recognition of the principle of equality, the primary basis of distribution is not merit but equality, substantive or procedural.

It is worth mentioning, in view of the many recent discussions of "the distribution of education," first, that, strictly speaking, society cannot distribute education but only the means of and opportunities for education, and, second, that it cannot distribute these in accordance with excellence or merit, since the achievement of excellence or merit presupposes a process of education. To this it may be replied that educational means and opportunities are to be distributed, not equally, but according to capacity. But then we may rejoin by pointing out that people's capacities can be determined only by educating them in some way, and that basic educational means and opportunities must therefore be distributed equally, since all must be given an equal chance to show their capacities if their capacities are to be used as a basis for determining their shares of other things. It follows, of course, from such premises, that a program of merit scholarships is fully just only if all of the candidates have had equal educational opportunities of the relevant kinds, though it may be a good thing anyway, as I believe it is.

None of what I have said is meant to imply that merit is not an acceptable basis of distribution in some contexts. I believe, indeed, that it is just to recognize and reward merit or excellence in certain ways; I have been trying to show only that merit cannot reasonably be regarded as our most *basic* criterion of distribution, as meritarians think.

Excellence is an excellent thing, but, if it is not taken to be its own sole reward, we must all equally be given the chance to attain it so far as we are able.

In this discussion I have been identifying merit with excellence, intellectual or moral; but there are, of course, other things that it may be taken to mean, for example, contribution to society or to the welfare of mankind, and it may be proposed that we should employ one of these things as our basis of distribution. What I have just said applies, however, to these further forms of merit also; they may be acceptable as secondary grounds of distributive policy, but they will not do as primary ones. It should be added that at least one of the reasons for rewarding merit in these and other forms is that doing so is useful, that is, conducive to the public good. But to argue that merit should be rewarded because it is *useful* to do so is not yet to show that *justice* requires us to reward it. What is useful may be right to do, but it is not *ipso facto* a requirement of justice, though it need not be unjust either. This *may* be one of the meanings of the puzzling parable of the workers in the vineyard.

It may be objected that we have been neglecting an important theory of social justice, one which may have more subscribers, if we count both sides of the Iron Curtain, than any other, namely, that the just society is that which takes from each according to his ability and gives to each according to his needs. This theory sounds like a form of inequalitarianism, since it is obvious that people's abilities and needs differ widely. It may, however, be contended that it presupposes a basic equalitarianism, and this contention seems to be supported by the fact that those who accept the theory mean to be equalitarians at least in principle. One of the good things about this ability-need theory, whether one accepts it or not, is its recognition that duties and tasks are to be distributed, as well as opportunities, rights, and goods. But what is involved in the notion that tasks are to be distributed according to ability? Not a belief in inequality, but precisely the reverse. For we do not treat people equally if we ask of them exactly the same performance. To some a given task is easy, to others it is difficult, and hence, to ask the same of everyone is actually to treat them unequally, asking sacrifices from some that others are not required to make. To ask from each according to his ability, then, is to ask the same *proportionate* effort and sacrifice from each, in an effort to leave all as nearly equally well off as possible. In the same way, since needs differ, to give equally to all does not entail giving exactly the same thing to each. Shakespeare is surely unjust when he tells us in *The Merchant of Venice* not to trust

The man that hath no music in himself,
Nor is not moved with concord of sweet sounds,

but it would not be unjust to give such a man a pair of skis when everyone else is being given a violin or a set of the latest Beatles recordings. To give to each according to his need is, again, to make the same *proportionate* contribution to the welfare of each, in an effort to make all as nearly equally well off as possible. The ability-need theory is therefore reasonable only if it presupposes an equalitarian goal or ideal.

IV.

If what has been said is correct, then we may reasonably regard inequalitarian views about the basic material principle of distributive justice as unsatisfactory, even if we cannot claim to have "disproved" them. The basic principle is that of equality, as Aristotle's democrats thought. Merit and other Q's which men have unequally may serve acceptably as secondary criteria of distribution, but the basic framework must be the principle of equality. This we may now state. It is the principle that matters are to be so disposed, that is, P is to be so distributed, that everyone has an equal chance of achieving the best life he is capable of. This is the foundational principle of social justice. Of course, to apply this principle we must have some defensible conception of what the good life is, and which lives are better than others, and these are not easy matters; but they must be left for another occasion.

For what it is worth, it may be pointed out that at least one leading meritarian, Aristotle, sometimes seems to presuppose the principle of equality just stated. For example, he regards slavery as justified because he believes that there are people who can enjoy the best lives they are capable of only if they are slaves of some master. In fact, more generally, he seems at his best to define the ideal state as one in which each member enjoys the highest happiness—the most excellent activity—he is capable of attaining.

To avoid misunderstanding, I should add that I do not mean to suggest that no extra attention should be given either to handicapped persons on the one hand, or to gifted individuals on the other. I have no wish to attack enterprises like Project Head Start, fellowship programs, etcetera. All that the principle of equal justice requires is that everyone be given an equal chance to enjoy the best life he is capable of, but it may be that doing this entails our giving what seems to be extra attention to certain sorts of people. Such attention seems extra only because it involves more effort or money, but it is not really extra (unjust), since it is necessary if we are to make the same *proportionate* contribution to the best of life of everyone. Some people simply are by nature harder to help on their way, and others easier, and we are, therefore, not unjust if we put more effort or money into helping some than we do into helping others, as long as all are enabled to make the same *relative* advance toward the good life.

One might object here that social justice consists, not in making possible the same relative advance for everyone, but rather in bringing everyone up to the same absolute level. One might contend, for example, that it is unjust for society to put anything extra into its gifted individuals until all the others, whether handicapped or not, have been brought up to the highest level possible for them, and that even then it is not unjust if it does not do anything extra for them. To deal with this objection we must distinguish two things a society might do for its members: (1) it might provide them with a certain level of material goods, (2) it might promote a certain level of goodness of life for them. These two things may overlap, but they are not the same. I am somewhat inclined to agree that society should try to make available to everyone the same general level of material possessions, at least up to a certain point. But material possessions are only externally connected with goodness of life, and it is the latter that society should be mainly concerned with. Now, some people just *are* capable of leading better lives than others; these are, in fact, the "gifted" ones. Should not society, in justice, do what it can to help these members achieve the best lives they are capable of (provided it also helps the others), at least after and perhaps even before the others have reached their peaks? A few remarks may perhaps serve to guide further thinking on this matter.

(a) It certainly seems only just that they should be helped if necessary, at least *after* the less gifted have reached their peaks. We must remember, however, that a just society will also be a free one, and that in a free society such individuals can and will do much to help themselves. (b) It is obviously conducive to the good, not only of the gifted individuals, but of others,

if the gifted are aided even *before* the others have gone as high as they can. For, like Plato's rulers, they can then put their gifts to the social use of helping the others. (c) It would seem clear, at any rate, that a just society must at least *permit* exceptional individuals to realize themselves, insofar as this is compatible with others' doing so. (d) Since a just society must provide the utmost freedom for each individual consistent with the freedom and welfare of others, it must even run the *risk* that some, in seeking their own best life, will endanger those of others. (e) In practice, perhaps, any society that seeks to be just must work on two fronts all the time: that of making possible the achievement by the gifted of the best lives they can attain and that of making *sure* that others also are so positioned as to be able to attain the best lives open to them by virtue of their potentialities.

V.

Now, having steered the good ship Justice safely though the straits of inequalitarianism into the haven of equalitarianism, we must ask what side of the harbor we are to anchor on, that of substantive or that of procedural equalitarianism. As was indicated earlier, the difficulty in substantive equalitarianism is that there seems to be no factual respect in which all human beings are equal, no Q which they all have in the same degree and form. (There is the further point that, even if there were such a Q, it still might not follow that all men ought to be treated as equals; but this is balanced by the fact that, if there is no such Q, it also does not follow that men ought not to be treated as equals.) As Benn and Peters put it,[12]

... if we strip away [from human nature] all the qualities in respect of which men differ, what is left? ... we are left with an undifferentiated potentiality ... 'Human nature' implies a varying potentiality for a certain limited range of qualities ... ; it is not another quality that all men posses equally, on account of which they should in some positive way be treated alike.

Benn and Peters conclude that equalitarianism must take a procedural form.[13]

... What we really demand, when we say that all men are equal, is that *none shall be held to have a claim to better treatment than another, in advance of good grounds being produced. . . .* Understood in this way, the principle of equality does not prescribe positively that all human beings be treated alike; it is a presumption against treating them differently, in any respect, until grounds for distinction have been shewn. It does not assume, therefore, a quality which all men have to the same degree, which is the ground of the presumption, for to say that there is a presumption means that no grounds need be shewn. The onus of justification rests on whoever would make distinctions. To act justly, then, is to treat all men alike except where there are relevant differences between them. . . . Presume equality until there is reason to presume otherwise.

With some qualifications, I am inclined to agree with this view of the matter. It still seems reasonable, however, to ask why we should adopt this procedural principle in the case of *all* the beings who are *human,* if they are not equal in any factual sense. The answer, I think, has two parts. (1) One part is that it seems to be a rule of reason to deal with similar things in similar ways. Thus, inductive reasoning may be thought of as depending on a presumption that we are to make similar assertions about similar things, unless we have evidence to the contrary. To quote Perelman:

The fact is, the rule of justice results from a tendency, natural to the human mind, to regard as normal and rational, and so as requiring no supplementary justification, a course of behaviour in conformity with precedent.[14]

This view may be substantiated somewhat by reference to the work of Piaget on the moral judgment of children.[15] But it does not suffice as an answer to our question. For, as we saw, and as Perelman recognizes, this rule of reason—treat similar cases similarly—is purely formal. Besides, even though, in our geological inductions, we must presume that what is true of one rock is true of others unless there is evidence to the contrary, we hardly need draw the conclusion that, in our behavior, we ought to *treat* all rocks in the same way unless we can show good reasons for treating them differently. Why then should we treat all *human* beings equally until we have good reasons for not doing so? (2) The reply, it seems to me, must be that human beings are different from rocks, they have desires, emotions, and minds, and are capable, as rocks are not, of having lives

that are good or bad. It is this fact that all men are similarly capable of experiencing a good or bad life, not the fact that they are equal in some respect (if they are), that justifies the presumption that they are to be treated as equals. With this, somewhat hesitantly, I drop anchor on the procedural equalitarian side.

VI.

Many problems remain, but we can take up only two of them, and then only briefly. (1) An equalitarian might hold, not only that justice requires us to treat all human beings equally (in the sense explained above, in which giving A a violin and B a pair of skis may be treating them equally, not in the sense of treating them exactly alike), but that any departure from equality, any unequal treatment is *ipso facto* unjust and wrong. But few equalitarians have had the temerity to espouse this position, nor have I, though I should point out that it is much more plausible to maintain that it is never just or right to treat people *unequally* than that it is never just or right to treat them differently. If one does not adopt this position, however, one must allow that unequal treatment is sometimes just or right, that the differences among people sometimes justify treating them unequally. And then the question arises: what differences among humans justify treating them unequally? What differences are relevant to questions of distribution? This is not an easy question, and it is sometimes felt that the relevant differences are so many and so various as to render the principle of equality of no effect. An inequalitarian must answer the question, too; but he *could* say that all differences are relevant, if not, prove why not; whereas the equalitarian must claim that the relevant differences can be limited in some way. Now, I have already intimated that in various kinds of context various kinds of considerations are relevant to questions of distribution, for example, that differences in height or color of skin may be relevant to decisions about the distribution of costumes and roles in plays. In a sense, then, if we abstract from context, the variety of relevant considerations, like that of evil spirits, is indeed legion. In another sense, however, each context determines what considerations are relevant and limits them; not all considerations are relevant in all contexts. Differences in sex, color, height, or dramatic ability may be relevant to decisions about casting players, but they are not always relevant; indeed they seem obviously irrelevant to most questions of social policy of the kind that a theory of distributive justice is primarily concerned to provide for. For such questions, I suggest, the relevant features of people are not such things as color, height, and the like, but only those features that bear, directly or indirectly, on the goodness or badness of the lives of which they are capable, for example, differences in ability or need.

(2) The last question is somewhat different, and may be put roughly by asking, "Why should we be just?" More accurately put, it is this: Why is justice, conceived as treating people equally in the sense explained, right?[16] One traditional answer is that of the deontologist in ethics, namely, that justice or equality of treatment is right in itself, as keeping promises is, or telling the truth. Another standard answer is that of the utilitarian, that justice or equal treatment is right because it is necessary for or at least conducive to the greatest general good or the greatest general happiness. As between these two views I should say that the first is essentially correct and the second mistaken. I should like, however, to propose a third mediating possibility. If we ask what the Ideal state of affairs would be, then, as far as I can see, the deontologist and the utilitarian can both accept the following statement:

The Ideal is that state of affairs in which *every person* (or perhaps every sentient being) has the best life he is capable of.

If this formulation of the Ideal is correct, as I believe it is, then we can plausibly argue that justice in the sense of equal treatment is right because it is a constitutive condition of the Ideal. For then, as Bentham declared, it is an essential aspect of the Ideal that everybody be counted as one and nobody as more than one. In the Ideal, as thus formulated, everyone is equally well off in the sense that everyone has the best life he is

capable of, which is all that can reasonably be asked for. An even more ideal equality would be realized, it is true, in a state of affairs in which everyone had the ideally best life or at least the best life that any human being is capable of; but such a state of affairs would be wholly impractical and Utopian as an ideal. It could only be wished, not worked, for. Logically, of course, one could reject even the more practical Ideal sketched in my statement, since "questions of ultimate ends do not admit of proof";[17] but it is hard to believe that anybody would in fact reject it if he were fully informed and completely reasonable,

> ... whose even-balanced soul
> From first youth tested up to extreme old age,
> Business could not make dull, nor passion wild;
> Who saw life steadily, and saw it whole ...[18]

NOTES

1. See W. K. Frankena, "The Concept of Social Justice," in R. B. Brandt (ed.), *Social Justice* (Englewood Cliffs, N.J., 1962); W. K. Frankena, *Ethics* (Englewood Cliffs, N.J., 1963), ch. 3.
2. Cf. J. S. Mill, *Utilitarianism,* Ch. V.
3. *The Idea of Justice and the Problem of Argument* (London, 1963), pp. 15–16.
4. *Ibid.,* pp. 27–28.
5. Cf. *ibid.,* p. 11. But see also pp. ix–x.
6. *Op. cit.,* near end of Ch. I.
7. See *Nicomachean Ethics,* Bk. V; *Politics,* Bk. III, Ch. IX, XII, XIII.
8. See S. I. Benn and R. S. Peters, *Social Principles and the Democratic State* (London, 1959), pp. 108–111.
9. *Matt.* 13:12.
10. W. D. Ross, *The Right and the Good* (Oxford, 1930), pp. 135–138.
11. Cf. *Ethics,* p. 40.
12. *Op. cit.,* p. 109.
13. *Ibid.,* pp. 110–111; cf. M. Ginsberg, *On Justice in Society* (Pelican Books, 1965), p. 79.
14. *Op. cit.,* p. 86. For the point I am borrowing, see pp. 79–87. Cf. J. N. Findlay, *Language, Mind and Value* (London, 1963), p. 250.
15. Jean Piaget, *The Moral Judgment of the Child* (New York, 1948). Perelman refers to Piaget's *Apprentissage et connaissance,* p. 42.
16. Meritarians have a corresponding question: why is justice, conceived as treating people according to their merits, right? They too can give either deontological or utilitarian answers.
17. Mill, *op. cit.,* opening sentence of Ch. IV.
18. Matthew Arnold, "To a Friend."

JOEL FEINBERG

Noncomparative Justice *

Suppose a cautious, empirically minded philosopher who lacks any one central insight, or any one basic analytic principle, nevertheless undertakes to write a systematic treatise on the nature of justice.[1] Such a person would naturally wish to get a preliminary idea of the land by searching through the data from which he must eventually extract his principles. What would he find? Without doubt, an enormous diversity of things. To begin with, there is a great variety of kinds of human activity in which questions of justice can arise: distributions of goods and evils, requitals of desert, compensation for loss, appraisals of worth, judgments of criticism, administration and enforcement of rules and regulations, games of amusement, settlements of disputes (by bargaining, voting, flipping coins), contracting, buying, selling, and more.

One way of imposing unity on the data of justice is to classify these diverse activities into more general kinds. Thus, from the Scholastic period on, philosophers have spoken of allocations, punishments, and exchanges under the rubrics "distributive," "retributive," and "commutative" justice, respectively. But from the point of view of theory, this classification does not cut very deep at all, and the inference from three general kinds of human activity to three distinct and theoretically interesting forms of justice would be a *non sequitur.* At best the traditional headings constitute a useful way of ordering a survey or dividing a book into chapters. An equally useful way of classifying the data of justice and one which promises more rewarding theoretical insights is that which divides injustices [2] into those that discriminate invidiously, those that exploit their victims, and those that wrong their victims by means of false derogatory judgments about them. This is a distinction among types of wrongs that are called injustices, and cuts across the distinctions among occasions or contexts of justice.

* From *The Philosophical Review,* Vol. 83 (1974), pp. 297–338. Reprinted by permission of the publisher.

Whatever the activity, whatever the institutional background, any injustice properly so called will be, I believe, a wrong of one of these three types.

A way of achieving still more unity is to separate the data of justice as neatly as possible into two categories. Perhaps this can be done in a variety of ways, but the one in which I am interested here sorts the various contexts, criteria, and principles of justice into those which essentially involve comparisons between various persons and those which do not. In all cases, of course, justice consists in giving a person his due, but in some cases one's due is determined independently of that of other people, while in other cases, a person's due is determinable *only* by reference to his relations to other persons. I shall refer to contexts, criteria, and principles of the former kind as *noncomparative,* and those of the latter sort as *comparative.* My aim in this paper will be to clarify the contrast between comparative and noncomparative justice, and also to investigate that which they might have in common, and in virtue of which the name of justice has come to apply to both.

I

In recent years, comparative justice has received far more attention than noncomparative justice, partly because writers have been able to agree about its general nature. Surprisingly many philosophers [3] have even gone so far as to claim that all justice *consists* (essentially) in the absence of arbitrary inequalities in the distribution of goods and evils, thus ignoring completely the many and diverse contexts for justice which are nondistributive in character. There is no denying, of course, that the problems of comparative justice are real and pressing; my concern here is only to correct the imbalance of emphasis resulting from the exclusive attention lavished upon them. Let us consider first, however, some typical occasions for comparative justice: *(i)* when competitive prizes are to be awarded, *(ii)* when burdens and benefits are to be distributed, and *(iii)* when general rules are to be made, administered, or enforced.

It is illustrative to notice how competitive prizes differ from grades and rewards. We can know that a grade or reward is improperly assigned without knowing anything about the claims or deserts of persons other than the assignee, whereas a prize, having the avowed purpose of selecting out the best in some competition (or, in the case of "booby prizes," the worst) or the exact ranking of contestants against one another, cannot be seen to be justly or unjustly awarded to one person prior to an examination of the credentials of all the others. Thus the awarding of prizes is an occasion for comparative justice, whereas the assigning of grades and rewards is typically noncomparative.

All comparative justice involves, in one way or another, equality in the treatment accorded all the members of a class; but whether that equality be absolute or "proportional," whether it be equality of share, equality of opportunity, or equality of consideration, depends on the nature of the goods and evils awarded or distributed, and the nature of the class in which the assignments and allocations take place. Comparative injustice consists in arbitrary and invidious discrimination of one kind or another: a departure from the requisite form of equal treatment without good reason. When the occasion for justice is the distribution of divisible but limited goods or the assignment of divisible but limited chores, *how much will be left for the others* is always pertinent to the question of how much it would be just for any particular individual to get. And where the occasion for justice is the application or enforcement of general rules, comparative justice requires that the judge or administrator give precisely the same treatment to each person who falls within a class specified by the rule.

These observations, of course, are by now boring and commonplace. My only purpose in making them here is to help make clear the contrast between comparative and noncomparative justice. Consider now the various noncomparative occasions for justice. When our problem is to make assignments, ascriptions, or awards in accordance with noncomparative justice, what is "due" the other person is not a share or portion of some divisible benefit or burden; hence it is not necessary for us to know what is due others in order to know what is due the person with whom we are dealing. *His* rights-or-deserts alone determine what is due him; and once we have come to a judgment of *his* due, that judgment cannot be logically affected by subsequent knowledge of the condition of other parties. We may decide, on the basis of information about other parties, to withhold from him his due; but no new data can upset our judgment of what in fact *is* his due. That judgment is based exclusively upon data about him and is incorrigible, as a judgment, by new information about others. When our task is to do noncomparative justice to each of a large number of individuals, we do not compare them with each other, but rather we compare each in turn with an objective standard and judge each (as we say) "on his merits." It follows that equality of treatment is no part of the concept of noncomparative justice, even though it is, of course, a central element in comparative justice. If we treat *everybody* unfairly, but equally and impartially so, we have done each an injustice that is, at best, only mitigated [4] by the equal injustice done all the others.

The clearest examples of noncomparative injustices are cases of unfair punishments and rewards, merit grading, and derogatory judgments. Of these three kinds of activities, the third seems the most basic from the point of view of justice, and since it has been largely neglected in recent discussions, it will be the main object of attention in the remainder of this essay. First, however, I shall briefly consider possible examples of noncomparative injustices in so-called commutative and retributive contexts. It might seem at first sight that when agreements, transactions, and transfers between free and equal bargainers are unfair, or when promises are wrongfully broken, the injustice is primarily noncomparative, for in such cases the agreement reached or the promise breached is unjust because it denies one of the parties his due, quite apart from the way in which others are treated or have been treated by the actor in question or by other actors. A businessman to whom a commercial promise is made and then broken, for example, is treated unfairly not because of the contrast between his treatment and that of others (though, of course, when such a comparison is made it may serve to aggravate the sense of injury and show that there is a derivative injustice resting on another, comparative, ground); he is treated unfairly in any case, so it would seem, because his rights, determined independently of any such comparison, have been violated. If these cases are indeed instances of noncomparative injustice, however, they are not the clearest or purest examples. Not all cases of wrongful promise-breaking are instances of injustice of any kind (*pace* Hobbes). One can, after all, mistreat a person with being particularly unfair to him. Broken promises typically *are* unfair, however, because, like cheating and much lying, they are forms of *exploitation*, of one party taking advantage of another, or promoting his own gain wrongfully at the expense of his victim. When exploitation occurs, the balance of advantages is upset, and benefits and losses are redistributed. Injustice becomes manifest in these cases when a *comparison* is made between the resultant condition of the exploiter and that of his victim. The point applies a fortiori to bargains that are unfair in the first place.[5]

Purer cases of noncomparative injustice are encountered in retributive contexts. It should be obvious, for example, that to punish an innocent person or a lawbreaker who was not responsible for what he did is to commit an injustice to the one punished irrespective of similar treatment accorded all other offenders of his class. There is, to be sure, an element of comparative injustice in the situation where a guilty person goes free and an innocent one is punished for his crime, but punishment of the innocent person would be unjust to him even if the guilty party were also punished, or suffered a fate even worse than punishment.

The category of noncomparative justice to which I shall devote major attention I propose to call *the justice of judgments*. The importance of judgment in the theory has been insufficiently acknowledged, I think, by writers who (like Plato and Aristotle) concentrate on the *virtue* of justice or (like the modern utilitarians and their enemies) on the justice and injustice of *acts* and *rules*. The idea of judgmental injustice is familiar enough. In everyday discourse statements and the opinions and judgments they express are commonly called just or unjust. Sometimes one person's opinion of another may not "do him justice"; it may not be "fair to him," as we say. When judgments (as distinct from actions) are said to be

unfair to the person judged, the injustice alleged is typically the noncomparative kind. When an innocent man is pronounced guilty, the record about him is falsified to the disadvantage of his reputation and to the detriment of the cause of truth. This is an injustice to him and remains so even if his sentence is suspended and no further hardship is imposed upon him. The injustice in this case consists precisely in the falsity of the derogatory allegation. It can also consist in the falsity of what is believed about the unjustly convicted man. Beliefs and opinions are often said to be unfair to those they are about, even if they are rarely voiced or disseminated to others. Similarly, if a book reviewer writes of a witty book that it is dull, or of a thorough discussion that it is superficial, or of a valid argument that it is invalid, he has not "done justice" to the book or its author. The injustice again is noncomparative. It can be discovered by anyone who reads the book in question, and depends in no way upon the other critical judgments that have been made by this and other critics about other books by this and other authors.

A hard case for the distinction between comparative and noncomparative justice is posed by judgments which are themselves comparative in form. For example, it is unfair to say that "*A* has more merit than *B*" when in fact *B* has more merit than *A*. So far, my definitional criteria are not precise enough to classify this injustice as either comparative or noncomparative. If a comparative injustice is an injustice that can be ascertained as such only after a comparison of *some kind or other* between the person unfairly treated and others, then of course the case at hand is comparative, for to establish the facts which would show the judgment in question to be true or false, *we must compare* the relevant traits of *A* with the relevant traits of *B*. On the other hand, the example differs from all the examples of comparative justice considered so far in a respect which is not without importance. All the other examples of comparative injustice require *comparisons of two kinds*—not only *(i)* comparison of the relevant characteristics, merits, or performances of the individual in question, which are the basis of his claim, with those of the relevant comparison group, but also *(ii)* comparison of consequent "treatments" (for example, prizes, grades, allocative shares, rewards, penalties, and, in this case, *judgments* about) accorded this individual claimant with the "treatments" (in this case, other judgments) made about relevant others. In all the cases of comparative justice considered thus far, a critic can find that justice was done when (as Aristotle might have said) the ratio between compared claims (in this case, merits) equals the ratio between compared treatments (in this case, judgments). But in the example at hand (the judgment "*A* has more merit than *B*") we can know that the judgment is unfair to *B* simply by learning if *it* is false—that is, by ascertaining that the relational fact it asserts does not hold in reality. We do not have to compare this judgment with *other judgments* about these or other persons, as we might in other contexts have to compare a present penalty, or prize, or allocative share with corresponding "treatments" (to use the generic term) of these or other persons. In short, the injustice is not like the comparative injustices already considered because it requires a critic to make only one, not two comparisons—a comparison of the merits of claimants but not a comparison of various treatments of (or judgments about) them.

This difference, I think, is sufficiently significant to warrant the classification of invidiously false comparative judgments as cases of noncomparative injustice. This can be done by simply appending an exceptive clause to our earlier definition, as follows. When the injustice done a person is noncomparative, no comparison of any kind is required to ascertain it *except* when the treatment in question consists of a *judgment* which is itself *comparative in form* so that a comparison of the claims (characteristics or past performances) of the person judged with those of others is required simply to confirm or disconfirm its truth. In contrast, when the treatment that is unjust to John Doe is unjust in the comparative sense, we must make two sorts of comparisons to ascertain it—namely, comparisons of Doe's claims with those of others, and comparison of this treatment of Doe with various treatments of others. When these two investigations uncover an Aristotelian "disproportion" between compared claims and treatments that is disadvantageous to Doe, then the treatment in question was unfair (in the comparative sense) to Doe.

A more thorough discussion of judgmental justice would have to distinguish between *(i)* the justice or injustice of the judgments themselves

which, like their truth or falsity, are properties that belong to them quite independently of who comes to believe them (indeed, even if no one comes to believe them); *(ii)* the justice or injustice of the "mental act" of forming a judgment or of simply holding or believing the judgment; and *(iii)* the justice or injustice of expressing a judgment in language, or symbolically in one's conduct. It is admittedly very misleading to assimilate *(i)* or *(ii)* to the justice or injustice of treatments of persons, even when the word "treatment" is self-consciously draped in quotation marks. At best, only *(iii)*, the actual communication of a derogatory judgment to an audience, could count as the treatment of a person in the same sense as that in which the awarding of a prize and the inflicting of a punishment clearly are treatments. This qualification, however, does not prevent me from reaching the conclusion that the justice or injustice of comparative judgments in cases *(i)* and *(ii)* as well as *(iii)*, is best classified as belonging to the noncomparative category, because if there are no treatments of the usual kind in their case, then it cannot be true that treatments must be compared; and, furthermore, as we have seen, it is not necessary in their case that the judgments in question be compared with other judgments of their kind.

Still another kind of barrier in the way of a cut and dried application of the distinction between comparative and noncomparative justice is that which results from the complexity of our institutionalized practices themselves. The awarding of prizes, for example, often is a process that involves elements of grading and rewarding. Rewards, too, are often similarly complex. In the simpler cases, we reward people with gifts that they will presumably value quite apart from their symbolism as rewards. We do this as a way of expressing our appreciation or admiration for some good deed, but sometimes that deed is the manifesting of merit through winning a contest of skill. In that case, the distinction between reward and prize is blurred. In other cases, prizes have no value to the winners except through their symbolism as prizes. Thus a blue ribbon won at the pie-baking contest at the State Fair is a pure prize, with no element of reward, whereas ten thousand dollars given to the winner of a professional golf tournament is both a prize and a reward. Moreover, prizes are often assigned as a consequence of a process of grading and, like grades, can often be understood as expressions of judgments. Grades, moreover, can be valued by their recipients as much as prizes or rewards, a fact that tends to blur these distinctions further.

Now suppose that Mary wins the first prize (a blue ribbon) and Jane the second prize (a red ribbon) even though Jane's pie in fact was better than Mary's. Since mere ribbons have no value in themselves, there is hardly an element of reward, in any strict sense, in this situation. The awardings of the prizes, however, are expressions of judgments, in this case false comparative judgments, about the relative merits of the two pies. As such, they are unfair to Jane. As a case of judgmental injustice, pure and simple, the unfairness is noncomparative, since only one comparison (that between the two pies) is required to establish it. Still, in classifying the ribbon as a prize, and not *merely* the expression of a comparative judgment, we are ascribing to it a value that the mere public utterance of words would not have. Other ways of expressing judgments are relatively ephemeral; the prize is a judgment in the form of an enduring trophy that can be possessed and exhibited. It is not a reward because its value is not even partially independent of the judgment it symbolizes (as the value of a money prize would be); but, on the other hand, it is more than the judgment it embodies, having the character of a permanent tangible record or proof. Thus, the awarding of a prize *is* a kind of "treatment" of a person, as the mere making of a judgment is not, and in virtue of symbolic conventions, the blue-ribbon award is a better treatment than the red. Thus, injustice in the awarding of prizes can be established (only) by comparison of treatments as well as claim bases, and thereby qualifies as comparative injustice.

Before moving to the topic of *grades* as kinds of judgments, I shall obviate one important misunderstanding of the justice of judgments: noncomparative injustice is not done to a person by the expression of a judgment that treats him *better* than he deserves. The "injustice" done by undeservedly favorable criticism, for example, is injustice of another category: either indirect comparative injustice done to all other authors, invidiously aggravating the hurt done to the poorly reviewed ones and debasing the currency in which praise is given to the favorably reviewed ones, or else noncomparative injustice of a "Platonic" or other "cosmic" kind (of which I shall speak shortly). But such treatment is hardly an injustice to the lucky recipient of the undeserved praise. He has not been wronged; he has no personal grievance, no complaint coming.

Grading, too, can be subsumed under the "justice of judgments" rubric. When the object of a grading system is simply to assess as accurately as possible the degree to which a person has some talent, knowledge, or other estimable quality, then the fairness or unfairness of a given grade assessment is of the noncomparative sort. Indeed, the grade itself can be taken to express a *judgment* (or assessment, or appraisal) of a person, and thus is fair or unfair to him in precisely the same manner as other judgments. When grades come to be used as the basis for subsequent job assignments, opportunities, competitive honors, and other benefits, then an undeservedly low grade can cause *further* injustice of a comparative kind, or of a different noncomparative kind analogous to the punishing of the innocent, or else, again, the "Platonic" injustice of preventing the square peg from entering the square hole it fits so well.

Sometimes, a grading system is understood to have a different aim. Instead of producing accurate assessments of each individual in a class, it may aim to stimulate a competition among the members of the class for positions of high rank relative to the other members of the class, as, for example, when students are "marked on a curve" so that it is a priori impossible that they all get high grades. The aim of such grading practices is to produce an accurate ranking of persons in respect to their possession of a given trait. The individual "curve grades," like all grades, are the expressions of judgments—in the case comparative judgments—and since the ascertainment of injustices requires only the limited single comparisons necessary for the confirmation or disconfirmation of the expressed assessments, unfair curve grades are unjust in the noncomparative sense. When, however, the avowed purpose of curve grading is to stimulate competition, and the curve restrictions are well known and consented to in advance, the graded performances resemble the elements of a rule-governed game or contest, with the higher grades taken as *prizes.* In that case, the injustices resemble those of the comparative kind since they deprive their victims of something like their "fair share" of a divisible good of limited supply—the highly prized, better grades.[6]

What I have called "Platonic justice" deserves just a word in this place. (Otherwise I shall not have "done justice" to the subject.) I have no doubt that a conception of justice much like that of Plato and the pre-Socratics survives and lives side by side in our moral consciousness with its more prominent descendants. The Platonic notion, as I shall understand it, is a noncomparative one. When "functions," whether of an internal psychological kind, or a social kind, or a more general natural kind, are not performed by the thing or person best fitted by its (his) own nature to perform them, there is injustice done, at least from the cosmic point of view, whether or not any assignable individual is denied his due. The Greeks thought of all nature (as Plato thought of the state or all society) as a kind of organic system, on the model of a machine, or a living organism, in which the macroscopic functioning of the larger system is causally dependent on the proper discharging of the functions of the component subsystems and, to some extent, vice versa. Thus when a component "organ" or "mechanism" fails to function properly, the larger system of which it is a part is thrown out of kilter. (Combine this conception with the idea, also Greek in origin, that human beings have *moral* functions upon which the normal working of cosmic process depends, and the Shakespearean notion of a foul murder throwing the universe "out of joint" becomes almost intelligible.) There is no point in trying to make this inherently vague conception more precise. My aim here is simply to point out that there is such a notion and that it is a noncomparative one, the perceived injustice not being suffered by those whose proper role is usurped (*that* injustice is the more common comparative kind) but rather by the badly used "function," and the organic cosmos in which it plays a part. "Cosmic injustice" is conceived as injustice suffered, *inter alia,* by the cosmos itself.[7]

The noncomparative conception of injustice is sometimes implied, I think, in our talk of *states of affairs* as "not right." It is part of the conventional wisdom in Anglo-American analytic ethics that the distinction between "right" and "good" in ordinary language consists partly in the fact that "right" applies to actions only, whereas "good" is used more generally to appraise not only actions and things but any state of affairs.[8] On the contrary, we do sometimes speak of states of affairs as right or wrong, and when we do, we do not intend to say merely that they are good or bad in different but equivalent language. We say, "It is not right that such and such should be the case," and this is a stronger and sharper complaint than simply stating that it is not a good thing that such and such is the case. Moreover, we sometimes say with confidence that things are not right even when there is no individual we know to be especially wronged, and no other individual to be blamed, and even no actions known by us to have the quality or effect of injustice. "It's just not right and fitting that the President of this great country should be such a little man," we might complain, while ignorant of the identity of some bigger man who was wronged by the voters, or even while unwilling to blame the voters for their choice. When we determine that a state of affairs as such is not right, or that the universe of which it is a part is "out of joint" in something like the Platonic fashion, without reference to the claims of wronged parties, our judgment is noncomparative.

II

Applying the distinction between comparative and noncomparative justice to the real world is not easily done. The distinction between concepts may be clear enough, but instances of each are rarely pure, any given example of one being likely also to have elements of the other. This contributes not only to conceptual confusion but also to moral perplexity. On many occasions for justice, both comparative and noncomparative principles apply. Comparative principles all share the form of the Aristotelian paradigm: justice requires that relevantly similar cases be treated similarly and relevantly dissimilar cases be treated dissimilarly in direct proportion to the relevant differences between them. Noncomparative principles, on the other hand, are irreducibly diverse in form as well as number. Some condemn punishment of the innocent or those who acted involuntarily; some require that reasonable expectations not be disappointed; others proscribe false derogatory judgments. When principles of both kinds apply to a particular case, often enough the duplication is benign, and what is just according to one principle is also the treatment prescribed by the other. On other occasions, the relevant comparative and noncomparative principles cut in opposite ways to the stupefaction of "the sense of justice."

To treat another person in contravention of both comparative and noncomparative principles when those principles coincide and reinforce one another is to inflict a kind of "double injustice" upon him. This is a point well appreciated by A. D. Woozley, who writes that "A man's getting less than he deserved for what he did [as remuneration for his labor] is doubly unjust if somebody else got more than he, but it would still be unjust if nobody else got more, even if nobody else was involved at all." [9] The underpayment of a worker, suggested by Woozley's example, does seem to be a double injustice to him, but it is not a clear example of the duplication of comparative and noncomparative principles. The principles of "commutative justice" which determine what is a "fair wage" might themselves be comparative principles, in which case Woozley's worker is treated unfairly on two grounds: he is paid less than his relevantly similar fellow worker at the same job, and he is paid less than a national "standard worker" at his trade, and therefore "less than he deserved." In that case, he is seen to be discriminated against when *compared* with a fellow worker in his own plant and also when *compared* with workers in relevantly similar jobs throughout the country, but no noncomparative principles seem to apply to his case at all. Perhaps, however, the commutative principles that determine a fair wage for a given job, like their counterparts in the area of retributive justice that determine a fair punishment for a given crime, are in part noncomparative. If beheading and disembowelment became the standard punishment for overtime parking, as the result of duly enacted statutes, the penalty as applied in a given case would be unjust (because too severe) even though it were applied uniformly and without discrimination to all offenders. Moreover, it would be unjust even if it were the mildest penalty in the whole system of criminal law, with more serious offenses punished with proportionately greater severity still (torture, punishment of the offender's family, and so forth). In short, it is possible for *every* punishment in a system of criminal law to be unjust because too severe, which shows that criminal desert is in part noncomparative. If the analogy between commutative and retributive justice holds in this respect, then it should be similarly conceivable that *all* of

the wages in a hypothetical economy are too low, so that any given worker is getting less than he deserves, not as determined by a comparison between his wages and those of other workers, but rather as determined by the merits of his own case. The analogy seems to fail, however, in one respect. The underpaid workers are surely treated unfairly as *compared* to their employers whose *share* of the wealth produced must be disproportionately great if theirs is disproportionately small. (This is the respect in which all *exploitation* is a comparative injustice.)

There can nevertheless be an element of noncomparative injustice in Woozley's example. Suppose, for example, that the case is one of racial bias, and the underpaid worker is discriminated against because he is black, though he is told (what is not true) that he is paid less because his work is inferior. On the one hand, this is unfair discrimination against one worker (or class of workers) among many, and thus is condemned by comparative principles. On the other hand, in so far as it is given the specious justification that it is based on assessments of ability, it can be taken to be an expression of nonrecognition of ability, a *judgment* that is unfair to the excluded worker who in fact has high ability, in which case, like all judgmental injustices, it is noncomparative.

When relevantly applicable comparative and noncomparative principles yield opposite judgments, there are, of course, two possibilities: what is condoned by the comparative principle is condemned by the noncomparative one, or what is endorsed by the noncomparative principle is declared unjust by the comparative one. Pure examples of the former kind are not easy to come by. The example of a slave society in which masters uniformly and impartially deprive their subjects of their due (as determined by the merits of their own cases) comes close, but even there the disparity between the resultant conditions of the privileged and deprived would be unjust on comparative grounds. A purer example is that suggested above of a system of criminal law, effectively and impartially administered, in which all penalties are disproportionate to actual culpability, for in that case (unlike the example of slavery) the judges, jurors, and jailers would not directly profit from the unjust treatments imposed on criminals; hence punishments would be unjust on noncomparative grounds, but not on comparative ones (at any rate, not if the punished offenders are compared only with each other). Even that example, however, is not perfectly pure, since comparisons of the excessive punishments of criminals may also be made to the nonpunishments of various noncriminals.

That the existence of comparative injustice is relative to the comparison class examined is a point whose importance is vividly shown by the perplexing case of a hypothetical system of criminal law in which people are punished even for involuntary infractions of rules. Imagine a system in which penalties are all exactly proportionate to moral guilt (whatever that might mean) or, in the case of "involuntary crimes," proportionate to the guilt that would have been involved had the infraction been voluntary. The courts in this imaginary system, with consistent impartiality, hold infants and insane people liable for crimes, and punish others for unavoidable accidents and innocent mistakes. These practices are, of course, grossly unfair to those who are punished, and the unfairness seems at least noncomparative. It might seem at first, however, that no element of comparative injustice need be involved at all, for none of these unfortunates would be in a position to complain of discrimination, prejudice, or favoritism in the enforcement of the law. Similar cases (involuntary wrongdoing) are rigorously treated, so it would seem, in similar ways (punished) so that the Aristotelian formula is satisfied. A quite different judgment results, however, when the comparison is made between different comparison classes. When all involuntary criminals are compared with each other in all relevant respects (their infraction of rules) and all voluntary noncriminals are compared with each other in all relevant respects (their compliance with rules), no invidious treatments can be discerned. But when all involuntary criminals are compared with all voluntary criminals of the same category, the result is quite different, for we soon discover that involuntary criminals are treated the same as voluntary ones even though they are *different in a morally relevant respect*—namely, that one group acted voluntarily and the other involuntarily. But why is voluntariness morally relevant? Simply because it is unfair to a person, any person, on noncomparative grounds, to punish him for his involuntary behavior. So this intriguing

example illustrates another point of importance, that comparative and noncomparative principles can dovetail in such a way that they are conceptually linked. In the case at hand, a noncomparative principle of justice determines the criterion of relevance for the application of the otherwise formal principle of comparative justice for certain contexts.

The more common examples of genuine conflict are provided by instances of treatment condoned by noncomparative principles but condemned as unjust by comparative ones. Consider something like the Augustinian theory of salvation. No man considered entirely on his own merits, prior to or independently of Divine Grace, deserves to be saved, since all men by their very natures are totally depraved. In each case, then, noncomparative justice would be served by damnation and consignment to hell-fire. Nevertheless, God, out of His infinite mercy, exercises something like executive clemency, and allows His grace to touch the souls of an arbitrarily selected minority of men, permitting them to achieve their own (undeserved) [10] salvations. The others then *are* consigned to hell, but noncomparative principles, at least, allow them no just complaint, since they are sinners simply getting what they deserve according to the canons of retributive justice. Yet if they think about their equally sinful but luckier comrades, they are likely to feel at least somewhat aggrieved at what they can only take to be unjust discrimination in plain contravention of comparative principles.

The more we ponder cases of the above kind, the more confused we become; for justice and injustice seem alternately to flit in and out of focus like the pictures in an optical illusion, depending upon whether we consider comparative or noncomparative factors. And such cases are not confined to theological speculation. They arise whenever an authority makes an "example" or an "exception" of one or more out of a class of subjects whose individual deserts are alike. When all the students in a class or all the soldiers in a barracks are equally guilty and only one is punished (as a threat to the others) or only one is left unpunished (out of favoritism) then the punished ones have no grievance on noncomparative grounds, since they are guilty after all, but they can complain against discriminatory treatment.[11]

Cases of this general kind also include instances of gratuitous benefaction. No person has a right to another person's charity, and yet if a charitable benefactor distributes his largesse to nine persons in a group of ten, arbitrarily withholding it from the tenth for no good reason, his behavior seems in some important way unfair to the tenth. Still, the benefactor might reply to the charge of arbitrary exclusion with the reminder that, morally speaking, he did not *have to* contribute to any of the group, and that his aid to nine was a net gain above and beyond the call of duty. The poor excluded beggar, his sense of justice confused, will feel aggrieved and unaggrieved in rapid alternation. There is no right to charity, or grace, or clemency, or any other form of gratuitous good treatment, and yet arbitrary inconsistency or favoritism in the distribution of these goods can seem unjust to those neglected or deprived of them.

A similar example of conflict between comparative and noncomparative principles is found in the case of the distribution of a *surplus* among a group of recipients after justice has already been done to each proper individual claim. According to Woozley: "If a father in the bequests which he makes to his sons *A* and *B* has fairly met their needs, he does no injustice to *B* if he leaves the whole of the rest of the estate to *A* —unless there is some further respect, other than need, in which the distinction between like cases is unjust." [12] Let us suppose, filling in Woozley's example, that *A* and *B* are roughly of the same age, size, health, appearance, abilities, beliefs, and ideals, that each has the same basic financial needs and that the bequests more than fulfill them in each case, but that the father leaves everything else after those basic needs have been met—say, one million unsuspected dollars—to *A,* simply because he likes *A* better (there being no other reason available). [13] We can suppose further that the existence of the "extra" one million dollars was totally unknown to the sons, so that neither of them had expectation or hope of inheriting any part of it. After individual claims based on needs, deserts, and "reasonable expectations" have been satisfied, injustice, by noncomparative standards at any rate, cannot be done. Yet comparative considerations might still properly agitate the sense of injustice (*pace* Woozley) of the "deprived" son.

The oppositions between comparative and noncomparative principles illustrated by these examples are not radical conflicts originating in the concept of justice itself of the kind that would render the very coherence of that concept suspect. I have given no examples where it is conceptually impossible to have justice both ways, cases in which satisfaction of a noncomparative principle requires violation of a comparative one, or vice versa. [14] All that the examples show is that it is sometimes possible to satisfy a principle of the one kind while violating a principle of the other kind. Such occasional and contingent opposition is one of the weaker senses in which principles can be said to conflict. In these cases of conflict, something less than perfect justice has been achieved, but that does not show that perfect justice is an impossible ideal. It is especially awkward sometimes to satisfy comparative principles, and we are tempted to take short cuts, for example, by punishing only some but not all members of a very large class of rule violators. In that event, we may choose for good reasons to compromise comparative justice for the sake of efficiency and convenience, and when we have already given noncomparative justice its due (that is, we have punished *only* the guilty) we might take our short cut with a relatively easy conscience. Still, we can easily *conceive* of what it would be like in cases of this kind to satisfy both comparative and noncomparative justice, so that the "conflict" between the two is by no means logically unavoidable. Since both noncomparative and comparative justice make valid claims on us, and since it is in principle possible for both to be satisfied, we must conclude that *in so far as a given act or arrangement fails to satisfy one or the other of the two kinds of principles, it is not as just as it could be.*

Another message to be inferred, I think, from our examples is that injustice by noncomparative standards tends to be a much more serious thing than comparative injustice. The right to be given one's due, where one's due is not merely an allotment or a share, but rather is determined (say) by prior agreements or by personal desert, is a more important right than the right not to be discriminated against. If a tyrant treats all his underlings "like dogs," then the injustice done underling John Doe is far more serious than he would suffer if he were given his due but everyone else were treated "like kings." Similarly, to be punished for a crime one did not commit is a greater outrage than to be punished for a crime one did commit while others who are equally guilty are let go. (The Dreyfus case was a greater injustice by far than the Calley case.)

Indeed, the superiority of the claims of non-comparative to comparative justice in some cases is so striking that one might well raise the question whether comparative justice, in those cases, makes any claims at all. Suppose an employer pays all his employees more than the prevailing scale in his industry, indeed more than any of them deserves by any reasonable noncomparative standard, but he pays Doe, a worker of only average skills and seniority, more than he pays Roe, a worker with superior skills and high seniority. If there is any injustice at all in this situation, it must consist entirely in the discriminatory character of the treatment. But where is the wrong in discrimination as such? In this example, no man is treated badly; in fact, each is getting more than his due. How then can Roe have *any* complaint? Why not describe the situation as one in which Roe is treated fairly but Doe gets *more* than his due? But to give a man more than his due is not to wrong him, and if no one is wronged, how can there be injustice? Much the same questions can be raised about the other examples considered above where noncomparative justice is satisfied and only discrimination remains to offend the sense of justice: punishment of the guilty when others equally guilty are let go, arbitrary exceptions to gratuitous benefactions, assignments of surplus goods after individual claims have been satisfied.[15]

Still, there is no doubt that arbitrary discrimination as such, even in the absence of any other violated claims, strikes most of us as wrong, and not merely wrong, but unfair. The explanation of this near-universal reaction involves two elements. In the first place, as a matter of psychological fact, people are *hurt* by discriminatory treatment whether or not they are wronged according to some additional standard, and secondly, the hurt is perceived to be in some important way *"offensive to reason"*—absurd, arbitrary, disproportionate, or inconsistent. These two elements, I suspect, are sufficient to account for our use of the vocabulary of "unfairness," and the spontaneous offense to our sense of justice, in cases of the kind under consideration. That it hurts to be singled out or pointedly excluded by discriminatory treatment is a plain fact which itself calls for a full psychological explanation, but a plain fact still, however it is to be accounted for. The sting of discrimination is most painful in cases of double injustice where it adds salt to other moral wounds. When one is a member of an enslaved minority, for example, it is the enslavement that does one the greatest wrong, but the perceived contrast between one's own condition and that of others not enslaved, let us suppose only because of their race, while adding nothing to the primary wrong, tends to exacerbate its immediate effect. When nearly everyone is enslaved, and cruel rules are enforced equally across the board, then the element of having been selected out for special treatment is missing. That condition is no less unjust, but it will in most cases be less constantly before the mind, less pointed in its application, and less intensely resented. So powerful is the psychological tendency to resent discriminatory treatment that it manifests itself even in cases where the discrimination is the whole of the wrong suffered and is disadvantageous only in a relative way.

The more important part of the explanation why discrimination as such is unjust, however, consists in its absolute groundlessness,[16] or grounding on morally irrelevant criteria, and the characteristic sort of offensiveness these features engender, for the general characteristic this form of injustice shares with all the others is that, quite apart from any other harm, or hurt, or wrong it might bring to the one who suffers it, it offends against impersonal reason itself. As many writers have pointed out,[17] the principle that relevantly similar cases should be treated in similar ways, put in just that general way, is a principle of reason, in much the same way as Aristotle's principles of identity, contradiction, and excluded middle are "laws of thought." It is *absurd* to treat relevantly similar cases in dissimilar ways, to ascribe different geometrical properties to identical isosceles triangles, or to assign unequal wages to relevantly equal workers.[18] Individual triangles, however, have no feelings and no interests; they do not recognize pointedly selective treatment, or partiality, or exclusion; they cannot be hurt, or harmed, or treated in relatively disadvantageous ways. For those reasons discrimination among triangles is *merely* absurd, whereas discrimination that affects the balance of advantages among beings with interests and feelings is unfair.

The moral offensiveness of discrimination is *sui generis*. In particular, it is not wholly derived from consideration of the motives of the wrong-doer, though such consideration is capable of intensifying the irritation it produces. Often discriminatory treatment strikes its victim as having something "personal" in it, an element of malice, or unprovoked insult. In other cases, like exemplary punishment, the victim may feel badly used, a mere instrument for another's purposes. But when the personal and exploitative elements are clearly missing—as, for example, when one is deprived of a shared benefit not for a morally shady motive, but for no apparent motive at all—then invidious treatment can be even more maddening.

III

It is natural enough to respond to hurt with anger, but when the hurt seems to have been arbitrarily inflicted in the manner characteristic of unjust discrimination, anger is transmuted into moral indignation. Because the treatment is offensive to reason as well as hurtful, responsive anger borrows some of the authority of reason; it becomes righteous and impersonal, free of self-doubt, and yet disinterested and free of mere self-preference. This moralized anger is by no means peculiar to discrimination among the various modes of injustice. It is, in fact, the common element in reactions to all injustices, whether comparative or noncomparative, whether actions, rules, or judgments. Perhaps more than anything else, it distinguishes the apprehension of injustice from awareness of other kinds of wrong or harmful conduct. John Stuart Mill was perhaps the first important writer to make much of this distinctive emotion.[19] No analysis of the concept of justice is complete, he claimed, without a supplementary analysis of what he called the "sentiment of justice." Mill's own analysis, however, failed to account for the element of righteousness I have noted. He analyzed the sentiment of justice (more accurately, the sentiment of injustice) into an impulse to retaliate for injury, which he took to be a kind of animal instinct, plus a distinctively human feeling of sympathy that enables us to identify imaginatively

with other victims of wrongdoing and respond angrily on their behalf as we would to our own injuries. Perhaps such elements *are* commonly part of the sentiment of injustice, but they would also be present, I should think, when we apprehend wrongdoing of other kinds, or even when we perceive harm caused to persons in an innocent or accidental way. Those elements peculiar to the sentiment of injustice that endow it with its uniquely righteous flavor have not been mentioned in Mill's account.

The sources of the sentiment of injustice are readily found in the experiences of childhood. Moral indignation in small children (in their own behalf, of course) is largely restricted, I think, to three kinds of contexts. In the first, outraged protest is directed at what is taken to be *favoritism*. Its characteristic formulae are: "He got more than I did," or "You punished me but not him, and he did it too," or "Why does he have a privilege or benefit and not me?" Impelled originally by jealousy, children learn both to accuse others of special treatment, and to defend themselves from such charges, to find analogies and disanalogies between cases, to invoke precedents and appeal to consistency. In these exercises are found the roots of the sense of comparative justice. Personal anger directed at favoritism comes to be anger felt on behalf of, or from the perspective of, impartiality. When the feeling occasioned by hurt expands its target to include inconsistency, disproportion, anomaly, and other elements similarly offensive to reason, it becomes full-blown moral indignation, and not mere animal anger sympathetically projected.

A second source of the sentiment of injustice does not appear until the stage of peer-group orientation and co-operative play, starting at about age six.[20] A new object of juvenile wrath at that stage is *exploitation*—taking unfair advantage of another's handicaps or placing another at a disadvantage in competitive or cooperative undertakings. In competitive games, one player can secure unfair advantage over another either by exploiting natural inequalities inconsistent with the game's purpose—for example, larger size or greater age—or else by creating inequalities through cheating, bribing, or lying. In co-operative undertakings one can exploit a partner's trust by free-loading, betraying him for personal gain, or otherwise letting him down. Before the age of five or six, the child has no firm concept of a regulated competition for fun or gain in which "players" trust each other to obey the rules that are meant to nullify inappropriate influences on the outcome; nor does he have a firm concept of a joint undertaking by co-operative partners each of whom trusts all the others to do their share of the work that is necessary to their common gain. Once the child becomes preoccupied, however, with games of skill and chance, with team sports and "team spirit," and with group chores and quotas assigned by parents or teachers, the streets echo with charges and rebuttals of unfairness not previously heard in the nursery.

Few six-year-olds have sufficient skill at abstract thinking to arrive at the philosophical views that will one day tempt most of them as adults: that all life is a competitive game or, alternatively, that all society is one large co-operative undertaking in which each and every partner has his assigned dues and his proper shares. The latter view is that of G. H. von Wright, who points to a respect in which *all* social wrongdoing is unjust in the manner of exploitation.[21] In von Wright's usage, escaping harm from others is the "share" which each member of a moral community has in the common good, whereas not harming others is the "price" one pays, or each member's "due share" of the price, for that good. Any time one member harms another, then, he tries to have his cake and eat it to—that is, to "have his share without paying his due," and this way of taking advantage of others, which is morally akin to cheating and free-loading, von Wright calls "the basic form of injustice." [22]

An interesting feature of von Wright's analysis in his suggestion of how exploitative injustice, too, contains an element that is offensive to reason:

One can ask questions like this: "What right have you got to put yourself in a privileged position? If you get your share without paying your due, then somebody else, who is equally anxious to get his share, will necessarily be without it. Don't you see that this is unfair?" One could almost call this appeal to a man's sense of justice an appeal to a man's sense of symmetry.[23]

The "asymmetry" referred to by von Wright is common to exploitation, distributive injustice, and discrimination. All create inequalities between relevantly equal cases, and all are offensive to reason in similar ways. Exploitation leads necessarily to unequal results that are in a way doubly unjust: the exploiter gets more than he deserves and his victim less. Like children on a seesaw, the one goes up by the same increment as the other goes down. The imbalance produced by exploitation rests on no correlated differences in which disinterested reason can find satisfaction. There are no relevant differences between the occupants of the up and down positions that underlie and justify the outcome. The crucial difference between them was a morally "irrelevant" one—worse, a morally inappropriate one; the gainer cheated or lied and the other did not.

Von Wright's bold claim that all social wrongdoing is essentially exploitative is an overstated insight. In the paradigm case of egregious exploitation that is apparently before his mind, *A* secures a gain for himself at the cost of a loss to *B*, and he does this by betraying *B*'s trust. This model fits far more cases than one might realize before reflecting, but it surely does not fit *all* cases of social wrongdoing. Some wrongs (for example, tax evasion) lack a determinate victim, or produce a trivial harm to "society" while producing a great gain to the wrongdoer. In other cases, *A* wrongfully harms *B* without any hope of gain for himself. In typical debauched or psychopathic crimes, nobody gains anything, and in cases of self-destructive malice, both parties lose. In still other cases, there need have been no prior trust relation between an aggressor and his victim. *A* and *B* may have been enemies constantly on the alert for the other's mischief. When their animosity erupts into combat one or the other of them is wrongfully injured. It is implausible to think of all these examples as instances of exploitation. Von Wright would probably insist, however, that in a great many cases of social wrongdoing that do not at first sight seem to involve duplicity, cheating, or free-loading, there is nevertheless an element, however attenuated, of exploitative injustice. Since the concept of injustice is somewhat diluted in this very general application, perhaps it would be wise to refer to "injustice in the weak sense." Then we can still ask how we can make out a contrast between those "unjust acts" which are also unjust in a specific stronger way and those which are not. My answer to that question is that the pointedly unjust acts (in the strong sense) are either those which are directly and obviously exploitative (for example, those involving cheating) or those which are invidiously discriminatory, or those expressive of derogatory falsehood. The "sentiment of injustice" in these cases is directed at the element of "asymmetry," "inconsistency," or "falsehood," all of which are, in a manner insufficiently appreciated by Mill, "offensive to reason."

IV

In a third kind of context for juvenile indignation, moral outrage stems neither from the awareness of exploitative "asymmetry" nor from the awareness of disadvantageous discrimination between like cases, for only one "case"—the child's own—may be involved. Rather the child reacts furiously to what he confidently believes to be a false judgment that is injurious to his esteem, or degrading to his status, or which simply misrepresents him in some respect that is important to him. Consider a typical example. An older child answers a parental question correctly. A younger sibling remarks that he too knew the answer, but that he did not have a chance to speak up in time. To this, the older child replies that the younger child did not know the answer and was silent only because of his ignorance. What a torrent of rage and frustration this will produce in the younger child if he *knows* that he knew the answer! In that case he has direct possession of the truth and cannot prove it to anyone. His rage, however, will not be merely an expression of his frustrated hope of presenting evidence. Nor will it be merely his reaction to the sting of an insult, for the imputation of specific ignorance in this context may not be very insulting, and much greater defamations (in the child's eyes) will not evoke the same response if they happen to be true. "You wet your bed last night," said accusingly by the older child, will, if true, evoke shame and humiliation. If false, it will produce the righteous anger characteristic of the outraged sense of (noncomparative) justice. What provides the special flavor in the child's response to the false allegation is the sense that not only he but *the truth itself* has been injured. His anger is righteous because it is not only in his own behalf; it is also and primarily in the name of the truth, or on behalf of *the way things really are.*

There is no doubt that an interest in the truth as such retains its central place in the moral outlook of adults. However we may disagree about other duties, all of us, upon reflection, will acknowledge a kind of transcendent and impersonal duty to the truth, and will also claim a kind of corresponding right to be truly ("fairly" here is a synonym of "truly") judged in matters that are relevant to our esteem. We do not insist with equal vehemence upon a right to be truly described in respects that are indifferent to esteem or to interest—for example, in respect to the color of our eyes or the shape of our fingerprints. If you describe my brown eyes as blue you will have said something false about me but not unfair to me.

The virtue of people who honor their duties of judgmental justice and respect the rights of others to be fairly appraised is called "fair-mindedness." Whatever job our voiced and written judgments may do, whatever changes they may effect in the world, they also form part of the human record, and all persons, or at least all fair-minded persons, have a double stake in that record. Everyone will wish to make his own record as good as possible, but all fair-minded persons will also wish the record itself to be accurate and untarnished, partly as a matter of common interest, but also, as we say, as *a matter of justice,* and justice in a quite basic and underivative sense. Nothing makes the head spin more than the death and burial of a known truth. Those who have read the passages about rewriting history in Orwell's *1984* will understand the "dizziness" which another writer, Albert Camus, cites as his response to "the absolute murder of a truth." [24] Our concern for the truth is also at the root of that feeling which is sometimes called "guilt", and is prominent in the consciousness of fair-minded people who sense that their own position in life implies a judgment of their merits that is too favorable, that they are therefore posing as something that they are not in fact. The moral principle behind these phenomena is that every person has a right to be treated and judged as the kind of being he is, and since this principle derives its persuasiveness and its impersonal authority from the alliance between interest and the objective truth, it also imposes a duty to accept no more favorable judgments from others than those that are in truth warranted. The alliance between personal interest and the truth may not always be present, and even where it exists, it may be short-lived, but the truth itself is timeless, and it is the truth's prestige that supports judgmental justice even when all connection with personal interests is severed. James Flexner writes that it is "unfair" to call George Washington a racist, given that he ardently and conscientiously opposed the institution of slavery.[25] Notice how the biographer naturally thinks of doing justice to his subject well after the subject, having long been dead, has any personal stake in the record.

Judgmental injustice is very commonly found to be an element of a complex injustice that includes as another element undeservedly injurious treatment. Sometimes rather subtle analysis is required to separate out injustice to the truth (and to the victim's "double interest" in the truth) from undeserved damage to other interests of the victim. Suppose, for example, that the rules of my club "allow expulsion for cheating and I am expelled [for cheating] without having cheated."[26] Note the two distinct ways in which the expulsion is unjust to me in these circumstances. On the one hand, it is an unwarranted deprivation of benefits, a hurt inflicted upon me that I have not deserved (though, of course, that deprivation, in itself, may not hurt very much if I do not particularly care for the club anyway); on the other hand the expulsion upholds, endorses, and affirms an unfair judgment—namely, the false charge that I have cheated. That affirmation would be unjust in itself even without the infliction of any further penalty.

Similarly, one player's cheating in a game may put his rival at an unfair competitive disadvantage, and that, of course, is a kind of injury to the rival's interests which may cause hurt and resentment, but the sense of injustice will be greatly magnified by the official judgment of the referee, or even the critical judgments of spectators and journalists, that there was no cheating in the first place. That judgment offends not only the player's interest in winning his match, but also it offends against the facts and involves the impersonal authority of truth as a reinforcement to the sense of merely private injury. This sort of phenomenon, which must surely provide for the philosopher one of his basic paradigms of injustice, finds a hundred illustrations in the official verdicts and decrees of courts and public tribunals. The Kent State murders, for example, angered and saddened most of us; yet the words "cruel" and "wanton" seem to describe those ter-rible events more naturally than the words "unjust" or "unfair" do. There was a different quality of responsive feeling, however, to the outrageous Ohio grand jury verdicts from that of the response to the actual primary happenings. Those official judgments added a new dimension of unfairness to the events they misrepresented, and thus rasped and rankled the sense of injustice as only the awareness of violated truth can.

V

Our legal system protects persons from the harm caused by certain kinds of false judgments by permitting them to sue their defamers for damages. But defamation (the generic legal term for libel and slander), while often involving judgmental injustice, is not simply to be identified with that moral category. It is useful to chart the differences between the two if only for the sake of getting clearer about what judgmental injustice is. Moreover, as so often happens when moral notions are compared with conceptual models drawn from the law,[27] we shall find that very precise questions can be raised within the framework of the law of defamation whose counterparts in the "natural" context of judgmental justice have no clear and easy answer. Some of these questions cannot simply be dismissed. In the interest of ultimate coherence, either precise answers should be stipulated for them through a reasoned process of "moral legislation," or else reasoned explanations should be given why such questions fail to make sense outside a narrow institutional setting.

Although defamation and judgmental injustice differ in crucial respects, there are several elements common to both. In the first place, both are propositional. Both essentially involve statements or judgments about persons of a kind that could be either true or false, but are in fact false. Prosser is especially emphatic in restricting the scope of defamation to exclude insults:

The courts . . . have held that mere words of abuse, indicating that the defendant dislikes the plaintiff and has a low opinion of him, but without suggesting any specific charge against him, are not to be treated as defamatory. A certain amount of vulgar name-calling is tolerated on the theory that it will necessarily be understood to amount to nothing more.[28]

Thus one can defame a man by calling him a

drunkard, a wifebeater, or a tax-evader, but not by calling him a rat, or a son of a bitch. There may be elements of exploitative, distributive, or even retributive injustice when a victim is made to suffer wrath or humiliation by an unwarranted insult, but judgmental injustice requires some judgment of fact, as opposed to the mere hurling of epithets.

A second element, common to defamation and judgmental injustice, is the derogatory character of the propositions affirmed by each. The propositions involved are imputations of fault, demerit, and responsibility for wrongdoing, of characteristics or actions that are somehow substandard. It is not defamatory to print in a newspaper that a man is dead,[29] although it might well seem to a living man that a widespread premature belief in his death ill serves his interests. That belief, however, makes no one think any the worse of him; a man's reputation will easily survive him, if the report of his death carries no further information to his discredit. Similarly, the premature report of a person's death may harm him (in some interest other than his interest in a good reputation), but as a proposition simply, it can hardly be unfair to him.

Defamation and judgmental injustice are also similar in that they are primarily unjust to the persons they are about, not to listeners or readers who are led to have false opinions. The essence of judgmental injustice is not deception, not being lied to. Indeed, one can express an unfair judgment in all good faith with no intent to deceive. Unjust judgments are like some other unjust actions in this respect. The justice or injustice of their effect on others can be determined independently of the motive or intention with which they are made.[30] Of course, where one does deceive by lying, this may be a kind of exploitation of the listener and therefore unfair, on other grounds, to him, too.

The first of the distinguishing differences between defamation and judgmental injustice is that defamation requires communication. Indeed, defamation is a relation among at least three parties. It consists of a judgment made by one person about another person and communicated to at least one other person. A judgment, however, need not even be spoken or written to be unjust simply as a judgment. If someone comes to believe an unjust judgment, then he has

an unjust belief, however blamelessly he comes to adopt it, however well supported it is by the evidence, however faithfully he keeps it entirely to himself. If John Doe has a belief that is unfair to Richard Roe and he voices it directly to Roe, then he expresses an unfair judgment, but he does not defame Roe, because he has not expressed that judgment to any third parties. Similarly, Doe may hold a belief that is unfair to himself, but even though he gives impulsive statement to that belief as he stares moodily at his image in the shaving mirror, he does not—indeed he cannot—defame himself.

A second difference has to do with the source of the injustice in the two cases. Although defamation usually (but not necessarily) commits judgmental injustice, the source of the legal wrong is not simply the unfairness of the communication but the harm it tends to cause. The harm in question must be suffered directly by the victim's reputation,[31] but a reputation itself may be valued for its own sake or for the sake of some ulterior interest, social, professional, or pecuniary, and sometimes the law requires proof of damage to one of these ulterior interests, too, before allowing recovery. Harms to reputation and dependent interests may vary in a large number of respects so that legal policies need to be formulated for grading the relative seriousness of different dimensions. So, for example, a defamatory utterance may make a major or a minor imputation of fault; the fault can be imputed with emphatic certainty or tentative probability; the imputation can be widely or narrowly disseminated; it can be communicated to an important or unimportant audience (friends or strangers, customers or creditors), and belief in its truth can threaten pocketbook interest or interests of another kind. "He is a butcher," said of a surgeon, may affect his medical practice and lower his income, whereas "He has syphilis," said about a rich playboy, hurts almost exclusively his interest in seducing women. A court of law can estimate pecuniary losses with reasonable exactitude and assign a compensatory fee to injured plaintiffs in a nonarbitrary way. Deciding on a fee to pay the playboy in compensation for his deprivation, on the other hand, requires a judgment of the relative seriousness of this harm compared to harms that carry non-arbitrary price tags, a comparison that is bound to be inexact at best.

In contrast, the source of judgmental injustice as such is not harm, but rather simple derogatory misrepresentation, harmful or not. Most normal persons do have an interest in not being thought worse of by others than they deserve. If only a half-dozen widely scattered persons falsely believe that I am a wife-beater or a plagiarizer, my interest in reputation is just to that extent damaged, and in a perfectly intelligible sense I am harmed, even though no other practical interest of mine is damaged as a consequence. In the extreme case, where the public record is forever falsified and everyone is convinced that I am (say) a murderer, I am harmed to an extreme extent by the opinions and judgments that are unfair to me. But those false opinions and judgments would be unfair to me in any case even if they did not cause me any harm.

Suppose a speaker stands up at a Harvard philosophical colloquium and accuses Professor Willard Van Orman Quine of being "the real and original Boston Strangler." I doubt whether this false derogatory judgment would do Professor Quine's reputation any harm. Nor would it be likely to distress him any. It is too patently absurd a judgment to have much of any effect at all, except perhaps to cause general amusement. And yet considered as a judgment simply, since it misrepresents the person it judges in a way that matters, it is unfair to him. Furthermore, if anyone were to come to believe it, then he would have a belief that is unfair to the person it is about.

I come finally to the differences between defamation and judgmental injustice that generate philosophical perplexities. These have to do with the nature of the standards employed in the two areas. Even within the law, there are disagreements over "the problem of the standard." "It has been held in England," Prosser tells us, "that the communication must tend to defame the plaintiff in the eyes of the community in general, or at least of a reasonable man, rather than in the opinion of any particular group or class." [32] The standard used in American courts, on the other hand, has been more realistic, "recognizing that the plaintiff may suffer real damage if he is lowered in the esteem of any substantial and respectable group, even though it be a minority one, with ideas that are not necessarily reasonable." [33] The class of persons whose esteem is lowered may be quite small, but not "so small as to be negligible."

One plaintiff recovered damages as a consequence of a defendant's false public statement that her father was a murderer though clearly not many persons, and no reasonable persons, would think less of *her,* even if they believed the allegation about her father. On the other hand, no one today, not even a debutante, could recover damages for a false public allegation that her father was a coal miner or a factory worker. Hardly any person could admit without embarrassment that he thought less of her because of *that.* When the size of the group whose esteem is at issue is "substantial and respectable," however, its standards of value need not be reasonable at all. There have been many cases, in southern courts especially, for example, in which a white man has recovered damages for the assertion or insinuation, in print, that he is a Negro. [34] While the esteeming group need not be reasonable, however, it must be minimally "respectable." No professional criminal could sue successfully for defamation on the ground that he had been falsely described as a police informer, even though that allegation may have utterly smashed his reputation with other criminals.

Whatever the correct policy decision about the standard for determining defamation, there is no reason a priori to expect it to apply also to determinations of judgmental unfairness. Indeed, as we have seen in the example of the white man who was defamed by the insinuation that he was a Negro, a genuinely defamatory utterance need not be judgmentally unfair at all. What then is the standard for judgmental injustice as such? This is a question which we should handle gingerly, since we have no guarantee in advance that it can be answered in as clear and precise a fashion as its legal counterpart. The problem requires the choice among standards of three kinds. We can choose a *subjective standard* for judgmental injustice, an *objective standard,* or the *standard of actual truth.* And there are choices within these categories. Within the subjective category, we can allow judgmental unfairness to be determined by the evaluative standards of the person judging, the person judged about, or the audience (if any) to whom the judgment is communicated. The latter possibility, while plausible enough for the determination of defamation, will not do for judgmental injustice; since we are after a standard that will apply to any judgment, expressed or not, we could hardly settle for a standard that applies to a judgment only when it is expressed. Similarly, we can eliminate the standards of the person making the judgment, for that would leave us with an anarchically relativistic result. One and the same false proposition—say, that John Doe is a Communist—would be unfair to Doe when believed by one person—say, Richard Nixon—and not at all unfair when believed by another—say, Angela Davis. This result cannot be ruled out dogmatically, but it does contradict a presupposition of our inquiry—namely, that propositions about persons can be unfair in themselves, just as they are true or false in themselves, quite independently of who believes, affirms, or asserts them. The most plausible of the subjective answers to our question is that the appropriate standard for judgmental injustice is the standard of the subject about whom the judgment is made. I shall return to it below.

Objective standards are not necessarily those that are actually employed by any given subject or group of subjects. Rather they are those that ought to be employed by any subjects, those that would be employed by all subjects if they were reasonable. Wherever the common law uses an objective standard, it refers therefore to the standard of "the reasonable man." If we had used an objective standard for defamation, as the English do, then Dunnigan should not have won his suit against the *Natchez Times* for insinuating falsely that he was a Negro, for surely he would not be lowered in the estimation of any reasonable man just for being thought to be a Negro. That is just another way of saying, of course, that racial prejudice is unreasonable. Applying objective criteria is not always that easy, especially if we permit our standard to be tailored somewhat to the circumstances, as indeed we often do in other contexts, when we consider that many of the evaluative standards of actual reasonable men do not correspond to those we would ascribe to a hypothetical ideal person whose values transcend the limitations of a particular culture at a particular time and place. With which human characteristics should we endow our hypothetical reasonable man if he is not to seem superhuman? Is he simply the normal man of average insight and sensitivity, like most of our neighbors? That is not a terribly attractive idea, but it may be a realistic one unless we wish to hold most of our

neighbors themselves to a standard that is beyond their reach. Supposing we give the reasonable man standards of judgment that are a good deal closer to an ideal of correctness than the average, what other characteristics should we give him? Is he a reasonable Southerner or a reasonable Northerner? Does he know a lot of history, psychology, and economics, or is his knowledge defective in the manner of most of our neighbors in those respects?

When we are dealing with various purely legal matters including the question of defamation, we will often wish to soften an objective standard by bringing in certain subjective elements. So, for example, the law of negligence holds a blind man to the standard of a "reasonably careful and prudent blind man," not to the more elevated standard of a reasonable man with normal vision. Similarly in the law of criminal homicide, under some rules,[35] a defendant is entitled to the mitigating defense of "provocation" if he can show that he killed a man in circumstances that would have caused even a reasonable man to lose control of himself. Such rules attribute an emotional side to the reasonable man, and even a tendency in certain rare circumstances to very human passionate anger.[36] The introduction of softening elements into objective legal standards is a concession to common human frailties intended to prevent the unfairness of holding specific persons to standards they cannot meet. In the law of defamation the softening process increases the protection given to prospective plaintiffs, but toughens the requirements imposed on prospective defendants, for it permits some plaintiffs to collect damages for false statements that would not diminish their standing in the eyes of an ideal transcultural reasonable man, but would diminish the esteem of a reasonable man of deep southern background and affiliation, say, or of Orthodox Jewish religious commitment, or whatever. But when we apply a standard of judgmental unfairness quite outside of legal contexts, there are no "plaintiffs" or "defendants" to consider, nor even subjects or objects of spoken utterances or written statements to specific audiences in concrete circumstances. Here, we deal not with persons who might later complain of harsh treatment, but with *propositions* about people, and propositions have no human frailties to consider. Here if anywhere we should expect our standards to be as free as possible of subjective elements.

The most objective standard we could possibly employ would be that of actual truth: a false statement is unfair to a person if it is *truly derogatory* of him—that is, if it would lower the esteem of a hypothetical reasonable man who employed only correct evaluative standards. If we then ascribe to our ideally reasonable man complete empirical knowledge of all matters relevant to evaluations, we would be very close to identifying the reasonable man with God. In a way this is the easiest solution to our problem, for it allows us to evade difficult questions about the evaluation of human character. Unlike its alternative solutions to the problem of the standard for judgmental unfairness, this one is not merely partially but completely formal, needing to be filled in by a thorough account of what the true standards for admiring and disrespecting *are*—in short, by a long and systematic treatise in what Kant called *Tugendlehre,* or the theory of virtue.

Nonetheless, the standard of actual truth is prima facie the most plausible one for our limited purposes here. It seems to be the standard presupposed by our intuitions in clear cases, explaining, for example, why it is unfair to Quine to judge or believe him to be the Boston Strangler, even though there are few if any actual contexts in which the assertion of that proposition would defame him. An ideally reasonable man who employed only the correct principles of character appraisal would give Quine very low points indeed if he believed him to be a strangler. There may be possible if not actual cultures or subcultures which exercise such strong influences on their members that even generally reasonable men among them would think *more* of Quine for his extracurricular violence, but whatever the opinions of "reasonable *machos*" like that, our intuitions are unwavering: the proposition in question is unfair to Quine. Similarly, it would be false but not unfair to Quine to believe him to be a Negro, whatever the reaction of some hypothetically localized and humanized "reasonable man."

It would be satisfyingly simple, and superficially plausible, to leave the matter at that, but as usual in philosophy there are troublesome counterexamples and looming complications. Suppose we assume, merely for the sake of an example, that the analytic-synthetic distinction is perfectly sensible and that the arguments so far mustered against it are muddled one and all. On that assumption, would it be unfair to Quine to believe that he is a great *defender* of the analytic-synthetic distinction? If we communicated this belief to audiences of certain kinds, Quine would probably feel defamed, but that is at least partly because he believes the analytic-synthetic distinction to be untenable. Suppose, however, that an angel of the Lord comes to Quine near the end of his days and reveals to him the truth that the analytic-synthetic distinction is quite tenable, so that Quine is forced to change his mind about it. Even then, I suspect, Quine could hardly be content with the false judgment, communicated or not, that his career had been spent defending the tenability, now vindicated, of the distinction. Indeed, I should think he might even feel *wronged* by the judgment, though neither defamed, nor otherwise harmed, nor disparaged, nor belittled by it. To be misdescribed in a way that is very basic to one's conception of oneself, one might think, is to be judged or treated unfairly, even though not in any obvious way derogated or discredited.

There are better examples, often involving less controversial assumptions, that can be drawn from history's catalogue of lost causes. Those of us who are liberals might well understand how it is unfair to Bill Buckley to judge him to be a liberal, and even a doctrinaire socialist will appreciate the judgmental injustice in the false claim that T. S. Eliot was a socialist. It is unfair to any person who has conscientiously believed in a proposition, taken it to heart, advocated and campaigned for it, and in the extreme case even built his life upon it, to deny that he believed that proposition, even though in fact that proposition is false. Thus, even though God might think better of Bertrand Russell if He believed him to be a devout Christian, that belief about Russell would be unfair to him, and unfair even if atheism, his actual conviction, should be false.

The conclusion I draw from these examples is that the standard for judgmental injustice is necessarily disjunctive in form. A false judgment or belief about a person is unfair to that person if *either* it is truly derogatory of him *or else* it severely misrepresents him in a way which is fundamental to his own conception of himself. (Unfairness by the second criterion would have to be restricted to violations of self-conceptions that fall within wide limits of reasonableness. The sincere subjective standards respected by that criterion cannot be so highly eccentric as to be irrational.) A judgment or belief about a person is unfair to him according to the second criterion even though it misrepresents him in a way that would elevate his standing in the eyes of an ideally reasonable being.

The disjunctive criterion suggests that we have duties of at least two kinds in respect to our beliefs about other persons. Corresponding to the first disjunct is a duty to try to avoid believing objectively derogatory things about others in the absence of firm evidence. That is a duty to give others the benefit of one's doubts, to avoid thinking ill of them without warrant—in short, to be generous. The second duty, however, cuts the other way, for in some cases it would have us also be careful to avoid believing too well of a person in the absence of firm evidence, because of the danger that a false generous belief might misrepresent him in a respect which is crucial to his own conception of himself. To take this second duty seriously, then, would be to create a disposition that would tend to counterbalance that created by the first, at least for a certain class of cases.

The morality of belief and judgment is subtle enough to begin with, and this disjunctive criterion of judgmental injustice makes it even more difficult. That result, however, should not be alarming. Given that we run such complicated moral risks when we judge falsely about our fellows, we had better make all the more sure that our beliefs and judgments are true.

NOTES

1. I have profited from positive suggestions and sharp criticisms of earlier versions of this paper from Jonathan Bennett, Bernard Gert, T. Y. Henderson, Saul Kripke, Phillip Montague, Joshua Rabinowitz, Robert Richman, Arthur Schafer, Harry Silverstein, and especially David Lyons.

2. As many writers have observed, it is much more convenient, when doing moral philosophy, to speak of injustice than to keep to the positive term, justice. That greater convenience is an undeniable fact, but I shall not speculate here whether it has any theoretical significance.

3. E.g., Richard Brandt, *Ethical Theory* (Englewood Cliffs, N.J., 1959), p. 410; S. I. Benn and Richard Peters, *Social Principles and the Democratic State* (London, 1959), chs. 5 and 6; Chaim Perelman, *The Idea of Justice and the Problem of Argument* (New York, 1963), pp. 16 ff.; and Morris Ginsberg, *On Justice in Society* (Harmondsworth, Middlesex, 1965), p. 70 *et passim*.

4. "Mitigated" in the sense that its sting might not hurt as much in a given case, not in the sense that the degree of (noncomparative) injustice in a given case is actually reduced.

5. I discuss exploitation more fully below in Part III.

6. The curve-grading situation, for similar reasons, has much in common with typical distributive contexts—for example, the dividing up of a pie. To give one person an undeservedly large portion is necessarily to deprive someone else of his proper share, so the just distributor will have to compare the claims of all the pie-eaters, and make the relation between his "treatments" (allocations) mirror the relation between their claims. Curve-grading is often more like prize-awarding than like pie-distributing, however, in that its treatments must mirror claims only in respect to their ranking order; the "size" of the grades cannot be modified to reflect close or wide differences between the strength of claims, whereas in principle one can make a piece of pie have any size at all short of the whole pie. In another respect, however, curve-grading is more like pie-distributing, for everybody gets assigned some "share" or other, whether it be an *A, B, C, D,* or *E*. To preserve a near-perfect analogy with prizes, we should have to interpret *every* grade as either a positive or negative prize, and each grade as a better prize than the one behind it and a worse prize than the one ahead of it in the ranking. At any rate, to the extent that grading is a kind of public exercise, with rule-determined risks and opportunities understood in advance by graders and those they grade alike, the curve-grading context is a comparative one, even though an individual grade as such is essentially an assessment—that is, the expression of a judgment. This is a complicated result, but I think there is no contradiction in it. We can say that in so far as *C*-minus is taken to be a judgment merely, even a comparative judgment, the injustice of its assignment when undeserved is noncomparative, and in so far as the assignment of *C*-minus to one of the better students in the class deprives him of the "prize" or "share" he deserves, and awards it (necessarily) to someone else instead, the injustice is comparative. "Double injustices," as I claim in Section II in the text, are frequent occurrences.

7. A quite different conception of cosmic injustice should be distinguished from the one described above. Cosmic injustice is sometimes conceived as injustice *caused* (as opposed to suffered) by the cosmos. When the best runner in the race fails to win the prize because he pulls up lame or suffers some other bad luck, a kind of injustice is done, but the unlucky runner has no grievance in that case against the judges or against his competitors. *They* have not done him wrong, and in fact his rights have not been infringed by any assignable person. If he nevertheless rails against his undeserved fate, he may conceive his grievance as holding against the laws of nature, the fates, the gods, or whatever. The conception of "cosmic injustice" which this suggests, unlike the one described in the text, is a comparative one: the winner's ability does not stand in the same "ratio" to the unlucky loser's ability as the winner's "treatment" (awarding him first prize) stands to the unlucky loser's treatment (awarding him a lesser prize or no prize at all).

8. See, *inter alia*, W. D. Ross, *The Right and the Good* (Oxford, 1931), pp. 2–3, and Michael Stocker, "Rightness and Goodness: Is There a Difference?," *American Philosophical Quarterly*, 10 (1973), 93 *et passim*.

9. A. D. Woozley, "Injustice," *American Philosophical Quarterly Monograph,* 7 (1973), 115–116.

10. One might choose to say "otherwise undeserved salvations" here to suggest that God confers on the elect not only their salvation, but also their desert of salvation. But this, I think, would render the concept of desert incoherent. Even

though omnipotent, God can no more make the undeserving deserving *by fiat* than He can make $2 + 2 = 5$.

11. Cf. A. M. Honoré: "If a rule forbids parking in a certain area, it is unfair to *A* who has parked in that area that he should be fined for doing so, whilst *B*, who has done the same thing is not punished" ("Social Justice," *McGill Law Journal*, 8 [1962], 67).

12. Woozley, *op. cit.*, pp. 112–113.

13. The import of the example would be changed, I think, if the father, preferring to have the whole (remaining) fortune in one set of hands than divided (and this for non-arbitrary reasons), selects *A* by flipping a coin.

14. There are easily imagined circumstances, on the other hand, in which it is *practically* impossible to do both comparative and noncomparative justice. E.g., suppose I owe *A*, *B*, *C*, and *D* each $100, but I have only $100 all together. If I pay $25 to each, there will be no comparative injustice (discrimination), but a "commutative injustice" will be done to each. But if I pay $100 to *A* and nothing to the others, then both comparative and noncomparative injustice is done to the others, but no injustice by any standard to *A*. Whatever I do, in this example, will have the effect of injustice *somewhere*.

It should be noted that I am concerned throughout this essay with the "effect" and not the "quality" of injustice. The distinction is Aristotle's. See the *Nicomachean Ethics*, V. For a convincing argument that justice in effect (justice *to* someone or other) is a more basic notion than justice as a quality of actions reflecting the virtue of the agent, see Josef Pieper, *Justice* (London, 1957). Pieper there paraphrases Aquinas: "in the realm of justice, good and evil are judged purely on the basis of the deed itself, regardless of the inner disposition of the doer; the point is not how the deed accords with the doer, but rather, how it affects 'the other person' " (pp. 36–37).

15. Still another example is that suggested by the biblical parable of the laborers in the vineyard, Ch. XX of the Gospel According to St. Matthew.

16. There are contexts, of course, in which comparative justice is not only compatible with arbitrariness but actually requires it. Sometimes distributive justice calls for purely arbitrary—that is, random—procedures for allocating indivisible goods or burdens. (See David Lyons, *The Forms and Limits of Utilitarianism* [Oxford, 1965], pp. 161–177.) In these cases, however, there is an intelligible rationale for the procedure, whereas in the case of unjust discrimination, there is either an irrelevant criterion employed, or else there is no "procedure" and no "rationale," but only arbitrariness through and through.

17. E.g., Isaiah Berlin, "Equality as an Ideal," *Proceedings of the Aristotelian Society*, vol. LVI (1955–1956).

18. It is, of course, even more absurd to assign unequal wages to relevantly unequal workers in *inverse* proportion to their relevant differences—that is, to pay more to the less deserving and less to the more deserving.

19. J. S. Mill, *Utilitarianism*, Ch. V, pars. 16–24.

20. See Jean Piaget, *The Moral Judgment of the Child*, trans. by Marjorie Gabain (London, 1932).

21. G. H. von Wright, *The Varieties of Goodness* (London,

1963), Ch. X. Cf. also Herbert Morris, "Persons and Punishment," *The Monist*, vol. 52 (October, 1968).

22. *Ibid.*, p. 208.

23. *Ibid.*, p. 210.

24. Albert Camus, *The Fall*, trans. by Justine O'Brien (New York, 1956), p. 90.

25. James Flexner, "Washington and Slavery," *New York Times*, Feb. 22, 1973, p. 39.

26. The example is from Brian Barry, *Political Argument* (London, 1965), p. 99.

27. See my *Doing and Deserving* (Princeton, 1970), Chs. 2–4.

28. William L. Prosser, *Handbook of the Law of Torts*, 2nd ed. (St. Paul, 1955), p. 576.

29. *Ibid.*, p. 574. See *Cohen* v. *New York Times Co.*, 1912, 153 App. Div. 242, 138 N.Y.S. 206, and *Lemmer* v. *The Tribune*, 1915, 50 Mont. 559, 148 P. 338.

30. Cf. Pieper, *op. cit.*, pp. 35–40.

31. Prosser defines defamation as "an invasion of the interest in reputation and good name by communication to others which tends to diminish the esteem [elsewhere he writes 're-spect,' 'good will,' or 'confidence'] in which the plaintiff is held, or to excite adverse feelings or opinions against him" (*op. cit.*, p. 572).

32. Prosser, *op. cit.*, p. 577.

33. *Loc. cit.*

34. One of the more recent cases is *Natchez Times Publishing Co.* v. *Dunnigan*, Mississippi, 1954, 72 So. 2d 681. See also *Spencer* v. *Looney*, Virginia, 1914, 116 Va. 767, 82 S.E. 745, and *Jones* v. *R. L. Polk & Co.* Alabama, 1915, 190 Ala. 243, 67 So. 577.

35. E.g., Great Britain's Homicide Act (1957), Sec. 3: "Where on a charge of murder there is evidence on which the jury can find that the person charged was provoked (whether by things done or by things said or by both together) to lose his self-control, the question whether the provocation was enough to make a reasonable man do as he did shall be left to be determined by the jury."

36. Such rules are by no means unanimously approved by legal commentators. Glanville Williams writes: "Surely the true view of provocation is that it is a concession to 'the frailty of human nature' in those exceptional cases where the legal prohibition fails of effect. It is a compromise, neither conceding the propriety of the act nor exacting the full penalty for it. This being so, how can it be admitted that that paragon of virtue, the reasonable man, gives way to provocation?" ("Provocation and the Reasonable Man," *Criminal Law Review* [1954], p. 742). The authors of the *Model Penal Code*, in their Comments on Tentative Draft No. 9 (1959), p. 47, argue that "To require, as the rule is sometimes stated, that the provocation be enough to make a reasonable man do as the defendant did is patently absurd; the reasonable man quite plainly does not kill. . . . But even the correct and the more common statement of the rule, that the provocative circumstances must be sufficient to deprive a reasonable or an ordinary man of self-control, leaves much to be desired since it totally excludes any attention to the special situation of the actor."

DAVID HUME

Of Justice *

PART I

That Justice is useful to society, and consequently that *part* of its merit, at least, must arise from that consideration, it would be a superfluous undertaking to prove. That public utility is the *sole* origin of justice, and that reflections on the beneficial consequences of this virtue are the *sole* foundation of its merit; this proposition, being more curious and important, will better deserve our examination and enquiry.

Let us suppose, that nature has bestowed on the human race such profuse *abundance* of all *external* conveniencies, that, without any uncertainty in the event, without any care or industry on our part, every individual finds himself fully provided with whatever his most voracious appetites can want, or luxurious imagination wish or desire. His natural beauty, we shall suppose, surpasses all acquired ornaments: The perpetual clemency of the seasons renders useless all cloaths or covering: The raw herbage affords him the most delicious fare; the clear fountain, the richest beverage. No laborious occupation required: No tillage: No navigation. Music, poetry, and contemplation form his sole business: Conversation, mirth, and friendship his sole amusement.

It seems evident, that, in such a happy state, every other social virtue would flourish, and receive tenfold encrease; but the cautious, jealous virtue of justice would never once have been dreamed of. For what purpose make a partition of goods, where every one has already more than enough? Why give rise to property, where there cannot possibly be any injury? Why call this object *mine,* when, upon the seizing of it by another, I need but stretch out my hand to possess myself of what is equally valuable? Justice, in that case, being totally USELESS, would be an idle

ceremonial, and could never possibly have place in the catalogue of virtues.

We see, even in the present necessitous condition of mankind, that, wherever any benefit is bestowed by nature in an unlimited abundance, we leave it always in common among the whole human race, and make no subdivisions of right and property. Water and air, though the most necessary of all objects, are not challenged as the property of individuals; nor can any man commit injustice by the most lavish use and enjoyment of these blessings. In fertile extensive countries, with few inhabitants, land is regarded on the same footing. And no topic is so much insisted on by those, who defend the liberty of the seas, as the unexhausted use of them in navigation. Were the advantages, procured by navigation, as inexhaustible, these reasoners had never had any adversaries to refute; nor had any claims ever been advanced of a separate, exclusive dominion over the ocean.

It may happen, in some countries, at some periods, that there be established a property in water, none in land; [1] if the latter be in greater abundance than can be used by the inhabitants, and the former be found, with difficulty, and in very small quantities.

Again; suppose, that, though the necessities of human race continue the same as at present, yet the mind is so enlarged, and so replete with friendship and generosity, that every man has the utmost tenderness for every man, and feels no more concern for his own interest than for that of his fellows: It seems evident, that the USE of justice would, in this case, be suspended by such an extensive benevolence, nor would the divisions and barriers of property and obligation have ever been thought of. Why should I bind another, by a deed or promise, to do me any good office, when I know that he is already prompted, by the strongest inclination, to seek my happiness, and would, of himself, perform the desired service;

---

* Section III of *An Enquiry Concerning the Principles of Morals,* first published in London in 1751.

except the hurt, he thereby receives, be greater than the benefit accruing to me? in which case, he knows, that, from my innate humanity and friendship, I should be the first to oppose myself to his imprudent generosity. Why raise landmarks between my neighbour's field and mine, when my heart has made no division between our interests; but shares all his joys and sorrows with the same force and vivacity as if originally my own? Every man, upon this supposition, being a second self to another, would trust all his interests to the discretion of every man; without jealousy, without partition, without distinction. And the whole human race would form only one family; where all would lie in common, and be used freely, without regard to property; but cautiously too, with as entire regard to the necessities of each individual, as if our own interests were most intimately concerned.

In the present disposition of the human heart, it would, perhaps, be difficult to find compleat instances of such enlarged affections; but still we may observe, that the case of families approaches towards it; and the stronger the mutual benevolence is among the individuals, the nearer it approaches; till all distinction of property be, in a great measure, lost and confounded among them. Between married persons, the cement of friendship is by the laws supposed so strong as to abolish all division of possessions: and has often, in reality, the force ascribed to it. And it is observable, that, during the ardour of new enthusiasms, when every principle is inflamed into extravagance, the community of goods has frequently been attempted: and nothing but experience of its inconveniencies, from the returning or disguised selfishness of men, could make the imprudent fanatics adopt anew the ideas of justice and of separate property. So true is it, that this virtue derives its existence entirely from its necessary *use* to the intercourse and social state of mankind.

To make this truth more evident, let us reverse the foregoing suppositions; and carrying every thing to the opposite extreme, consider what would be the effect of these new situations. Suppose a society to fall into such want of all common necessaries, that the utmost frugality and industry cannot preserve the greater number from perishing, and the whole from extreme misery: It will readily, I believe, be admitted, that the strict laws of justice are suspended, in such a

pressing emergence, and give place to the stronger motives of necessity and self-preservation. Is it any crime, after a shipwreck, to seize whatever means or instrument of safety one can lay hold of, without regard to former limitations of property? Or if a city besieged were perishing with hunger; can we imagine, that men will see any means of preservation before them, and lose their lives, from a scrupulous regard to what, in other situations, would be the rules of equity and justice? The USE and TENDENCY of that virtue is to procure happiness and security, by preserving order in society: But where the society is ready to perish from extreme necessity, no greater evil can be dreaded from violence and injustice; and every man may now provide for himself by all the means, which prudence can dictate, or humanity permit. The public, even in less urgent necessities, opens granaries, without the consent of proprietors; as justly supposing, that the authority of magistracy may, consistent with equity, extend so far: But were any number of men to assemble, without the tye of laws or civil jurisdiction; would an equal partition of bread in a famine, though effected by power and even violence, be regarded as criminal or injurious?

Suppose likewise, that it should be a virtuous man's fate to fall into the society of ruffians, remote from the protection of laws and government; what conduct must he embrace in that melancholy situation? He sees such a desperate rapaciousness prevail; such a disregard to equity, such contempt of order, such stupid blindness to future consequences, as must immediately have the most tragical conclusion, and must terminate in destruction to the greater number, and in a total dissolution of society to the rest. He, mean while, can have no other expedient than to arm himself, to whomever the sword he seizes, or the buckler, may belong: To make provision of all means of defence and security: And his particular regard to justice being no longer of USE to his own safety or that of others, he must consult the dictates of self-preservation alone, without concern for those who no longer merit his care and attention.

When any man, even in political society, renders himself, by his crimes, obnoxious to the public, he is punished by the laws in his goods and person; that is, the ordinary rules of justice are, with regard to him, suspended for a moment, and it becomes equitable to inflict on him, for the *benefit* of society, what, otherwise, he could not suffer without wrong or injury.

The rage and violence of public war; what is it but a suspension of justice among the warring parties, who perceive, that this virtue is now no longer of any *use* or advantage to them? The laws of war, which then succeed to those of equity and justice, are rules calculated for the *advantage* and *utility* of that particular state, in which men are now placed. And were a civilized nation engaged with barbarians, who observed no rules even of war; the former must also suspend their observance of them, where they no longer serve to any purpose; and must render every action or rencounter as bloody and pernicious as possible to the first aggressors.

Thus, the rules of equity or justice depend entirely on the particular state and condition, in which men are placed, and owe their origin and existence to that UTILITY, which results to the public from their strict and regular observance. Reverse, in any considerable circumstance, the condition of men: Produce extreme abundance or extreme necessity: Implant in the human breast perfect moderation and humanity, or perfect rapaciousness and malice: By rendering justice totally *useless,* you thereby totally destroy its essence, and suspend its obligation upon mankind.

The common situation of society is a medium amidst all these extremes. We are naturally partial to ourselves, and to our friends; but are capable of learning the advantage resulting from a more equitable conduct. Few enjoyments are given us from the open and liberal hand of nature; but by art, labour, and industry, we can extract them in great abundance. Hence the ideas of property become necessary in all civil society: Hence justice derives its usefulness to the public: And hence alone arises its merit and moral obligation.

These conclusions are so natural and obvious, that they have not escaped even the poets, in their descriptions of the felicity, attending the golden age or the reign of SATURN. The seasons, in that first period of nature, were so temperate, if we credit these agreeable fictions, that there was no necessity for men to provide themselves with cloaths and houses, as a security against the violence of heat and cold: The rivers flowed with wine and milk: The oaks yielded honey; and nature spontaneously produced her greatest delicacies. Nor were these the chief advantages of that happy age. Tempests were not alone removed from nature; but those more furious tempests were unknown to human breasts, which now cause such uproar, and engender such confusion. Avarice, ambition, cruelty, selfishness, were never heard of: Cordial affection, compassion, sympathy, were the only movements with which the mind was yet acquainted. Even the punctilious distinction of *mine* and *thine* was banished from among that happy race of mortals, and carried with it the very notion of property and obligation, justice and injustice.

This *poetical* fiction of the *golden age* is, in some respects, of a piece with the *philosophical* fiction of the *state of nature;* only that the former is represented as the most charming and most peaceable condition, which can possibly be imagined; whereas the latter is painted out as a state of mutual war and violence, attended with the most extreme necessity. On the first origin of mankind, we are told, their ignorance and savage nature were so prevalent, that they could give no mutual trust, but must each depend upon himself, and his own force or cunning for protection and security. No law was heard of: No rule of justice known: No distinction of property regarded: Power was the only measure of right; and a perpetual war of all against all was the result of men's untamed selfishness and barbarity.[2]

Whether such a condition of human nature could ever exist, or if it did, could continue so long as to merit the appellation of a *state,* may justly be doubted. Men are necessarily born in a family-society, at least; and are trained up by their parents to some rule of conduct and behaviour. But this must be admitted, that, if such a state of mutual war and violence was ever real, the suspension of all laws of justice, from their absolute inutility, is a necessary and infallible consequence.

The more we vary our views of human life, and the newer and more unusual the lights are, in which we survey it, the more shall we be convinced, that the origin here assigned for the virtue of justice is real and satisfactory.

Were there a species of creatures, intermingled with men, which, though rational, were possessed of such inferior strength, both of body and mind, that they were incapable of all resistance, and could never, upon the highest provocation, make us feel the effects of their resentment; the necessary consequence, I think, is, that we should be bound, by the laws of humanity, to give gentle usage to these creatures, but should not, properly speaking, lie under any restraint of justice with regard to them, nor could they possess any right or property, exclusive of such arbitrary lords. Our intercourse with them could not be called society, which supposes a degree of equality; but absolute command on the one side, and servile obedience on the other. Whatever we covet, they must instantly resign: Our permission is the only tenure, by which they hold their possessions: Our compassion and kindness the only check, by which they curb our lawless will: And as no inconvenience ever results from the exercise of a power, so firmly established in nature, the restraints of justice and property, being totally *useless,* would never have place in so unequal a confederacy.

This is plainly the situation of men, with regard to animals; and how far these may be said to possess reason, I leave it to others to determine. The great superiority of civilized EUROPEANS above barbarous INDIANS, tempted us to imagine ourselves on the same footing with regard to them, and made us throw off all restraints of justice, and even of humanity, in our treatment of them. In many nations, the female sex are reduced to like slavery, and are rendered incapable of all property, in opposition to their lordly masters. But though the males, when united, have, in all countries, bodily force sufficient to maintain this severe tyranny; yet such are the insinuation, address, and charms of their fair companions, that women are commonly able to break the confederacy, and share with the other sex in all the rights and privileges of society.

Were the human species so framed by nature as that each individual possessed within himself every faculty, requisite both for his own preservation and for the propagation of his kind: Were all society and intercourse cut off between man and man, by the primary intention of the supreme Creator: It seems evident, that so solitary a being would be as much incapable of justice, as of social discourse and conversation. Where mutual regards and forbearance serve to no manner of purpose, they would never direct the conduct of any

reasonable man. The headlong course of the passions would be checked by no reflection on future consequences. And as each man is here supposed to love himself alone, and to depend only on himself and his own activity for safety and happiness, he would, on every occasion, to the utmost of his power, challenge the preference above every other being, to none of which he is bound by any ties, either of nature or of interest.

But suppose the conjunction of the sexes to be established in nature, a family immediately arises; and particular rules being found requisite for its subsistence, these are immediately embraced; though without comprehending the rest of mankind within their prescriptions. Suppose, that several families unite together into one society, which is totally disjoined from all others, the rules, which preserve peace and order, enlarge themselves to the utmost extent of that society; but becoming then entirely useless, lose their force when carried one step farther. But again suppose, that several distinct societies maintain a kind of intercourse for mutual convenience and advantage, the boundaries of justice still grow larger, in proportion to the largeness of men's views, and the force of their mutual connexions. History, experience, reason sufficiently instruct us in this natural progress of human sentiments, and in the gradual enlargement of our regards to justice, in proportion as we become acquainted with the extensive utility of that virtue.

PART II

If we examine the *particular* laws, by which justice is directed, and property determined; we shall still be presented with the same conclusion. The good of mankind is the only object of all these laws and regulations. Not only it is requisite, for the peace and interest of society, that men's possessions should be separated; but the rules, which we follow, in making the separation, are such as can best be contrived to serve farther the interests of society.

We shall suppose, that a creature, possessed of reason, but unacquainted with human nature, deliberates with himself what RULES of justice or property would best promote public interest, and establish peace and security among mankind: His most obvious thought would be, to assign the largest possessions to the most extensive virtue, and give every one the power of doing good, proportioned to his inclination. In a perfect theocracy, where a being, infinitely intelligent, governs by particular volitions, this rule would certainly have place, and might serve to the wisest purposes: But were mankind to execute such a law; so great is the uncertainty of merit, both from its natural obscurity, and from the self-conceit of each individual, that no determinate rule of conduct would ever result from it; and the total dissolution of society must be the immediate consequence. Fanatics may suppose, *that dominion is founded on grace,* and *that saints alone inherit the earth;* but the civil magistrate very justly puts these sublime theorists on the same footing with common robbers, and teaches them by the severest discipline, that a rule, which, in speculation, may seem the most advantageous to society, may yet be found, in practice, totally pernicious and destructive.

That there were *religious* fanatics of this kind in ENGLAND, during the civil wars, we learn from history; though it is probable, that the obvious *tendency* of these principles excited such horror in mankind, as soon obliged the dangerous enthusiasts to renounce, or at least conceal their tenets. Perhaps, the *levellers,* who claimed an equal distribution of property, were a kind of *political* fanatics, which arose from the religious species, and more openly avowed their pretensions; as carrying a more plausible appearance, of being practicable in themselves, as well as useful to human society.

It must, indeed, be confessed, that nature is so liberal to mankind, that, were all her presents equally divided among the species, and improved by art and industry, every individual would enjoy all the necessaries, and even most of the comforts of life; nor would ever be liable to any ills, but such as might accidentally arise from the sickly frame and constitution of his body. It must also be confessed, that, wherever we depart from this equality, we rob the poor of more satisfaction than we add to the rich, and that the slight gratification of a frivolous vanity, in one individual, frequently costs more than bread to many families, and even provinces. It may appear withal, that the rule of equality, as it would be highly *useful,* is not altogether *impracticable;* but has taken place, at least in an imperfect degree, in some republics; particularly that of SPARTA; where it was attended, it is said, with the most beneficial consequences. Not to mention, that the AGRARIAN laws, so frequently claimed in ROME, and carried into execution in many GREEK cities, proceeded, all of them, from a general idea of the utility of this principle.

But historians, and even common sense, may inform us, that, however specious these ideas of *perfect* equality may seem, they are really, at bottom, *impracticable;* and were they not so, would be extremely *pernicious* to human society. Render possessions ever so equal, men's different degrees of art, care, and industry will immediately break that equality. Or if you check these virtues, you reduce society to the most extreme indigence; and instead of preventing want and beggary in a few, render it unavoidable to the whole community. The most rigorous inquisition too is requisite to watch every inequality on its first appearance; and the most severe jurisdiction, to punish and redress it. But besides, that so much authority must soon degenerate into tyranny, and be exerted with great partialities; who can possibly be possessed of it, in such a situation as is here supposed? Perfect equality of possessions, destroying all subordination, weakens extremely the authority of magistracy, and must reduce all power nearly to a level, as well as property.

We may conclude, therefore, that, in order to establish laws for the regulation of property, we must be acquainted with the nature and situation of man; must reject appearances, which may be false, though specious; and must search for those rules, which are, on the whole, most *useful* and *beneficial.* Vulgar sense and slight experience are sufficient for this purpose; where men give not way to too selfish avidity, or too extensive enthusiasm.

Who sees not, for instance, that whatever is produced or improved by a man's art or industry ought, for ever, to be secured to him, in order to give encouragement to such *useful* habits and accomplishments? That the property ought also to descend to children and relations, for the same *useful* purpose? That it may be alienated by consent, in order to beget that commerce and intercourse, which is so *beneficial* to human society? And that all contracts and promises ought carefully to be fulfilled, in order to secure mutual trust and confidence, by which the general *interest* of mankind is so much promoted?

Examine the writers on the laws of nature; and

you will always find, that, whatever principles they set out with, they are sure to terminate here at last, and to assign, as the ultimate reason for every rule which they establish, the convenience and necessities of mankind. A concession thus extorted, in opposition to systems, has more authority, than if it had been made in prosecution of them.

What other reason, indeed, could writers ever give, why this must be *mine* and that *yours;* since uninstructed nature, surely, never made any such distinction? The objects, which receive those appellations, are, of themselves, foreign to us; they are totally disjoined and separated from us; and nothing but the general interests of society can form the connexion.

Sometimes, the interests of society may require a rule of justice in a particular case; but may not determine any particular rule, among several, which are all equally beneficial. In that case, the slightest *analogies* are laid hold of, in order to prevent that indifference and ambiguity, which would be the source of perpetual dissention. Thus possession alone, and first possession, is supposed to convey property, where no body else has any preceding claim and pretension. Many of the reasonings of lawyers are of this analogical nature, and depend on very slight connexions of the imagination.

Does any one scruple, in extraordinary cases, to violate all regard to the private property of individuals, and sacrifice to public interest a distinction, which had been established for the sake of that interest? The safety of the people is the supreme law: All other particular laws are subordinate to it, and dependant on it: And if, in the *common* course of things, they be followed and regarded; it is only because the public safety and interest *commonly* demand so equal and impartial an administration.

Sometimes both *utility* and *analogy* fail, and leave the laws of justice in total uncertainty. Thus, it is highly requisite, that prescription or long possession should convey property; but what number of days or months or years should be sufficient for that purpose, it is impossible for reason alone to determine. *Civil laws* here supply the place of the natural *code,* and assign different terms for prescription, according to the different *utilities,* proposed by the legislator. Bills of exchange and promissory notes, by the laws of most countries, prescribe sooner than bonds, and mortgages, and contracts of a more formal nature.

In general, we may observe, that all questions of property are subordinate to authority of civil laws, which extend, restrain, modify, and alter the rules of natural justice, according to the particular *convenience* of each community. The laws have, or ought to have, a constant reference to the constitution of government, the manners, the climate, the religion, the commerce, the situation of each society. A late author [3] of genius, as well as learning, has prosecuted this subject at large, and has established, from these principles, a system of political knowledge, which abounds in ingenious and brilliant thoughts, and is not wanting in solidity. [4]

What is a man's property? Any thing, which it is lawful for him, and for him alone, to use. *But what rule have we, by which we can distinguish these objects?* Here we must have recourse to statutes, customs, precedents, analogies, and a hundred other circumstances; some of which are constant and inflexible, some variable and arbitrary. But the ultimate point, in which they all professedly terminate, is, the interest and happiness of human society. Where this enters not into consideration, nothing can appear more whimsical, unnatural, and even superstitious, than all or most of the laws of justice and of property.

Those, who ridicule vulgar superstitions, and expose the folly of particular regards to meats, days, places, postures, apparel, have an easy task; while they consider all the qualities and relations of the objects, and discover no adequate cause for that affection or antipathy, veneration or horror, which have so mighty an influence over a considerable part of mankind. A SYRIAN would have starved rather than taste pigeon; an EGYPTIAN would not have approached bacon: But if these species of food be examined by the senses of sight, smell, or taste, or scrutinized by the sciences of chymistry, medicine, or physics; no difference is ever found between them and any other species, nor can that precise circumstance be pitched on, which may afford a just foundation for the religious passion. A fowl on Thursday is lawful food; on Friday abominable: Eggs, in this house, and in this diocese, are permitted during Lent; a hundred paces farther, to eat them is a damnable sin. This earth or building, yesterday was profane; to-day, by the muttering of certain words, it has become holy and sacred. Such reflections as these, in the mouth of a philosopher, one may safely say, are too obvious to have any influence; because they must always, to every man, occur at first sight; and where they prevail not, of themselves, they are surely obstructed by education, prejudice, and passion, not by ignorance or mistake.

It may appear to a careless view, or rather a too abstracted reflection, that there enters a like superstition into all the sentiments of justice; and that, if a man expose its object, or what we call property, to the same scrutiny of sense and science, he will not, by the most accurate enquiry, find any foundation for the difference made by moral sentiment. I may lawfully nourish myself from this tree; but the fruit of another of the same species, ten paces off, it is criminal for me to touch. Had I worne this apparel an hour ago, I had merited the severest punishment; but a man, by pronouncing a few magical syllables, has now rendered it fit for my use and service. Were this house placed in the neighbouring territory, it had been immoral for me to dwell in it; but being built on this side of the river, it is subject to a different municipal law, and,[5] by its becoming mine, I incur no blame or censure. The same species of reasoning, it may be thought, which so successfully exposes superstition, is also applicable to justice; nor is it possible, in the one case more than in the other, to point out, in the object, that precise quality or circumstance, which is the foundation of the sentiment.

But there is this material difference between *superstition* and *justice,* that the former is frivolous, useless, and burdensome; the latter is absolutely requisite to the well-being of mankind and existence of society. When we abstract from this circumstance (for it is too apparent ever to be overlooked) it must be confessed, that all regards to right and property, seem entirely without foundation, as much as the grossest and most vulgar superstition. Were the interests of society nowise concerned, it is as unintelligible, why another's articulating certain sounds implying consent, should change the nature of my actions with regard to a particular object, as why the reciting of a liturgy by a priest, in a certain habit and posture, should dedicate a heap of brick and timber, and render it, thenceforth and for ever, sacred.[6]

These reflections are far from weakening the obligations of justice, or diminishing any thing from the most sacred attention to property. On the contrary, such sentiments must acquire new force from the present reasoning. For what stronger foundation can be desired or conceived for any duty, than to observe, that human society, or even human nature could not subsist, without the establishment of it; and will still arrive at greater degrees of happiness and perfection, the more inviolable the regard is, which is paid to that duty?[7]

The dilemma seems obvious: As justice evidently tends to promote public utility and to support civil society, the sentiment of justice is either derived from our reflecting on that tendency, or like hunger, thirst, and other appetites, resentment, love of life, attachment to offspring, and other passions, arises from a simple original instinct in the human breast, which nature has implanted for like salutary purposes.[8] If the latter be the case, it follows, that property, which is the object of justice, is also distinguished by a simple, original instinct, and is not ascertained by any argument or reflection. But who is there that ever heard of such an instinct? Or is this a subject, in which new discoveries can be made? We may as well attempt to discover, in the body, new senses, which had before escaped the observation of all mankind.

But farther, though it seems a very simple proposition to say, that nature, by an instinctive sentiment, distinguishes property, yet in reality we shall find, that there are required for that purpose ten thousand different instincts, and these employed about objects of the greatest intricacy and nicest discernment. For when a definition of *property* is required, that relation is found to resolve itself into any possession acquired by occupation, by industry, by prescription, by inheritance, by contract, &c. Can we think, that nature, by an original instinct, instructs us in all these methods of acquisition?

These words too, inheritance and contract, stand for ideas infinitely complicated; and to define them exactly, a hundred volumes of laws, and a thousand volumes of commentators, have not been found sufficient. Does nature, whose instincts in men are all simple, embrace such complicated and artificial objects, and create a rational creature, without trusting any thing to the operation of his reason?

But even though all this were admitted, it would not be satisfactory. Positive laws can certainly transfer property. Is it by another original instinct, that we recognize the authority of kings and senates, and mark all the boundaries of their jurisdiction? Judges too, even though their sentence be erroneous and illegal, must be allowed, for the sake of peace and order, to have decisive authority, and ultimately to determine property. Have we original, innate ideas of prætors and chancellors and juries? Who sees not, that all these institutions arise merely from the necessities of human society?

All birds of the same species, in every age and country, build their nests alike: In this we see the force of instinct. Men, in different times and places, frame their houses differently: Here we perceive the influence of reason and custom. A like inference may be drawn from comparing the instinct of generation and the institution of property.

How great soever the variety of municipal laws, it must be confessed, that their chief outlines pretty regularly concur; because the purposes, to which they tend, are every where exactly similar. In like manner, all houses have a roof and walls, windows and chimneys; though diversified in their shape, figure, and materials. The purposes of the latter, directed to the conveniencies of human life, discover not more plainly their origin from reason and reflection, than do those of the former, which point all to a like end.

I need not mention the variations, which all the rules of property receive from the finer turns and connexions of the imagination, and from the subtilties and abstractions of law-topics and reasonings. There is no possibility of reconciling this observation to the notion of original instincts.

What alone will beget a doubt concerning the theory, on which I insist, is the influence of education and acquired habits, by which we are so accustomed to blame injustice, that we are not, in every instance, conscious of any immediate reflection on the pernicious consequences of it. The views the most familiar to us are apt, for that very reason, to escape us; and what we have very frequently performed from certain motives, we are apt likewise to continue mechanically, without recalling, on every occasion, the reflections,

which first determined us. The convenience, or rather necessity, which leads to justice, is so universal, and every where points so much to the same rules, that the habit takes place in all societies; and it is not without some scrutiny, that we are able to ascertain its true origin. The matter, however, is not so obscure, but that, even in common life, we have, every moment, recourse to the principle of public utility, and ask, *What must become of the world, if such practices prevail? How could society subsist under such disorders?* Were the distinction or separation of possessions entirely useless, can any one conceive, that it ever should have obtained in society?

Thus we seem, upon the whole, to have attained a knowledge of the force of that principle here insisted on, and can determine what degree of esteem or moral approbation may result from reflections on public interest and utility. The necessity of justice to the support of society is the SOLE foundation of that virtue; and since no moral excellence is more highly esteemed, we may conclude, that this circumstance of usefulness has, in general, the strongest energy, and most entire command over our sentiments. It must,·therefore, be the source of a considerable part of the merit ascribed to humanity, benevolence, friendship, public spirit, and other social virtues of that stamp; as it is the SOLE source of the moral approbation paid to fidelity, justice, veracity, integrity, and those other estimable and useful qualities and principles. It is entirely agreeable to the rules of philosophy, and even of common reason; where any principle has been found to have a great force and energy in one instance, to ascribe to it a like energy in all similar instances.[9] This indeed is NEWTON's chief rule of philosophizing.[10]

NOTES

1. *Genesis,* chap. xiii. and xxi.
2. This fiction of a state of nature, as a state of war, was not first started by Mr. HOBBES, as is commonly imagined. PLATO endeavours to refute an hypothesis very like it in the 2nd, 3rd, and 4th books de republica. CICERO, on the contrary, supposes it certain and universally acknowledged in the following passage.* 'Quis enim vestrûm, judices, ignorat, ita naturam rerum tulisse, ut quodam tempore homines, nondum neque naturali, neque civili jure descripto, fusi per agros, ac dispersi vagarentur tantumque haberent quantum manu ac viribus, per cædem ac vulnera, aut eripere, aut retinere potuissent? Qui igitur primi virtute et consilio præstanti exstiterunt, ii perspecto genere humanæ docilitatis atque ingenii, dissipatos, unum in locum congregarunt, eosque ex feritate illa ad justitiam ac mansuetudinem transduxerunt. Tum res ad

communem utilitatem, quas publicas appellamus, tum couventicula hominum, quæ postea civitates nominatæ sunt, tum domicilia conjuncta, quas urbes dicamus, invento et divino et humano jure, mœnibus sepserunt. Atque inter hanc vitam, perpolitam humanitate, et illam immanem, nihil tam interest quam JUS atque VIS. Horum utro uti nolimus, altero est utendum. Vim volumus extingui? Jus valeat necesse est, id est, judicia, quibus omne jus continetur. Judicia displicent, aut nulla sunt? Vis dominetur necesse est. Hæc vident omnes.' *Pro Sext.* 1. 42. [* Editions G to N add: Which is the only authority I shall cite for these reasonings: not imitating in this the example of PUFFENDORF, nor even that of GROTIUS, who think a verse from OVID or PLAUTUS or PETRONIUS a necessary warrant for every moral truth; or the example of Mr. WOOLASTON, who has constant recourse to HEBREW and ARABIC authors for the same purpose.]

3. [Editions G and K read: Of great genius as well as extensive learning,—the best system of political knowledge, that, perhaps, has ever yet been communicated to the world.]

4. The author of *L'Esprit des Loix.* This illustrious writer, however, sets out with a different theory, and supposes all right to be founded on certain *rapports* or relations; which is a system, that, in my opinion, never will be reconciled with true philosophy. Father MALEBRANCHE, as far as I can learn, was the first that started this abstract theory of morals which was afterwards adopted by * CUDWORTH, CLARKE, and others; and as it excludes all sentiment, and pretends to found every thing on reason, it has not wanted followers in this philosophic age. See Section 1, and Appendix I. With regard to justice, the virtue here treated of, the inference against this theory seems short and conclusive. Property is allowed to be dependent on civil laws; civil laws are allowed to have no other object, but the interest of society: This therefore must be allowed to be the sole foundation of property and justice. Not to mention, that our obligation itself to obey the magistrate and his laws is founded on nothing but the interests of society.

If the ideas of justice, sometimes, do not follow the dispositions of civil law: we shall find, that these cases, instead of objections, are confirmations of the theory delivered above. Where a civil law is so perverse as to cross all the interests of society, it loses all its authority, and men judge by the ideas of natural justice, which are conformable to those interests. Sometimes also civil laws, for useful purposes, require a ceremony or form to any deed; and where that is wanting, their decrees run contrary to the usual tenour of justice; but one who takes advantage of such chicanes, is not commonly regarded as an honest man. Thus, the interests of society require, that contracts be fulfilled; and there is not a more material article either of natural or civil justice: But the omission of a trifling circumstance will often, by law, invalidate a contract, *in foro humano,* but not *in foro conscientiæ,* as divines express themselves. In these cases, the magistrate is supposed only to withdraw his power of enforcing the right, not to have altered the right. Where his intention extends to the right, and is conformable to the interests of society; it never fails to alter the right; a clear proof of the origin of justice and of property, as assigned above. [* The reference to CUDWORTH was added in Edition O.]

5. [By its becoming mine: added in Edition Q.]

6. It is evident, that the will or consent alone never transfers property, nor causes the obligation of a promise (for the same reasoning extends to both) but the will must be expressed by words or signs, in order to impose a tye upon any man. The expression being once brought in as subservient to the will, soon becomes the principal part of the promise; nor will a man be less bound by his word, though he secretly give a different direction to his intention, and with-hold the assent

of his mind. But though the expression makes, on most occasions, the whole of the promise, yet it does not always so; and one who should make use of any expression, of which he knows not the meaning, and which he uses without any sense of the consequences, would not certainly be bound by it. Nay, though he know its meaning, yet if he use it in jest only, and with such signs as evidently show, that he has no serious intention of binding himself, he would not lie under any obligation of performance; but it is necessary, that the words be a perfect expression of the will, without any contrary signs. Nay, even this we must not carry so far as to imagine, that one, whom, by our quickness of understanding, we conjecture, from certain signs, to have an intention of deceiving us, is not bound by his expression or verbal promise, if we accept of it; but must limit this conclusion to those cases where the signs are of a different nature from those of deceit. All these contradictions are easily accounted for, if justice arise entirely from its usefulness to society; but will never be explained on any other hypothesis.

It is remarkable, that the moral decisions of the *Jesuits* and other relaxed casuists, were commonly formed in prosecution of some such subtilties of reasoning as are here pointed out, and proceed as much from the habit of scholastic refinement as from any corruption of the heart, if we may follow the authority of Mons. BAYLE. See his Dictionary, article LOYOLA. And why has the indignation of mankind risen so high against these casuists; but because every one perceived, that human society could not subsist were such practices authorized, and that morals must always be handled with a view to public interest, more than philosophical regularity? If the secret direction of the intention, said every man of sense, could invalidate a contract; where is our security? And yet a metaphysical schoolman might think, that where an intention was supposed to be requisite, if that intention really had not place, no consequence ought to follow, and no obligation be imposed. The casuistical subtilties may not be greater than the subtilties of lawyers, hinted at above; but as the former are *pernicious,* and the latter *innocent* and even *necessary,* this is the reason of the very different reception they meet with from the world.

* It is a doctrine of the church of ROME, that the priest, by a secret direction of his intention, can invalidate any sacrament. This position is derived from a strict and regular prosecution of the obvious truth, that empty words alone, without any meaning or intention in the speaker, can never be attended with any effect. If the same conclusion be not admitted in reasonings concerning civil contracts, where the affair is allowed to be of so much less consequence than the eternal salvation of thousands, it proceeds entirely from men's sense of the danger and inconvenience of the doctrine in the former case: And we may thence observe, that however positive, arrogant, and dogmatical any superstition may appear, it never can convey any thorough persuasion of the reality of its objects, or put them, in any degree, on a balance with the common incidents of life, which we learn from daily observation and experimental reasoning. [* This paragraph was added in Edition O.]

7. [Edition G omits all between this point and the concluding paragraph of the section.]

8. [Edition N omits the preceding sentence, and reads: If justice arose from a simple, original instinct in the human breast, without any reflection, even on those obvious interests of society, which absolutely require that virtue, it follows, &c.]

9. [This sentence is printed as a note in Editions G to P; and they also call it the *second* rule.]

10. Principia, lib. iii.

JOHN STUART MILL

On the Connection Between Justice and Utility*

In all ages of speculation, one of the strongest obstacles to the reception of the doctrine that Utility or Happiness is the criterion of right and wrong, has been drawn from the idea of Justice. The powerful sentiment and apparently clear perception which that word recalls, with a rapidity and certainty resembling an instinct, have seemed to the majority of thinkers to point to an inherent quality in things, to show that the Just must have an existence in nature as something absolute, generically distinct from every variety of the Expedient and, in idea, opposed to it, though (as is commonly acknowledged) never, in the long run, disjoined from it in fact.

In the case of this, as of our other moral sentiments, there is no necessary connection between the question of its origin and that of its binding force. That a feeling is bestowed on us by Nature does not necessarily legitimate all its promptings. The feeling of justice might be a peculiar instinct, and might yet require, like our other instincts, to be controlled and enlightened by a higher reason. If we have intellectual instincts leading us to judge in a particular way, as well as animal instincts that prompt us to act in a particular way, there is no necessity that the former should be more infallible in their sphere than the latter in theirs; it may as well happen that wrong judgments are occasionally suggested by those, as wrong actions by these. But though it is one thing to believe that we have natural feelings of justice and another to acknowledge them as an ultimate criterion of conduct, these two opinions are very closely connected in point of fact. Mankind are always predisposed to believe that any subjective feeling not otherwise accounted for, is a revelation of some objective reality. Our present object is to determine whether the reality to which the feeling of justice corresponds, is one which needs any such special revelation, whether the justice or injustice of an action is a thing intrinsically peculiar, and distinct from all its other qualities, or only a combination of certain of those qualities, presented under a peculiar aspect. For the purpose of this inquiry, it is practically important to consider whether the feeling itself of justice and injustice is *sui generis* like our sensations of color and taste, or a derivative feeling, formed by a combination of others. And this it is the more essential to examine, as people are in general willing enough to allow that, objectively, the dictates of Justice coincide with a part of the field of General Expediency; but inasmuch as the subjective mental feeling of Justice is different from that which commonly attaches to simple expediency and, except in the extreme cases of the latter, is far more imperative in its demands, people find it difficult to see, in Justice, only a particular kind or branch of general utility, and think that its superior binding force requires a totally different origin.

To throw light upon this question, it is necessary to attempt to ascertain what is the distinguishing character of justice or of injustice; what is the quality, or whether there is any quality, attributed in common to all modes of conduct designated as unjust (for justice, like many other moral attributes, is best defined by its opposite), and distinguishing them from such modes of conduct as are disapproved, but without having that particular epithet of disapprobation applied to them. If, in everything which men are accustomed to characterize as just or unjust, some one common attribute or collection of attributes is always present, we may judge whether this particular attribute, or combination of attributes, would be capable of gathering round it a sentiment of that peculiar character and intensity by

*Chapter 5 (complete) of *Utilitarianism.* First published in 1861.

virtue of the general laws of our emotional constitution, or whether the sentiment is inexplicable and requires to be regarded as a special provision of nature. If we find the former to be the case, we shall, in resolving this question, have resolved also the main problem; if the latter, we shall have to seek for some other mode of investigating it.

To find the common attributes of a variety of objects, it is necessary to begin by surveying the objects themselves in the concrete. Let us therefore avert successively to the various modes of action, and arrangements of human affairs, which are classed, by universal or widely spread opinion, as Just or Unjust. The things well known to excite the sentiments associated with those names are of a very multifarious character. I shall pass them rapidly in review, without studying any particular arrangement.

In the first place, it is mostly considered unjust to deprive any one of his personal liberty, his property, or any other thing which belongs to him by law. Here, therefore, is one instance of the application of the terms Just and Unjust in a perfectly definite sense, namely, that it is just to respect, unjust to violate, the *legal rights* of any one. But this judgment admits of several exceptions, arising from the other forms in which the notions of justice and injustice present themselves. For example: The person who suffers the deprivation may (as the phrase is) have *forfeited* the rights which he is so deprived of; a case to which we shall return presently. But also,

Secondly, The legal rights of which he is deprived may be rights which *ought* not to have belonged to him; in other words, the law which confers on him these rights may be a bad law. When it is so, or when (which is the same thing for our purpose) it is supposed to be so, opinions will differ as to the justice or injustice of infringing it. Some maintain that no law, however bad, ought to be disobeyed by an individual citizen, that his opposition to it, if shown at all, should only be shown in endeavoring to get it altered by competent authority. This opinion (which condemns many of the most illustrious benefactors of mankind, and would often protect pernicious institutions against the only weapons which, in the state of things existing at the time, have any chance of succeeding against them) is defended, by those who hold it, on grounds of expediency,

principally on that of the importance, to the common interest of mankind, of maintaining inviolate the sentiment of submission to law. Other persons, again, hold the directly contrary opinion that any law judged to be bad may blamelessly be disobeyed, even though it be not judged to be unjust, but only inexpedient, while others would confine the license of disobedience to the case of unjust laws. But, again, some say that all laws which are inexpedient are unjust, since every law imposes some restriction on the natural liberty of mankind, which restriction is an injustice, unless legitimated by tending to their good. Among these diversities of opinion, it seems to be universally admitted that there may be unjust laws, and that law, consequently, is not the ultimate criterion of justice, but may give to one person a benefit, or impose on another an evil, which justice condemns. When, however, a law is thought to be unjust, it seems always to be regarded as being so in the same way in which a breach of law is unjust—namely, by infringing somebody's right; which, as it cannot in this case be a legal right, receives a different appellation and is called a moral right. We may say, therefore, that a second case of injustice consists in taking or withholding from any person that to which he has a *moral right.*

Thirdly, It is universally considered just that each person should obtain that (whether good or evil) which he *deserves,* and unjust, that he should obtain a good, or be made to undergo an evil, which he does not deserve. This is, perhaps, the clearest and most emphatic form in which the idea of justice is conceived by the general mind. As it involves the notion of desert, the question arises, What constitutes desert? Speaking in a general way, a person is understood to deserve good if he does right, evil, if he does wrong; and, in a more particular sense, to deserve good from those to whom he does or has done good, and evil from those to whom he does or has done evil. The precept of returning good for evil has never been regarded as a case of the fulfilment of justice, but as one in which the claims of justice are waived, in obedience to other considerations.

Fourthly, It is confessedly unjust to *break faith* with any one, to violate an engagement, either express or implied, or disappoint expectations raised by our own conduct, at least if we have raised those expectations knowingly and voluntarily. Like the other obligations of justice already spoken of, this one is not regarded as absolute, but as capable of being overruled by a stronger obligation of justice on the other side, or by such conduct on the part of the person concerned as is deemed to absolve us from our obligation to him and to constitute a *forfeiture* of the benefit which he has been led to expect.

Fifthly, It is, by universal admission, inconsistent with justice to be *partial,* to show favor or preference to one person over another in matters to which favor and preference do not properly apply. Impartiality, however, does not seem to be regarded as a duty in itself, but rather as instrumental to some other duty, for it is admitted that favor and preference are not always censurable, and indeed the cases in which they are condemned are rather the exception than the rule. A person would be more likely to be blamed than applauded for giving his family or friends no superiority in good offices over strangers, when he could do so without violating any other duty, and no one thinks it unjust to seek one person in preference to another as a friend, connection, or companion. Impartiality, where rights are concerned, is of course obligatory, but this is involved in the more general obligation of giving to every one his right. A tribunal, for example, must be impartial, because it is bound to award, without regard to any other consideration, a disputed object to the one of two parties who has the right to it. There are other cases in which impartiality means, being solely influenced by desert, as with those who, in the capacity of judges, preceptors, or parents, administer reward and punishment as such. There are cases, again, in which it means being solely influenced by consideration for the public interest, as in making a selection among candidates for a government employment. Impartiality, in short, as an obligation of justice, may be said to mean being exclusively influenced by the considerations which it is supposed ought to influence the particular case in hand, and resisting the solicitation of any motives which prompt to conduct different from what those considerations would dictate.

Nearly allied to the idea of impartiality is that of *equality,* which often enters as a component part both into the conception of justice and into the practice of it and, in the eyes of many persons, constitutes its essence. But, in this still more than in any other case, the notion of justice varies in different persons, and always conforms in its variations to their notion of utility. Each person maintains that equality is the dictate of justice, except where he thinks that expediency requires inequality. The justice of giving equal protection to the rights of all is maintained by those who support the most outrageous inequality in the rights themselves. Even in slave countries, it is theoretically admitted that the rights of the slave, such as they are, ought to be as sacred as those of the master, and that a tribunal which fails to enforce them with equal strictness is wanting in justice, while, at the same time, institutions which leave to the slave scarcely any rights to enforce are not deemed unjust, because they are not deemed inexpedient. Those who think that utility requires distinctions of rank do not consider it unjust that riches and social privileges should be unequally dispensed, but those who think this inequality inexpedient think it unjust also. Whoever thinks that government is necessary sees no injustice in as much inequality as is constituted by giving to the magistrate powers not granted to other people. Even among those who hold leveling doctrines, there are as many questions of justice as there are differences of opinion about expediency. Some Communists consider it unjust that the produce of the labor of the community should be shared on any other principle than that of exact equality, others think it just that those should receive most whose wants are greatest, while others hold that those who work harder, or who produce more, or whose services are more valuable to the community, may justly claim a larger quota in the division of the produce. And the sense of natural justice may be plausibly appealed to in behalf of every one of these opinions.

Among so many diverse applications of the term Justice, which yet is not regarded as ambiguous, it is a matter of some difficulty to seize the mental link which holds them together, and on which the moral sentiment adhering to the term essentially depends. Perhaps, in this embarrassment, some help may be derived from the history of the word, as indicated by its etymology.

[In most, if not all languages, the etymology of the word which corresponds to Just points distinctly to an origin connected with the ordinance of law. *Justum* is a form of *jussum*—that which has been ordered. Δίκαιον comes directly from δίκη, a suit at law. *Recht,* from which came *right* and *righteous,* is synonymous with law. The courts of justice, the administration of justice, are the courts and administration of law. *La justice,* in French, is the established term for judicature. I am not commiting the fallacy imputed with some show of truth to Horne Tooke, of assuming that a word must still continue to mean what it originally meant. Etymology is slight evidence of what the idea now signified is, but the very best evidence of how it sprang up.] There can, I think, be no doubt that the *idée mère,* the primitive element, in the formation of the notion of justice, was conformity to law. It constituted the entire idea among the Hebrews up to the birth of Christianity, as might be expected in the case of a people whose laws attempted to embrace all subjects on which precepts were required, and who believed those laws to be a direct emanation from the Supreme Being. But other nations, and in particular the Greeks and Romans, who knew that their laws had been made originally, and still continued to be made, by men, were not afraid to admit that those men might make bad laws, might do, by law, the same things, and from the same motives, which, if done by individuals without the sanction of law, would be called unjust. And hence the sentiment of justice came to be attached, not to all violations of law, but only to violations of such laws as *ought* to exist, including such as ought to exist, but do not, and to laws themselves, if supposed to be contrary to what ought to be law. In this manner, the idea of law and of its injunctions was still predominant in the notion of justice, even when the laws actually in force ceased to be accepted as the standard of it.

It is true that mankind consider the idea of justice and its obligations as applicable to many things which neither are, nor is it desired that they should be, regulated by law. Nobody desires that laws should interfere with the whole detail of private life, yet every one allows that, in all daily conduct, a person may and does show himself to be either just or unjust. But even here, the idea of the breach of what ought to be law still lingers in a modified shape. It would always give us pleasure, and chime in with our feelings of fitness, that acts which we deem unjust should be punished, though we do not always think it expedient that this should be done by the tribunals. We forego that gratification on account of incidental inconveniences. We should be glad to see just conduct enforced, and injustice repressed, even in the minutest details, if we were not with reason afraid of trusting the magistrate with so unlimited an amount of power over individuals. When we think that a person is bound in justice to do a thing, it is an ordinary form of language to say that he ought to be compelled to do it. We should be gratified to see the obligation enforced by anybody who had the power. If we see that its enforcement by law would be inexpedient, we lament the impossibility, we consider the impunity given to injustice as an evil, and strive to make amends for it by bringing a strong expression of our own and the public disapprobation to bear upon the offender. Thus the idea of legal constraint is still the generating idea of the notion of justice, though undergoing several transformations before that notion, as it exists in an advanced state of society, becomes complete.

The above is, I think, a true account, as far as it goes, of the origin and progressive growth of the idea of justice. But we must observe that it contains, as yet, nothing to distinguish that obligation from moral obligation in general. For the truth is that the idea of penal sanction, which is the essence of law, enters not only into the conception of injustice, but into that of any kind of wrong. We do not call anything wrong, unless we mean to imply that a person ought to be punished in some way or other for doing it, if not by law, by the opinion of his fellow-creatures, if not by opinion, by the reproaches of his own conscience. This seems the real turning point of the distinction between morality and simple expediency. It is a part of the notion of Duty in every one of its forms that a person may rightfully be compelled to fulfill it. Duty is a thing which may be *exacted* from a person, as one exacts a debt. Unless we think that it may be exacted from him, we do not call it his duty. Reasons of prudence, or the interest of other people, may militate against actually exacting it, but the person himself, it is clearly understood, would not be entitled to complain. There are other things, on the contrary, which we wish that people should do, which we like or admire them for doing, perhaps dislike or despise them for not doing, but yet admit that they are not bound to do; it is not a case of moral obligation; we do not blame them, that is, we do not think that they are proper objects of punishment. How we come by these ideas of deserving and not deserving punishment, will appear, perhaps, in the sequel; but I think there is no doubt that this distinction lies at the bottom of the notions of right and wrong, that we call any conduct wrong, or employ instead some other term of dislike or disparagement, according as we think that the person ought or ought not to be punished for it, and we say it would be right to do so and so, or merely that it would be desirable or laudable, according as we would wish to see the person whom it concerns compelled, or only persuaded and exhorted, to act in that manner.[1]

This, therefore, being the characteristic difference which marks off, not justice but morality in general, from the remaining provinces of Expediency and Worthiness, the character is still to be sought which distinguishes justice from other branches of morality. Now, it is known that ethical writers divide moral duties into two classes, denoted by the ill-chosen expressions, duties of perfect and of imperfect obligation; the latter being those in which, though the act is obligatory, the particular occasions of performing it are left to our choice, as in the case of charity or beneficence, which we are indeed bound to practice, but not towards any definite person, nor at any prescribed time. In the more precise language of philosophic jurists, duties of perfect obligation are those duties in virtue of which a correlative *right* resides in some person or persons; duties of imperfect obligation are those moral obligations which do not give birth to any right. I think it will be found that this distinction exactly coincides with that which exists between justice and the other obligations of morality. In our survey of the various popular acceptations of justice, the term appeared generally to involve the idea of personal right—a claim on the part of one or more individuals, like that which the law gives when it confers a proprietary or other legal right. Whether the injustice consists in depriving a person of a possession, or in breaking faith with him, or in treating him worse than he deserves, or worse than other people who have no greater claims, in each case the supposition implies two things—a wrong done, and some assignable person who is wronged. Injustice may also be done by treating a person better than others, but the wrong in this case is to his competitors, who are also assignable persons. It seems to me that this feature in the case—a right in some person, correlative to the moral obligation—constitutes the specific difference between justice and generosity or beneficence. Justice implies something which it is not only right to do and wrong not to do, but which some individual person can claim from us as his moral right. No one has a moral right to our generosity or beneficence, because we are not morally bound to practice those virtues towards any given individual. And it will be found, with respect to this as to every correct definition, that the instances which seem to conflict with it are those which most confirm it, for if a moralist attempts, as some have done, to make out that mankind generally, though not any given individual, have a right to all the good we can do them, he at once, by that thesis, includes generosity and beneficence within the category of justice. He is obliged to say that our utmost exertions are *due* to our fellow creatures, thus assimilating them to a debt, or that nothing less can be a sufficient *return* for what society does for us, thus classing the case as one of gratitude, both of which are acknowledged cases of justice. Wherever there is a right, the case is one of justice, and not of the virtue of beneficence, and whoever does not place the distinction between justice and morality in general where we have now placed it will be found to make no distinction between them at all, but to merge all morality in justice.

Having thus endeavored to determine the distinctive elements which enter into the composition of the idea of justice, we are ready to enter on the inquiry, whether the feeling which accompanies the idea is attached to it by a special dispensation of nature, or whether it could have grown up by any known laws out of the idea itself, and, in particular, whether it can have originated in considerations of general expediency.

I conceive that the sentiment itself does not arise from anything which would commonly or correctly be termed an idea of expediency, but that, though the sentiment does not, whatever is moral in it does.

We have seen that the two essential ingredients in the sentiment of justice are the desire to punish a person who has done harm, and the knowledge or belief that there is some definite individual or individuals to whom harm has been done.

Now, it appears to me that the desire to punish a person who has done harm to some individual is a spontaneous outgrowth from two sentiments, both in the highest degree natural, and which either are or resemble instincts—the impulse of self-defense, and the feeling of sympathy.

It is natural to resent, and to repel or retaliate, any harm done or attempted against ourselves or against those with whom we sympathize. The origin of this sentiment it is not necessary here to discuss. Whether it be an instinct or a result of intelligence, it is, we know, common to all animal nature, for every animal tries to hurt those who have hurt, or who it thinks are about to hurt, itself or its young. Human beings, on this point, only differ from other animals in two particulars: first, in being capable of sympathizing, not solely with their offspring or, like some of the more noble animals, with some superior animal who is kind to them, but with all human and even with all sentient beings; secondly, in having a more developed intelligence, which gives a wider range to the whole of their sentiments, whether self-regarding or sympathetic. By virtue of his superior intelligence, even apart from his superior range of sympathy, a human being is capable of apprehending a community of interest between himself and the human society of which he forms a part, such that any conduct which threatens the security of the society generally is threatening to his own, and calls forth his instinct (if instinct it be) of self-defense. The same superiority of intelligence, joined to the power of sympathizing with human beings generally, enables him to attach himself to the collective idea of his tribe, his country, or mankind, in such a manner that any act hurtful to them raises his instinct of sympathy, and urges him to resistance.

The sentiment of justice, in that one of its elements which consists of the desire to punish, is thus, I conceive, the natural feeling of retaliation or vengeance, rendered by intellect and sympathy applicable to those injuries—that is, to those hurts—which wound us through, or in common with, society at large. This sentiment in itself has nothing moral in it; what is moral is the exclusive subordination of it to the social sympathies, so as to wait on and obey their call. For the natural feeling would make us resent indiscriminately whatever any one does that is disagreeable to us, but, when moralized by the social feeling, it only acts in the directions conformable to the general good: just persons resenting a hurt to society,

though not otherwise a hurt to themselves, and not resenting a hurt to themselves, however painful, unless it be of the kind which society has a common interest with them in the repression of.

It is no objection against this doctrine to say that, when we feel our sentiment of justice outraged, we are not thinking of society at large, or of any collective interest, but only of the individual case. It is common enough, certainly, though the reverse of commendable, to feel resentment merely because we have suffered pain, but a person whose resentment is really a moral feeling—that is, who considers whether an act is blamable before he allows himself to resent it—such a person, though he may not say expressly to himself that he is standing up for the interest of society, certainly does feel that he is asserting a rule which is for the benefit of others as well as for his own. If he is not feeling this, if he is regarding the act solely as it affects him individually—he is not consciously just, he is not concerning himself about the justice of his actions. This is admitted even by anti-utilitarian moralists. When Kant (as before remarked) propounds as the fundamental principle of morals, "So act that thy rule of conduct might be adopted as a law by all rational beings," he virtually acknowledges that the interest of mankind collectively, or at least of mankind indiscriminately, must be in the mind of the agent when conscientiously deciding on the morality of the act. Otherwise he uses words without a meaning, for that a rule even of utter selfishness could not *possibly* be adopted by all rational beings—that there is any insuperable obstacle in the nature of things to its adoption—cannot be even plausibly maintained. To give any meaning to Kant's principle, the sense put upon it must be that we ought to shape our conduct by a rule which all rational beings might adopt *with benefit to their collective interest.*

To recapitulate: The idea of justice·supposes two things—a rule of conduct and a sentiment which sanctions the rule. The first must be supposed common to all mankind, and intended for their good; the other (the sentiment) is a desire that punishment may be suffered by those who infringe the rule. There is involved, in addition, the conception of some definite person who suffers by the infringement, whose rights (to use the expression appropriated to the case) are violated by it. And the sentiment of justice appears to me to be the animal desire to repel or retaliate a hurt or damage to one's self or to those with whom one sympathizes, widened so as to include all persons, by the human capacity of enlarged sympathy, and the human conception of intelligent self-interest. From the latter elements, the feeling derives its morality; from the former, its peculiar impressiveness and energy of self-assertion.

I have throughout treated the idea of a *right* residing in the injured person, and violated by the injury, not as a separate element in the composition of the idea and sentiment, but as one of the forms in which the other two elements clothe themselves. These elements are a hurt to some assignable person or persons on the one hand, and a demand for punishment on the other. An examination of our own minds, I think, will show that these two things include all that we mean when we speak of violation of a right. When we call any thing a person's right, we mean that he has a valid claim on society to protect him in the possession of it, either by the force of law, or by that of education and opinion. If he has what we consider a sufficient claim, on whatever account, to have something guaranteed to him by society, we say that he has a right to it. If we desire to prove that anything does not belong to him by right, we think this done as soon as it is admitted that society ought not to take measures for securing it to him, but should leave him to chance or to his own exertions. Thus a person is said to have a right to what he can earn in fair professional competition, because society ought not to allow any other person to hinder him from endeavoring to earn in that manner as much as he can. But he has not a right to three hundred a year, though he may happen to be earning it, because society is not called on to provide that he shall earn that sum. On the contrary, if he owns ten thousand pounds three-per-cent stock, he *has* a right to three hundred a year, because society has come under an obligation to provide him with an income of that amount.

To have a right then is, I conceive, to have something which society ought to defend me in the possession of. If the objector goes on to ask why it ought, I can give him no other reason than general utility. If that expression does not seem to convey a sufficient feeling of the strength of the obligation, nor to account for the peculiar energy of the feeling, it is because there goes to the composition of the sentiment, not a rational only but also an animal element—the thirst for retaliation, and his thirst derives its intensity, as well as its moral justification, from the extraordinarily important and impressive kind of utility which is concerned. The interest involved is that of security, to every one's feelings, the most vital of all interests. All other earthly benefits are needed by one person, not needed by another, and many of them can, if necessary, be cheerfully foregone, or replaced by something else. But security no human being can possibly do without; on it we depend for all our immunity from evil, and for the whole value of all and every good, beyond the passing moment, since nothing but the gratification of the instant could be of any worth to us if we could be deprived of everything the next instant by whoever was momentarily stronger than ourselves. Now, this most indispensable of all necessaries, after physical nutriment, cannot be had, unless the machinery for providing it is kept unintermittedly in active play. Our notion, therefore, of the claim we have on our fellow creatures to join in making safe for us the very groundwork of our existence, gathers feelings around it so much more intense than those concerned in any of the more common cases of utility, that the difference in degree (as is often the case in psychology) becomes a real difference in kind. The claim assumes that character of absoluteness, that apparent infinity and incommensurability with all other considerations, which constitute the distinction between the feeling of right and wrong and that of ordinary expediency and inexpediency. The feelings concerned are so powerful, and we count so positively on finding a responsive feeling in others (all being alike interested), that *ought* and *should* grow into *must,* and recognized indispensability becomes a moral necessity, analogous to physical, and often not inferior to it in binding force.

If the preceding analysis, or something resembling it, be not the correct account of the notion of justice, if justice be totally independent of utility, and be a standard *per se,* which the mind can recognize by simple introspection of itself—it is hard to understand why that internal oracle is so ambiguous, and why so many things appear either just or unjust, according to the light in which they are regarded.

We are continually informed that Utility is an uncertain standard, which every different person interprets differently, and that there is no safety but in the immutable, ineffaceable, and unmistakable dictates of Justice, which carry their evidence in themselves and are independent of the fluctuations of opinion. One would suppose from this that, on questions of justice, there could be no controversy, that, if we take that for our rule, its application to any given case could leave us in as little doubt as a mathematical demonstration. So far is this from being the fact, that there is as much difference of opinion and as much discussion about what is just as about what is useful to society. Not only have different nations and individuals different notions of justice but, in the mind of one and the same individual, justice is not some one rule, principle, or maxim, but many, which do not always coincide in their dictates, and, in choosing between which, he is guided either by some extraneous standard, or by his own personal predilections.

For instance: There are some who say that it is unjust to punish any one for the sake of example to others, that punishment is just, only when intended for the good of the sufferer himself. Others maintain the extreme reverse, contending that to punish persons who have attained years of discretion, for their own benefit, is despotism and injustice, since, if the matter at issue is solely their own good, no one has a right to control their own judgment of it, but that they may justly be punished to prevent evil to others, this being the exercise of the legitimate right of self-defense. Mr. Owen, again, affirms that it is unjust to punish at all, for the criminal did not make his own character; his education, and the circumstances which surrounded him, have made him a criminal, and for these he is not responsible. All these opinions are extremely plausible, and so long as the question is argued as one of justice simply, without going down to the principles which lie under justice, and are the source of its authority, I am unable to see how any of these reasoners can be refuted. For, in truth, every one of the three builds upon rules of justice of singling out an individual, and making him a sacrifice, without his consent, for other people's benefit. The second relies on the acknowledged justice of self-defense,

and the admitted injustice of forcing one person to conform to another's notions of what constitutes his good. The Owenite invokes the admitted principle that it is unjust to punish any one for what he cannot help. Each is triumphant so long as he is not compelled to take into consideration any other maxims of justice than the one he has selected but, as soon as their several maxims are brought face to face, each disputant seems to have exactly as much to say for himself as the others. No one of them can carry out his own notion of justice without trampling upon another equally binding. These are difficulties, they have always been felt to be such, and many devices have been invented to turn rather than to overcome them. As a refuge from the last of the three, men imagined what they called the "freedom of the will," fancying that they could not justify punishing a man whose will is in a thoroughly hateful state, unless it be supposed to have come into that state through no influence of anterior circumstances. To escape from the other difficulties, a favorite contrivance has been the fiction of a contract, whereby, at some unknown period all the members of society engaged to obey the laws, and consented to be punished for any disobedience to them, thereby giving to their legislators the right, which it is assumed they would not otherwise have had, of punishing them, either for their own good or for that of society. This happy thought was considered to get rid of the whole difficulty, and to legitimate the infliction of punishment, in virtue of another received maxim of justice, *volenti non fit injuria,* "That is not unjust which is done with the consent of the person who is supposed to be hurt by it." I need hardly remark that, even if the consent were not a mere fiction, this maxim is not superior in authority to the others which it is brought in to supersede. It is, on the contrary, an instructive specimen of the loose and irregular manner in which supposed principles of justice grow up. This particular one evidently came in use as a help to the coarse exigencies of courts of law, which are sometimes obliged to be content with very uncertain presumptions, on account of the greater evils which would often arise from any attempt on their part to cut finer. But even courts of law are not able to adhere consistently to the maxim, for they allow voluntary engagements to be set aside on the ground of fraud, and sometimes on that of mere mistake or misinformation.

Again: when the legitimacy of inflicting punishment is admitted, how many conflicting conceptions of justice come to light in discussing the proper apportionment of punishments to offenses! No rule on the subject recommends itself so strongly to the primitive and spontaneous sentiment of justice, as the *lex talionis,* "An eye for an eye, and a tooth for a tooth." Though this principle of the Jewish and of the Mohammedan law has been generally abandoned in Europe as a practical maxim, there is, I suspect, in most minds, a secret hankering after it and, when retribution accidentally falls on an offender in that precise shape, the general feeling of satisfaction evinced bears witness how natural is the sentiment to which this repayment in kind is acceptable. With many, the test of justice in penal infliction is that the punishment should be proportioned to the offence; meaning that it should be exactly measured by the moral guilt of the culprit (whatever be their standard for measuring moral guilt): the consideration, what amount of punishment is necessary to deter from the offense, having nothing to do with the question of justice, in their estimation: while there are others to whom that consideration is all in all; who maintain that it is not just, at least for man, to inflict on a fellow-creature, whatever may be his offences, any amount of suffering beyond the least that will suffice to prevent him from repeating, and others from imitating, his misconduct.

To take another example from a subject already once referred to. In a co-operative industrial association, is it just or not that talent or skill should give a title to superior remuneration? On the negative side of the question it is argued, that whoever does the best he can, deserves equally well, and ought not in justice to be put in a position of inferiority for no fault of his own; that superior abilities have already advantages more than enough, in the admiration they excite, the personal influence they command, and the internal sources of satisfaction attending them, without adding to these a superior share of the world's goods; and that society is bound in justice rather to make compensation to the less favoured, for this unmerited inequality of advantages, than to aggravate it. On the contrary side it is contended, that society receives more from the more efficient labourer; that his services being more useful, society owes him a larger return for them; that a greater share of the joint result is actually his work, and not to allow his claim to it is a kind of robbery; that if he is only to receive as much as others, he can only be justly required to produce as much, and to give a smaller amount of time and exertion, proportioned to his superior efficiency. Who shall decide between these appeals to conflicting principles of justice? Justice has in this case two sides to it, which it is impossible to bring into harmony, and the two disputants have chosen opposite sides; the one looks to what it is just that the individual should receive, the other to what it is just that the community should give. Each, from his own point of view, is unanswerable; and any choice between them, on grounds of justice, must be perfectly arbitrary. Social utility alone can decide the preference.

How many, again, and how irreconcilable, are the standards of justice to which reference is made in discussing the repartition of taxation. One opinion is that payment to the State should be in numerical proportion to pecuniary means. Others think that justice dictates what they term graduated taxation; taking a higher percentage from those who have more to spare. In point of natural justice a strong case might be made for disregarding means altogether, and taking the same absolute sum (whenever it could be got) from every one: as the subscribers to a mess, or to a club, all pay the same sum for the same privileges, whether they can all equally afford it or not. Since the protection (it might be said) of law and government is afforded to, and is equally required by all, there is no injustice in making all buy it at the same price. It is reckoned justice, not injustice, that a dealer should charge to all customers the same price for the same article, not a price varying according to their means of payment. This doctrine, as applied to taxation, finds no advocates because it conflicts so strongly with man's feelings of humanity and of social expediency: but the principle of justice which it invokes is as true and as binding as those which can be appealed to against it. Accordingly it exerts a tacit influence on the line of defence employed for other modes of assessing taxation. People feel obliged to argue that the State does more for the rich than for the poor, as a justification for its taking more from them: though this is in reality not true, for the rich would be far better able to protect themselves, in the absence of law or government, than the poor, and indeed would probably be successful in converting the poor into their slaves. Others again, so far defer to the same conception of justice, as to maintain that all should pay an equal capitation tax for the protection of their persons (these being of equal value to all), and an unequal tax for the protection of their property, which is unequal. To this others reply, that the all of one man is as valuable to him as the all of another. From these confusions there is no other mode of extrication than the utilitarian.

Is, then, the difference between the Just and the Expedient a merely imaginary distinction? Have mankind been under a delusion in thinking that justice is a more sacred thing than policy, and that the latter ought only to be listened to after the former has been satisfied? By no means. The exposition we have given of the nature and origin of the sentiment recognizes a real distinction, and no one of those who profess the most sublime contempt for the consequences of actions as an element in their morality attaches more importance to the distinction than I do. While I dispute the pretensions of any theory which sets up an imaginary standard of justice not grounded on utility, I account the justice which is grounded on utility to be the chief part, and incomparably the most sacred and binding part, of all morality. Justice is a name for certain classes of moral rules which concern the essentials of human well-being more nearly, and are therefore of more absolute obligation, than any other rules for the guidance of life, and the notion which we have found to be of the essence of the idea of justice, that of a right residing in an individual, implies and testifies to this more binding obligation.

The moral rules which forbid mankind to hurt one another (in which we must never forget to include wrongful interference with each other's freedom) are more vital to human well-being than any maxims, however important, which only point out the best mode of managing some department of human affairs. They have also the peculiarity that they are the main element in determining the whole of the social feelings of mankind. It is their observance which alone preserves peace among human beings; if obedience to them were not the rule, and disobedience the exception, every one would see in every one else an enemy, against whom he must be perpetually guarding himself. What is hardly less important, these are the precepts which mankind have the strongest and the most direct inducements for impressing upon one another. By merely giving to each other prudential instruction or exhortation, they may gain, or think they gain, nothing; in inculcating on each other the duty of positive beneficence, they have an unmistakable interest, but far less in degree: a person may possibly not need the benefits of others, but he always needs that they should not do him hurt. Thus the moralities which protect every individual from being harmed by others, either directly or by being hindered in his freedom of pursuing his own good, are at once those which he himself has most at heart, and those which he has the strongest interest in publishing and enforcing by word and deed. It is by a person's observance of these, that his fitness to exist as one of the fellowship of human beings, is tested and decided; for on that depends his being a nuisance or not to those with whom he is in contact. Now it is these moralities primarily, which compose the obligations of justice. The most marked cases of injustice, and those which give the tone to the feeling of repugnance which characterizes the sentiment, are acts of wrongful aggression, or wrongful exercise of power over some one; the next are those which consist in wrongfully witholding from him something which is his due; in both cases, inflicting on him a positive hurt, either in the form of direct suffering, or of the privation of some good which he had reasonable ground either of a physical or of a social kind, for counting upon.

The same powerful motives which command the observance of these primary moralities, enjoin the punishment of those who violate them; and as the impulses of self-defence, of defence of others, and of vengeance, are all called forth against such persons, retribution, or evil for evil, becomes closely connected with the sentiment of justice, and is universally included in the idea. Good for good is also one of the dictates of justice; and this, though its social utility is evident, and though it carries with it a natural human feeling, has not at first sight that obvious connexion with hurt or injury, which, existing in the most elementary cases of just and unjust, and is the source of the characteristic intensity of the sentiment. But the connexion, though less obvious, is not less real. He who accepts benefits, and denies a return of them when needed, inflicts a real hurt, by disappointing one of the most natural and reasonable of expectations, and one which he must at least tacitly have encouraged, otherwise the benefits would seldom have been conferred. The important rank, among human evils and wrongs, of the disappointment of expectation, is shown in the fact that it constitutes the principal criminality of two such highly immoral acts as a breach of friendship and a breach of promise. Few hurts which human beings can sustain are greater, and none wound more, than when that on which they habitually and with full assurance relied, fails them in the hour of need; and few wrongs are greater than this mere witholding of good; none excite more resentment, either in the person suffering, or in a sympathizing spectator. The principle, therefore, of giving to each what they deserve—that is, good for good, as well as evil for evil—is not only included within the idea of Justice as we have defined it, but is a proper object of that intensity of sentiment which places the Just, in human estimation, above the simply Expedient.

Most of the maxims of justice current in the world, and commonly appealed to in its transactions, are simply instrumental to carrying into effect the principles of justice which we have now spoken of. That a person is only responsible for what he has done voluntarily, or could voluntarily have avoided, that it is unjust to condemn any person unheard, that the punishment ought to be proportioned to the offense, and the like—are maxims intended to prevent the just principle of evil for evil from being perverted to the infliction of evil without that justification. The greater part of these common maxims have come into use from the practice of courts of justice, which have been naturally led to a more complete recognition and elaboration than was likely to suggest itself to others, of the rules necessary to enable them to fulfill their double function, of inflicting punishment when due, and of awarding to each person his right.

That first of judicial virtues, impartiality, is an obligation of justice, partly for the reason last mentioned, as being a necessary condition of the fulfillment of the other obligations of justice. But this is not the only source of the exalted rank, among human obligations, of those maxims of equality and impartiality, which, both in popular estimation and in that of the most enlightened, are included among the precepts of justice. In one point of view, they may be considered as corollaries from the principles already laid down. If it is a duty to do to each according to his deserts, returning good for good as well as repressing evil by evil, it necessarily follows that we should treat all equally well (when no higher duty forbids) who have deserved equally well of *us,* and that society should treat all equally well who have deserved equally well of *it*—that is, who have deserved equally well absolutely. This is the highest abstract standard of social and distributive justice, towards which all institutions, and the efforts of all virtuous citizens, should be made in the utmost possible degree to converge. But this great moral duty rests upon a still deeper foundation, being a direct emanation from the first principle of morals, and not a mere logical corollary from secondary or derivative doctrines. It is involved in the very meaning of Utility, or the Greatest-happiness Principle. That principle is a mere form of words without rational signification, unless one person's happiness, supposed equal in degree (with the proper allowance made for kind), is counted for exactly as much as another's. Those conditions being supplied, Bentham's dictum, "Everybody to count for one, nobody for more than one," might be written under the principle of utility as an explanatory commentary.[2] The equal claim of everybody to happiness, in the estimation of the moralist and the legislator, involves an equal claim to all the means of happiness, except in so far as the inevitable conditions of human life, and the general interest, in which that of every individual is included, set limits to the maxim, and those limits ought to be strictly construed. As every other maxim of justice, so this, is by no means applied or held applicable universally; on the contrary, as I have already remarked, it bends to every person's ideas of social expediency. But, in whatever case it is deemed applicable at all, it is held to be the dictate of justice. All persons are deemed to have a *right* to equality of treatment, except when some recognized social expediency requires the reverse. And hence all social inequalities, which have ceased to be considered expedient, assume the character, not of simple inexpediency but of injustice, and appear so tyrannical that people are apt to wonder how they ever could have been tolerated, forgetful that they themselves perhaps tolerate other inequalities under an equally mistaken notion of expediency, the correction of which would make that which they approve seem quite as monstrous as what they have at last learnt to condemn. The entire history of social improvement has been a series of transitions, by which one custom or institution after another, from being a supposed primary necessity of social existence, has passed into the rank of an universally stigmatized injustice and tyranny. So it has been with the distinctions of slaves and freemen, nobles and serfs, patricians and plebeians, and so it will be, and in part already is, with the aristocracies of color, race, and sex.

It appears, from what has been said, that justice is a name for certain moral requirements which, regarded collectively, stand higher in the scale of social utility, and are therefore of more paramount obligation, than any others, though particular cases may occur in which some other social duty is so important as to overrule any one of the general maxims of justice. Thus, to save a life, it may not only be allowable, but a duty, to steal, or take by force, the necessary food or medicine, or to kidnap and compel to officiate, the only qualified medical practitioner. In such cases, we do not call any thing justice which is not a virtue, we usually say, not that justice must give way to some other moral principle, but that what is just in ordinary cases is, by reason of that other principle, not just in the particular case. By this useful accommodation of language, the character of indefeasibility attributed to justice is kept up, and we are saved from the necessity of maintaining that there can be laudable injustice.

The considerations which have now been adduced, resolve, I conceive, the only real difficulty in the utilitarian theory of morals. It has always been evident that all cases of justice are also cases of expediency; the difference is in the peculiar sentiment which attaches to the former, as contradistinguished from the latter. If this characteristic sentiment has been sufficiently accounted for, if there is no necessity to assume for it any peculiarity of origin, if it is simply the natural feeling of resentment, moralized by being made coextensive with the demands of social good, and if this feeling not only does but ought to exist in all the classes of cases to which the idea of justice corresponds—that idea no longer presents itself as a stumbling-block to the utilitarian ethics. Justice remains the appropriate name for certain social utilities which are vastly more important, and therefore more absolute and imperative, than any others are as a class (though not more so than others may be in particular cases), and which therefore ought to be, as well as naturally are, guarded by a sentiment not only different in degree, but also in kind, distinguished from the milder feeling which attaches to the mere idea of promoting human pleasure or convenience, at once by the more definite nature of its commands, and by the sterner character of its sanctions.

NOTES

1. See this point enforced and illustrated by Professor Bain, in an admirable chapter (entitled "The Ethical Emotions, or the Moral Sense") of the second of the two treatises composing his elaborate and profound work on the Mind.

2. This implication, in the first principle of the utilitarian scheme, of perfect impartiality between persons is regarded by Mr. Herbert Spencer (in his *Social Statics*) as a disproof of the pretensions of utility to be a sufficient guide to right, since (he says) the principle of utility presupposes the anterior principle, that everybody has an equal right to happiness. It may be more correctly described as supposing that equal amounts of happiness are equally desirable, whether felt by the same or by different persons. This, however, is not a *pre*-supposition, not a premise needful to support the principle of utility, but the very principle itself; for what is the principle of utility, if it be not that "happiness" and "desirable" are synonymous terms? If there is any anterior principle implied, it can be no other than this—that the truths of arithmetic are applicable to the valuation of happiness, as of all other measurable quantities.

[Mr. Herbert Spencer, in a private communication on the subject of the preceding note, objects to being considered an opponent of Utilitarianism, and states that he regards happiness as the ultimate end of morality; but deems that end only partially attainable by empirical generalizations from the observed results of conduct, and completely attainable only by deducing, from the laws of life and the conditions of existence, what kinds of action necessarily tend to produce happiness, and what kinds to produce unhappiness. With the exception of the word "necessarily," I have no dissent to express from this doctrine, and (omitting that word) I am not aware that any modern advocate of Utilitarianism is of a different opinion. Bentham certainly, to whom, in the *Social Statics,* Mr. Spencer particularly referred, is, least of all writers, chargeable with unwillingness to deduce the effect of actions on happiness from the laws of human nature and the universal conditions of human life. The common charge against him is of relying too exclusively upon such deductions, and declining altogether to be bound by the generalizations from specific experience which Mr. Spencer thinks that utilitarians generally confine themselves to. My own opinion (and, as I collect, Mr. Spencer's) is, that in ethics, as in all other branches of scientific study, the consilience of the results of both these processes, each corroborating and verifying the other, is requisite to give to any general proposition the kind and degree of evidence which constitutes scientific proof.]

BRIAN BARRY

Justice and Fairness*

PROCEDURAL FAIRNESS, BACKGROUND FAIRNESS AND LEGAL JUSTICE

PROCEDURAL FAIRNESS

To say that a procedure is being fairly operated is to say that the formalities which define the procedure have been correctly adhered to. A fair race, for example, is one in which the competitors start together (nobody 'jumps the gun'), do not elbow one another or take short cuts, and in which the first person past the line and not disqualified is recognized as the winner; a fair fight is one in which the contestants are not allowed to get away with fouls; and so on. Fairness in the operation of the authoritative determination procedure has more or less content according to the detail with which the procedure is specified in any given case. A 'fair trial', for example, must satisfy elaborate procedural safeguards, whereas a 'fair administrative decision' need mean only that the official taking it was impartial or 'fair minded'.[1] In terms of formalities an administrative tribunal or an official inquiry occupy an intermediate position.[2] The fair application of a chance procedure requires the procedure to be genuinely random (a true die, for example) so as to give everyone a 'fair chance'. A 'fair election' rules out ballot stuffing, double voting, miscounts, etc.

This leaves the first three procedures. 'Fair war' has no use (though 'just war' has): 'All's fair in love and war.' The explanation is that war does not specify rules to be followed before what is happening can be called 'war'; indeed, it is the negation of orderly procedures.[3] War in its fullest sense is an attempt to impose one's will on another by violence; as soon as conventions come in

* From *Political Argument* by Brian Barry (London: Routledge & Kegan Paul, 1965), pp. 97–106. Reprinted by permission of the author and the publishers, Routledge & Kegan Paul (London) and Humanities Press, Inc. (New Jersey).

(if you capture place *A* or man *B* you win) an element of contest enters in. Winning becomes not merely *being in a position* to impose your will but *being allowed* to impose your will in virtue of having satisfied a certain standard.[4] A duel is a contest just as a boxing match is, because if it settles, say, who gets the lady, it does so by convention: 'Let the best man win.'[5]

The notion of 'fair discussion on merits' also has no obvious use, again because there are no prescribed formalities to be observed; nor has 'fair bargaining' in general any use, since if threats are included it is simply the verbal counterpart to combat. Under more restricted conditions, however, considerations of procedural fairness can be invoked. Thus, in a context where threats are supposed to be ruled out it is 'unfair' to make threats. More subtly, in a context which is supposed to be one of 'perfect competition' it is unfair for a rich company to sell below cost in order to drive out its competitors. 'Fair trade', the traditional name for all restrictive practices aimed at protecting the inefficient producer and retailer, in theory usually means this, while in practice it normally degenerates into an attempt to guarantee 'cost plus' all around.[6] It is also used in connection with the closely similar proposal of tariffs against foreign 'dumping', which again generally comes to mean 'effective foreign competition'.

BACKGROUND FAIRNESS

While still concentrating on the way the procedure works, some evaluations in terms of 'fairness' dig a little deeper and ask whether the background conditions are satisfactory. Some examples should make the notion of 'background conditions' clear. Procedural fairness rules out one boxer having a piece of lead inside his gloves, but background fairness would also rule out any undue disparity in the weight of the boxers; similarly background fairness would rule out sailing boats or cars of different sizes being raced against one another unless suitably handicapped. In a court case the fact that one side's counsel showed far greater forensic skill than the other's would be grounds for complaint under the rubric of background fairness but not procedural fairness. Background fairness in voting might be thought to require that the opportunities available to those supporting the different sides should be equal, or roughly proportional to their strength among the voters. On these grounds one might well object to the two-to-one superiority in resources of Republicans and Conservatives or to de Gaulle's use of the government monopoly in radio and television to further his referenda. Chance has no room for background fairness alongside procedural fairness, nor, except in a loose sense, has bargaining. Exactly why this is will be examined in Section 3 when I consider the justification of evaluations in terms of procedural and background fairness.

LEGAL JUSTICE

Procedural fairness and background fairness are concerned respectively with whether the prescribed formalities have been observed and whether the initial position of the parties was right. There is a third type of evaluation which is based on the working of procedures: legal or (more generally) rule-based justice.

Henry Sidgwick noted that one of the clearest and most frequent uses of 'justice' is in a legal context: A verdict is just when it is a correct application of the relevant rule of law. He also noted that it is not the *only* use of 'justice' because we can for example say (Hobbes notwithstanding) that a law is itself unjust.[7] The restriction to legal rules does not correspond to any difference in terms or evaluations; if the rules of the club allow expulsion for cheating and I am expelled without having cheated this is unjust in exactly the same way as a punishment inflicted by a court can be unjust. I shall therefore use the same term 'legal justice' whether the rule in question is a rule of law or not.[8]

The criterion of legal justice can be employed only where a decision is reached in the light of some rule(s), held by those taking the decision to give the answer in cases of that kind. It can there-fore be used only in conjunction with the authoritative determination procedure. There may also perhaps be a marginal application to contest: a bad interpretation of the rules could at a pinch be called unjust; but it is more natural to say that it was unfair. This is closely bound up with a point made in the previous chapter: a referee does not determine the result of a football match in the same way as a judge determines the result of a trial. A bad decision by the referee only gives an 'unfair advantage' to one side; the other side may still win. When I try to think of a referee's decision for which I should feel 'unjust' to be the appropriate epithet, I immediately light on something like sending a man off the field or recommending his suspension, which are of course examples of a direct effect on the player rather than (or at least in addition to) an indirect effect on the result of the game.[9]

JUSTIFICATIONS

LEGAL JUSTICE

So far I have simply presented procedural and background fairness and legal justice. It must now be asked why the honorific names of 'fair' and 'just' should be applied to the correct carrying out of procedures and the correct application of rules. Unless one is a 'rule worshipper' one must presumably ask for a justification of these procedural considerations in terms of conduciveness to some more general consideration, either aggregative or distributive.[10]

I shall begin by advancing three reasons of this more general kind for taking legal justice seriously. One argument is that any consistent application of a rule creates a primitive variety of equity—like cases being treated alike—though this is a rather weak sort of distributive principle because the basis of 'likeness' is stipulated by the rule and it may be outrageous. Another argument is that if known rules are applied, everyone can if he chooses avoid the consequences of infringing them; this applies to any rule, good or bad, unless it prescribes penalties for something nobody can do anything about (such as being a Jew or a Negro) or for past voluntary actions done before the rule was promulgated (such as having joined the Communist Party in the nineteen thirties). Both distributive and aggregative justifications underlie this second argument. Reasoning on aggregative premises one may say that following rules of the required kind prevents insecurity (the knock on the door in the early morning) and allows punishment to be deterrent rather than a dead loss of total want-satisfaction. On distributive premises one may say that if the required kinds of rule are followed then at least nobody will suffer for something he could not have helped doing, and this is at least a *part* of the criteria for 'desert'.

Finally, legal justice tends to reduce the incidence of unfulfilled expectations. The principle that unfulfilled expectations should be avoided if possible can itself be justified on both aggregative and distributive grounds, and then applies to legal justice as a special case.[11] The aggregative argument, for what it is worth, was elaborately worked out by Bentham in his analysis of the competing (utilitarian) claims of security and equality.

. . . 'the *advantage of gaining* cannot be compared with the *evil of losing.*' This proposition is itself deduced from two others. On the one hand every man naturally expects to preserve what he has; the feeling of expectation is natural to man and is founded on the ordinary course of events, since, taking the whole sum of men, acquired wealth is not only preserved but even increased. All loss is therefore unexpected, and gives rise to deception, which is a pain—the pain of frustrated expectation. On the other hand the deduction (or addition) of a portion of wealth will produce in the sum of happiness of each individual a deduction (or an addition) more or less great according to the portion deducted and the remaining or original proportion.[12]

The distributive argument is of more limited import and refers specifically to cases where people have invested money, changed jobs, moved house, etcetera, in the belief that the state of affairs which induced them to do so would continue indefinitely. If they have, then it is wrong for this state of affairs to be suddenly changed.[13]

When a legislature passes a law, not for any temporary purposes, nor limited as to the time of its operation, and which therefore may be reasonably expected to be permanent,—and persons, confiding in its permanency, embark their capital, bestow their labour, or shape the course of their life, so that their only hope of success is founded on the existence of the law,—the rights which they have acquired in the reliance upon its continuance are termed 'vested rights'; and persons in this situation are considered as having a moral claim on the legislature for the maintenance of the law, or at least for the allowance of a sufficient time to withdraw their investments, and to take the measures necessary for guarding against the loss consequent on so large a change.[14]

PROCEDURAL AND BACKGROUND FAIRNESS

Now take procedural and background fairness. What, first of all, is the relation between a fair trial and a just verdict? The answer seems to me to be the empirical one that fair trials tend to produce just verdicts more often than unfair trials and that the more respects in which a trial is fair the more likely it is to eventuate in a just verdict.[15] The value of fairness is thus a subordinate to that of justice: Fair procedures and background conditions are to be valued for their tendency to produce (rule-based) justice. Procedural fairness provides the minimum conditions while background fairness constitutes a refinement.[16]

Now consider contest. Again the criteria of fairness are empirically related to a tendency for fair contests to produce the 'right' results; and it is even clearer than before that the criteria for fairness are drawn with this requirement in mind. In Section 2 and again above, I have used the expression 'the right result', and this bears the same relation to the contest procedure as 'rule-based justice' does to 'rule-based authoritative determination'. But whereas one can define 'justice' as 'conformity with the rule', one cannot give a general characterization of 'the right result' except as 'a result which is an accurate index of the quality which the contest was supposed to be testing'.

Procedural fairness (conformity with the procedural rules) is always more likely than not to produce the 'right results'—whatever they may be—because it merely specifies that everyone does the same thing. Whatever it is that the race is supposed to be testing, it is hard to see how its reliability would be improved if some competitors got away with jumping the gun, except in the perverse case where the race is a blind and the real test is in gun-jumping ability.

The criteria of background fairness, on the other hand, vary according to the 'right result'. If all that is being tested is ability to knock out an opponent, there is no need for any limits on disparity of size between boxers; but if the boxing match is supposed to be a test of skill, 'background fairness' must be brought in to specify the maximum disparity beyond which skill is secondary in determining the result to brute force. Again, if an examination is supposed to be testing *effort,* a different method of marking will be required from that necessary to test *ability.*

As with rule-based authoritative determination, the main justification for procedural and background fairness lies in its tendency to produce certain results. If these results are good then fairness, as a means to them, is also good; if not, not. The results of contest are to match rewards and deprivations (perhaps only immaterial ones such as prestige and chagrin) to performance, and for this to be desirable the scale of rewards and deprivations must be such that when it is adhered to they are appropriate to the performances. 'Equality of opportunity' (the honorific name for background and procedural fairness) is not very important if the achievements which are rewarded are base or trifling.[17] However, as before, we can suggest that there are certain virtues in procedural and background fairness in a contest regardless of the result to which the contest is directed. These are, as before, the minimal equity of like cases being treated alike (even though 'likeness' may be defined in any way) and the fact that contestants at least know what they are supposed to be trying to do. It must be allowed that these general considerations seem to be a good deal weaker than those raised in connection with rule-based authoritative determination.

The link between justifying procedural and background fairness and justifying the use of the procedure itself comes out even more clearly if we look at voting. If we suppose that the object of the voting procedure is to ascertain the opinions of the voters then plainly the formal requirements are a necessary condition of this. If in addition we say that the object is to secure their informed opinions we have to introduce the background conditions as well. If these objects are good then the means to them are good.

I have now covered the three procedures of whose operation both procedural and background fairness can be predicated. Of the rest, chance, I remarked, is liable to procedural fairness (or unfairness) only. This follows from the rather peculiar fact that there is no end in view when a chance procedure is employed beyond settling something on a random basis.[18] Since the end is identified with the actual mechanical procedure there is no room for background fairness. Indeed, procedural and substantive fairness are merged since the distributive value *is* the randomness.

I also suggested that bargaining is in the reverse position. It cannot be procedurally fair (or unfair) but at least in a loose sense background fairness (or unfairness) can sometimes be attributed to it. Indeed, I may add that the same can sometimes be said of combat. This odd state of affairs arises whenever something which those taking part in it define to themselves as combat is at the same time being evaluated by a third party as if it were a contest. This observer, but not the combatants, may then speak of fairness—but only loosely and perhaps one might even say improperly.[19]

So far I have dealt with justifications for fairness taking one procedure at a time; but are there general reasons for following a prescribed form which applies to *any* form? I can suggest two. One is the argument (offered by Rawls) from 'fair play'.[20] This is essentially a distributive argument, which runs as follows: If you have accepted benefits arising from a certain practice then (unless you have given notice to the contrary) it is only fair that you should continue to adhere to it even when in some specific case it would suit you better not to. The other is an aggregative argument to the effect that the more a society is divided on substantive values, the more precious as a means of preserving social peace is any agreement that can be reached on procedure. The connection between liberalism and an emphasis on 'due process' is not fortuitous. Procedures cannot be justified by the results they produce because a result which one approves of another disapproves; the adherence to procedures is justified instead by saying that everyone agrees on them and this is the only thing on which everyone does agree. Whether these considerations are sufficiently universal or compelling to account for the importance which is often attached to a meticulous adherence to prescribed forms I shall not guess. Perhaps there is an element of 'rule worship' which can be supported by neither aggregative nor distributive principles; but the rationality of general adherence to prescribed forms is high on almost any principles.

NOTES

1.   'Impartiality as an obligation of justice may be said to mean being exclusively influenced by considerations which it is supposed ought to influence the particular case in hand, and resisting the solicitation of any motives which prompt to conduct different from what these considerations would dictate.' J. S. Mill, *Utilitarianism,* Chapter V.

2.   See the Franks Report (Cmnd 218, 1957), *passim.*

3.   It is quite correct for the old saw to include 'love' in the same category, at least if it is taken to mean 'attaining the object of sexual desire'. There are no rules, no formal requirements, to satisfy before you can get your girl (or your man); you may have all the virtues but if you don't happen to have appeal you don't win.

4.   I am not saying that war, still less combat in general, cannot be limited in its means (or in its ends) but that there cannot, by my definitions, be a conventional connection between achieving a certain feat and winning; the only connection can be that the other side in fact gives up. A strike or a lockout, for example, can be limited in means (no shooting, no sabotage) and ends (a rise of 5 per cent or a reduction of 5 per cent). But it is still combat and not contest because each is aiming directly at changing the attitude of the other, not at some separate standard of achievement which is then taken as settling the dispute. A contest would occur if the trade union and the employer agreed in advance that whichever side was the first to cost the other a million pounds should get its demand fulfilled.

5.   A duel *à l'outrance* of course removes the loser not conventionally but necessarily; but the removal is still in the course of an activity with formal rules. If we have a duel fixed for tomorrow it would still be 'unfair' for me to shoot you in the back today as you walk along the street.

6.   E.g., the 'Codes of Fair Practice' produced under the NRA, in the New Deal.

7.   H. Sidgwick, *The Methods of Ethics,* Book III, Chapter V.

8.   Sidgwick indeed extended the term 'legal justice' to cover promises and similar social obligations.

9.   The *result* of a match may be unjust in that it does not reflect the relative merits of the teams, but this is a different use of 'unjust' bound up with desert. An unjust result in this sense may be due equally to a bad decision or an unlucky gust of wind.

10.   See J. J. C. Smart, *An Outline of a System of Utilitarian Ethics* (Melbourne, 1961). Smart's 'utilitarianism' appears to be *entirely* made up of a rejection of 'rule worship'. Not only is the position he defends not (necessarily) hedonistic; it is not even aggregative. This—formerly, I should have thought, the sole distinguishing mark of nonhedonistic utilitarianism—is abandoned when Smart admits that different utilitarians may disagree on distributive questions.

11.   Sidgwick, in *The Methods of Ethics* suggests that the avoiding of unfulfilled expectations constitutes most of the Common Sense idea of 'justice' but (at least nowadays) 'justice' does not seem to be used so widely. There still seems to be agreement that there *is* a value in not frustrating expectations, however. Consider the contrasting attitudes of many people to death duties on one hand and a capital levy on the other. (I am referring to the opinions of those who are naïve enough to believe that death duties, as currently operated in the UK, are effective in reducing fortunes.)

12.   In Halévy, *The Growth of Philosophical Radicalism* (Beacon, 1955), p. 40. Note that the second argument would sometimes *favour* redistribution. Take £10 from a man with £1,000 and give it to one with £100. You decrease the happiness of the former by 1 per cent, but increase the happiness of the latter by 10 per cent. The argument in any case rests on a peculiar assumption about the marginal utility of money —far more questionable than the simple diminishing marginal utility idea.

13.   Sidgwick's claim that 'just' is used to refer to fulfilling expectations would be more plausible if restricted to cases which fall under this argument.

14.   Sir George Cornewall Lewis, *Remarks on the Use and Abuse of Some Political Terms* (London, 1832), p. 25.

15.   When I say that this is a matter of fact I do not mean that the dovetailing of fair procedures and just results is an accident, for the criteria of a fair trial are selected with an eye on this dovetailing. What I am denying is any analytic connection between the two such that a just verdict entails a fair trial or a fair trial entails a just verdict: there can be fair trials which still produce unjust verdicts.

16.   Indeed, it is quite plausible to suggest that background fairness is only relevant to trials inasfar as they partake of contest, by their use of the adversary system which thus places a premium on equally matched counsel. Courts do not *have* to be so organized. See Sybille Bedford, *The Faces of Justice* (London, 1961).

17.   Compare 'equality before the law', the honorific name for procedural fairness in connection with rule-based authoritative determination: 'Equality before the law' does not guarantee that outrageous actions are not rewarded and good ones punished. It should hardly need saying that neither form of procedural 'equality' has anything to do with substantial equality though the possibility of confusion is convenient for those who prefer the rhetoric to the reality of equality. (See, e.g., C. A. R. Crosland, *The Future of Socialism* (London, 1956)). Plato in *The Republic* and Michael Young in *The Rise of the Meritocracy* (Penguin Books, 1961) have both given us pictures of extremely hierarchical societies based on 'equality of opportunity'.

18.   An apparent exception would be the use of a random device in the belief that God will arrange for a substantively good result; but then the arrangement is not (in the eyes of the people operating it) to be regarded as invoking a *chance* mechanism.

19.   This point is pursued in the context of J. K. Galbraith's 'concept of countervailing power'.

20.   John Rawls, 'Justice as Fairness', *Philosophical Review,* LXVII (1958).

JOHN RAWLS

Justice as Fairness*

I

It might seem at first sight that the concepts of justice and fairness are the same, and that there is no reason to distinguish them, or to say that one is more fundamental than the other. I think that this impression is mistaken. In this paper I wish to show that the fundamental idea in the concept of justice is fairness; and I wish to offer an analysis of the concept of justice from this point of view. To bring out the force of this claim, and the analysis based upon it, I shall then argue that it is this aspect of justice for which utilitarianism, in its classical form, is unable to account, but which is expressed, even if misleadingly, by the idea of the social contract.

To start with I shall develop a particular conception of justice by stating and commenting upon two principles which specify it, and by considering the circumstances and conditions under which they may be thought to arise. The principles defining this conception, and the conception itself, are, of course, familiar. It may be possible, however, by using the notion of fairness as a framework, to assemble and to look at them in a new way. Before stating this conception, however, the following preliminary matters should be kept in mind.

Throughout I consider justice only as a virtue of social institutions, or what I shall call practices.[1] The principles of justice are regarded as formulating restrictions as to how practices may define positions and offices, and assign thereto powers and liabilities, rights, and duties. Justice as a virtue of particular actions or of persons I do not take up at all. It is important to distinguish these various subjects of justice, since the meaning of the concept varies according to whether it is applied to practices, particular actions, or persons. These meanings are, indeed, connected, but they are not identical. I shall confine my discussion to the sense of justice as applied to practices, since this sense is the basic one. Once it is understood, the other senses should go quite easily.

Justice is to be understood in its customary sense as representing but *one* of the many virtues of social institutions, for these may be antiquated, inefficient, degrading, or any number of other things, without being unjust. Justice is not to be confused with an all-inclusive vision of a good society; it is only one part of any such conception. It is important, for example, to distinguish that sense of equality which is an aspect of the concept of justice from that sense of equality which belongs to a more comprehensive social ideal. There may well be inequalities which one concedes are just, or at least not unjust, but which, nevertheless, one wishes, on other grounds, to do away with. I shall focus attention, then, on the usual sense of justice in which it is essentially the elimination of arbitrary distinctions and the establishment, within the structure of a practice, of a proper balance between competing claims.

Finally, there is no need to consider the principles discussed below as *the* principles of justice. For the moment it is sufficient that they are typical of a family of principles normally associated with the concept of justice. The way in which the principles of this family resemble one another, as shown by the background against which they may be thought to arise, will be made clear by the whole of the subsequent argument.

*From *The Philosophical Review,* Vol. 67 (1958), pp. 164–94. Reprinted by permission of the author and the publisher. An abbreviated version of this paper (less than one-half the length) was presented in a symposium with the same title at the American Philosophical Association, Eastern Division, December 28, 1957, and appeared in the *Journal of Philosophy,* LIV, 653–662. Footnotes have been renumbered.

II

The conception of justice which I want to develop may be stated in the form of two principles as follows: First, each person participating in a practice, or affected by it, has an equal right to the most extensive liberty compatible with a like liberty for all; and second, inequalities are arbitrary unless it is reasonable to expect that they will work out for everyone's advantage, and provided the positions and offices to which they attach, or from which they may be gained, are open to all. These principles express justice as a complex of three ideas: liberty, equality, and reward for services contributing to the common good.[2]

The term "person" is to be construed variously depending on the circumstances. On some occasions it will mean human individuals, but in others it may refer to nations, provinces, business firms, churches, teams, and so on. The principles of justice apply in all these instances, although there is a certain logical priority to the case of human individuals. As I shall use the term "person," it will be ambiguous in the manner indicated.

The first principle holds, of course, only if other things are equal: That is, while there must always be a justification for departing from the initial position of equal liberty (which is defined by the pattern of rights and duties, powers and liabilities, established by a practice), and the burden of proof is placed on him who would depart from it, nevertheless, there can be, and often there is, a justification for doing so. Now, that similar particular cases, as defined by a practice, should be treated similarly as they arise, is part of the very concept of a practice; it is involved in the notion of an activity in accordance with rules.[3] The first principle expresses an analogous conception, but as applied to the structure of practices themselves. It holds, for example, that there is a presumption against the distinctions and classifications made by legal systems and other practices to the extent that they infringe on the original and equal liberty of the persons participating them. The second principle defines how this presumption may be rebutted.

It might be argued at this point that justice requires only an equal liberty. If, however, a greater liberty were possible for all without loss or conflict, then it would be irrational to settle on a lesser liberty. There is no reason for circumscribing rights unless their exercise would be incompatible, or would render the practice defining them less effective. Therefore no serious distortion of the concept of justice is likely to follow from including within it the concept of the greatest equal liberty.

The second principle defines what sorts of inequalities are permissible; it specifies how the presumption laid down by the first principle may be put aside. Now by inequalities it is best to understand not *any* differences between offices and positions, but differences in the benefits and burdens attached to them either directly or indirectly, such as prestige and wealth, or liability to taxation and compulsory services. Players in a game do not protest against there being different positions, such as batter, pitcher, catcher, and the like, nor to there being various privileges and powers as specified by the rules; nor do the citizens of a country object to there being the different offices of government such as president, senator, governor, judge, and so on, each with its special rights and duties. It is not differences of this kind that are normally thought of as inequalities, but differences in the resulting distribution established by a practice, or made possible by it, of the things men strive to attain or avoid. Thus they may complain about the pattern of honors and rewards set up by a practice (for example, the privileges and salaries of government officials) or they may object to the distribution of power and wealth which results from the various ways in which men avail themselves of the opportunities allowed by it (for example, the concentration of wealth which may develop in a free price system allowing large entrepreneurial or speculative gains).

It should be noted that the second principle holds that an inequality is allowed only if there is reason to believe that the practice with the inequality, or resulting in it, will work for the advantage of *every* party engaging in it. Here it is important to stress that *every* party must gain from the inequality. Since the principle applies to practices, it implies that the representative man in every office or position defined by a practice, when he views it as a going concern, must find it reasonable to prefer his condition and prospects with the inequality to what they would be under the practice without it. The principle excludes, therefore, the justification of inequalities on the grounds that the disadvantages of those in one position are outweighed by the greater advantages of those in another position. This rather simple restriction is the main modification I wish to make in the utilitarian principle as usually understood. When coupled with the notion of a practice, it is a restriction of consequence[4], and one which some utilitarians, for example, Hume and Mill, have used in their discussions of justice without realizing apparently its significance, or at least without calling attention to it.[5] Why it is a significant modification of principle, changing one's conception of justice entirely, the whole of my argument will show.

Further, it is also necessary that the various offices to which special benefits or burdens attach are open to all. It may be, for example, to the common advantage, as just defined, to attach special benefits to certain offices. Perhaps by doing so the requisite talent can be attracted to them and encouraged to give its best efforts. But any offices having special benefits must be won in a fair competition in which contestants are judged on their merits. If some offices were not open, those excluded would normally be justified in feeling unjustly treated, even if they benefited from the greater efforts of those who were allowed to compete for them. Now if one can assume that offices are open, it is necessary only to consider the design of practices themselves and how they jointly, as a system, work together. It will be a mistake to focus attention on the varying relative positions of particular persons, who may be known to us by their proper names, and to require that each such change, as a once for all transaction viewed in isolation, must be in itself just. It is the system of practices which is to be judged, and judged from a general point of view: Unless one is prepared to criticize it from the standpoint of a representative man holding some particular office, one has no complaint against it.

III

Given these principles one might try to derive them from a priori principles of reason, or claim that they were known by intuition. These are familiar enough steps and, at least in the case of the first principle, might be made with some success. Usually, however, such arguments, made at this point, are unconvincing. They are not likely to lead to an understanding of the basis of the principles of justice, not at least as principles of justice. I wish, therefore, to look at the principles in a different way.

Imagine a society of persons amongst whom a certain system of practices is *already* well established. Now suppose that by and large they are mutually self-interested; their allegiance to their established practices is normally founded on the prospect of self-advantage. One need not assume that, in all senses of the term "person," the persons in this society are mutually self-interested. If the characterization as mutually self-interested applies when the line of division is the family, it may still be true that members of families are bound by ties of sentiment and affection and willingly acknowledge duties in contradiction to self-interest. Mutual self-interestedness in the relations between families, nations, churches, and the like, is commonly associated with intense loyalty and devotion on the part of individual members. Therefore, one can form a more realistic conception of this society if one thinks of it as consisting of mutually self-interested families, or some other association. Further, it is not necessary to suppose that these persons are mutually self-interested under all circumstances, but only in the usual situations in which they participate in their common practices.

Now suppose also that these persons are rational: they know their own interests more or less accurately; they are capable to tracing out the likely consequences of adopting one practice rather than another; they are capable of adhering to a course of action once they have decided upon it; they can resist present temptations and the enticements of immediate gain; and the bare knowledge or perception of the difference between their condition and that of others is not, within certain limits and in itself, a source of great dissatisfaction. Only the last point adds anything to the usual definition of rationality. This defination should allow, I think, for the idea that a rational man would not be greatly downcast from knowing, or seeing, that others are in a better position than himself, unless he thought their being so was the result of injustice, or the consequence of letting chance work itself out for no useful common purpose, and so on. So if these persons strike us as unpleasantly egoistic, they are at least free in some degree from the fault of envy.[6]

Finally, assume that these persons have roughly similar needs and interests, or needs and interests in various ways complementary, so that fruitful cooperation amongst them is possible; and suppose that they are sufficiently equal in power and ability to guarantee that in normal circumstances none is able to dominate the others. This condition (as well as the others) may seem excessively vague; but in view of the conception of justice to which the argument leads, there seems no reason for making it more exact here.

Since these persons are conceived as engaging in their common practices, which are already established, there is no question of our supposing them to come together to deliberate as to how they will set these practices up for the first time. Yet we can imagine that from time to time they discuss with one another whether any of them has a legitimate complaint against their established institutions. Such discussions are perfectly natural in any normal society. Now suppose that they have settled on doing this in the following way. They first try to arrive at the principles by which complaints, and so practices themselves, are to be judged. Their procedure for this is to let each person propose the principles upon which he wishes his complaints to be tried with the understanding that, if acknowledged, the complaints of others will be similarly tried, and that no complaints will be heard at all until everyone is roughly to one mind as to how complaints are to be judged. They each understand further that the principles proposed and acknowledged on this occasion are binding on future occasions. Thus each will be wary of proposing a principle which would give him a peculiar advantage, in his present circumstances, supposing it to be accepted. Each person knows that he will be bound by it in future circumstances the peculiarities of which cannot be known, and which might well be such that the principle is then to his disadvantage. The idea is that everyone should be required to make *in advance* a firm commitment, which others also may reasonably be expected to make, and that no one be given the opportunity to tailor the canons of a legitimate complaint to fit his own special condition, and then to discard them when they no longer suit his purpose. Hence each per-

son will propose principles of a general kind which will, to a large degree, gain their sense from the various applications to be made of them, the particular circumstances of which being as yet unknown. These principles will express the conditions in accordance with which each is the least unwilling to have his interests limited in the design of practices, given the competing interests of the others, on the supposition that the interests of others will be limited likewise. The restrictions which would so arise might be thought of as those a person would keep in mind if he were designing a practice in which his enemy were to assign him his place.

The two main parts of his conjectural account have a definite significance. The character and respective situations of the parties reflect the typical circumstances in which questions of justice arise. The procedure whereby principles are proposed and acknowledged represents constraints, analogous to those of having a morality, whereby rational and mutually self-interested persons are brought to act reasonably. Thus the first part reflects the fact that questions of justice arise when conflicting claims are made upon the design of a practice and where it is taken for granted that each person will insist, as far as possible, on what he considers his rights. It is typical of cases of justice to involve persons who are pressing on one another their claims, between which a fair balance or equilibrium must be found. On the other hand, as expressed by the second part, having a morality must at least imply the acknowledgment of principles as impartially applying to one's own conduct as well as to another's, and moreover principles which may constitute a constraint, or limitation, upon the pursuit of one's own interests. There are, of course, other aspects of having a morality: The acknowledgment of moral principles must show itself in accepting a reference to them as reasons for limiting one's claims, in acknowledging the burden of providing a special explanation, or excuse, when one acts contrary to them, or else in showing shame and remorse and a desire to make amends, and so on. It is sufficient to remark here that having a morality is analogous to having made a firm commitment in advance; for one must acknowledge the principles of morality even when to one's disadvantage.[7] A man whose moral judgments always coincided with his interests could be suspected of having no morality at all.

Thus the two parts of the foregoing account are intended to mirror the kinds of circumstances in which questions of justice arise and the constraints which having a morality would impose upon persons so situated. In this way one can see how the acceptance of the principles of justice might come about, for given all these conditions as described, it would be natural if the two principles of justice were to be acknowledged. Since there is no way of anyone to win special advantages for himself, each might consider it reasonable to acknowledge equality as an initial principle. There is, however, no reason why they should regard this position as final; for if there are inequalities which satisfy the second principle, the immediate gain which equality would allow can be considered as intelligently invested in view of its future return. If, as is quite likely, these inequalities work as incentives to draw out better efforts, the members of this society may look upon them as concessions to human nature: they, like us, may think that people ideally should want to serve one another. But as they are mutually self-interested, their acceptance of these inequalities is merely the acceptance of the relations in which they actually stand, and a recognition of the motives which lead them to engage in their common practices. *They* have no title to complain of one another. And so provided that the conditions of the principle are met, there is no reason why they should not allow such inequalities. Indeed, it would be short-sighted of them to do so, and could result, in most cases, only from their being dejected by the bare knowledge, or perception, that others are better situated. Each person will, however, insist on an advantage to himself, and so on a common advantage, for none is willing to sacrifice anything for the others.

These remarks are not offered as a proof that persons so conceived and circumstanced would settle on the two principles, but only to show that these principles could have such a background, and so can be viewed as those principles which mutually self-interested and rational persons, when similarly situated and required to make in advance a firm commitment, could acknowledge as restrictions governing the assignment of rights and duties in their common practices, and thereby accept as limiting their rights against one another. The principles of justice may, then, be regarded as those principles which arise when the constraints of having a morality are imposed upon parties in the typical circumstances of justice.

IV

These ideas are, of course, connected with a familiar way of thinking about justice which goes back at least to the Greek Sophists, and which regards the acceptance of the principles of justice as a compromise between persons of roughly equal power who would enforce their will on each other if they could, but who, in view of the equality of forces amongst them and for the sake of their own peace and security, acknowledge certain forms of conduct insofar as prudence seems to require. Justice is thought of as a pact between rational egoists the stability of which is dependent on a balance of power and a similarity of circumstances.[8] While the previous account is connected with this tradition, and with its most recent variant, the theory of games,[9] it differs from it in several important respects which, to forestall misinterpretations, I will set out here.

First, I wish to use the previous conjectural account of the background of justice as a way of analyzing the concept. I do not want, therefore, to be interpreted as assuming a general theory of human motivation: When I suppose that the parties are mutually self-interested, and are not willing to have their (substantial) interests sacrificed to others, I am referring to their conduct and motives as they are taken for granted in cases where questions of justice ordinarily arise. Justice is the virtue of practices where there are assumed to be competing interests and conflicting claims, and where it is supposed that persons will press their rights on each other. That persons are mutually self-interested in certain situations and for certain purposes is what gives rise to the question of justice in practices covering those circumstances. Amongst an association of saints, if such a community could really exist, the disputes about justice could hardly occur; for they would all work selflessly together for one end, the glory of God as defined by their common religion, and reference to this end would settle every question of right. The justice of practices does not come up until there are several different parties (whether we think of these as individuals, associations, or nations and so on, is irrelevant) who do press their claims on one another, and who do regard themselves as representatives of interests which deserve to be considered. Thus the previous account involves no general theory of human motivation. Its intent is simply to incorporate into the conception of justice the relations of men to one another which set the stage for questions of justice. It makes no difference how wide or general these relations are, as this matter does not bear on the analysis of the concept.

Again, in contrast to the various conceptions of the social contract, the several parties do not establish any particular society or practice; they do not convenant to obey a particular sovereign body or to accept a given constitution.[10] Nor do they, as in the theory of games (in certain respects a marvelously sophisticated development of this tradition), decide on individual strategies adjusted to their respective circumstances in the game. What the parties do is to *jointly* acknowledge certain *principles* of appraisal relating to their common *practices* either as already established or merely proposed. They accede to standards of judgment, not to a given practice; they do not make any specific agreement, or bargain, or adopt a particular strategy. The subject of their acknowledgment is, therefore, very general indeed; it is simply the acknowledgment of certain principles of judgment, fulfilling certain general conditions, to be used in criticizing the arrangement of their common affairs. The relations of mutual self-interest [among] the parties who are similarly circumstanced mirror the conditions under which questions of justice arise, and the procedure by which the principles of judgment are proposed and acknowledged reflects the constraints of having a morality. Each aspect, then, of preceding hypothetical account serves the purpose of bringing out a feature of the notion of justice. One could, if one liked, view the principles of justice as the "solution" of this highest order "game" of adopting, subject to the procedure described, principles of argument for all coming particular "games" whose peculiarities one can in no way foresee. But this comparison, while no doubt helpful, must not obscure the fact that this highest order "game" is of a special sort.[11] Its significance is that its various pieces represent aspects of the concept of justice.

Finally, I do not, of course, conceive the several parties as necessarily coming together to establish their common practices for the first time. Some institutions may, indeed, be set up *de novo;* but I have framed the preceding account so that it will apply when the full complement of social institutions already exists and represents the result of a long period of development. Nor is the account in any way fictitious. In any society where people reflect on their institutions they will have an idea of what principles of justice would be acknowledged under the conditions described, and there will be occasions when the questions of justice are actually discussed in this way. Therefore if their practices do not accord with these principles, this will affect the quality of their social relations. For in this case there will be some recognized situations wherein the parties are mutually aware that one of them is being forced to accept what the other would concede is injust. The foregoing analysis may then be thought of as representing the actual quality of relations [among] persons as defined by practices accepted as just. In such practices the parties will acknowledge the principles on which it is constructed, and the general recognition of this fact shows itself in the absence of resentment and in the sense of being justly treated. Thus one common objection to the theory of the social contract, its apparently historical and fictitious character, is avoided.

V

That the principles of justice may be regarded as arising in the manner described illustrates an important fact about them. Not only does it bring out the idea that justice is a primitive moral notion in that it arises once the concept of morality is imposed on mutually self-interested agents similarly circumstanced, but it emphasizes that, fundamental to justice, is the concept of fairness which relates to right dealing between persons who are cooperating with or competing against one another, as when one speaks of fair games, fair competition, and fair bargains. The question of fairness arises when free persons, who have no authority over one another, are engaging in a joint activity and amongst themselves settling or acknowledging the rules which define it and which determine the respective shares in its benefits and burdens. A practice will strike the parties as fair if none feels that, by participating in it, they or any of the others are taken advantage of, or forced to give in to claims, which they do not regard as legitimate. This implies that each has a conception of legitimate claims which he thinks it reasonable for others as well as himself to acknowledge. If one thinks of the principles of justice as arising in the manner described, then they do define this sort of conception. A practice is just or fair, then, when it satisfies the principles which those who participate in it could propose to one another for mutual acceptance under the aforementioned circumstances. Persons engaged in a just, or fair, practice can face one another openly and support their respective positions, should they appear questionable, by reference to principles which it is reasonable to expect each to accept.

It is this notion of the possibility of mutual acknowledgment of principles by free persons who have no authority over one another which makes the concept of fairness fundamental to justice. Only if such acknowledgment is possible can there be true community between persons in their common practices; otherwise their relations will appear to them as founded to some extent on force. If, in ordinary speech, fairness applies more particularly to practices in which there is a choice whether to engage or not (for example, in games, business competition), and justice to practices in which there is no choice (for example, in slavery), the element of necessity does not render the conception of mutual acknowledgment inapplicable, although it may make it much more urgent to change unjust than unfair institutions. For one activity in which one can always engage is that of proposing and acknowledging principles to one another supposing each to be similarly circumstanced; and to judge practices by the principles so arrived at is to apply the standard of fairness to them.

Now if the participants in a practice accept its rules as fair, and so have no complaint to lodge against it, there arises a prima facie duty (and a corresponding prima facie right) of the parties to each other to act in accordance with the practice when it falls upon them to comply. When any number of persons engage in a practice, or conduct a joint undertaking according to rules, and thus restrict their liberty, those who have submitted to these restrictions when required have the right to a similar acquiescence on the part of those who have benefited by their submission. These conditions will obtain if a practice is correctly acknowledged to be fair, for in this case all who participate in it will benefit from it. The rights and duties so arising are special rights and duties in that they depend on previous actions voluntarily undertaken, in this case on the parties having engaged in a common practice and knowingly accepted its benefits.[12] It is not, however, an obligation which presupposes a deliberate performative act in the sense of a promise, or contract, and the like.[13] An unfortunate mistake of proponents of the idea of the social contract was to suppose that political obligation does require some such act, or at least to use language which suggests it. It is sufficient that one has knowingly participated in and accepted the benefits of a practice acknowledged to be fair. This prima facie obligation may, of course, be overridden: It may happen, when it comes one's turn to follow a rule, that other considerations will justify not doing so. But one cannot, in general, be released from this obligation by denying the justice of the practice only when it falls on one to obey. If a person rejects a practice, he should, so far as possible, declare his intention in advance, and avoid participating in it or enjoying its benefits.

This duty I have called that of fair play, but it should be admitted that to refer to it in this way is, perhaps, to extend the ordinary notion of fairness. Usually acting unfairly is not so much the breaking of any particular rule, even if the infraction is difficult to detect (cheating), but taking advantage of loopholes or ambiguities in rules, availing oneself of unexpected or special circumstances which make it impossible to enforce them, insisting that rules be enforced to one's advantage when they should be suspended, and more generally, acting contrary to the intention of a practice. It is for this reason that one speaks of the sense of fair play: Acting fairly requires more than simply being able to follow rules; what is fair must often be felt, or perceived, one wants to say. It is not, however, an unnatural extension of the duty of fair play to have it include the obligation which participants who have knowingly accepted the benefits of their common practice owe to each other to act in accordance with it when their performance falls due; for it is usually considered unfair if someone accepts the benefits of a practice but refuses to do his part in maintaining it. Thus one might say of the tax-dodger that he violates the duty of fair play: He accepts the benefits of government but will not do his part in releasing resources to it; and members of labor unions often say that fellow workers who refuse to join are being unfair: They refer to them as "free riders," as persons who enjoy what are the supposed benefits of unionism, higher wages, shorter hours, job security, and the like, but who refuse to share in its burdens in the form of paying dues, and so on.

The duty of fair play stands beside other prima facie duties such as fidelity and gratitude as a basic moral notion; yet it is not to be confused with them.[14] These duties are all clearly distinct, as would be obvious from their definitions. As with any moral duty, that of fair play implies a constraint on self-interest in particular cases; on occasion it enjoins conduct which a rational egoist strictly defined would not decide upon. So while justice does not require of anyone that he sacrifice his interests in that *general position* and procedure whereby the principles of justice are proposed and acknowledged, it may happen that in particular situations, arising in the context of engaging in a practice, the duty of fair play will often cross his interests in the sense that he will be required to forego particular advantages which the peculiarities of his circumstances might permit him to take. There is, of course, nothing surprising in this. It is simply the consequence of the firm commitment which the parties may be supposed to have made, or which they would make, in the general position, together with the fact that they have participated in and accepted the benefits of a practice which they regard as fair.

Now the acknowledgment of this constraint in particular cases, which is manifested in acting fairly or wishing to make amends, feeling ashamed, and the like, when one has evaded it, is one of the forms of conduct by which participants in a common practice exhibit their recognition of each other as persons with similar interests and capacities. In the same way that, failing a special explanation, the criterion for the recognition of suffering is helping one who suffers, acknowledging the duty of fair play is a necessary part of the criterion of recognizing another as a person with similar interests and feelings as oneself.[15] A person who never under any circumstances showed a wish to help others in pain would show, at the same time, that he did not recognize that they were in pain; nor could he have any feelings of affection or friendship for anyone; for having these feelings implies, failing special circumstances, that he comes to their aid when they are suffering. Recognition that another is a person in pain shows itself in sympathetic action; this primitive natural response of compassion is one of those responses upon which the various forms of moral conduct are built.

Similarly, the acceptance of the duty of fair play by participants in a common practice is a reflection in each person of the recognition of the aspirations and interests of the others to be realized by their joint activity. Failing a special explanation, their acceptance of it is a necessary part of the criterion for their recognizing one another as persons with similar interests and capacities, as the conception of their relations in the general position supposes them to be. Otherwise they would show no recognition of one another as persons with similar capacities and interests, and indeed, in some cases perhaps hypothetical, they would not recognize one another as persons at all, but as complicated objects involved in a complicated activity. To recognize another as a person one must respond to him and act towards him in certain ways; and these ways are intimately connected with the various prima facie duties. Acknowledging these duties in *some* degree, and so having the elements of morality, is not a matter of choice, or of intuiting moral qualities, or a matter of the expression of feelings or attitudes (the three interpretations between which philosophical opinion frequently oscillates); it is simply the possession of one of the forms of conduct in which the recognition of others as persons is manifested.

These remarks are unhappily obscure. Their main purpose here, however, is to forestall, together with the remarks in section IV, the misinterpretation that, on the view presented, the acceptance of justice and the acknowledgment of the duty of fair play depends in every day life solely on their being a *de facto* balance of forces between the parties. It would indeed be foolish to underestimate the importance of such a balance in securing justice; but it is not the only basis thereof. The recognition of one another as persons with similar interests and capacities engaged in a common practice must, failing a special explanation, show itself in the acceptance of the principles of justice and the acknowledgment of the duty of fair play.

The conception at which we have arrived, then, is that the principles of justice may be thought of as arising once the constraints of having a morality are imposed upon rational and mutually self-interested parties who are related and situated in a special way. A practice is just if it is in accordance with the principles which all who participate in it might reasonably be expected to propose or to acknowledge before one another when they are similarly circumstanced and required to make a firm commitment in advance without knowledge of what will be their peculiar condition, and thus when it meets standards which the parties could accept as fair should occasion arise for them to debate its merits. Regarding the participants themselves, once persons knowingly engage in a practice which they acknowledge to be fair and accept the benefits of doing so, they are bound by the duty of fair play to follow the rules when it comes their turn to do so, and this implies a limitation on their pursuit of self-interest in particular cases.

Now one consequence of this conception is that, where it applies, there is no moral value in the satisfaction of a claim incompatible with it. Such a claim violates the conditions of reciprocity and community amongst persons, and he who presses it, not being willing to acknowledge it when pressed by another, has no grounds for complaint when it is denied; whereas he against whom it is pressed can complain. As it cannot be mutually acknowledged it is a resort to coercion; granting the claim is possible only if one party can compel acceptance of what the other will not admit. But it makes no sense to concede claims the denial of which cannot be complained of in preference to claims the denial of which can be objected to. Thus in deciding on the justice of a practice it is not enough to ascertain that it answers to wants and interests in the fullest and most effective manner. For if any of these conflict with justice, they should not be counted, as their satisfaction is no reason at all for having a practice. It would be irrelevant to say, even if true, that it resulted in the greatest satisfaction of desire. In tallying up the merits of a practice one must toss out the satisfaction of interests the

claims of which are incompatible with the principles of justice.

VI

The discussion so far has been excessively abstract. While this is perhaps unavoidable, I should now like to bring out some of the features of the conception of justice as fairness by comparing it with the conception of justice in classical utilitarianism as represented by Bentham and Sidgwick, and its counterpart in welfare economics. This conception assimilates justice to benevolence and the latter in turn to the most efficient design of institutions to promote the general welfare. Justice is a kind of efficiency.[16]

Now it is said occasionally that this form of utilitarianism puts no restrictions on what might be a just assignment of rights and duties in that there might be circumstances which, on utilitarian grounds, would justify institutions highly offensive to our ordinary sense of justice. But the classical utilitarian conception is not totally unprepared for this objection. Beginning with the notion that the general happiness can be represented by a social utility function consisting of a sum of individual utility functions with identical weights (this being the meaning of the maxim that each counts for one and no more than one),[17] it is commonly assumed that the utility functions of individuals are similar in all essential respects. Differences [among] individuals are ascribed to accidents of education and upbringing, and they should not be taken into account. This assumption, coupled with that of diminishing marginal utility, results in a prima facie case for equality, for example, of equality in the distribution of income during any given period of time, laying aside indirect effects on the future. But even if utilitarianism is interpreted as having such restrictions built into the utility function, and even if it is supposed that these restrictions have in practice much the same result as the application of the principles of justice (and appear, perhaps, to be ways of expressing these principles in the language of mathematics and psychology), the fundamental idea is very different from the conception of justice as fairness. For one thing, that the principles of justice should be accepted is interpreted as the contingent result of a higher order administrative decision. The form of this decision is regarded as being similar to that of an entrepreneur deciding how much to produce of this or that commodity in view of its marginal revenue, or to that of someone distributing goods to needy persons according to the relative urgency of their wants. The choice between practices is thought of as being made on the basis of the allocation of benefits and burdens to individuals (these being measured by the present capitalized value of their utility over the full period of the practice's existence), which results from the distribution of rights and duties established by a practice.

Moreover, the individuals receiving these benefits are not conceived as being related in any way: They represent so many different directions in which limited resources may be allocated. The value of assigning resources to one direction rather than another depends solely on the preferences and interests of individuals as individuals. The satisfaction of desire has its value irrespective of the moral relations between persons, say as members of a joint undertaking, of the claims which, in the name of these interests, they are prepared to make on one another;[18] and it is this value which is to be taken into account by the (ideal) legislator who is conceived as adjusting the rules of the system from the center so as to maximize the value of the social utility function.

It is thought that the principles of justice will not be violated by a legal system so conceived provided these executive decisions are correctly made. In this fact the principles of justice are said to have their derivation and explanation; they simply express the most important general features of social institutions in which the administrative problem is solved in the best way. These principles have, indeed, a special urgency because, given the facts of human nature, so much depends on them; and this explains the peculiar quality of the moral feelings associated with justice.[19] This assimilation of justice to a higher order executive decision, certainly a striking conception, is central to classical utilitarianism; and it also brings out its profound individualism, in one sense of this ambiguous word. It regards persons as so many *separate* directions in which benefits and burdens may be assigned; and the value of the satisfaction or dissatisfaction of desire is not thought to depend in any way on the moral relations in which individuals stand, or on the

kinds of claims which they are willing, in the pursuit of their interests, to press on each other.

VII

Many social decisions are, of course, of an administrative nature. Certainly this is so when it is a matter of social utility in what one may call its ordinary sense: that is, when it is a question of the efficient design of social institutions for the use of common means to achieve common ends. In this case either the benefits and burdens may be assumed to be impartially distributed, or the question of distribution is misplaced, as in the instance of maintaining public order and security or national defense. But as an interpretation of the basis of the principles of justice, classical utilitarianism is mistaken. It *permits* one to argue, for example, that slavery is unjust on the grounds that the advantages to the slaveholder as slaveholder do not counterbalance the disadvantages to the slave and to society at large burdened by a comparatively inefficient system of labor. Now the conception of justice as fairness, when applied to the practice of slavery with its offices of slaveholder and slave, would not allow one to consider the advantages of the slaveholder in the first place. As that office is not in accordance with principles which could be mutually acknowledged, the gains accruing to the slaveholder, assuming them to exist, cannot be counted as in *any* way mitigating the injustice of the practice. The question whether these gains outweigh the disadvantages to the slave and to society cannot arise, since in considering the justice of slavery these gains have no weight at all which requires that they be overridden. Where the conception of justice as fairness applies, slavery is *always* unjust.

I am not, of course, suggesting the absurdity that the classical utilitarians approved of slavery. I am only rejecting a type of argument which their view allows them to use in support of their disapproval of it. The conception of justice as derivative from efficiency implies that judging the justice of a practice is always, in principle at least, a matter of weighing up advantages and disadvantages, each having an intrinsic value or disvalue as the satisfaction of interests, irrespective of whether or not these interests necessarily involve acquiescence in principles which could not be mutually acknowledged. Utilitarianism cannot account for the fact that slavery is always unjust, nor for the fact that it would be recognized as irrelevant in defeating the accusation of injustice for one person to say to another, engaged with him in a common practice and debating its merits, that nevertheless it allowed of the greatest satisfaction of desire. The charge of injustice cannot be rebutted in this way. If justice were derivative from a higher order executive efficiency, this would not be so.

But now, even if it is taken as established that, so far as the ordinary conception of justice goes, slavery is always unjust (that is, slavery by definition violates commonly recognized principles of justice), the classical utilitarian would surely reply that these principles, as other moral principles subordinate to that of utility, are only generally correct. It is simply for the most part true that slavery is less efficient than other institutions; and while common sense may define the concept of justice so that slavery is unjust, nevertheless, where slavery would lead to the greatest satisfaction of desire, it is not wrong. Indeed, it is then right, and for the very same reason that justice, as ordinarily understood, is usually right. If, as ordinarily understood, slavery is always unjust, to this extent the utilitarian conception of justice might be admitted to differ from that of common moral opinion. Still the utilitarian would want to hold that, as a matter of moral principle, his view is correct in giving no special weight to considerations of justice beyond that allowed for by the general presumption of effectiveness. And this, he claims, is as it should be. The everyday opinion is morally in error, although, indeed, it is a useful error, since it protects rules of generally high utility.

The question, then relates not simply to the analysis of the concept of justice as common sense defines it, but the analysis of it in the wider sense as to how much weight considerations of justice, as defined, are to have when laid against other kinds of moral considerations. Here again I wish to argue that reasons of justice have a *special* weight for which only the conception of justice as fairness can account. Moreover, it belongs to the concept of justice that they do have this special weight. While Mill recognized that this was so, he thought that it could be accounted for by the special urgency of the moral feelings which naturally support principles of such high utility. But it is a mistake to resort to the urgency of feeling;

as with the appeal to intuition, it manifests a failure to pursue the question far enough. The special weight of considerations of justice can be explained from the conception of justice as fairness. It is only necessary to elaborate a bit what has already been said as follows.

If one examines the circumstances in which a certain tolerance of slavery is justified, or perhaps better, excused, it turns out that these are of a rather special sort. Perhaps slavery exists as an inheritance from the past and it proves necessary to dismantle it piece by piece; at times slavery may conceivably be an advance on previous institutions. Now while there may be some excuse for slavery in special conditions, it is never an excuse for it that it is sufficiently advantageous to the slaveholder to outweigh the disadvantages to the slave and to society. A person who argues in this way is not perhaps making a wildly irrelevant remark; but he is guilty of a moral fallacy. There is disorder in his conception of the ranking of moral principles. For the slaveholder, by his own admission, has no moral title to the advantages which he receives as a slaveholder. He is no more prepared than the slave to acknowledge the principle upon which is founded the respective positions in which they both stand. Since slavery does not accord with principles which they could mutually acknowledge, they each may be supposed to agree that it is unjust: it grants claims which it ought not to grant and in doing so denies claims which it ought not to deny. Amongst persons in a general position who are debating the form of their common practices, it cannot, therefore, be offered as a reason for a practice that, in conceding these very claims that ought to be denied, it nevertheless meets existing interests more effectively. By their very nature the satisfaction of these claims is without weight and cannot enter into any tabulation of advantages and disadvantages.

Furthermore, it follows from the concept of morality that, to the extent that the slaveholder recognizes his position vis-à-vis the slave to be unjust, he would not choose to press his claims. His not wanting to receive his special advantages is one of the ways in which he shows that he thinks slavery is unjust. It would be fallacious for the legislator to suppose, then, that it is a ground for having a practice that it brings advantages greater than disadvantages, if those for whom the practice is designed, and to whom the advantages flow, acknowledge that they have no moral title to them and do not wish to receive them.

For these reasons the principles of justice have a special weight; and with respect to the principle of the greatest satisfaction of desire, as cited in the general position amongst those discussing the merits of their common practices, the principles of justice have an absolute weight. In this sense they are not contingent; and this is why their force is greater than can be accounted for by the general presumption (assuming that there is one) of the effectiveness, in the utilitarian sense, of practices which in fact satisfy them.

If one wants to continue using the concepts of classical utilitarianism, one will have to say, to meet this criticism, that at least the individual or social utility functions must be so defined that no value is given to the satisfaction of interests the representative claims of which violate the principles of justice. In this way it is no doubt possible to include these principles within the form of the utilitarian conception; but to do so is, of course, to change its inspiration altogether as a moral conception. For it is to incorporate within it principles which cannot be understood on the basis of a higher order executive decision aiming at the greatest satisfaction of desire.

It is worth remarking, perhaps, that this criticism of utilitarianism does not depend on whether or not the two assumptions, that of individuals having similar utility functions and that of diminishing marginal utility, are interpreted as psychological propositions to be supported or refuted by experience, or as moral and political principles expressed in a somewhat technical language. There are, certainly, several advantages in taking them in the latter fashion.[20] For one thing, one might say that this is what Bentham and others really meant by them, as least as shown by how they were used in arguments for social reform. More importantly, one could hold that the best way to defend the classical utilitarian view is to interpret these assumptions as moral and political principles. It is doubtful whether, taken as psychological propositions, they are true of men in general as we know them under normal conditions. On the other hand, utilitarians would not have wanted to propose them merely as practical working principles of legislation, or as expedient maxims to guide reform, given the egalitarian

sentiments of modern society.[21] When pressed they might well have invoked the idea of a more or less equal capacity of men in relevant respects if given an equal chance in a just society. But if the argument above regarding slavery is correct, then granting these assumptions as moral and political principles makes no difference. To view individuals as equally fruitful lines for the allocation of benefits, even as a matter of moral principle, still leaves the mistaken notion that the satisfaction of desire has value in itself irrespective of the relations between persons as members of a common practice, and irrespective of the claims upon one another which the satisfaction of interests represents. To see the error of this idea one must give up the conception of justice as an executive decision altogether and refer to the notion of justice as fairness: that participants in a common practice be regarded as having an original and equal liberty and that their common practices be considered unjust unless they accord with principles which persons so circumstanced and related could freely acknowledge before one another, and so could accept as fair. Once the emphasis is put upon the concept of the mutual recognition of principles by participants in a common practice the rules of which are to define their several relations and give form to their claims on one another, then it is clear that the granting of a claim the principle of which could not be acknowledged by each in the general position (that is, in the position in which the parties propose and acknowledge principles before one another) is not a reason for adopting a practice. Viewed in this way, the background of the claim is seen to exclude it from consideration; that it can represent a value in itself arises from the conception of individuals as separate lines for the assignment of benefits, as isolated persons who stand as claimants on an administrative or benevolent largesse. Occasionally persons do so stand to one another; but this is not the general case, nor, more importantly, is it the case when it is a matter of the justice of practices themselves in which participants stand in various relations to be appraised in accordance with standards which they may be expected to acknowledge before one another. Thus however mistaken the notion of the social contract may be as history, and however far it may overreach itself as a general theory of social and political obligation, it does express, suitably interpreted, an essential part of the concept of justice.[22]

VIII

By way of conclusion I should like to make two remarks: first, the original modification of the utilitarian principle (that it require of practices that the offices and positions defined by them be equal unless it is reasonable to suppose that the representative man in *every* office would find the inequality to his advantage), slight as it may appear at first sight, actually has a different conception of justice standing behind it. I have tried to show how this is so by developing the concept of justice as fairness and by indicating how this notion involves the mutual acceptance, from a general position, of the principles on which a practice is founded, and how this in turn requires the exclusion from consideration of claims violating the principles of justice. Thus the slight alteration of principle reveals another family of notions, another way of looking at the concept of justice.

Second, I should like to remark also that I have been dealing with the *concept* of justice. I have tried to set out the kinds of principles upon which judgments concerning the justice of practices may be said to stand. The analysis will be successful to the degree that it expresses the principles involved in these judgments when made by competent persons upon deliberation and reflection.[23] Now every people may be supposed to have the concept of justice, since in the life of every society there must be at least some relations in which the parties consider themselves to be circumstanced and related as the concept of justice as fairness requires. Societies will differ from one another not in having or in failing to have this notion but in the range of cases to which they apply it and in the emphasis which they give to it as compared with other moral concepts.

A firm grasp of the concept of justice itself is necessary if these variations, and the reasons for them, are to be understood. No study of the development of moral ideas and of the differences between them is more sound than the analysis of the fundamental moral concepts upon which it must depend. I have tried, therefore, to give an analysis of the concept of justice which should apply generally, however large a part the concept may have in a given morality, and which can be used in explaining the course of men's thoughts about justice and its relations to other moral concepts. How it is to be used for this purpose is a large topic which I cannot, of course, take up here. I mention it only to emphasize that I have been dealing with the concept of justice itself and to indicate what use I consider such an analysis to have.

NOTES

1. I use the word "practice" throughout as a sort of technical term meaning any form of activity specified by a system of rules which defines offices, roles, moves, penalties, defenses, and so on, and which gives the activity its structure. As examples one may think of games and rituals, trials and parliaments, markets and systems of property. I have attempted a partial analysis of the notion of a practice in a paper "Two Concepts of Rules," *Philosophical Review*, LXIV (1955), 3–32.

2. These principles are, of course, well known in one form or another and appear in many analyses of justice even where the writers differ widely on other matters. Thus if the principle of equal liberty is commonly associated with Kant (see *The Philosophy of Law*, tr. by W. Hastie, Edinburgh, 1887, pp. 56 f.), it may be claimed that it can also be found in J. S. Mill's *On Liberty* and elsewhere, and in many other liberal writers. Recently H. L. A. Hart has argued for something like it in his paper "Are There Any Natural Rights?" *Philosophical Review*, LXIV (1955), 175–191. The injustice of inequalities which are not won in return for a contribution to the common advantage is, of course, widespread in political writings of all sorts. The conception of justice here discussed is distinctive, if at all, only in selecting these two principles in this form; but for another similar analysis, see the discussion by W. D. Lamont, *The Principles of Moral Judgment* (Oxford, 1946), ch. v.

3. This point was made by Sidgwick, *Methods of Ethics*, 6th ed. (London, 1901), Bk. III, ch. v, sec. 1. It has recently been emphasized by Sir Isaiah Berlin in a symposium, "Equality," *Proceedings of the Aristotelian Society*, n.s. LVI (1955–56), 305 f.

4. In the paper referred to above, footnote 1, I have tried to show the importance of taking practices as the proper subject of the utilitarian principle. The criticisms of so-called "restricted utilitarianism" by J. J. C. Smart, "Extreme and Restricted Utilitarianism," *Philosophical Quarterly*, VI (1956), 344–354, and by H. J. McCloskey, "An Examination of Restricted Utilitarianism," *Philosophical Review*, LXVI (1957), 466–485, do not affect my argument. These papers are concerned with the very general proposition, which is attributed (with what justice I shall not consider) to S. E. Toulmin and P. H. Nowell-Smith (and in the case of the latter paper, also, apparently, to me); namely, the proposition that particular moral actions are justified by appealing to moral rules, and moral rules in turn by reference to utility. But clearly I meant to defend no such view. My discussion of the concept of rules as maxims is an explicit rejection of it. What I did argue was that, in the *logically special* case of practices (although actually quite a common case) where the rules have special features and are not moral rules at all but legal rules or rules of games and the like (except, perhaps, in the case of promises), there is a peculiar force to the distinction between justifying particular actions and justifying the system of rules themselves. Even then I claimed only that restricting the

utilitarian principle to practices as defined strengthened it. I did not argue for the position that this amendment alone is sufficient for a complete defense of utilitarianism as a general theory of morals. In this paper I take up the question as to how the utilitarian principle itself must be modified, but here, too, the subject of inquiry is not all of morality at once, but a limited topic, the concept of justice.

5. It might seem as if J. S. Mill, in paragraph 36 of Chapter v of *Utilitarianism*, expressed the utilitarian principle in this modified form, but in the remaining two paragraphs of the chapter, and elsewhere, he would appear not to grasp the significance of the change. Hume often emphasizes that *every* man must benefit. For example, in discussing the utility of general rules, he holds that they are requisite to the "wellbeing of every individual"; from a stable system of property "every individual person must find himself a gainer in balancing the account. . . . " "Every member of society is sensible of this interest; everyone expresses this sense to his fellows along with the resolution he has taken of squaring his actions by it, on the conditions that others will do the same." *A Treatise of Human Nature*, Bk. III, Pt. II, Section II, paragraph 22.

6. It is not possible to discuss here this addition to the usual conception of rationality. If it seems peculiar, it may be worth remarking that it is analogous to the modification of the utilitarian principle which the argument as a whole is designed to explain and justify. In the same way that the satisfaction of interests, the representative claims of which violate the principles of justice, is not a reason for having a practice (see sec. VII), unfounded envy, within limits, need not to be taken into account.

7. The idea that accepting a principle as a moral principle implies that one generally acts on it, failing a special explanation, has been stressed by R. M. Hare, *The Language of Morals* (Oxford, 1952). His formulation of it needs to be modified, however, along the lines suggested by P. L. Gardiner, "On Assenting to a Moral Principle," *Proceedings of the Aristotelian Society*, n.s. LV (1955), 23–44. See also C. K. Grant, "Akrasia and the Criteria of Assent to Practical Principles," *Mind*, LXV (1956), 400–407, where the complexity of the criteria for assent is discussed.

8. Perhaps the best known statement of this conception is that given by Glaucon at the beginning of Book II of Plato's *Republic*. Presumably it was, in various forms, a common view among the Sophists; but that Plato gives a fair representation of it is doubtful. See K. R. Popper, *The Open Society and Its Enemies*, rev. ed. (Princeton, 1950), pp. 112–118. Certainly Plato usually attributes to it a quality of manic egoism which one feels must be an exaggeration; on the other hand, see the Melian Debate in Thucydides, *The Peloponnesian War*, Book V, ch. vii, although it is impossible to say to what extent the views expressed there reveal any current philosophical opinion. Also in this tradition are the remarks of Epicurus on justice in *Principal Doctrines*, XXXI–XXXVIII. In modern times elements of the conception appear in a more sophisticated form in Hobbes's *The Leviathan* and in Hume's *A Treatise of Human Nature*, Book III, Pt. II, as well as in the writings of the school of natural law such as Pufendorf's *De jure naturae et gentium*. Hobbes and Hume are especially instructive. For Hobbe's argument see Howard Warrender's *The Political Philosophy of Hobbes* (Oxford, 1957). W. J. Baumol's *Welfare Economics and the Theory of the State* (London, 1952), is valuable in showing the wide applicability of Hobbes's fundamental idea (interpreting his natural law as principles of prudence), although in this book it is traced back only to Hume's *Treatise*.

9. See J. von Neumann and O. Morgenstern, *The Theory of Games and Economic Behavior*, 2nd ed. (Princeton, 1947). For a comprehensive and not too technical discussion of the developments since, see R. Duncan Luce and Howard Raiffa, *Games and Decisions: Introduction and Critical Survey* (New York, 1957). Chs. vi and xiv discuss the developments most obviously related to the analysis of justice.

10. For a general survey see J. W. Gough, *The Social Contract*, 2nd ed. (Oxford, 1957), and Otto von Gierke, *The Development of Political Theory*, tr. by B. Freyd (London, 1939), Pt. II, ch. II.

11. The difficulty one gets into by a mechanical application of the theory of games to moral philosophy can be brought out by considering among several possible examples, R. B. Braithwaite's study, *Theory of Games as a Tool for the Moral Philosopher* (Cambridge, 1955). On the analysis there given, it turns out that the fair division of playing time between Matthew and Luke depends on their preferences, and these in turn are connected with the instruments they wish to play. Since Matthew has a threat advantage over Luke, arising purely from the fact that Matthew, the trumpeter, prefers both of them playing at once to neither of them playing, whereas Luke, the pianist, prefers silence to cacophony, Matthew is alloted 26 evenings of play to Luke's 17. If the situation were reversed, the threat advantage would be with Luke. See pp. 36 f. But now we have only to suppose that Matthew is a jazz enthusiast who plays the drums, and Luke a violinist who plays sonatas, in which case it will be fair, on this analysis, for Matthew to play whenever and as often as he likes, assuming, of course, as it is plausible to assume, that he does not care whether Luke plays or not. Certainly something has gone wrong. To each according to his threat advantage is hardly the principle of fairness. What is lacking is the concept of morality, and it must be brought into the conjectural account in some way or other. In the text this is done by the form of the procedure whereby principles are proposed and acknowledged (section III). If one starts directly with the particular case as known, and if one accepts as given and definitive the preferences and relative positions of the parties, whatever they are, it is impossible to give an analysis of the moral concept of fairness. Braithwaite's use of the theory of games, insofar as it is intended to analyze the concept of fairness, is, I think, mistaken. This is not, of course, to criticize in any way the theory of games as a mathematical theory, to which Braithwaite's book certainly contributes, nor as an analysis of how rational (and amoral) egoists might behave (and so as an analysis of how people sometimes actually do behave). But it is to say that if the theory of games is to be used to analyze moral concepts, its formal structure must be interpreted in a special and general manner as indicated in the text. Once we do this, though, we are in touch again with a much older tradition.

12. For the definition of this prima facie duty, and the idea that it is a special duty, I am indebted to H. L. A. Hart. See his paper "Are There Any Natural Rights?" *Philosophical Review*, LXIV (1955), 185 f.

13. The sense of "performative" here is to be derived from J. L. Austin's paper in the symposium, "Other Minds," *Proceedings of the Aristotelian Society*, Supplementary Volume (1946), pp. 170–174.

14. This, however, commonly happens. Hobbes, for example, when invoking the notion of a "tacit covenant," appeals not to the natural law that promises should be kept but to his fourth law of nature, that of gratitude. On Hobbes's shift from fidelity to gratitude, see Warrender, *Political Philosophy of Hobbes* (footnote 8), pp. 51–52, 233–237. While it is not a serious criticism of Hobbes, it would have improved his argument had he appealed to the duty of fair play. On his premises he is perfectly entitled to do so. Similarly Sidgwick

thought that a principle of justice, such as every man ought to receive adequate requital for his labor, is like gratitude universalized. See *Methods of Ethics,* Bk. III, ch. v, Sec. 5. There is a gap in the stock of moral concepts used by philosophers into which the concept of the duty of fair play fits quite naturally.

15.   I am using the concept of criterion here in what I take to be Wittgenstein's sense. See *Philosophical Investigations,* (Oxford, 1953); and Norman Malcolm's review, "Wittgenstein's *Philosophical Investigations," Philosophical Review,* LXIII (1954), 543–547. That the response of compassion, under appropriate circumstances, is part of the criterion for whether or not a person understands what "pain" means, is, I think, in the *Philosophical Investigations.* The view in the text is simply an extension of this idea. I cannot, however, attempt to justify it here. Similar thoughts are to be found, I think, in Max Scheler, *The Nature of Sympathy,* tr. by Peter Heath (New Haven, 1954). His way of writing is often so obscure that I cannot be certain.

16.   While this assimilation is implicit in Bentham's and Sidgwick's moral theory, explicit statements of it as applied to justice are relatively rare. One clear instance in *The Principles of Morals and Legislation* occurs in ch. x, footnote 2 to section XL: ". . . justice, in the only sense in which it has a meaning, is an imaginary personage, feigned for the convenience of discourse, whose dictates are the dictates of utility, applied to certain particular cases. Justice, then, is nothing more than an imaginary instrument, employed to forward on certain occasions, and by certain means, the purposes of benevolence. The dictates of justice are nothing more than a part of the dictates of benevolence, which, on certain occasions, are applied to certain subjects. . . ." Likewise in *The Limits of Jurisprudence Defined,* ed. by C. W. Everett (New York, 1945), pp. 117 f., Bentham criticizes Grotius for denying that justice derives from utility; and in *The Theory of Legislation,* ed. by C. K. Ogden (London, 1931), p. 3, he says that he uses the words "just" and "unjust" along with other words "simply as collective terms including the ideas of certain pains or pleasures." That Sidgwick's conception of justice is similar to Bentham's is admittedly not evident from his discussion of justice in Book III, ch. v of *Methods of Ethics.* But it follows, I think, from the moral theory he accepts. Hence C. D. Broad's criticism of Sidgwick in the matter of distributive justice in *Five Types of Ethical Theory* (London, 1930), pp. 249–253, do not rest on a misinterpretation.

17.   This maxim is attributed to Bentham by J. S. Mill in *Utilitarianism,* ch. v, paragraph 36. I have not found it in Bentham's writings, nor seen such a reference. Similarly James Bonar, *Philosophy and Political Economy* (London, 1893), p. 234 n. But it accords perfectly with Bentham's ideas. See the hitherto unpublished manuscript in David Baumgardt, *Bentham and the Ethics of Today* (Princeton, 1952), Appendix IV. For example, "the total value of the stock of pleasure belonging to the whole community is to be obtained by multiplying the number expressing the value of it as respecting any one person, by the number expressing the multitude of such individuals" (p. 556).

18.   An idea essential to the classical utilitarian conception of justice. Bentham is firm in his statement of it: "It is only upon that principle [the principle of asceticism], and not from the principle of utility, that the most abominable pleasure which the vilest of malefactors ever reaped from his crime would be reprobated, if it stood alone. The case is, that it never does stand alone; but is necessarily followed by such a quantity of pain (or, what comes to the same thing, such a chance for a certain quantity of pain) that the pleasure in comparison of it, is as nothing: and this is the true and sole, but perfectly sufficient, reason for making it a ground for punishment" (*The Principles of Morals and Legislation,* ch. II, sec. iv. See also ch. x, sec. x, footnote I). The same point is made in *The Limits of Jurisprudence Defined,* pp. 115 f. Although much recent welfare economics, as found in such important works as I. M. D. Little, *A Critique of Welfare Economics,* 2nd ed. (Oxford, 1957) and K. J. Arrow, *Social Choice and Individual Values* (New York, 1951), dispenses with the idea of cardinal utility, and uses instead the theory of ordinal utility as stated by J. R. Hicks, *Value and Capital,* 2nd ed. (Oxford, 1946), Pt. I, it assumes with utilitarianism that individual preferences have value as such, and so accepts the idea being criticized here. I hasten to add, however, that this is no objection to it as a means of analyzing economic policy, and for that purpose it may, indeed, be a necessary simplifying assumption. Nevertheless it is an assumption which cannot be made insofar as one is trying to analyze moral concepts, especially the concept of justice, as economists would, I think, agree. Justice is usually regarded as a separate and distinct part of any comprehensive criterion of economic policy. See, for example, Tibor Scitovsky, *Welfare and Competition* (London, 1952), pp. 59–69, and Little, *Critique of Welfare Economics* (this footnote), ch. VII.

19.   See J. S. Mill's argument in *Utilitarianism,* ch. v, pars. 16–25.

20.   See D. G. Ritchie, *Natural Rights* (London, 1894), pp. 95 ff., 249 ff. Lionel Robbins has insisted on this point on several occasions. See *An Essay on the Nature and Significance of Economic Science,* 2nd ed. (London, 1935), pp. 134–43, "Interpersonal Comparisons of Utility: A Comment," *Economic Journal,* XLVIII (1938), 635–41, and more recently, "Robertson on Utility and Scope," *Economica,* n.s. XX (1953), 108 f.

21.   As Sir Henry Maine suggested Bentham may have regarded them. See *The Early History of Institutions* (London, 1875), pp. 398 ff.

22.   Thus Kant was not far wrong when he interpreted the original contract merely as an "Idea of Reason"; yet he still thought of it as a *general* criterion of right and as providing a general theory of political obligation. See the second part of the essay, "On the Saying 'That may be right in theory but has no value in practice' " (1793), in *Kant's Principles of Politics,* tr. by W. Hastie (Edinburgh, 1891). I have drawn on the contractarian tradition not for a general theory of political obligation but to clarify the concept of justice.

23.   For a further discussion of the idea expressed here, see my paper, "Outline of a Decision Procedure for Ethics," in the *Philosophical Review,* LX (1951), 177–197. For an analysis, similar in many respects but using the notion of the ideal observer instead of that of the considered judgment of a competent person, see Roderick Firth, "Ethical Absolutism and the Ideal Observer," *Philosophy and Phenomenological Research,* XII (1952), 317–345. While the similarities between these two discussions are more important than the differences, an analysis based on the notion of a considered judgment of a competent person, as it is based on a kind of judgment, may prove more helpful in understanding the features of moral judgment than an analysis based on the notion of an ideal observer, although this remains to be shown. A man who rejects the conditions imposed on a considered judgment of a competent person could no longer profess to *judge* at all. This seems more fundamental than his rejecting the conditions of observation, for these do not seem to apply, in an ordinary sense, to making a moral judgment.

ROBERT NOZICK

The Principle of Fairness *

A principle suggested by Herbert Hart, which (following John Rawls) we shall call the *principle of fairness,* would be of service here if it were adequate. This principle holds that when a number of persons engage in a just, mutually advantageous, cooperative venture according to rules and thus restrain their liberty in ways necessary to yield advantages for all, those who have submitted to these restrictions have a right to similar acquiescence on the part of those who have benefited from their submission.[1] Acceptance of benefits (even when this is not a giving of express or tacit undertaking to cooperate) is enough, according to this principle, to bind one. If one adds to the principle of fairness the claim that the others to whom the obligations are owed or their agents may *enforce* the obligations arising under this principle (including the obligation to limit one's actions), then groups of people in a state of nature who agree to a procedure to pick those to engage in certain acts will have legitimate rights to prohibit "free riders." Such a right may be crucial to the viability of such agreements. We should scrutinize such a powerful right very carefully, especially as it seems to make *unanimous* consent to coercive government in a state of nature *unnecessary!* Yet a further reason to examine it is its plausibility as a counterexample to my claim that no new rights "emerge" at the group level, that individuals in combination cannot create new rights which are not the sum of preexisting ones. A right to enforce others' obligation to limit their conduct in specified ways might stem from some special feature of the obligation or might be thought to follow from some general principle that all obligations owed to others may be enforced. In the absence of argument for the

special enforcement-justifying nature of the obligation supposedly arising under the principle of fairness, I shall consider first the principle of the enforceability of all obligations and then turn to the adequacy of the principle of fairness itself. If either of these principles is rejected, the right to enforce the cooperation of others in these situations totters. I shall argue that *both* of these principles must be rejected.

Herbert Hart's argument for the existence of a natural right [2] depends upon particularizing the principle of the enforceability of all obligations: someone's being under a special obligation to you to do *A* (which might have arisen, for example, by their promising to you that they would do *A*) gives you, not only the right that they do *A,* but also the right to force them to do *A*. Only against a background in which people may not force you to do *A* or other actions you may promise to do can we understand, says Hart, the *point* and purpose of special obligations. Since special obligations do have a point and purpose, Hart continues, there is a natural right not to be forced to do something unless certain specified conditions pertain; this natural right is built into the background against which special obligations exist.

This well-known argument of Hart's is puzzling. I may release someone from an obligation not to force me to do *A*. ("I now release you from the obligation not to force me to do *A*. You now are free to force me to do *A*.") Yet so releasing them does *not* create in me an obligation to them to do *A*. Since Hart supposes that my being under an obligation to someone to do *A* gives him (entails that he has) the right to force me to do *A,* and since we have seen the converse does not hold, we may consider that component of being under an obligation to someone to do something over and above his having the right to force you to do it. (May we suppose there is this distinguishable component without facing the charge of "logical atomism"?) An alternative view which rejects Hart's inclusion of the right to force in the

* From pp. 90–95 of *Anarchy, State and Utopia* by Robert Nozick, © 1974 by Basic Books, Inc., Publishers, New York. Reprinted by permission of the author and publishers, Basic Books (New York) and Basil Blackwell & Mott Ltd. (Oxford, England).

notion of being owed an obligation might hold that this additional component is the *whole* of the content of being obligated to someone to do something. If I don't do it, then (all things being equal) I'm doing something wrong; control over the situation is in his hands; he has the power to release me from the obligation unless he's promised to someone else that he won't, and so on. Perhaps all this looks too *ephemeral* without the additional presence of rights of enforcement. Yet rights of enforcement are themselves merely *rights;* that is, permissions to do something and obligations on others not to interfere. True, one has the right to enforce these further obligations, but it is not clear that including *rights* of enforcing really shores up the whole structure if one assumes it to be insubstantial to begin with. Perhaps one must merely take the moral realm seriously and think one component amounts to something even without a connection to enforcement. (Of course, this is not to say that this component *never* is connected with enforcement!) On this view, we can explain the point of obligations without bringing in rights of enforcement and hence without supposing a general background of obligation not to force from which this stands out. (Of course, even though Hart's argument does not demonstrate the existence of such an obligation not to force, it may exist nevertheless.)

Apart from these general considerations against the principle of the enforceability of all special obligations, puzzle cases can be produced. For example, if I promise to you that I will not murder someone, this does not *give* you the right to force me not to, for you already have this right, though it does create a particular obligation *to you.* Or, if I cautiously insist that you first promise to me that you won't force me to do *A* before I will make my promise to you to do *A,* and I do receive this promise from you first, it would be implausible to say that in promising I give you the right to force me to do *A.* (Though consider the situation which results if I am so foolish as to release you unilaterally from your promise to me.)

If there were cogency to Hart's claim that only against a background of required nonforcing can we understand the point of special rights, then there would seem to be equal cogency to the claim that only against a background of *permitted* forcing can we understand the point of *general*

rights. For according to Hart, a person has a general right to do *A* if and only if for all persons *P* and *Q, Q* may not interfere with *P*'s doing *A* or force him not to do *A,* unless *P* has acted to give *Q* a special right to do this. But not every act can be substituted for "*A*"; people have general rights to do only particular types of action. So, one might argue, if there is to be a point to having general rights, to having rights to do a particular type of act *A,* to other's being under an obligation not to force you not to do *A,* then it must be against a contrasting background, in which there is *no* obligation on people to refrain from forcing you to do, or not to do, things, that is, against a background in which, for actions generally, people do *not* have a general right to do them. If Hart can argue to a presumption against forcing from there being a point to particular rights, then it seems he can equally well argue to the absence of such a presumption from there being a point to general rights.[3]

An argument for an enforceable obligation has two stages: the first leads to the existence of the obligation, and the second, to its enforceability. Having disposed of the second stage (at least insofar as it is supposed generally to follow from the first), let us turn to the supposed obligation to cooperate in the joint decisions of others to limit their activities. The principle of fairness, as we stated it following Hart and Rawls, is objectionable and unacceptable. Suppose some of the people in your neighborhood (there are 364 other adults) have found a public address system and decide to institute a system of public entertainment. They post a list of names, one for each day, yours among them. On his assigned day (one can easily switch days) a person is to run the public address system, play records over it, give news bulletins, tell amusing stories he has heard, and so on. After 138 days on which each person has done his part, your day arrives. Are you obligated to take your turn? You *have* benefited from it, occasionally opening your window to listen, enjoying some music or chuckling at someone's funny story. The other people *have* put themselves out. But must you answer the call when it is your turn to do so? As it stands, surely not. Though you benefit from the arrangement, you may know all along that 364 days of entertainment supplied by others will not be worth your giving up *one* day. You would rather not have any of it and not give up a day than have it all and spend one of your days at it. Given these preferences, how can it be that you are required to participate when your scheduled time comes? It would be nice to have philosophy readings on the radio to which one could tune in at any time, perhaps late at night when tired. But it may not be nice enough for you to want to give up one whole day of your own as a reader on the program. Whatever you want, can others create an obligation for you to do so by going ahead and starting the program themselves? In this case you can choose to forego the benefit by not turning on the radio; in other cases the benefits may be unavoidable. If each day a different person on your street sweeps the entire street, must you do so when your time comes? Even if you don't care that much about a clean street? Must you imagine dirt as you traverse the street, so as not to benefit as a free rider? Must you refrain from turning on the radio to hear the philosophy readings? Must you mow your front lawn as often as your neighbors mow theirs?

At the very least one wants to build into the principle of fairness the condition that the benefits to a person from the actions of the others are greater than the costs to him of doing his share. How are we to imagine this? Is the condition satisfied if you do enjoy the daily broadcasts over the PA system in your neighborhood but would prefer a day off hiking, rather than hearing these broadcasts all year? For you to be obligated to give up your day to broadcast mustn't it be true, at least, that there is nothing you could do with a day (with that day, with the increment in any other day by shifting some activities to that day) which you would prefer to hearing broadcasts for the year? If the only way to get the broadcasts was to spend the day participating in the arrangement, in order for the condition that the benefits outweigh the costs to be satisfied, you would have to be willing to spend it on the broadcasts rather than to gain *any* other available thing.

If the principle of fairness were modified so as to contain this very strong condition, it still would be objectionable. The benefits might only barely be worth the costs to you of doing your share, yet others might benefit from *this* institution much more than you do; they all treasure listening to the public broadcasts. As the person least benefited by the practice, are you obligated to do an equal amount for it? Or perhaps you would prefer that all cooperated in *another* ven-

ture, limiting their conduct and making sacrifices for *it*. It is true, *given* that they are not following your plan (and thus limiting what other options are available to you), that the benefits of their venture *are* worth to you the costs of your cooperation. However, you do not wish to cooperate, as part of your plan to focus their attention on your alternative proposal which they have ignored or not given, in your view at least, its proper due. (You want them, for example, to read the Talmud on the radio instead of the philosophy they are reading.) By lending the institution (their institution) the support of your cooperating in it, you will only make it harder to change or alter.[4]

On the face of it, enforcing the principle of fairness is objectionable. You may not decide to give me something, for example a book, and then grab money from me to pay for it, even if I have nothing better to spend the money on. You have, if anything, even less reason to demand payment if your activity that gives me the book also benefits you; suppose that your best way of getting exercise is by throwing books into people's houses, or that some other activity of yours thrusts books into people's houses as an unavoidable side effect. Nor are things changed if your inability to collect money or payments for the books which unavoidably spill over into others' houses makes it inadvisable or too expensive for you to carry on the activity with this side effect. One cannot, whatever one's purposes, just act so as to give people benefits and then demand (or seize) payment. Nor can a group of persons do this. If you may not charge and collect for benefits you bestow without prior agreement, you certainly may not do so for benefits whose bestowal costs you nothing, and most certainly people need not repay you for costless-to-provide benefits which yet *others* provided them. So the fact that we partially are "social products" in that we benefit from current patterns and forms created by the multitudinous actions of a long string of long-forgotten people, forms which include institutions, ways of doing things, and language (whose social nature may involve our current use depending upon Wittgensteinian matching of the speech of others), does not create in us a general floating debt which the current society can collect and use as it will.

Perhaps a modified principle of fairness can be stated which would be free from these and similar difficulties. What seems certain is that any such principle, if possible, would be so complex and involuted that one could not combine it with a special principle legitimating *enforcement* within a state of nature of the obligations that have arisen under it. Hence, even if the principle could be formulated so that it was no longer open to objection, it would not serve to obviate the need for other persons' *consenting* to cooperate and limit their own activities.

NOTES

1. Herbert Hart, "Are There Any Natural Rights?" *Philosophical Review,* 1955; John Rawls, *A Theory of Justice* (Cambridge, Mass.: Harvard University Press, 1971), sect. 18. My statement of the principle stays close to Rawls.' The argument Rawls offers for this principle constitutes an argument only for the narrower principle of fidelity (bona fide promises are to be kept). Though if there were no way to avoid "can't get started" difficulties about the principle of fidelity (p. 349) other than by appealing to the principle of fairness, it *would* be an argument for the principle of fairness.

2. Hart, "Are There Any Natural Rights?"

3. I have formulated my remarks in terms of the admittedly vague notion of there being a "point" to certain kinds of rights because this, I think, gives Hart's argument its most plausible construction.

4. I have skirted making the institution one that you didn't get a fair say in setting up or deciding its nature, for here Rawls would object that it doesn't satisfy his two principles of justice. Though Rawls does not require that every microinstitution satisfy his two principles of justice, but only the basic structure of the society, he seems to hold that a microinstitution must satisfy these two principles if it is to give rise to obligations under the principle of fairness.

ROBERT NOZICK

Distributive Justice *

The minimal state is the most extensive state that can be justified. Any state more extensive violates people's rights. Yet many persons have put forth reasons purporting to justify a more extensive state. It is impossible within the compass of this book to examine all the reasons that have been put forth. Therefore, I shall focus upon those generally acknowledged to be most weighty and influential, to see precisely wherein they fail. In this chapter we consider the claim that a more extensive state is justified, because necessary (or the best instrument) to achieve distributive justice; in the next chapter we shall take up diverse other claims.

The term "distributive justice" is not a neutral one. Hearing the term "distribution," most people presume that some thing or mechanism uses some principle or criterion to give out a supply of things. Into this process of distributing shares some error may have crept. So it is an open question, at least, whether redistribution should take place; whether we should do again what has already been done once, though poorly. However, we are not in the position of children who have been given portions of pie by someone who now makes last minute adjustments to rectify careless cutting. There is no *central* distribution, no person or group entitled to control all the resources, jointly deciding how they are to be doled out. What each person gets, he gets from others who give to him in exchange for something, or as a gift. In a free society, diverse persons control different resources, and new holdings arise out of the voluntary exchanges and actions of persons. There is no more a distributing or distribution of shares than there is a distributing of mates in a society in which persons choose whom they shall marry. The total result is the product of many individual decisions which the different individuals involved are entitled to make. Some uses of the term "distribution," it is true, do not imply a previous distributing appropriately judged by some criterion (for example, "probability distribution"); nevertheless, despite the title of this chapter, it would be best to use a terminology that clearly is neutral. We shall speak of people's holdings; a principle of justice in holdings describes (part of) what justice tells us (requires) about holdings. I shall state first what I take to be the correct view about justice in holdings, and then turn to the discussion of alternate views.[1]

SECTION I

THE ENTITLEMENT THEORY

The subject of justice in holdings consists of three major topics. The first is the *original acquisition of holdings,* the appropriation of unheld things. This includes the issues of how unheld things may come to be held; the process, or processes, by which unheld things may come to be held, the things that may come to be held by these processes, the extent of what comes to be held by a particular process, and so on. We shall refer to the complicated truth about this topic, which we shall not formulate here, as the principle of justice in acquisition. The second topic concerns the *transfer of holdings* from one person to another. By what processes may a person transfer holdings to another? How may a person acquire a holding from another who holds it? Under this topic come general descriptions of voluntary exchange, and gift and (on the other hand) fraud, as well as reference to particular conventional details fixed upon in a given society. The complicated truth about this subject (with placeholders for conventional details) we shall call the principle of justice in transfer. (And we shall suppose it also includes principles governing how a person may divest himself of a holding, passing it into an unheld state.)

* From pp. 149–163 of *Anarchy, State and Utopia* by Robert Nozick, © 1974 by Basic Books, Inc., Publishers, New York. Reprinted by permission of the author and publishers, Basic Books (New York) and Basil Blackwell & Mott Ltd. (Oxford, England). (Footnotes renumbered.)

If the world were wholly just, the following inductive definition would exhaustively cover the subject of justice in holdings.

1. A person who acquires a holding in accordance with the principle of justice in acquisition is entitled to that holding.
2. A person who acquires a holding in accordance with the principle of justice in transfer, from someone else entitled to the holding, is entitled to the holding.
3. No one is entitled to a holding except by (repeated) applications of 1 and 2.

The complete principle of distributive justice would say simply that a distribution is just if everyone is entitled to the holdings they possess under the distribution.

A distribution is just if it arises from another just distribution by legitimate means. The legitimate means of moving from one distribution to another are specified by the principle of justice in transfer. The legitimate first "moves" are specified by the principle of justice in acquisition.[2] Whatever arises from a just situation by just steps is itself just. The means of change specified by the principle of justice in transfer preserve justice. As correct rules of inference are truth-preserving, and any conclusion deduced via repeated application of such rules from only true premises is itself true, so the means of transition from one situation to another specified by the principle of justice in transfer are justice-preserving, and any situation actually arising from repeated transitions in accordance with the principle from a just situation is itself just. The parallel between justice-preserving transformations and truth-preserving transformations illuminates where it fails as well as where it holds. That a conclusion could have been deduced by truth-preserving means from premises that are true suffices to show its truth. That from a just situation a situation *could* have arisen via justice-preserving means does *not* suffice to show its justice. The fact that a thief's victims voluntarily *could* have presented him with gifts does not entitle the thief to his ill-gotten gains. Justice in holdings is historical; it depends upon what actually has happened. We shall return to this point later.

Not all actual situations are generated in accordance with the two principles of justice in holdings: the principle of justice in acquisition and the principle of justice in transfer. Some people steal from others, or defraud them, or enslave them, seizing their product and preventing them from living as they choose, or forcibly exclude others from competing in exchanges. None of these are permissible modes of transition from one situation to another. And some persons acquire holdings by means not sanctioned by the principle of justice in acquisition. The existence of past injustice (previous violations of the first two principles of justice in holdings) raises the third major topic under justice in holdings: the rectification of injustice in holdings. If past injustice has shaped present holdings in various ways, some identifiable and some not, what now, if anything, ought to be done to rectify these injustices? What obligations do the performers of injustice have toward those whose position is worse than it would have been had the injustice not been done? Or, than it would have been had compensation been paid promptly? How, if at all, do things change if the beneficiaries and those made worse off are not the direct parties in the act of injustice, but, for example, their descendants? Is an injustice done to someone whose holding was itself based upon an unrectified injustice? How far back must one go in wiping clean the historical slate of injustices? What may victims of injustice permissibly do in order to rectify the injustices being done to them, including the many injustices done by persons acting through their government? I do not know of a thorough or theoretically sophisticated treatment of such issues.[3] Idealizing greatly, let us suppose theoretical investigation will produce a principle of rectification. This principle uses historical information about previous situations and injustices done in them (as defined by the first two principles of justice and rights against interference), and information about the actual course of events that flowed from these injustices, until the present, and it yields a description (or descriptions) of holdings in the society. The principle of rectification presumably will make use of its best estimate of subjunctive information about what would have occurred (or a probability distribution over what might have occurred, using the expected value) if the injustice had not taken place. If the actual description of holdings turns out not to be one of the descriptions yielded by the principle, then one of the descriptions yielded must be realized.[4]

The general outlines of the theory of justice in holdings are that the holdings of a person are just if he is entitled to them by the principles of justice in acquisition and transfer, or by the principle of rectification of injustice (as specified by the first two principles). If each person's holdings are just, then the total set (distribution) of holdings is just. To turn these general outlines into a specific theory we would have to specify the details of each of the three principles of justice in holdings: the principle of acquisition of holdings, the principle of transfer of holdings, and the principle of rectification of violations of the first two principles. I shall not attempt that task here. (Locke's principle of justice in acquisition is discussed below.)

HISTORICAL PRINCIPLES AND END-RESULT PRINCIPLES

The general outlines of the entitlement theory illuminate the nature and defects of other conceptions of distributive justice. The entitlement theory of justice in distribution is *historical;* whether a distribution is just depends upon how it came about. In contrast, *current time-slice principles* of justice hold that the justice of a distribution is determined by how things are distributed (who has what) as judged by some *structural* principle(s) of just distribution. A utilitarian who judges between any two distributions by seeing which has the greater sum of utility and, if the sums tie, applies some fixed equality criterion to choose the more equal distribution, would hold a current time-slice principle of justice. As would someone who had a fixed schedule of trade-offs between the sum of happiness and equality. According to a current time-slice principle, all that needs to be looked at, in judging the justice of a distribution, is who ends up with what; in comparing any two distributions one need look only at the matrix presenting the distributions. No further information need be fed into a principle of justice. It is a consequence of such principles of justice that any two structurally identical distributions are equally just. (Two distributions are structurally identical if they present the same profile, but perhaps have different persons occupying the particular slots. My having ten and your having five, and my having five and your having ten are structurally identical distributions.) Welfare economics is the theory of current time-slice principles of justice. The subject is conceived as operating on matrices representing only current information about distribution. This, as well as some of the usual conditions (for example, the choice of distribution is invariant under relabeling of columns), guarantees that welfare economics will be a current time-slice theory, with all of its inadequacies.

Most persons do not accept current time-slice principles as constituting the whole story about distributive shares. They think it relevant in assessing the justice of a situation to consider not only the distribution it embodies, but also how that distribution came about. If some persons are in prison for murder or war crimes, we do not say that to assess the justice of the distribution in the society we must look only at what this person has, and that person has, and that person has, . . . at the current time. We think it relevant to ask whether someone did something so that he *deserved* to be punished, deserved to have a lower share. Most will agree to the relevance of further information with regard to punishments and penalties. Consider also desired things. One traditional socialist view is that workers are entitled to the product and full fruits of their labor; they have earned it; a distribution is unjust if it does not give the workers what they are entitled to. Such entitlements are based upon some past history. No socialist holding this view would find it comforting to be told that because the actual distribution *A* happens to coincide structurally with the one he desires *D, A* therefore is no less just than *D;* it differs only in that the "parasitic" owners of capital receive under *A* what the workers are entitled to under *D,* and the workers receive under *A* what the owners are entitled to under *D,* namely very little. This socialist rightly, in my view, holds onto the notions of earning, producing, entitlement, desert, and so forth, and he rejects current time-slice principles that look only to the structure of the resulting set of holdings. (The set of holdings resulting from what? Isn't it implausible that how holdings are produced and come to exist has no effect at all on who should hold what?) His mistake lies in his view of what entitlements arise out of what sorts of productive processes.

We construe the position we discuss too narrowly by speaking of *current* time-slice principles. Nothing is changed if structural principles operate upon a time sequence of current time-slice profiles and, for example, give someone more now to counterbalance the less he has had earlier. A utilitarian or an egalitarian or any mixture of the two over time will inherit the difficulties of his more myopic comrades. He is not helped by the fact that *some* of the information others consider relevant in assessing a distribution is reflected, unrecoverably, in past matrices. Henceforth, we shall refer to such unhistorical principles of distributive justice, including the current time-slice principles, as *end-result principles* or *end-state principles.*

In contrast to end-result principles of justice, *historical principles* of justice hold that past circumstances or actions of people can create differential entitlements or differential deserts to things. An injustice can be worked by moving from one distribution to another structurally identical one, for the second, in profile the same, may violate people's entitlements or deserts; it may not fit the actual history.

PATTERNING

The entitlement principles of justice in holdings that we have sketched are historical principles of justice. To better understand their precise character, we shall distinguish them from another subclass of the historical principles. Consider, as an example, the principle of distribution according to moral merit. This principle requires that total distributive shares vary directly with moral merit; no person should have a greater share than anyone whose moral merit is greater. (If moral merit could be not merely ordered but measured on an interval or ratio scale, stronger principles could be formulated.) Or consider the principle that results by substituting "usefulness to society" for "moral merit" in the previous principle. Or instead of "distribute according to moral merit," or "distribute according to usefulness to society," we might consider "distribute according to the weighted sum of moral merit, usefulness to society, and need," with the weights of the different dimensions equal. Let us call a principle of distribution *patterned* if it specifies that a distribution is to vary along with some natural dimension, weighted sum of natural dimensions, or lexicographic ordering of natural dimensions. And let us say a distribution is patterned if it accords with some patterned principle. (I speak of natural dimensions, admittedly without a general criterion for them, because for any set of holdings some artificial dimensions can be gimmicked up to vary along with the distribution of

the set.) The principle of distribution in accordance with moral merit is a patterned historical principle, which specifies a patterned distribution. "Distribute according to I.Q." is a patterned principle that looks to information not contained in distributional matrices. It is not historical, however, in that it does not look to any past actions creating differential entitlements to evaluate a distribution; it requires only distributional matrices whose columns are labeled by I.Q. scores. The distribution in a society, however, may be composed of such simple patterned distributions, without itself being simply patterned. Different sectors may operate different patterns, or some combination of patterns may operate in different proportions across a society. A distribution composed in this manner, from a small number of patterned distributions, we also shall term "patterned." And we extend the use of "pattern" to include the overall designs put forth by combinations of end-state principles.

Almost every suggested principle of distributive justice is patterned: to each according to his moral merit, or needs, or marginal product, or how hard he tries, or the weighted sum of the foregoing, and so on. The principle of entitlement we have sketched is *not* patterned.[5] There is no one natural dimension or weighted sum or combination of a small number of natural dimensions that yields the distributions generated in accordance with the principle of entitlement. The set of holdings that results when some persons receive their marginal products, others win at gambling, others receive a share of their mate's income, others receive gifts from foundations, others receive interest on loans, others receive gifts from admirers, others receive returns on investment, others make for themselves much of what they have, others find things, and so on, will not be patterned. Heavy strands of patterns will run through it; significant portions of the variance in holdings will be accounted for by pattern-variables. If most people most of the time choose to transfer some of their entitlements to others only in exchange for something from them, then a large part of what many people hold will vary with what they held that others wanted. More details are provided by the theory of marginal productivity. But gifts to relatives, charitable donations, bequests to children, and the like, are not best conceived, in the first instance, in this manner. Ignoring the strands of pattern, let us suppose for the moment that a distribution actually arrived at by the operation of the principle of entitlement is random with respect to any pattern. Though the resulting set of holdings will be unpatterned, it will not be incomprehensible, for it can be seen as arising from the operation of a small number of principles. These principles specify how an initial distribution may arise (the principle of acquisition of holdings) and how distributions may be transformed into others (the principle of transfer of holdings). The process whereby the set of holdings is generated will be intelligible, though the set of holdings itself that results from this process will be unpatterned.

The writings of F. A. Hayek focus less than is usually done upon what patterning distributive justice requires. Hayek argues that we cannot know enough about each person's situation to distribute to each according to his moral merit (but would justice demand we do so if we did have this knowledge?); and he goes on to say, "our objection is against all attempts to impress upon society a deliberately chosen pattern of distribution, whether it be an order of equality or of inequality." [6] However, Hayek concludes that in a free society there will be distribution in accordance with value rather than moral merit; that is, in accordance with the perceived value of a person's actions and services to others. Despite his rejection of a patterned conception of distributive justice, Hayek himself suggests a pattern he thinks justifiable: distribution in accordance with the perceived benefits given to others, leaving room for the complaint that a free society does not realize exactly this pattern. Stating this patterned strand of a free capitalist society more precisely, we get "To each according to how much he benefits others who have the resources for benefiting those who benefit them." This will seem arbitrary unless some acceptable initial set of holdings is specified, or unless it is held that the operation of the system over time washes out any significant effects from the initial set of holdings. As an example of the latter, if almost anyone would have bought a car from Henry Ford, the supposition that it was an arbitrary matter who held the money then (and so bought) would not place Henry Ford's earnings under a cloud. In any event, *his* coming to hold it is not arbitrary. Distribution according to benefits to others *is* a major patterned strand in a free capitalist society,

as Hayek correctly points out, but it is only a strand and does not constitute the whole pattern of a system of entitlements (namely, inheritance, gifts for arbitrary reasons, charity, and so on) or a standard that one should insist a society fit. Will people tolerate for long a system yielding distributions that they believe are unpatterned? [7] No doubt people will not long accept a distribution they believe is *unjust*. People want their society to be and to look just. But must the look of justice reside in a resulting pattern rather than in the underlying generating principles? We are in no position to conclude that the inhabitants of a society embodying an entitlement conception of justice in holdings will find it unacceptable. Still, it must be granted that were people's reasons for transferring some of their holdings to others always irrational or arbitrary, we would find this disturbing. (Suppose people always determined what holdings they would transfer, and to whom, by using a random device.) We feel more comfortable upholding the justice of an entitlement system if most of the transfers under it are done for reasons. This does not mean necessarily that all deserve what holdings they receive. It means only that there is a purpose or point to someone's transferring a holding to one person rather than to another; that usually we can see what the transferrer thinks he's gaining, what cause he thinks he's serving, what goals he thinks he's helping to achieve, and so forth. Since in a capitalist society people often transfer holdings to others in accordance with how much they perceive these others benefiting them, the fabric constituted by the individual transactions and transfers is largely reasonable and intelligible. [8] (Gifts to loved ones, bequests to children, charity to the needy also are nonarbitrary components of the fabric.) In stressing the large strand of distribution in accordance with benefit to others, Hayek shows the point of many transfers, and so shows that the system of transfer of entitlements is not just spinning its gears aimlessly. The system of entitlements is defensible when constituted by the individual aims of individual transactions. No overarching aim is needed, no distributional pattern is required.

To think that the task of a theory of distributive justice is to fill in the blank in "to each according to his ____" is to be predisposed to search for a pattern; and the separate treatment of "from each according to his ____" treats production and distribution as two separate and independent issues. On an entitlement view these are *not* two separate questions. Whoever makes something, having bought or contracted for all other held resources used in the process (transferring some of his holdings for these cooperating factors), is entitled to it. The situation is *not* one of something's getting made, and there being an open question of who is to get it. Things come into the world already attached to people having entitlements over them. From the point of view of the historical entitlement conception of justice in holdings, those who start afresh to complete "to each according to his ____" treat objects as if they appeared from nowhere, out of nothing. A complete theory of justice might cover this limit case as well; perhaps here is a use for the usual conceptions of distributive justice.[9]

So entrenched are maxims of the usual form that perhaps we should present the entitlement conception as a competitor. Ignoring acquisition and rectification, we might say:

From each according to what he chooses to do, to each according to what he makes for himself (perhaps with the contracted aid of others) and what others choose to do for him and choose to give him of what they've been given previously (under this maxim) and haven't yet expended or transferred.

This, the discerning reader will have noticed, has its defects as a slogan. So as a summary and great simplification (and not as a maxim with any independent meaning) we have:

From each as they choose, to each as they are chosen.

HOW LIBERTY UPSETS PATTERNS

It is not clear how those holding alternative conceptions of distributive justice can reject the entitlement conception of justice in holdings. For suppose a distribution favored by one of these nonentitlement conceptions is realized. Let us suppose it is your favorite one and let us call this distribution D_1; perhaps everyone has an equal share, perhaps shares vary in accordance with some dimension you treasure. Now suppose that Wilt Chamberlain is greatly in demand by basketball teams, being a great gate attraction. (Also suppose contracts run only for a year, with players being free agents.) He signs the following sort of contract with a team: In each home game,

twenty-five cents from the price of each ticket of admission goes to him. (We ignore the question of whether he is "gouging" the owners, letting them look out for themselves.) The season starts, and people cheerfully attend his team's games; they buy their tickets, each time dropping a separate twenty-five cents of their admission price into a special box with Chamberlain's name on it. They are excited about seeing him play; it is worth the total admission price to them. Let us suppose that in one season one million persons attend his home games, and Wilt Chamberlain winds up with $250,000, a much larger sum than the average income and larger even than anyone else has. Is he entitled to this income? Is this new distribution D_2, unjust? If so, why? There is *no* question about whether each of the people was entitled to the control over the resources they held in D_1; because that was the distribution (your favorite) that (for the purposes of argument) we assumed was acceptable. Each of these persons *chose* to give twenty-five cents of their money to Chamberlain. They could have spent it on going to the movies, or on candy bars, or on copies of *Dissent* magazine, or of *Monthly Review*. But they all, at least one million of them, converged on giving it to Wilt Chamberlain in exchange for watching him play basketball. If D_1 was a just distribution, and people voluntarily moved from it to D_2, transferring parts of their shares they were given under D_1 (what was it for if not to do something with?), isn't D_2 also just? If the people were entitled to dispose of the resources to which they were entitled (under D_1), didn't this include their being entitled to give it to, or exchange it with, Wilt Chamberlain? Can anyone else complain on grounds of justice? Each other person already has his legitimate share under D_1. Under D_1, there is nothing that anyone has that anyone else has a claim of justice against. After someone transfers something to Wilt Chamberlain, third parties *still* have their legitimate shares; *their* shares are not changed. By what process could such a transfer among two persons give rise to a legitimate claim of distributive justice on a portion of what was transferred, by a third party who had no claim of justice on any holding of the others *before* the transfer? [10] To cut off objections irrelevant here, we might imagine the exchanges occurring in a socialist society, after hours. After playing whatever basketball he does in his daily work, or doing whatever other daily work he does, Wilt Chamberlain decides to put in *overtime* to earn additional money. (First his work quota is set; he works time over that.) Or imagine it is a skilled juggler people like to see, who puts on shows after hours.

Why might someone work overtime in a society in which it is assumed their needs are satisfied? Perhaps because they care about things other than needs. I like to write in books that I read, and to have easy access to books for browsing at odd hours. It would be very pleasant and convenient to have the resources of Widener Library in my back yard. No society, I assume, will provide such resources close to each person who would like them as part of his regular allotment (under D_1). Thus, persons either must do without some extra things that they want, or be allowed to do something extra to get some of these things. On what basis could the inequalities that would eventuate be forbidden? Notice also that small factories would spring up in a socialist society, unless forbidden. I melt down some of my personal possessions (under D_1) and build a machine out of the material. I offer you, and others, a philosophy lecture once a week in exchange for your cranking the handle on my machine, whose products I exchange for yet other things, and so on. (The raw materials used by the machine are given to me by others who possess them under D_1, in exchange for hearing lectures.) Each person might participate to gain things over and above their allotment under D_1. Some persons even might want to leave their job in socialist industry and work full time in this private sector. I shall say something more about these issues in the next chapter. Here I wish merely to note how private property even in means of production would occur in a socialist society that did not forbid people to use as they wished some of the resources they are given under the socialist distribution D_1.[11] The socialist society would have to forbid capitalist acts between consenting adults.

The general point illustrated by the Wilt Chamberlain example and the example of the entrepreneur in a socialist society is that no end-state principle or distributional patterned principle of justice can be continuously realized without continuous interference with people's lives. Any favored pattern would be transformed into one unfavored by the principle, by people choosing to act in various ways; for example, by people exchanging goods and services with other people, or giving things to other people, things the transferrers are entitled to under the favored distributional pattern. To maintain a pattern one must either continually interfere to stop people from transferring resources as they wish to, or continually (or periodically) interfere to take from some persons resources that others for some reason chose to transfer to them. (But if some time limit is to be set on how long people may keep resources others voluntarily transfer to them, why let them keep these resources for *any* period of time? Why not have immediate confiscation?) It might be objected that all persons voluntarily will choose to refrain from actions which would upset the pattern. This presupposes unrealistically (1) that all will most want to maintain the pattern (are those who don't, to be "reeducated" or forced to undergo "self-criticism"?), (2) that each can gather enough information about his own actions and the ongoing activities of others to discover which of his actions will upset the pattern, and (3) that diverse and far-flung persons can coordinate their actions to dovetail into the pattern. Compare the manner in which the market is neutral among persons' desires, as it reflects and transmits widely scattered information via prices, and coordinates persons' activities.

It puts things perhaps a bit too strongly to say that every patterned (or end-state) principle is liable to be thwarted by the voluntary actions of the individual parties transferring some of their shares they receive under the principle. For perhaps some *very* weak patterns are not so thwarted.[12] Any distributional pattern with any egalitarian component is overturnable by the voluntary actions of individual persons over time; as is every patterned condition with sufficient content so as actually to have been proposed as presenting the central core of distributive justice. Still, given the possibility that some weak conditions or patterns may not be unstable in this way, it would be better to formulate an explicit description of the kind of interesting and contentful patterns under discussion, and to prove a theorem about their instability. Since the weaker the patterning, the more likely it is that the entitlement system itself satisfies it, a plausible conjecture is that any patterning either is unstable or is satisfied by the entitlement system.

NOTES

1. The reader who has looked ahead and seen that the second part of this chapter discusses Rawls' theory mistakenly may think that every remark or argument in the first part against alternative theories of justice is meant to apply to, or anticipate, a criticism of Rawls' theory. This is not so; there are other theories also worth criticizing.

2. Applications of the principle of justice in acquisition may also occur as part of the move from one distribution to another. You may find an unheld thing now and appropriate it. Acquisitions also are to be understood as included when, to simplify, I speak only of transitions by transfers.

3. See, however, the useful book by Boris Bittker, *The Case for Black Reparations* (New York: Random House, 1973).

4. If the principle of rectification of violations of the first two principles yields more than one description of holdings, then some choice must be made as to which of these is to be realized. Perhaps the sort of considerations about distributive justice and equality that I argue against play a legitimate role in *this* subsidiary choice. Similarly, there may be room for such considerations in deciding which otherwise arbitrary features a statute will embody, when such features are unavoidable because other considerations do not specify a precise line; yet a line must be drawn.

5. One might try to squeeze a patterned conception of distributive justice into the framework of the entitlement conception, by formulating a gimmicky obligatory "principle of transfer" that would lead to the pattern. For example, the principle that if one has more than the mean income one must transfer everything one holds above the mean to persons below the mean so as to bring them up to (but not over) the mean. We can formulate a criterion for a "principle of transfer" to rule out such obligatory transfers, or we can say that no correct principle of transfer, no principle of transfer in a free society will be like this. The former is probably the better course, though the latter also is true.

Alternatively, one might think to make the entitlement conception instantiate a pattern, by using matrix entries that express the relative strength of a person's entitlements as measured by some real-valued function. But even if the limitation to natural dimensions failed to exclude this function, the resulting edifice would *not* capture our system of entitlements to *particular* things.

6. F. A. Hayek, *The Constitution of Liberty* (Chicago: University of Chicago Press, 1960), p. 87.

7. This question does not imply that they will tolerate any and every patterned distribution. In discussing Hayek's views, Irving Kristol has recently speculated that people will not long tolerate a system that yields distributions patterned in accordance with value rather than merit. (" 'When Virtue Loses All Her Loveliness'—Some Reflections on Capitalism and 'The Free Society,' " *The Public Interest*, Fall 1970, pp. 3–15.) Kristol, following some remarks of Hayek's, equates the merit system with justice. Since some case can be made for the external standard of distribution in accordance with benefit to others, we ask about a weaker (and therefore more plausible) hypothesis.

8. We certainly benefit because great economic incentives operate to get others to spend much time and energy to figure out how to serve us by providing things we will want to pay for. It is not mere paradox mongering to wonder whether capitalism should be criticized for most rewarding and hence encouraging, not individualists like Thoreau who go about their own lives, but people who are occupied with serving others and winning them as customers. But to defend capitalism one need not think businessmen are the finest human types. (I do not mean to join here the general maligning of

businessmen, either.) Those who think the finest should acquire the most can try to convince their fellows to transfer resources in accordance with *that* principle.

9. Varying situations continuously from that limit situation to our own would force us to make explicit the underlying rationale of entitlements and to consider whether entitlement considerations lexicographically precede the considerations of the usual theories of distributive justice, so that the *slightest* strand of entitlement outweighs the considerations of the usual theories of distributive justice.

10. Might not a transfer have instrumental effects on a third party, changing his feasible options? (But what if the two parties to the transfer independently had used their holdings in this fashion?) I discuss this question below, but note here that this question concedes the point for distributions of ultimate intrinsic noninstrumental goods (pure utility experiences, so to speak) that are transferable. It also might be objected that the transfer might make a third party more envious because it worsens his position relative to someone else. I find it incomprehensible how this can be thought to involve a claim of justice. On envy, see Chapter 8.

Here and elsewhere in this chapter, a theory which incorporates elements of pure procedural justice might find what I say acceptable, *if* kept in its proper place; that is, if background institutions exist to ensure the satisfaction of certain conditions on distributive shares. But if these institutions are not themselves the sum or invisible-hand result of people's voluntary (nonaggressive) actions, the constraints they impose require justification. At no point does *our* argument assume any background institutions more extensive than those of the minimal night-watchman state, a state limited to protecting persons against murder, assault, theft, fraud, and so forth.

11. See the selection from John Henry MacKay's novel, *The Anarchists*, reprinted in Leonard Krimmerman and Lewis Perry, eds., *Patterns of Anarchy* (New York: Doubleday Anchor Books, 1966), in which an individualist anarchist presses upon a communist anarchist the following question: "Would you, in the system of society which you call 'free Communism' prevent individuals from exchanging their labor among themselves by means of their own medium of exchange? And further: Would you prevent them from occupying land for the purpose of personal use?" The novel continues: "[the] question was not to be escaped. If he answered 'Yes!' he admitted that society had the right of control over the individual and threw overboard the autonomy of the individual which he had always zealously defended; if on the other hand, he answered 'No!' he admitted the right of private property which he had just denied so emphatically. . . . Then he answered 'In Anarchy any number of men must have the right of forming a voluntary association, and so realizing their ideas in practice. Nor can I understand how any one could justly be driven from the land and house which he uses and occupies . . . every serious man must declare himself: for Socialism, and thereby for force and against liberty, or for Anarchism, and thereby for liberty and against force.' " In contrast, we find Noam Chomsky writing, "Any consistent anarchist must oppose private ownership of the means of production," "the consistent anarchist then . . . will be a socialist . . . of a particular sort." Introduction to Daniel Guerin, *Anarchism: From Theory to Practice* (New York: Monthly Review Press, 1970), pages xiii, xv.

12. Is the patterned principle stable that requires merely that a distribution be Pareto-optimal? One person might give another a gift or bequest that the second could exchange with a third to their mutual benefit. Before the second makes this exchange, there is not Pareto-optimality. Is a stable pattern presented by a principle choosing that among the Pareto-optimal positions that satisfies some further condition C? It

may seem that there cannot be a counterexample, for won't any voluntary exchange made away from a situation show that the first situation wasn't Pareto-optimal? (Ignore the implausibility of this last claim for the case of bequests.) But principles are to be satisfied over time, during which new possibilities arise. A distribution that at one time satisfies the criterion of Pareto-optimality might not do so when some new possibilities arise (Wilt Chamberlain grows up and starts play-ing basketball); and though people's activities will tend to move then to a new Pareto-optimal position, *this* new one need not satisfy the contentful condition *C*. Continual inter-ference will be needed to insure the continual satisfaction of *C*. (The theoretical possibility of a pattern's being maintained by some invisible-hand process that brings it back to an equi-librium that fits the pattern when deviations occur should be investigated.)

T . M . S C A N L O N

Distributive Justice and the Difference Principle *

Rawls is concerned with justice in only one of the many senses of the term. For him, questions of justice are questions of how the benefits and burdens of social cooperation are to be shared, and the principles of justice he develops are to apply in the first instance not to arbitrary distri-butions of goods but to the basic institutions of society which determine "the assignment of rights and duties and . . . regulate the distribu-tion of social and economic advantages." [1] Rawls' principles apply to particular distribu-tions only indirectly: a distribution may be called just if it is the result of just institutions working properly, but the principles provide no standard for appraising the justice of distributions in-dependent of the institutions effecting them. [2] Conceived of in this way, principles of justice are analogous to a specification of what constitutes a fair gamble. If a gamble is fair then its outcome, whatever it may be, is fair and cannot be com-plained of. But the notion of a fair gamble pro-vides no standard for judging particular distribu-tions (Smith and Harris win five dollars, Jones loses ten dollars) as fair or unfair when these are considered in isolation from particular gambles which bring them about.

The principle which Rawls offers for apprais-ing the distributive aspects of the basic structure of a society is his Second Principle of Justice which, considerations of the priority of liberty aside, is equivalent to what he calls the General Conception of Justice as Fairness. This principle is stated as follows: "Social and economic inequalities are to be arranged so that they are both (a) to the greatest benefit of the least advan-taged and (b) attached to offices and positions open to all under conditions of fair equality of opportunity." [3]

According to clause (a) of this principle, which Rawls refers to as the Difference Principle, a sys-tem of social and economic inequalities is just only if there is no feasible alternative institution under which the expectations of the worst-off group would be greater. The phrase "fair equality of opportunity" in clause (b) requires not only that no one be formally excluded from positions to which special benefits attach, but also that per-sons with similar talents and inclinations should have similar prospects of attaining these benefits "regardless of their initial place in the social sys-tem, that is, irrespective of the income class into which they are born." [4] The rationale behind this principle, particularly the motivation for clause (a), will be discussed at length below. First, how-ever, I will consider briefly how the principle is to be applied.

* From "Rawls' Theory of Justice," 121 *University of Penn-sylvania Law Review* (1973), pp. 1056–1069. Reprinted by permission of the author and publisher. (Footnotes renum-bered.)

A. THE DIFFERENCE PRINCIPLE AND ITS APPLICATION

The most natural examples of inequalities to which Rawls' principle might be applied involve the creation of new jobs or offices to which special economic rewards are attached or an increase in the income associated with an existing job. But the intended application of the principle is much broader than this. It is to apply not only to inequalities in wealth and income but to all inequalities in primary social goods, *e.g.* to the creation of positions of special political authority. Further, its application is not limited to "jobs" or "offices" in the narrow sense but includes all the most general features of the basic structure of a society that give rise to unequal shares of primary social goods. In the case of economic goods these will include the system of money and credit, the laws of contract, the system of property rights and the laws governing the exchange and inheritance of property, the system of taxation, the institutions for the provision of public goods, etc.

It is fairly clear how Rawls' principle is to apply to the creation of one new office to which special rewards are attached (or to the assignment of new rewards to one existing position) in an otherwise egalitarian society: such as inequality is just only if those who do not directly benefit from this inequality by occupying the office benefit indirectly with the result that they too are better off than they were before (and than they would be if the benefits in question were distributed in any alternative way). It is less obvious how the principle is to apply in the more general case of complex institutions with many separable inequality-generating features. Rawls deals with this problem by specifying that institutions are to be appraised as a whole from the perspective of representative members of each relevant social position. The Difference Principle requires that the total system of inequalities be so arranged as to maximize the expectations of a representative member of the class which the system leaves worst off.

The notions of relevant social position and the expectations of a representative person in such a position require explanation. Relevant social positions in Rawls' sense are those places in the basic structure of society which correspond to the main divisions in the distribution of primary social goods. (He mentions the role of "unskilled worker" as constituting such a position.[5]) Rawls believes that the distribution of other primary social goods will be closely enough correlated with income and wealth that the latter can be taken as an index for identifying the least advantaged group. Accordingly, he suggests that the class of least advantaged persons may be taken to include everyone whose income is no greater than the average income of persons in the lowest relevant social position (or alternatively everyone with less than half the median income and wealth in the society [6]). To compute the expectations of a representative member of a given social position one takes the average of the shares of primary social goods enjoyed by persons in that position. Thus, while the parties in the Original Position do not estimate the value to them of becoming a member of a given society by taking the likelihood of their being a member of a particular social position to be represented by the proportion of the total population that is in that position, they do estimate the expected value (in primary social goods) of being a member of a particular social position by taking the likelihood that they will have any particular feature affecting the distribution of primary social goods within that position to be represented by the fraction of persons in the position who have that feature. Rawls does not explicitly discuss his reasons for allowing averaging within a social position when he has rejected it in the more general case. A more extreme position eschewing averaging would require maximizing the expectations of the worst-off individual in society. The Difference Principle occupies a position somewhere between this extreme and the principle of maximizing the average share of primary social goods across the society as a whole, its exact position within this range depending on how broadly or narrowly the relevant social positions are defined. The resort to averaging seems to some extent to be dictated by practical considerations: a coherent and manageable theory cannot take into account literally every position in a society.[7] In addition, the theoretical case against the use of averaging (as opposed to some more conservative method of choice) is weaker when we are concerned with differences in expectation within a single social position rather than differences between such positions. For here we are not concerned with a single "gamble" with incomparably high stakes: intraposition differences are, by definition, limited, and each person's allotment is determined by a large number of independent factors, many of which are of approximately equal magnitude.[8]

There is a further problem about the notion of expectations which requires consideration. Rawls refers to the relevant social positions as "starting places," *i.e.* as the places in society people are born into.[9] Now the expectations of a person born into a family in a certain social position can be thought of as consisting of two components. First, there is the level of well-being he can expect to enjoy as a child. Presumably we may identify this with his parents' allotment of primary social goods. Second, there are his long term prospects as a member of society in his own right. If perfect fair equality of opportunity were attained then this latter component would not be substantially affected by the social and economic position of one's parents. As Rawls notes, however, such perfect equality of opportunity is unlikely, at least as long as the family is maintained,[10] so we may suppose that in general the second component will be heavily influenced by the first. One might conclude that the second component can be neglected entirely, reasoning that the distribution of social and economic advantages will influence the long term life prospects of a representative person born into the worst-off class mainly through its effect on the conditions in which such a person grows up. Taking this course would have the same consequences as deciding that what should be considered in applying the Difference Principle are not the expectations of a representative person born into the worst-off social position but the expectations of a representative person who winds up in that position after the social mechanism for assigning people to social roles has run its course.

But the principle which results from ignoring long term expectations seems to me unsatisfactory. Suppose we have a society in which there are 100 people in the lowest social position and twenty-five people in each of the two higher positions, and suppose it becomes known that the basic institutions of the society could be altered so that in later generations there would be fifty people in each of the three social positions, with

the levels of wealth, income, authority, etc. associated with these positions remaining the same as they are now. Now it seems to me that a person in the lowest social position in this society is apt to be strongly in favor of this change. And such a person could plausibly support this preference by saying that the expectations of a representative person born into his social position (in particular, the expectations of his children) would be better if this change were made than if it were not. This increase in expectations will not be captured by the interpretation of the Difference Principle just suggested or by any principle which focuses only on the levels of income, wealth, etc. associated with various positions in society while ignoring the way in which the population is distributed among these positions. Examples of this kind convince me that considerations of population distribution have to be incorporated in some way into Rawls' theory, and the most natural way to do this seems to me to be to bring them in through the notion of long term expectations.

But how is this to be done? The rule mentioned above that the expectations of a representative person in a given social position are to be determined by averaging the benefits enjoyed by persons in that position suggests that in a society with three relevant social positions whose average levels of income, wealth, authority, etc. can be indexed by p_1, p_2 and p_3, the long term prospects of a person born into the worst-off position should be represented by $a_1p_1 + a_2p_2 + a_3p_3$, where a_1, a_2 and a_3 are the fractions of people born into the worst-off position who wind up in each of the three places.

But the adoption of averaging as the method for computing long term expectations has unpleasant consequences for Rawls' theory. To the extent that the inequalities in childhood expectations resulting from the unequal economic and social positions of different families are eliminated (perhaps by eliminating the institution of the family itself), the first component in the expectations of a representative person will become the same for everyone regardless of the social position into which he is born, and Rawls' requirement that the expectations of a representative person in the lowest social position be maximized becomes the requirement that we maximize the second component of these expectations, *i.e.* the long term expectation $a_1p_2 +$

$a_2p_2 + a_3p_3$. Moreover, to the extent that fair equality of opportunity is achieved (and barring the formation of a genetic elite) the coefficients a_1, a_2 and a_3 in this polynomial will become the same for every representative person regardless of social class, and the polynomial will thus come to express the average share of primary goods enjoyed by members of the society in question. It follows that on the interpretation just suggested Rawls' Difference Principle will be distinct from the principle requiring us to maximize the average share of primary social goods only so long as the inequalities resulting from the institution of the family persist or the fair equality of opportunity required by clause (b) of the Second Principle is otherwise not achieved. Even if fair equality of opportunity is an unattainable ideal this conclusion seems to me unacceptable for Rawls' theory. As was pointed out above,[11] the principle of maximum average primary social goods is an extremely implausible one, much less plausible than the principle of maximum average utility. I see no reason to think that this principle would be acceptable even if perfect equality of opportunity were to obtain.

The problem here is how to give some weight to the way in which the population is distributed across social positions without introducing aggregative considerations in such a way that they take over the theory altogether (or would do so but for the "friction" introduced by imperfect equality of opportunity). One way of dealing with this problem which seems to me in the spirit of Rawls' theory would be to modify the Difference Principle to require the following:

First maximize the income, wealth, etc. of the worst-off representative person, then seek to minimize the number of people in his position (by moving them upwards); then proceed to do the same for the next worst-off social position, then the next and so on, finally seeking to maximize the benefits of those in the best-off position (as long as this does not affect the others).[12]

This seems to me a natural elaboration of what Rawls calls the Lexical Difference Principle.[13] It also has the advantage of dealing with the problem of population distribution without introducing the summing or averaging of benefits across relevant social positions. There are obviously many variations on this theme as well as many altogether different approaches.[14]

B. THE ARGUMENT FOR THE DIFFERENCE PRINCIPLE

I return now to the central question of the rationale behind the Difference Principle. The intuitive idea here is that a system of inequalities is just only if we can say to each person in the society, "Eliminating the advantages of those who have more than you would not enable us to improve the lot of any or all of the people in your position (or beneath it). Thus it is unavoidable that a certain number of people will have expectations no greater than yours, and no unfairness is involved in your being one of these people." The requirement that we be able to say this to *every* member of society, and not just to those in the worst-off group, corresponds to what Rawls calls the Lexical Difference Principle:

[I]n a basic structure with n relevant representatives, first maximize the welfare of the worst-off representative man; second, for equal welfare of the worst-off representative, maximize the welfare of the second worst-off representative man, and so on until the last case which is, for equal welfare of all the preceding n-1 representatives, maximize the welfare of the best-off representative man.[15]

This form of the principle is called "lexical" since "lexical priority" is given to the expectations of the worse-off: the fate of the second worst-off group is considered only to decide between arrangements which do equally well for the worst-off, and so on for the higher groups, working always from the bottom up. This asymmetry of concern in favor of the worse-off is a central feature of the theory. Rawls remarks a number of times in contrasting his theory with utilitarianism that under the Difference Principle no one is "expected . . . to accept lower prospects of life for the sake of others." [16] But what this means, as Rawls himself notes,[17] is that no one is expected to take *less than others receive* in order that the others may have a greater share. It seems likely, however, that those who are endowed with talents which are much in demand will receive less in a society governed by Rawls' Difference Principle than they would if allowed to press for all they could get on a free market. Thus, in a Rawlsian society these people will be asked to accept less than they might otherwise have had, and there is a clear sense in which they will be asked to accept these smaller shares "for the sake of others." What, then, can be said to these people?

Rawls' stated answer to this question consists in pointing out that the well-being of the better endowed, no less than that of the other members of society, depends on the existence of social cooperation, and that they can "ask for the willing cooperation of everyone only if the terms of the scheme are reasonable." [18] The Difference Principle, Rawls holds, represents the most favorable basis of cooperation the well-endowed could expect others to accept. Taken by itself this does not seem an adequate response to the complaint of the better endowed, for the question at issue is just what terms of cooperation are "reasonable."

The particular notion of "reasonable terms" that Rawls is appealing to here is one that is founded in the conception of social cooperation which he is propounding. The basis of this conception lies not in a particular bias in favor of the less advantaged but in the idea that economic institutions are reciprocal arrangements for mutual advantage in which the parties cooperate on a footing of equality. Their cooperative enterprise may be more or less efficient depending on the talents of the members and how fully these are developed, but since the value of these talents is something that is realized only in cooperation the benefits derived from these talents are seen as a common product on which all have an equal claim. Thus Rawls says of his Two Principles that they "are equivalent . . . to an undertaking to regard the distribution of natural abilities as a collective asset so that the more fortunate are to benefit only in ways that help those who have lost out." [19]

This same notion of the equality of the parties in a cooperative scheme is invoked in the following intuitive argument for the Difference Principle.

Now looking at the situation from the standpoint of one person selected arbitrarily, there is no way for him to win special advantages for himself. Nor, on the other hand, are there grounds for his acquiescing in special disadvantages. Since it is not reasonable for him to expect more than an equal share in the division of social goods, and since it is not rational for him to agree to less, the sensible thing for him to do is to acknowledge as the first principle of justice one requiring an equal distribution. Indeed, this principle is so obvious that we would expect it to occur to anyone immediately.

Thus, the parties start with a principle establishing equal liberty for all, including equality of opportunity, as well as an equal distribution of income and wealth. But there is no reason why this acknowledgment should be final. If there are inequalities in the basic structure that work to make everyone better off in comparison with the benchmark of initial equality, why not permit them? [20]

If one accepts equality as the natural first solution to the problem of justice then this argument strongly supports the conclusion that the Difference Principle marks the limit of acceptable inequality. More surprisingly, it also appears to show (whether or not one accepts equality as a first solution) that the Difference Principle is the most egalitarian principle it would be rational to adopt from the perspective of the Original Position. It is of course a difficult empirical question how much inequality in income and wealth the Difference Principle will in fact allow, i.e. how many economic inequalities will be efficient enough to "pay their own way" as the principle requires. The only theoretical limitation on such inequalities provided by Rawls' theory appears to be the possibility that glaring inequalities in material circumstances may give rise to (justified) feelings of loss of self-respect [21] on the part of those less advantaged, off-setting the material gains these inequalities bring them. One can thus make the Difference Principle more (or less) egalitarian by positing greater (or lesser) justified sensitivity to perceived inequality. But as far as I am able to determine there is no plausible candidate for adoption in Rawls' Original Position that is distinct from the Difference Principle and intermediate between it and strict equality. Since the inequalities allowed by the Difference Principle, while not great, may nonetheless be significant, this strikes me as a surprising fact. What it shows, perhaps, is that if one wishes to defend a position more egalitarian than Rawls' then one must abandon the perspective which takes the dominant moral problem of social cooperation to be that of justifying distributive institutions to mutually disinterested persons each of whose fundamental interest is in receiving the greatest possible share of the distributed goods.[22]

The ideal of social cooperation which Rawls presents is naturally contrasted with two alternative conceptions of justice. The first of these is what Rawls calls the system of natural liberty.[23]

This conception presupposes background institutions which guarantee equal liberties of citizenship in the sense of the First Principle and preserve formal equality of opportunity, *i.e.* "that all have at least the same legal rights of access to all advantaged social positions."[24] But no effort is made to compensate for the advantages of birth, *i.e.* of inherited wealth. Against the background provided by these institutions individuals compete in a free market and are free to press upon one another whatever competitive advantages derive from their different abilities and circumstances.

The second alternative is that of utilitarianism, understood broadly to include the two modified views presented at the end of the last section. The last of those views differed from the versions of utilitarianism criticized by Rawls in that it incorporated Rawls' principle that no one may be asked to accept a less than equal share in order that some others may enjoy correspondingly greater benefits. But even though it is not simply a maximizing conception, this view is like other forms of utilitarianism in holding it to be the duty of each person to make the greatest possible contribution to the welfare of mankind. Any asset one may have control over, whether a personal talent or a transferable good, one is bound to disburse in such a way as to make the greatest contribution to human well-being.[25] Utilitarianism is in this sense an asocial view; the relation taken as fundamental by the theory is that which holds between any two people when one has the capacity to aid the other. Relations between persons deriving from their position in common institutions, *e.g.* institutions of production and exchange, are in themselves irrelevant. It would be possible to maintain a view of this kind which focused only on the well-being of members of a particular society, but such a restriction would appear arbitrary. The natural tendency of utilitarian theories is to be global in their application.

Rawls' Difference Principle can be seen as occupying a position intermediate between these two extremes. Like the system of natural liberty and unlike utilitarianism, Rawls' conception of justice applies only to persons who are related to one another under common institutions. The problem of justice arises, according to Rawls, for people who are engaged in a cooperative enterprise for mutual benefit, and it is the problem of how *the benefits of their cooperation* are to be shared. What the parties in a cooperative scheme owe one another as a matter of justice is an equitable share of this social product, and neither the maximum attainable level of satisfaction nor the goods and services necessary, given their needs and disabilities, to bring them up to a certain level of well-being.

The qualification "as a matter of justice" is essential here since justice, central though it is, is not the only moral notion for Rawls, and other moral notions take account of need and satisfaction in a way that justice does not. Rawls speaks, for example, of the duty of mutual aid, "the duty of helping another when he is in need or jeopardy, provided that one can do so without excessive risk or loss to oneself."[26] Now it seems likely that those to whom we are bound by ties of justice will fare better at our hands (or at least have a stronger claim on us) than those to whom we owe only duties of mutual aid; for justice, which requires that our institutions be arranged so as to maximize the expectations of the worst-off group in our society, says nothing about others elsewhere with whom we stand in no institutional relation but who may be worse off than anyone in our society. If this is so, then it may make a great deal of difference on Rawls' theory where the boundary of society is drawn. Are our relations with the people of South Asia, for example (or the people in isolated rural areas of our own country), governed by considerations of justice or only by the duties which hold between any one human being and another? The only satisfactory solution to this problem seems to me to be to hold that considerations of justice apply at least wherever there is systematic economic interaction; for whenever there is regularized commerce there is an institution in Rawls' sense, *i.e.* a public system of rules defining rights and duties etc.[27] Thus the Difference Principle would apply to the world economic system taken as a whole as well as to particular societies within it.

In distinguishing justice from altruism and benevolence and taking it to apply only to arrangements for reciprocal advantage Rawls' theory is like the system of natural liberty. But a proponent of natural liberty takes "arrangements for reciprocal advantage" in the relevant sense to be arrangements arising out of explicit agreements. Such arrangements are just if they were in fact freely agreed to by the parties involved, and the background institutions of the system of natural liberty are designed to ensure justice in this sense. Since Rawls' Difference Principle constrains people to cooperate on terms other than those they would arrive at through a process of free bargaining on the basis of their natural assets, it is to be rejected. As Rawls says, the terms of this principle are equivalent to an undertaking to regard natural abilities as a common asset, and a proponent of natural liberty would say, I believe, that the terms of the principle apply only where such an undertaking has in fact been made.

Rawls holds, on the other hand, that one is born into a set of institutions whose basic structure largely determines one's prospects and opportunities. Background institutions of the kind described in the system of natural liberty are one example of such institutions; the various institutions satisfying the Difference Principle are another. Within the framework of such institutions one may enter into specific contractual arrangements with others, but these institutions themselves are not established by explicit agreement; they are present from birth and their legitimacy must have some other foundation. The test of legitimacy which Rawls proposes is, of course, the idea of hypothetical contract, as it is embodied in his Original Position construction.

The argument sketched here is obviously parallel to a familiar controversy about the bases of political obligation. The doctrine of natural liberty corresponds to the doctrine which seeks to found all political ties on explicit consent, and seems to me to inherit many of the problems of that view. For Rawls, on the other hand, the legitimacy of both political and economic institutions is to be analyzed in terms of a merely hypothetical agreement. (Indeed, Rawls does not separate the two cases.) The parallel between the problems of political institutions and those of economic institutions is often obscured because the political problem is thought of in terms of *obligation* while economic justice is thought of in terms of *distribution*.[28] But economic institutions, no less than political ones, must be capable of generating obligations, *viz.* obligations to cooperate on the terms these institutions provide in order to produce the shares to which others are entitled.[29]

The idea of such economic obligations raises a number of interesting issues which I can only mention here. Such an obligation to contribute would be violated, *e.g.*, by a person who, while wishing to receive benefits derived from the participation of others in a scheme of cooperation satisfying the Difference Principle, refused to contribute his own skills on the same terms, holding out for a higher level of compensation than the scheme provided. Presumably obligations of this kind do not in general prevent a person from opting out of a scheme of economic cooperation, any more than political obligation constitutes a general bar to emigration; but this does not mean (in either case) that people are always free to simply pick up and go. Further, there obviously are limits to what a just scheme can demand of those born into it and limits to how far their freedom to choose among different forms of contribution can be restricted. It seems likely that these limits would be defended, on Rawls' view, by appeal to an increasing marginal preference for "economic liberty" relative to other goods.

As I have argued above, the central thesis underlying the Difference Principle is the idea that the basic institutions of society are a cooperative enterprise in which the citizens stand as equal partners. This notion of equality is reflected in Rawls' particular Original Position construction in the fact that the parties are prevented by the veil of ignorance and the requirement that the principles they choose be general (*i.e.* contain no proper names or token reflexives) from framing principles which ensure them special advantages.[30] But the fact that it would be chosen under these conditions is not a conclusive argument for the Difference Principle since a person who favored the system of natural liberty would undoubtedly reject the notion that principles of justice must be chosen under these particular constraints. The situation here is similar to that of the argument against perfectionism: Rawls' defense of the Difference Principle must proceed in the main by setting out the ideal of social cooperation of which this principle is the natural expression. The advantages of this ideal—*e.g.* the fact that institutions founded on this ideal support the self-esteem of their members and provide a public expression of their respect for one another—can be set out, and its ability to account for our considered judgments of justice can be demonstrated, but in the end the adoption of an alternative view is not wholly precluded. A person who, finding that he has valuable talents, wishes to opt for the system of natural liberty is analogous to the person who, knowing his own conception of the good, prefers a perfectionist system organized around this conception to what I have called "co-operation on a footing of justice." In both cases one can offer reasons why cooperation with others on a basis all could agree to in a situation of initial equality is an important good, but one cannot expect to offer arguments which meet the objections of such a person and defeat them on their own grounds.

I do not regard this residual indeterminacy as a failing of Rawls' book or as a source for skepticism. The conception of justice which Rawls describes has an important place in our thought, and to have presented this conception as fully and displayed its deepest features as clearly as Rawls has done is a rare and valuable accomplishment. Almost no one will read the book without finding himself strongly drawn to Rawls' view at many points, and even those who do not share Rawls' conclusions will come to a deeper understanding of their own views as a result of his work.

NOTES

1. Rawls, *A Theory of Justice,* 61 (Hereinafter Rawls).
2. *Id.* 88.
3. *Id.* 83. Rawls' final formulation of this principle, *id.* 312, incorporates considerations of justice between generations which the present discussion leaves aside.
4. *Id.* 73.
5. *Id.* 98.
6. *Id.*
7. *Id.*
8. *Cf. id.* 169–71.
9. *Id.* 96.
10. *Id.* 74, 301.
11. *See* p. 1050 *supra.*
12. This solution was suggested to me by Bruce Ackerman.
13. Rawls 83. *See* text accompanying note 68 *infra.*
14. One would be to take the position a person is "born into" to be defined not only by the social and economic status of his family but also by his inborn talents and liabilities, *i.e.* those features which will enable him to prosper in the society or prevent him from doing so. Given this definition of the "starting places," one could employ averaging as a method for representing the long term expectations of a representative person born into the worst-off such place without fear that the theory would collapse into the doctrine of maximum average primary social goods if the institution of the family were eliminated. Modifying the Difference Principle in this way would bring Rawls closer (perhaps too close) to what he calls "the principle of redress," the principle that the distribution of social advantages must be arranged to compensate for un-

deserved inequalities such as the inequalities of birth and natural endowment. *See* Rawls 100–02.
15. *Id.* 83. I will regard this as the canonical formulation of Rawls' principle. When this version of the principle is fulfilled there is a clear sense in which prevailing inequalities are "to everyone's advantage" since there is no one who would benefit from their removal. Fulfillment of the simple Difference Principle (that inequalities must benefit the worst-off) insures fulfillment of the lexical principle only if expectations of members of the society are "close knit"—it is impossible to alter the expectations of one representative person without affecting the expectations of every other representative person—and "chain connected"—if an inequality favoring group *A* raises the expectations of the worst-off representative person *B* then it also raises the expectations of every representative person between *B* and *A. Id.* 80–82.
16. *Id.* 178, 180.
17. *Id.* 103.
18. *Id.*
19. *Id.* 179.
20. *Id.* 150–51.
21. Inequalities give rise to loss of self-respect in Rawls' sense to the extent that they give a person reason for lack of confidence in his own worth and in his abilities to carry out his life plans. *Id.* 535. Whether given inequalities have this effect will depend not only on their magnitude but also on the public reasons offered to justify them. Rawls believes that effects of this kind will not be a factor in a society governed by the Difference Principle since the inequalities in wealth and income in such a society will not be extreme and will "probably [be] less than those that have often prevailed." *Id.* 536. In addition, the justification offered for those inequalities that do prevail will be one which supports the self-esteem of the less advantaged since this justification must appeal to the tendency of these inequalities to advance their good.
22. A position of this kind was put forward, for example, by Kropotkin. *See* P. Kropotkin, *The Conquest of Bread* 62, ch. 13, *et passim* (Penguin ed. 1972). Kropotkin holds that if one accepts, as Rawls appears to, the view that the productive capacities of a society must be seen as the common property of its members, then one must reject the idea of wages (or any other way of tying distribution to social roles). Rather, the social product is to be held in common and used to provide facilities which meet the basic needs of all.
23. Rawls 72.
24. *Id.*
25. This aspect of utilitarianism is most clearly emphasized by William Godwin. *See* 2 W. *Godwin, Enquiry Concerning Political Justice* bk. VIII (3d ed. 1797) (facsim. ed. F. Priestley 1946).
26. Rawls 114.
27. *Id.* 55.
28. For a discussion of political obligation relevant to economic contribution as well, see M. Walzer, *Obligations* (1970).
29. *See* Rawls 313. The contribution side of the problem of economic justice is forcefully emphasized in R. Nozick, *Anarchy, State and Utopia (1974).* Nozick criticizes Rawls from the perspective of a purely contractarian view much more sophisticated and subtle than the system of natural liberty I have crudely described here.
30. These considerations alone, of course, do not ensure that the parties in the Original Position will arrive at a principle of equal distribution even as a first solution. Given that they have no way to ensure a larger share for themselves the question remains whether they should settle for the maximin solution represented by the Difference Principle or gamble on receiving a larger share under some other rule.

LOUIS KATZNER

Is the Favoring of Women and Blacks in Employment and Educational Opportunities Justified?*

There is presently a call to favor blacks and women in employment and educational opportunities because in the past many of them have been discriminated against in these areas. The basic concern of this paper is whether or not reverse discrimination in this sense is justified. Given that, as will be shown, all acts of reverse discrimination involve prejudgment, it is appropriate to scrutinize first the notion of discrimination itself. Next, the idea of reverse discrimination will be explicated by distinguishing among several different forms that it may take; and from this explication the set of conditions under which a bias of redress is justified will emerge. Finally, the situation of blacks and women in the United States will be examined to see what conclusions can be drawn concerning the justification of reverse discrimination for these two classes.

I. DISCRIMINATION

There are certain things that are relevant to the way people should be treated and certain things that are not. The size of one's chest is relevant to the size shirt he should have, but it has nothing to do with the size his shoes should be. The rate of one's metabolism is pertinent to the amount of food she should be served, but not to the color of the napkin she is given. People should be treated on the basis of their attributes and merits that are relevant to the circumstances. When they are, those who are similar are treated similarly and those who are dissimilar are treated differently. Although these distinctions do involve treating people differently (those with larger chests get larger shirts than those with smaller chests), it does not involve discrimination. For discrimination means treating people differently when they

are similar in the relevant respects or treating them similarly when they are different in the relevant respects.

It follows that to determine what constitutes discrimination in vocational and education opportunities, we must first determine what qualities are relevant to a career and the capacity to learn. People today generally seem to accept the principle of meritocracy—that is, that an individual's potential for success, which is a combination of his native and/or developed ability and the amount of effort he can be expected to put forth, is the sole criterion that should be used in hiring and college admissions practices. It may be that until recently many people did not accept this view, and it may be that there are some even today who do not accept it. Nevertheless, this is one of the basic principles of the "American Dream"; it is the foundation of the civil service system; it is a principle to which even the most ardent racists and sexists at least give lipservice; and it is the principle that most people seem to have in mind when they speak of the problem of discrimination in hiring and college admissions practices. And because it is generally agreed that people with the same potential should be treated similarly in employment and college admissions, and that those with more potential should receive preference over those with less, the discussion begins with this assumption.

II. REVERSE DISCRIMINATION

With the notion of discrimination clarified, it is now possible to see what is involved in the idea of reverse discrimination. Reverse discrimination is much more than a call to eliminate bias; it is a call to offset the effects of past acts of bias by skewing opportunity in the opposite direction. This paper will consider only the claims that blacks, women, etcetera, have been discriminated against in the past (that is, they have been

* This essay appeared in Feinberg and Gross, *Philosophy of Law,* 1975 (Encino, Calif.: Dickenson Publishing Co.), pp. 291–296.

treated as if they have less potential than they actually do); and that the only way to offset their subsequent disadvantages is to discriminate now in their favor (that is, to treat them as if they have more potential than they actually do).

It follows that those who are currently calling for the revision of admission standards at our colleges because they do not accurately reflect a student's chances of success there are not calling for reverse discrimination. They are merely saying that we should find a way of determining precisely who is qualified (that is, who has the potential) to go to college, and then admit the most qualified. On the other hand, those who are calling for us to admit students whom they allow are less qualified than others who are denied admission, and to provide these less qualified students with special tutorial help, are calling for reverse discrimination.

This example clearly illustrates the basic problem that any justification of reverse discrimination must come to grips with—viz., that every act of reverse discrimination is itself discriminatory. For every less qualified person who is admitted to a college, or hired for a job, there is a more qualified person who is being discriminated against, and who has a right to complain. Hence the justification of reverse discrimination must involve not only a justification of *discriminating for* those who are benefiting from it, it must also involve a justification of discriminating *against* those at whose expense the reverse discrimination is being practiced.

III. JUSTIFICATION OF REVERSE DISCRIMINATION: DIRECT

There are at least two significantly different kinds of situations in which reverse discrimination can be called for. On the one hand, a person might argue that he should be favored because he was arbitrarily passed over at some time in the past. Thus, for example, a Chicano might maintain that since he was denied a job for which he was the most qualified candidate simply because of his race, he should now be given one for which he is not the most qualified candidate, simply because he was discriminated against in the past. On the other hand, one might argue that he should be given preference because his ancestors (parents, grandparents, great-grandparents, et cetera) were discriminated against. In this case,

the Chicano would claim that he should be given a job for which he is not the most qualified applicant because his ancestors were denied jobs for which they were the most qualified.

In the former case, that of rectifying bias against an individual by unduly favoring him, there are several interesting points that can be made. First of all, the case for reverse discrimination of this type is strongest when the person to be passed over in the reverse discrimination is the same one who benefited from the initial discriminatory act. Suppose, for example, that when it comes time to appoint the vice-president of a company, the best qualified applicant (that is, the one who has the most potential) is passed over because of his race, and a less qualified applicant is given the job. Suppose that the following year the job of president in the same firm becomes open. At this point, the vice-president, because of the training he had as second in command, is the most qualified applicant for the job. It could be argued, however, that the presidency should go to the person who was passed over for the vice-presidency. For he should have been the vice-president, and if he had been he would probably now be the best-equipped applicant for the top post; it is only because he was passed over that the current vice-president is now the most qualified candidate. In other words, since the current vice-president got ahead at his expense, it is warranted for him to move up at the vice-president's expense. In this way the wrong that was done him will be righted.

There are two main problems with this argument. First of all, certainly to be considered is how well the individual who benefited from the initial act of discrimination exploited his break. If he used this opportunity to work up to his capacity, this would seem to be a good reason for not passing him over for the presidency. If, on the other hand, although performing very adequately as vice-president, he was not working up to the limits of his capacity, then perhaps the job of president should be given to the man who was passed over in the first place—even though the vice-president's experience in his job leads one to think that he is the one most qualified to handle the difficult tasks of the presidency. In other words, how much a person has made of the benefit he has received from an act of discrimination seems to be relevant to the question of whether or not he should be discriminated against so that the victim of that discrimination may now be benefited.

Secondly, there are so few cases of this kind that even if reverse discrimination is justified in such cases, this would not show very much. In most instances of reverse discrimination, the redress is at the expense of someone who did not benefit from the initial act of discrimination rather than someone who did.

One species of this form of reverse discrimination is that in which the victim of the proposed act of reverse discrimination has not benefited from *any* acts of discrimination. In such a case, what is in effect happening is that the burden of discrimination is being transferred from one individual who does not deserve it to another individual who does not deserve it. There is no sense in which "the score is being evened," as in the case above. Because there is no reason for saying that one of the individuals deserves to be penalized by prejudice while the other one does not, it is difficult to see how this kind of reverse discrimination can be justified.

The only argument that comes to mind as a justification for this species of reverse discrimination is the following: The burdens of discrimination should be shared rather than placed on a few. It is better that the liabilities of discrimination be passed from person to person than that they remain the handicap only of those who have been disfavored. It follows that if we find someone who has been discriminated against, we are warranted in rectifying that injustice by an act of reverse discrimination, as long as the victim of the reverse discrimination has not himself been discriminated against in the past.

But this is not a very persuasive argument. For one thing, the claim that discrimination should be shared does not seem a very compelling reason for discriminating against a totally innocent bystander. Secondly, even if this is viewed as a forceful reason, the image of society that emerges is a horrifying one. The moment someone is discriminated against, he seeks out someone who has not been unfairly barred, and asks for reverse discrimination against this person to rectify the wrong he has suffered. Such a procedure would seem to entrench rather than eliminate discrimination, and would produce an incredibly unstable society.

Another species of this form of reverse discrimination is that in which the victim of the proposed reverse bias has benefited from a previous unfair decision, although it is not the particular act that is being rectified. In other words, he did not get ahead at the expense of the individual to whom we are trying to "make things up" by reverse discrimination, but he has benefited from bias against other individuals. In such a case, there is a sense, admittedly extended, in which a score is being evened.

Now it appears that such cases are more like those in which the victim of the proposed act of reverse discrimination benefited from the initial instance of discrimination than those in which he is a completely innocent bystander, and hence in such cases reverse discrimination can be justified. Of course it would be preferable if we could find the beneficiary of the original act of discrimination—but very often this just is not possible. And we must make sure that the reverse discrimination is proportionate to both the liability suffered by the proposed beneficiary and the advantage previously gained by the proposed victim—a very difficult task indeed. But there does not seem to be any reason for saying that reverse discrimination can only be visited upon those who benefited from the particular discriminatory act that is being rectified. It seems more reasonable to say that reverse discrimination can be visited upon those who benefited from either the particular instance of discrimination being rectified or from roughly similar acts.

Although the conclusions drawn from this discussion of the various species of one form of reverse discrimination do not seem conclusive, this discussion has brought to light three conditions which are necessary for the justification of reverse discrimination: First, there must have been an act of discrimination that is being rectified. Second, the initial act of discrimination must have in some way handicapped its victim, for if he has not been handicapped or set back in some way, then there is nothing to "make up to him" through reverse discrimination. And third, the victim of the proposed reverse discrimination must have benefited from an act of discrimination (either the one that is being rectified or a similar one); otherwise it is unacceptable to say that he should now be disfavored.

IV. JUSTIFICATION OF REVERSE DISCRIMINATION: INDIRECT

Not all of the claims that are made for reverse discrimination, however, assume that the individual involved has himself been the victim of bias. In many cases what is being claimed is that an individual is entitled to benefit from a rectifying bias because his ancestors (parents, grandparents, great grandparents, etcetera) were unfairly denied opportunity. Keeping in mind the three conditions necessary for reverse discrimination that we have just developed, this form of reverse discrimination will be examined.

In a society in which wealth could not be accumulated or, even if it could, it did not give one access to a better education and/or job, and a good education did not give one access to a better job and/or greater wealth, it would be hard to see how educational and/or economic discrimination against one's ancestors could be a handicap. That is, if education was not a key to economic success, then the educational discrimination one's ancestors suffered could not handicap one in the search for a job. If wealth did not buy better teachers and better schools, then the fact that one's ancestors have been handicapped economically could not be a reason for his being educationally disadvantaged. If wealth could not start a business, buy into a business, or give one direct access to a good job, then the economic shackling one's ancestors endured could in no way handicap her in the economic realm. But if wealth and education do these things, as in our society they clearly do, and if because of discrimination some people were not allowed to accumulate the wealth that their talents normally would bring, then it is quite clear that their offspring are handicapped by the discrimination they have suffered.

It is important to note that this point in no way turns on the controversy that is currently raging over the relationship between IQ and race. For it is not being claimed that unless there is complete equality there is discrimination. The members of a suppressed group may be above, below, or equal to the other members of society with regard to potential. All that is being claimed is that to the extent that the members of a group have been denied a fair chance to do work commensurate with their capacities, and to the extent that this has handicapped subsequent members of that group, reverse discrimination may be justified to offset this handicap.

But, as we have already seen, for reverse discrimination to be justified, not only must the victims of discrimination be handicapped by the discrimination, those who will suffer from its reversal must have benefited from the original injustice. In this particular case, it may be that they are the children of the beneficiaries of discrimination who have passed these advantages on to them. Or it may be that they benefit in facing reduced competition for schooling and jobs, and hence they are able to get into a better school and land a better job than they would if those suffering the effects of discrimination were not handicapped. Or they may have benefited from discrimination in some other way. But the proposed victims of reverse discrimination must be the beneficiaries of previous discrimination.

In addition to all of this, however, it seems that there is one more condition that must be met for reverse discrimination to be justified. Assuming that if we eliminated all discrimination immediately, the people who have suffered from it could compete on an equal basis with all other members of society, then reverse discrimination would not be justified. This of course is trivially true if it is only being claimed that if the elimination of all discrimination entails the eradication of all the handicaps it creates, then only the elimination of discrimination (and not reverse discrimination) is justified. But the claim involves much more than this. What is being argued is that even if the immediate elimination of all discrimination does not allow all suppressed people to compete equally with other members of society, as long as it allows equal opportunity to all children born subsequent to the end of discrimination, then reverse discrimination is not justified—*not even for those who have been handicapped by discrimination.* In other words, reverse discrimination will not prevent its debilitating effects from being passed on to generations yet unborn.

The justification of this claim is a straightforward utilitarian one (it cannot be a justification in terms of justice since what is being countenanced is blatant injustice). The social cost of implementing a policy of reverse discrimination is very high. The problems in determining who are the victims of discrimination and how great their handicaps, and who are the beneficiaries of discrimination and how great their benefits, as well as the problems in both developing and administering policies that will lead to a proper rectification of discrimination, are not merely enormously complex, they are enormously costly to solve. Moreover, the benefits of ending all discrimination are very great. Not only will many people be hired for jobs and admitted to colleges otherwise barred to them because of discrimination, but many people who have themselves been handicapped by discrimination will take great satisfaction in the knowledge that their offspring will not be held back as they have. This, of course, in no way eliminates the injustice involved in allowing acts of reverse discrimination to go unrectified. All it shows is that given the tremendous cost of implementing a comprehensive program of reverse discrimination, and given the tremendous benefits that would accrue simply from the elimination of all discrimination, it is reasonable to claim that reverse discrimination is justified only if the elimination of discrimination will not prevent its debilitating effects from being passed on to generations yet unborn.

Thus there is a fourth condition that must be added to the list of conditions that are necessary for the justification of reverse discrimination. Moreover, the addition of this condition renders the list jointly sufficient for the justification of reverse discrimination. Thus, reverse discrimination is justified if, and only if, the following conditions are met:

1. There must have been an initial act of discrimination that the reverse discrimination is going to rectify.
2. The beneficiary of the proposed act of reverse discrimination must have been handicapped by the initial act—either directly, if he was the victim of the initial discrimination, or indirectly, if he is the offspring of a victim (and inherited the handicap).
3. The victim of the proposed act of reverse discrimination must have benefited from an act of discrimination—the one that is being rectified or a similar one—and either directly, if he was the beneficiary of an initial act of discrimination or indirectly, if he is the offspring of a beneficiary (and inherited the benefit).
4. It must be the case that even if all discrimination were ended immediately, the debilitating effects of discrimination would be passed on to generations yet unborn.

V. REVERSE DISCRIMINATION FAVORING WOMEN AND BLACKS

A partial answer, at least, to the question of whether or not reverse discrimination is justified in the case of women and blacks is now possible. Let us begin with blacks.

It seems clear that the situation of many blacks in this country meets the four conditions shown to be individually necessary and jointly sufficient for the justification of reverse discrimination. First, there can be no doubt that many blacks have been the victims of educational and vocational discrimination. Second, given the relationships existing between wealth, education, and vocation, there can be no doubt that the discrimination that blacks have met with has handicapped both themselves and their offspring. Third, it also seems clear that within our economic framework, if blacks had not been discriminated against, there are many whites (those who got an education or a job at the expense of a more qualified black or in competition with the handicapped offspring of disadvantaged blacks) who would be in far less advantageous educational and vocational situations than they currently are —that is, there are people who have benefited from discrimination. And finally, again given the relationships existing among wealth, education, and vocation, even if all discrimination against blacks were to cease immediately, many black children born subsequent to this time would not be able to compete for educational and vocational opportunities on the same basis that they would had there been no bias against their ancestors.

Of course this in no way shows that reverse discrimination for all blacks is justified. After all, there are some blacks who have not let themselves be handicapped by discrimination. There are also undoubtedly some whites who have not benefited from the discrimination against blacks. And finally, there are many whites who have endured discrimination in the same way blacks have. In other words, so far it has only been shown that all those who have been discriminated against in a way that meets the conditions established are entitled to reverse discrimination and that some blacks have been discriminated against in this way.

To move from this claim to the conclusion that blacks as a class are entitled to reverse discrimination, several additional things must be shown. First, it must be demonstrated that it is unfeasible to handle reverse discrimination on a case by case basis (for example, it might be argued that such a procedure would be far too costly). Second, it must be proven that the overwhelming percentage of blacks have been victimized by discrimination—that is, the number of blacks who would benefit from reverse discrimination, but who do not deserve to, must be very small. And finally, it must be shown that the overwhelming majority of the potential victims of bias of redress have benefited from the acts of discrimination (or similar acts) that are being rectified—that is, it must be that the number of whites who will suffer the effects of reverse discrimination, without deserving to, must also be very small. If these conditions are met, then although there will be some unwarranted discrimination resulting from the reverse discrimination in favor of blacks (that is, some blacks benefiting who were not victimized and some whites suffering who were not benefited), such cases will be kept to a bare minimum, and hence the basic result will be the offsetting of the handicaps with which blacks have unwarrantedly been saddled.

When it comes to the case of (white) women, however, the situation is quite different. There is little doubt that many women have been denied opportunity, and thus handicapped while many men have benefited from this discrimination (although I believe that discrimination has been far less pervasive in the case of women than it has been for blacks). But women generally do not constitute the kind of class in which the handicaps of discrimination are passed on to one's offspring. This is because, unlike blacks, they are not an isolated social group. Most women are reared in families in which the gains a father makes, even if the mother is limited by society's prejudice, work to the advantage of *all* offspring. (White) women have attended white schools and colleges and, even if they have been discriminated against, their children have attended these same schools and colleges. If all discrimination were ended tomorrow, there would be no external problem at all for most women in competing, commensurate with their potential, with the male population.

Two important things follow from this. First, it is illegitimate for most women to claim that they should be favored because their mothers were disfavored. Second, and most importantly, if all discrimination against women were ended immediately, in most cases none of its debilitating effects would be transmitted to the generations of women yet unborn; hence, for most women, the fourth condition necessary for the justification of reverse discrimination is not satisfied. Thus, reverse discrimination for women as a class cannot be justified, although there are undoubtedly some cases in which, for a particular woman, it can.

One must be careful, however, not to interpret this judgment too broadly. For one thing, the conclusion that reverse discrimination is not warranted for women as a class is contingent upon the immediate elimination of all discrimination. Hence it does not apply if discrimination against women continues. In other words, the conclusion does not show that reverse discrimination for women as a class is unjustified in the face of continuing bias against them. Under these circumstances, reverse discrimination may or may not be justified.

Secondly, as reverse discrimination has been described here, it involves offsetting the impact of a particular kind of discrimination (that is, in educational and job opportunities) by another instance of the same kind of discrimination (that is, preferential treatment in education and job opportunities). All our argument shows is that this is unwarranted for women as a class. One might, however, want to argue in favor of discriminating for women as a class in the area of education and jobs, not to offset previous discrimination in this area, but rather to counter the debilitating effects that institutionalized sexism has had on the female psyche. That is, one might argue that because our society has conditioned women to desire subservient roles (for example, that of a nurse rather than doctor, secretary rather than executive, housewife rather than breadwinner, and so on), even if all forms of discrimination were eliminated tomorrow, very few (or at least not enough) women would take advantage of the opportunities open to them. Hence we need (reverse) discrimination as a means of placing women in visible positions of success, so that other women will have models to emulate and will strive for success in these areas. Now although it is not clear whether or not such a program can legitimately be labelled "reverse discrimination," the important point is that this paper has not been addressed to this kind of problem, and hence has not shown that it is illegitimate to give preferential treatment to women (or blacks) for this reason.

SWEATT v. PAINTER

United States Supreme Court, 1950 *

Mr. Chief Justice Vinson delivered the opinion of the Court.

This case and *McLaurin* v. *Oklahoma State Regents, post*, p. 637, present different aspects of this general question: To what extent does the Equal Protection Clause of the Fourteenth Amendment limit the power of a state to distinguish between students of different races in professional and graduate education in a state university? Broader issues have been urged for our consideration, but we adhere to the principle of deciding constitutional questions only in the context of the particular case before the Court. We have frequently reiterated that this Court will decide constitutional questions only when necessary to the disposition of the case at hand, and that such decisions will be drawn as narrowly as possible. *Rescue Army* v. *Municipal Court,* 331 U.S. 549 (1947), and cases cited therein. Because of this traditional reluctance to extend constitutional interpretations to situations or facts which are not before the Court, much of the excellent research and detailed argument presented in these cases is unnecessary to their disposition.

In the instant case, petitioner filed an application for admission to the University of Texas Law School for the February, 1946 term. His application was rejected solely because he is a Negro.[1] Petitioner thereupon brought this suit for mandamus against the appropriate school officials, respondents here, to compel his admission. At that time, there was no law school in Texas which admitted Negroes.

The state trial court recognized that the action of the State in denying petitioner the opportunity to gain a legal education while granting it to others deprived him of the equal protection of the laws guaranteed by the Fourteenth Amendment. The court did not grant the relief requested, however, but continued the case for six months to allow the State to supply substantially equal facilities. At the expiration of the six months, in December, 1946, the court denied the writ on the showing that the authorized university officials had adopted an order calling for the opening of a law school for Negroes the following February. While petitioner's appeal was pending, such a school was made available, but petitioner refused to register therein. The Texas

Court of Civil Appeals set aside the trial court's judgment and ordered the cause "remanded generally to the trial court for further proceedings without prejudice to the rights of any party to this suit."

On remand, a hearing was held on the issue of the equality of the educational facilities at the newly established school as compared with the University of Texas Law School. Finding that the new school offered petitioner "privileges, advantages, and opportunities for the study of law substantially equivalent to those offered by the State to white students at the University of Texas," the trial court denied mandamus. The Court of Civil Appeals affirmed. 210 S. W. 2d 442 (1948). Petitioner's application for a writ of error was denied by the Texas Supreme Court. We granted certiorari, 338 U.S. 865 (1949), because of the manifest importance of the constitutional issues involved.

The University of Texas Law School, from which petitioner was excluded, was staffed by a faculty of sixteen full-time and three part-time professors, some of whom are nationally recognized authorities in their field. Its student body numbered 850. The library contained over 65,000 volumes. Among the other facilities available to the students were a law review, moot court facilities, scholarship funds, and Order of the Coif affiliation. The school's alumni occupy the most distinguished positions in the private practice of the law and in the public life of the State. It may properly be considered one of the nation's ranking law schools.

The law school for Negroes which was to have opened in February, 1947, would have had no independent faculty or library. The teaching was to be carried on by four members of the University of Texas Law School faculty, who were to maintain their offices at the University of Texas while teaching at both institutions. Few of the 10,000 volumes ordered for the library had arrived;[2] nor was there any full-time librarian. The school lacked accreditation.

Since the trial of this case, respondents report the opening of a law school at the Texas State University for Negroes. It is apparently on the road to full accreditation. It has a faculty of five full-time professors; a student body of 23; a library of some 16,500 volumes serviced by a full-time staff; a practice court and legal aid association; and one alumnus who has become a member of the Texas Bar.

* 339 U.S. 629 (1950).

Whether the University of Texas Law School is compared with the original or the new law school for Negroes, we cannot find substantial equality in the educational opportunities offered white and Negro law students by the State. In terms of number of the faculty, variety of courses and opportunity for specialization, size of the student body, scope of the library, availability of law review and similar activities, the University of Texas Law School is superior. What is more important, the University of Texas Law School possesses to a far greater degree those qualities which are incapable of objective measurement but which make for greatness in a law school. Such qualities, to name but a few, include reputation of the faculty, experience of the administration, position and influence of the alumni, standing in the community, traditions and prestige. It is difficult to believe that one who had a free choice between these law schools would consider the question close.

Moreover, although the law is a highly learned profession, we are well aware that it is an intensely practical one. The law school, the proving ground for legal learning and practice, cannot be effective in isolation from the individuals and institutions with which the law interacts. Few students and no one who has practiced law would choose to study in an academic vacuum, removed from the interplay of ideas and the exchange of views with which the law is concerned. The law school to which Texas is willing to admit petitioner excludes from its student body members of the racial groups which number 85% of the population of the State and include most of the lawyers, witnesses, jurors, judges and other officials with whom petitioner will inevitably be dealing when he becomes a member of the Texas Bar. With such a substantial and significant segment of society excluded, we cannot conclude that the education offered petitioner is substantially equal to that which he would receive if admitted to the University of Texas Law School.

It may be argued that excluding petitioner from that school is no different from excluding white students from the new law school. This contention overlooks realities. It is unlikely that a member of a group so decisively in the majority, attending a school with rich traditions and prestige which only a history of consistently maintained excellence could command, would claim that the opportunities afforded him for legal education were unequal to those held open to petitioner. That such a claim, if made, would be dishonored by the State, is no answer. "Equal protection of the laws is not achieved through indiscriminate imposition of inequalities." *Shelley* v. *Kraemer,* 334 U.S. 1, 22 (1948).

It is fundamental that these cases concern rights which are personal and present. This Court has stated

unanimously that "The State must provide [legal education] for [petitioner] in conformity with the equal protection clause of the Fourteenth Amendment and provide it as soon as it does for applicants of any other group." *Sipuel* v. *Board of Regents,* 332 U.S. 631, 633 (1948). That case "did not present the issue whether a state might not satisfy the equal protection clause of the Fourteenth Amendment by establishing a separate law school for Negroes." *Fisher* v. *Hurst,* 333 U.S. 147, 150 (1948). In *Missouri ex rel. Gaines* v. *Canada,* 305 U.S. 337, 351 (1938), the Court, speaking through Chief Justice Hughes, declared that "petitioner's right was a personal one. It was as an individual that he was entitled to the equal protection of the laws, and the State was bound to furnish him within its borders facilities for legal education substantially equal to those which the State there afforded for persons of the white race, whether or not other negroes sought the same opportunity." These are the only cases in this Court which present the issue of the constitutional validity of race distinctions in state-supported graduate and professional education.

In accordance with these cases, petitioner may claim his full constitutional right: legal education equivalent to that offered by the State to students of other races. Such education is not available to him in a separate law school as offered by the State. We cannot, therefore, agree with respondents that the doctrine of *Plessy* v. *Ferguson,* 163 U.S. 537 (1896), requires affirmance of the judgment below. Nor need we reach petitioner's contention that *Plessy* v. *Ferguson* should be reexamined in the light of contemporary knowledge respecting the purposes of the Fourteenth Amendment and the effects of racial segregation. See *supra,* p. 631.

We hold that the Equal Protection Clause of the Fourteenth Amendment requires that petitioner be admitted to the University of Texas Law School. The judgment is reversed and the cause is remanded for proceedings not inconsistent with this opinion.

Reversed.

NOTES

1. It appears that the University has been restricted to white students, in accordance with the State law. See Tex. Const., Art. VII, §§ 7, 14; Tex. Rev. Civ. Stat. (Vernon, 1925), Arts. 2643b (Supp. 1949), 2719, 2900.

2. "Students of the interim School of Law of the Texas State University for Negroes [located in Austin, whereas the permanent School was to be located at Houston] shall have use of the State Law Library in the Capitol Building. . . ." Tex. Laws 1947, c. 29, § 11, Tex. Rev. Civ. Stat. (Vernon, 1949 Supp.), note to Art. 2643b. It is not clear that this privilege was anything more than was extended to all citizens of the State.

DEFUNIS v. ODEGAARD

United States Supreme Court, 1974 *

Mr. Justice Douglas, dissenting.

I agree with MR. JUSTICE BRENNAN that this case is not moot, and because of the significance of the issues raised I think it is important to reach the merits.

I

The University of Washington Law School received 1,601 applications for admission to its first-year class beginning in September 1971. There were spaces available for only about 150 students, but in order to enroll this number the school eventually offered admission to 275 applicants. All applicants were put into two groups, one of which was considered under the minority admissions program. Thirty-seven of those offered admission had indicated on an optional question on their application that their "dominant" ethnic origin was either Black, Chicano, American Indian, or Filipino, the four groups included in the minority admissions program. Answers to this optional question were apparently the sole basis upon which eligibility for the program was determined. Eighteen of these 37 actually enrolled in the Law School.

In general, the admissions process proceeded as follows: An index called the Predicted First Year Average (Average) was calculated for each applicant on the basis of a formula combining the applicant's score on the Law School Admission Test (LSAT) and his grades in his last two years in college.[1] On the basis of its experience with previous years' applications, the admissions committee, consisting of faculty, administration, and students, concluded that the most outstanding applicants were those with averages above 77; the highest average of any applicant was 81. Applicants with averages above 77 were considered as their applications arrived by random distribution of their files to the members of the committee who would read them and report their recommendations back to the committee. As a result of the first three committee meetings in February, March, and April 1971, 78 applicants from this group were admitted, although virtually no other applicants were offered admission this early.[2] By the final conclusion of the admissions process in Au-

* 416 U.S. 312 (1974). This dissenting opinion appears at page 320.

gust 1971, 147 applicants with averages above 77 had been admitted, including all applicants with averages above 78, and 93 of 106 applicants with averages between 77 and 78.

Also beginning early in the admissions process was the culling out of applicants with averages below 74.5. These were reviewed by the Chairman of the Admissions Committee, who had the authority to reject them summarily without further consideration by the rest of the Committee. A small number of these applications were saved by the Chairman for committee consideration on the basis of information in the file indicating greater promise than suggested by the Average. Finally during the early months the Committee accumulated the applications of those with averages between 74.5 and 77 to be considered at a later time when most of the applications had been received and thus could be compared with one another. Since DeFunis' average was 76.23, he was in this middle group.

Beginning in their May meeting the Committee considered this middle group of applicants, whose folders had been randomly distributed to Committee members for their recommendations to the Committee. Also considered at this time were remaining applicants with averages below 74.5 who had not been summarily rejected, and some of those with averages above 77 who had not been summarily admitted, but instead held for further consideration. Each Committee member would consider the applications competitively, following rough guidelines as to the proportion who could be offered admission. After the Committee had extended offers of admission to somewhat over 200 applicants, a waiting list was constructed in the same fashion, and was divided into four groups ranked by the Committee's assessment of their applications. DeFunis was on this waiting list, but was ranked in the lowest quarter. He was ultimately told in August 1971 that there would be no room for him.

Applicants who had indicated on their application forms that they were either Black, Chicano, American Indian, or Filipino were treated differently in several respects. Whatever their averages, none were given to the Committee Chairman for consideration of summary rejection, nor were they distributed randomly among committee members for consideration along with the other applications. Instead, all applications of

Black students were assigned separately to two particular Committee members: a first-year Black law student on the Committee, and a professor on the Committee who had worked the previous summer in a special program for disadvantaged college students considering application to Law School.[3] Applications from among the other three minority groups were assigned to an assistant dean who was on the Committee. The minority applications, while considered competitively with one another, were never directly compared to the remaining applications, either by the subcommittee or by the full Committee. As in the admissions process generally, the Committee sought to find "within the minority category, those persons who we thought had the highest probability of succeeding in Law School."[4] In reviewing the minority applications, the Committee attached less weight to the Average "in making a total judgmental evaluation as to the relative ability of the particular applicant to succeed in law school." 82 Wash. 2d 11, 21, 507 P. 2d 1169, 1175. In its publicly distributed Guide to Applicants, the Committee explained that "[a]n applicant's racial or ethnic background was considered as one factor in our general attempt to convert formal credentials into realistic predictions."[5]

Thirty-seven minority applicants were admitted under this procedure. Of these, 36 had Averages below DeFunis' 76.23, and 30 had Averages below 74.5, and thus would ordinarily have been summarily rejected by the Chairman. There were also 48 nonminority applicants admitted who had Averages below DeFunis. Twenty-three of these were returning veterans, see n.2, *supra,* and 25 were others who presumably were admitted because of other factors in their applications that made them attractive candidates despite their relatively low Averages.

It is reasonable to conclude from the above facts that while other factors were considered by the Committee, and were on occasion crucial, the Average was for most applicants a heavily weighted factor, and was at the extremes virtually dispositive.[6] A different balance was apparently struck, however, with regard to the minority applicants. Indeed, at oral argument, the respondents' counsel advised us that were the minority applicants considered under the same procedure as was generally used, none of those who eventually enrolled at the Law School would have been admitted.

The educational policy choices confronting a university admissions committee are not ordinarily a subject for judicial oversight; clearly it is not for us but for the law school to decide which tests to employ, how heavily to weigh recommendations from professors or undergraduate grades, and what level of achievement on the chosen criteria are sufficient to demonstrate that the candidate is qualified for admission. What places this case in a special category is the fact that the school did not choose one set of criteria but two, and then determined which to apply to a given applicant on the basis of his race. The Committee adopted this policy in order to achieve "a reasonable representation" of minority groups in the Law School 82 Wash. 2d, at 20, 507 P. 2d, at 1175. Although it may be speculated that the Committee sought to rectify what it perceived to be cultural or racial biases in the LSAT or in the candidates' undergraduate records, the record in this case is devoid of any evidence of such bias, and the school has not sought to justify its procedures on this basis.

Although testifying that "[w]e do not have a quota . . ." the Law School dean explained that "[w]e want a reasonable representation. We will go down to reach it if we can," without "taking people who are unqualified in an absolute sense. . . ." (Statement of Facts 420.) By "unqualified in an absolute sense" the dean meant candidates who "have no reasonable probable likelihood of having a chance of succeeding in the study of law. . . ." *(Ibid.)* But the dean conceded that in "reaching," the school does take "some minority students who at least, viewed as a group, have a less such likelihood than the majority student group taken as a whole." *(Id.,* at 423.)

"Q. Of those who have made application to go to the law school, I am saying you are not taking the best qualified?
"A. In total?
"Q. In total.
"A. In using that definition, yes." *(Id.,* at 423–424.)

It thus appears that by the Committee's own assessment, it admitted minority students who, by the tests given, seemed less qualified than some white students who were not accepted, in order to achieve a "reasonable representation." In this regard it may be pointed out that for the year 1969–1970—the year before the class to which DeFunis was seeking admission—the Law School reported an enrollment of eight Black students out of a total of 356.[7] (Defendants' Ex. 7.) That percentage, approximately 2.2%, compares to a percentage of Blacks in the population of Washington of approximately 2.1%.[8]

II

There was a time when law schools could follow the advice of Wigmore, who believed that "the way to find out whether a boy has the makings of a competent lawyer is to see what he can do in a first year of law studies." Wigmore, Juristic Psychopoyemetrology —Or, How to Find Out Whether a Boy Has the Makings of a Lawyer, 24 Ill. L. Rev. 454, 463–464 (1929). In those days there were enough spaces to admit every applicant who met minimal credentials, and they all could be given the opportunity to prove themselves at law school. But by the 1920's many law schools found that they could not admit all minimally qualified applicants, and some selection process began.[9] The pressure to use some kind of admissions test mounted, and a number of schools instituted them. One early precursor to the modern day LSAT was the Ferson-Stoddard Law Aptitude examination. Wigmore conducted his own study of that test with 50 student volunteers, and concluded that it "had no substantial practical value." *Id.,* at 463. But his conclusions were not accepted, and the harried law schools still sought some kind of admissions test which would simplify the process of judging applicants, and in 1948 the LSAT was born. It has been with us ever since.[10]

The test purports to predict how successful the applicant will be in his first year of law school, and consists of a few hours' worth of multiple-choice questions. But the answers the student can give to a multiple-choice question are limited by the creativity and intelligence of the test-maker; the student with a better or more original understanding of the problem than the test-maker may realize that none of the alternative answers are any good, but there is no way for him to demonstrate his understanding. "It is obvious from the nature of the tests that they do not give the candidate a significant opportunity to express himself. If he is subtle in his choice of answers it will go against him; and yet there is no other way for him to show any individuality. If he is strong-minded, nonconformist, unusual, original, or creative—as so many of the truly important people are—he must stifle his impulses and conform as best he can to the norms that the multiple-choice testers set up in their unimaginative, scientific way. The more profoundly gifted the candidate is, the more his resentment will rise against the mental strait jacket into which the testers would force his mind." B. Hoffmann, The Tyranny of Testing 91–92 (1962).

Those who make the tests and the law schools which use them point, of course, to the high correlations between the test scores and the grades at law school the first year. *E. g.,* Winterbottom, Comments on "A Study of the Criteria for Legal Education and Admission to the Bar," An article by Dr. Thomas M. Goolsby, Jr., 21 J. Legal Ed. 75 (1968). Certainly the tests do seem to do better than chance. But they do not have the value that their deceptively precise scoring system suggests. The proponents' own data show that, for example, most of those scoring in the bottom 20% on the test do better than that in law school—indeed six of every 100 of them will be in the *top* 20% of their law school class. *Id.,* at 79. And no one knows how many of those who were not admitted because of their test scores would in fact have done well were they given the chance. There are many relevant factors, such as motivation, cultural backgrounds of specific minorities that the test cannot measure, and they inevitably must

impair its value as a predictor.[11] Of course, the law school that admits only those with the highest test scores finds that on the average they do much better, and thus the test is a convenient tool for the admissions committee. The price is paid by the able student who for unknown reasons did not achieve that high score—perhaps even the minority with a different cultural background. Some tests, at least in the past, have been aimed at eliminating Jews.

The school can safely conclude that the applicant with a score of 750 should be admitted before one with a score of 500. The problem is that in many cases the choice will be between 643 and 602 or 574 and 528. The numbers create an illusion of difference tending to overwhelm other factors. "The wiser testers are well aware of the defects of the multiple-choice format and the danger of placing reliance on any one method of assessment to the exclusion of all others. What is distressing is how little their caveats have impressed the people who succumb to the propaganda of the test-makers and use these tests mechanically as though they were a valid substitute for judgment." Hoffmann, *supra.* at 215.

Of course, the tests are not the only thing considered; here they were combined with the prelaw grades to produce a new number called the Average. The grades have their own problems; one school's A is another school's C. And even to the extent that this formula predicts law school grades, its value is limited. The law student with lower grades may in the long pull of a legal career surpass those at the top of the class. "[L]aw school admissions criteria have operated within a hermetically sealed system; it is now beginning to leak. The traditional combination of LSAT and GPA [undergraduate grade point average] may have provided acceptable predictors of likely performance in law school in the past. . . . [But] [t]here is no clear evidence that the LSAT and GPA provide particularly good evaluators of the intrinsic or enriched ability of an individual to perform as a law student or lawyer in a functioning society undergoing change. Nor is there any clear evidence that grades and other evaluators of law school performance, and the bar examination, are particularly good predicators of competence or success as a lawyer." Rosen, Equalizing Access to Legal Education: Special Programs for Law Students Who Are Not Admissible by Traditional Criteria, 1970 U. Tol. L. Rev. 321, 332–333.

But, by whatever techniques, the law school must make choices. Neither party has challenged the validity of the Average employed here as an admissions tool, and therefore consideration of its possible deficiencies is not presented as an issue. The Law School presented no evidence to show that adjustments in the process employed were used in order validly to compare applicants of different races; instead, it chose to avoid making such comparisons. Finally, although the Committee did consider other information in the files of all applicants, the Law School has made no effort to show that it was because of these additional factors that it admitted minority applicants who would otherwise have been rejected. To the contrary, the school appears to have conceded that by its own assessment—taking all factors into account—it admitted minority applicants who would have been rejected had they been white. We have no choice but to evaluate the Law School's case as it has been made.

III

The Equal Protection Clause did not enact a requirement that Law Schools employ as the sole criterion for admissions a formula based upon the LSAT and undergraduate grades, nor does it prohibit law schools from evaluating an applicant's prior achievements in light of the barriers that he had to overcome. A Black applicant who pulled himself out of the ghetto into a junior college may thereby demonstrate a level of motivation, perseverance and ability that would lead a fairminded admissions committee to conclude that he shows more promise for law study than the son of a rich alumnus who achieved better grades at Harvard. That applicant would not be offered admission because he is Black, but because as an individual he has shown he has the potential, while the Harvard man may have taken less advantage of the vastly superior opportunities offered him. Because of the weight of the prior handicaps, that Black applicant may not realize his full potential in the first year of law school, or even in the full three years, but in the long pull of a legal career his achievements may far outstrip those of his classmates whose earlier records appeared superior by conventional criteria. There is currently no test available to the Admissions Committee that can predict such possibilities with assurance, but the Committee may nevertheless seek to gauge it as best it can, and weigh this factor in its decisions. Such a policy would not be limited to Blacks, or Chicanos or Filipinos, or American Indians, although undoubtedly groups such as these may in practice be the principal beneficiaries of it. But a poor Appalachian white, or a second generation Chinese in San Francisco, or some other American whose lineage is so diverse as to defy ethnic labels, may demonstrate similar potential and thus be accorded favorable consideration by the committee.

The difference between such a policy and the one presented by this case is that the Committee would be making decisions on the basis of individual attributes, rather than according a preference solely on the basis of race. To be sure, the racial preference here was not absolute—the Committee did not admit all applicants from the four favored groups. But it did accord all such applicants a preference by applying, to an extent not precisely ascertainable from the record, different standards by which to judge their applications, with the result that the Committee admitted minority applicants who, in the school's own judgment, were less promising than other applicants who were rejected. Furthermore, it is apparent that because the Admissions Committee compared minority applicants only with one another, it was necessary to reserve some proportion of the class for them, even if at the outset a precise number of places were not set aside.[12] That proportion, apparently 15% to 20%, was chosen because the school determined it to be "reasonable," [13] although no explanation is provided as to how that number rather than some other was found appropriate. Without becoming embroiled in a semantic debate over whether this practice constitutes a "quota," it is clear that, given the limitation on the total number of applicants who could be accepted, this policy did reduce the total number of places for which DeFunis could compete—solely on account of his race. Thus, as the Washington Supreme Court concluded, whatever label one wishes to apply to it, "the minority admissions policy is certainly not benign with respect to nonminority students who are displaced by it." 82 Wash. 2d, at 32, 507 P. 2d, at 1182. A finding that the state school employed a racial classification in selecting its students subjects it to the strictest scrutiny under the Equal Protection Clause.

The consideration of race as a measure of an applicant's qualification normally introduces a capricious and irrelevant factor working an invidious discrimination, *Anderson* v. *Martin*, 375 U. S. 399, 402; *Loving* v. *Virginia*, 388 U.S. 1, 10; *Harper* v. *Virginia Board of Elections*, 383 U.S. 663, 668. Once race is a starting point educators and courts are immediately embroiled in competing claims of different racial and ethnic groups that would make difficult, manageable standards consistent with the Equal Protection Clause. "The clear and central purpose of the Fourteenth Amendment was to eliminate all official state sources of invidious racial discrimination in the States." *Loving, supra,* at 10. The Law School's admissions policy cannot be reconciled with that purpose, unless cultural standards of a diverse rather than a homogeneous society are taken into account. The reason is that professional persons, particularly lawyers, are not selected for life in a computerized society. The Indian who walks to the beat of Chief Seattle of the Muckleshoot Tribe in Washington [14] has a different culture from examiners at law schools.

The key to the problem is the consideration of each application *in a racially neutral way*. Since LSAT reflects questions touching on cultural backgrounds, the

Admissions Committee acted properly in my view in setting minority applications apart for separate processing. These minorities have cultural backgrounds that are vastly different from the dominant Caucasian. Many Eskimos, American Indians, Filipinos, Chicanos, Asian Indians, Burmese, and Africans come from such disparate backgrounds that a test sensitively tuned for most applicants would be wide of the mark for many minorities.

The melting pot is not designed to homogenize people, making them uniform in consistency. The melting pot as I understand it is a figure of speech that depicts the wide diversities tolerated by the First Amendment under one flag. See 2 S. Morison & H. Commager, The Growth of the American Republic, c. VIII (4th ed. 1950). Minorities in our midst who are to serve actively in our public affairs should be chosen on talent and character alone, not on cultural orientation or leanings.

I do know, coming as I do from Indian country in Washington, that many of the young Indians know little about Adam Smith or Karl Marx but are deeply imbued with the spirit and philosophy of Chief Robert B. Jim of the Yakimas, Chief Seattle of the Muckleshoots, and Chief Joseph of the Nez Perce which offer competitive attitudes towards life, fellow man, and nature.[15]

I do not know the extent to which Blacks in this country are imbued with ideas of African Socialism.[16] Leopold Senghor and Sékou Touré, most articulate of African leaders, have held that modern African political philosophy is not oriented either to Marxism or to capitalism.[17] How far the reintroduction into educational curricula of ancient African art and history has reached the minds of young Afro-Americans I do not know. But at least as respects Indians, Blacks, and Chicanos—as well as those from Asian cultures—I think a separate classification of these applicants is warranted, lest race be a subtle force in eliminating minority members because of cultural differences.

Insofar as LSAT tests reflect the dimensions and orientation of the Organization Man they do a disservice to minorities. I personally know that admissions tests were once used to eliminate Jews. How many other minorities they aim at I do not know. My reaction is that the presence of an LSAT test is sufficient warrant for a school to put racial minorities into a separate class in order better to probe their capacities and potentials.

The merits of the present controversy cannot in my view be resolved on this record. A trial would involve the disclosure of hidden prejudices, if any, against certain minorities and the manner in which substitute measurements of one's talents and character were employed in the conventional tests. I could agree with the majority of the Washington Supreme Court only if, on the record, it could be said that the Law School's selection was racially neutral. The case, in my view, should be remanded for a new trial to consider, *inter alia,* whether the established LSAT tests should be eliminated so far as racial minorities are concerned.

This does not mean that a separate LSAT test must be designed for minority racial groups, although that might be a possibility. The reason for the separate treatment of minorities as a class is to make more certain that racial factors do not militate *against an applicant or on his behalf.*[18]

There is no constitutional right for any race to be preferred. The years of slavery did more than retard the progress of Blacks. Even a greater wrong was done the whites by creating arrogance instead of humility and by encouraging the growth of the fiction of a superior race. There is no superior person by constitutional standards. A DeFunis who is white is entitled to no advantage by reason of that fact; nor is he subject to any disability, no matter what his race or color. Whatever his race, he had a constitutional right to have his application considered on its individual merits in a racially neutral manner.

The slate is not entirely clean. First, we have held that *pro rata* representation of the races is not required either on juries, see *Cassell* v. *Texas,* 339 U.S. 282, 286–287, or in public schools, *Swann* v. *Charlotte-Mecklenburg Board of Education,* 402 U.S. 1, 24. Moreover, in *Hughes* v. *Superior Court,* 339 U.S. 460, we reviewed the contempt convictions of pickets who sought by their demonstration to force an employer to prefer Negroes to whites in his hiring of clerks, in order to ensure that 50% of the employees were Negro. In finding that California could constitutionally enjoin the picketing there involved we quoted from the opinion of the California Supreme Court, which noted that the pickets would " 'make the right to work for Lucky dependent not on fitness for the work nor on an equal right of all, regardless of race, to compete in an open market, but, rather, on membership in a particular race. If petitioners were upheld in their demand then other races, white, yellow, brown and red, would have equal rights to demand discriminatory hiring on a racial basis.' " *Id.,* at 463–464. We then noted that

"[t]o deny to California the right to ban picketing in the circumstances of this case would mean that there could be no prohibition of picketing to secure proportional employment on ancestral grounds of Hungarians in Cleveland, of Poles in Buffalo, of Germans in Milwaukee, of Portuguese in New Bedford, of Mexicans in San Antonio, of the numerous minority groups in New York, and so on through the whole gamut of racial and religious concentrations in various cities." *Id.,* at 464.

The reservation of a proportion of the law school class for members of selected minority groups is fraught with similar dangers, for one must immediately determine which groups are to receive such favored treatment and which are to be excluded, the proportions of the class that are to be allocated to each, and even the criteria by which to determine whether an individual is a member of a favored group. There is no assurance that a common agreement can be reached, and first the schools, and then the courts, will be buffeted with the competing claims. The University of Washington included Filipinos, but excluded Chinese and Japanese; another school may limit its program to Blacks, or to Blacks and Chicanos. Once the Court sanctioned racial preferences such as these, it could not then wash its hands of the matter, leaving it entirely in the discretion of the school, for then we would have effectively overruled *Sweatt* v. *Painter,* 339 U.S. 629, and allowed imposition of a "zero" allocation.[19] But what standard is the Court to apply when a rejected applicant of Japanese ancestry brings suit to require the University of Washington to extend the same privileges to his group? The Committee might conclude that the population of Washington is now 2% Japanese, and that Japanese also constitute 2% of the Bar, but that had they not been handicapped by a history of discrimination, Japanese would now constitute 5% of the Bar, or 20%. Or, alternatively, the Court could attempt to assess how grievously each group has suffered from discrimination, and allocate proportions accordingly; if that were the standard the current University of Washington policy would almost surely fall, for there is no Western State which can claim that it has always treated Japanese and Chinese in a fair and even-handed manner. See, *e. g., Yick Wo* v. *Hopkins,* 118 U.S. 356; *Terrace* v. *Thompson,* 263 U.S. 197; *Oyama* v. *California,* 332 U.S. 633. This Court has not sustained a racial classification since the wartime cases of *Korematsu* v. *United States,* 323 U.S. 214 (1944), and *Hirabayashi* v. *United States,* 320 U.S. 81 (1943), involving curfews and relocations imposed upon Japanese-Americans.[20]

Nor obviously will the problem be solved if next year the Law School included only Japanese and Chinese, for then Norwegians and Swedes, Poles and Italians, Puerto Ricans and Hungarians, and all other groups which form this diverse Nation would have just complaints.

The key to the problem is consideration of such applications *in a racially neutral way.* Abolition of the LSAT would be a start. The invention of substitute tests might be made to get a measure of an applicant's cultural background, perception, ability to analyze, and his or her relation to groups. They are highly subjective, but unlike the LSAT they are not concealed, but in the open. A law school is not bound by any legal principle to admit students by mechanical criteria which are insensitive to the potential of such an applicant which may be realized in a more hospita-

ble environment. It will be necessary under such an approach to put more effort into assessing each individual than is required when LSAT scores and undergraduate grades dominate the selection process. Interviews with the applicant and others who know him is a time-honored test. Some schools currently run summer programs in which potential students who likely would be bypassed under conventional admissions criteria are given the opportunity to try their hand at law courses,[21] and certainly their performance in such programs could be weighed heavily. There is, moreover, no bar to considering an individual's prior achievements in light of the racial discrimination that barred his way, as a factor in attempting to assess his true potential for a successful legal career. Nor is there any bar to considering on an individual basis, rather than according to racial classifications, the likelihood that a particular candidate will more likely employ his legal skills to service communities that are not now adequately represented than will competing candidates. Not every student benefited by such an expanded admissions program would fall into one of the four racial groups involved here, but it is no drawback that other deserving applicants will also get an opportunity they would otherwise have been denied. Certainly such a program would substantially fulfill the Law School's interest in giving a more diverse group access to the legal profession. Such a program might be less convenient administratively than simply sorting students by race, but we have never held administrative convenience to justify racial discrimination.

The argument is that a "compelling" state interest can easily justify the racial discrimination that is practiced here. To many, "compelling" would give members of one race even more than *pro rata* representation. The public payrolls might then be deluged say with Chicanos because they are as a group the poorest of the poor and need work more than others, leaving desperately poor individual Blacks and whites without employment. By the same token large quotas of blacks or browns could be added to the Bar, waiving examinations required of other groups, so that it would be better racially balanced.[22] The State, however, may not proceed by racial classification to force strict population equivalencies for every group in every occupation, overriding individual preferences. The Equal Protection Clause commands the elimination of racial barriers, not their creation in order to satisfy our theory as to how society ought to be organized. The purpose of the University of Washington cannot be to produce Black lawyers for Blacks, Polish lawyers for Poles, Jewish lawyers for Jews, Irish lawyers for Irish. It should be to produce good lawyers for Americans and not to place First Amendment barriers against anyone.[23] That is the point at the heart of all our school desegregation cases, from *Brown* v. *Board of Educa-*

tion, 347 U.S. 483, through *Swann* v. *Charlotte-Meck-lenburg Board of Education*, 402 U.S. 1. A segregated admissions process creates suggestions of stigma and caste no less than a segregated classroom, and in the end it may produce that result despite its contrary intentions. One other assumption must be clearly disapproved, that Blacks or Browns cannot make it on their individual merit. That is a stamp of inferiority that a State is not permitted to place on any lawyer.

If discrimination based on race is constitutionally permissible when those who hold the reins can come up with "compelling" reasons to justify it, then constitutional guarantees acquire an accordionlike quality. Speech is closely brigaded with action when it triggers a fight, *Chaplinsky* v. *New Hampshire*, 315 U.S. 568, as shouting "fire" in a crowded theater triggers a riot. It may well be that racial strains, racial susceptibility to certain disease, racial sensitiveness to environmental conditions that other races do not experience, may in an extreme situation justify differences in racial treatment that no fairminded person would call "invidious" discrimination. Mental ability is not in that category. All races can compete fairly at all professional levels. So far as race is concerned, any state-sponsored preference to one race over another in that competition is in my view "invidious" and violative of the Equal Protection Clause.

The problem tendered by this case is important and crucial to the operation of our constitutional system; and educators must be given leeway. It may well be that a whole congeries of applicants in the marginal group defy known methods of selection. Conceivably, an admissions committee might conclude that a selection by lot of, say, the last 20 seats is the only fair solution. Courts are not educators; their expertise is limited; and our task ends with the inquiry whether, judged by the main purpose of the Equal Protection Clause—the protection against racial discrimination [24]—there has been an "invidious" discrimination.

We would have a different case if the suit were one to displace the applicant who was chosen in lieu of DeFunis. What the record would show concerning his potentials would have to be considered and weighed. The educational decision, provided proper guidelines were used, would reflect an expertise that courts should honor. The problem is not tendered here because the physical facilities were apparently adequate to take DeFunis in addition to the others. My view is only that I cannot say by the tests used and applied he was invidiously discriminated against because of his race.

I cannot conclude that the admissions procedure of the Law School of the University of Washington that excluded DeFunis is violative of the Equal Protection Clause of the Fourteenth Amendment. The judgment of the Washington Supreme Court should be vacated and the case remanded for a new trial.

APPENDIX TO OPINION OF DOUGLAS, J., DISSENTING

The following are excerpts from the Law School's current admissions policy, as provided to the Court by counsel for the respondents.

ADMISSIONS

A. Policy Statement Regarding Admission to Entering Classes of Juris Doctor Program—Adopted by the Law Faculty December 4, 1973.

§ 1. The objectives of the admissions program are to select and admit those applicants who have the best prospect of high quality academic work at the law school and, in the minority admissions program described below, the further objective there stated.

§ 2. In measuring academic potential the law school relies primarily on the undergraduate grade-point average and the performance on the Law School Admission Test (LSAT). The weighting of these two indicators is determined statistically by reference to past experience at this school. For most applicants the resulting applicant ranking is the most nearly accurate of all available measures of relative academic potential. In truly exceptional cases, *i. e.,* those in which the numerical indicators clearly appear to be an inaccurate measure of academic potential, the admission decision indicated by them alone may be altered by a consideration of the factors listed below. The number of these truly exceptional cases in any particular year should fall somewhere from zero to approximately forty. These factors are used, however, only as an aid in assessing the applicant's academic potential in its totality, without undue emphasis or reliance upon one or a few and without an attempt to quantify in advance the strength of their application, singly or as a whole, in a particular case. They are:

a) the difficulty or ease of the undergraduate curriculum track pursued;

b) the demanding or non-demanding quality of the undergraduate school or department;

c) the attainment of an advanced degree, the nature thereof, and difficulty or ease of its attainment;

d) the applicant's pursuits subsequent to attainment of the undergraduate degree and the degree of success therein, as bearing on the applicant's academic potential;

e) the possibility that an applicant many years away from academic work may do less well on the LSAT than his or her counterpart presently or recently in academic work;

f) substantial change in mental or physical health that indicates prospect for either higher or lower quality of academic work;

g) substantial change in economic pressures or other circumstances that indicates prospect for either higher or lower quality of academic work;

h) exceptionally good or bad performance upon the writing test ingredient of the LSAT, if the current year's weighting of the numerical indicators does not otherwise take the writing score into account;

i) the quality and strength of recommendations bearing upon the applicant's academic potential;

j) objective indicators of motivation to succeed at the academic study of law;

k) variations in the level of academic achievement over time; and

l) any other indicators that serve the objective stated above.

.   .   .   .   .

§ 6. Because certain ethnic groups in our society have historically been limited in their access to the legal profession and because the resulting underrepresentation can affect the quality of legal services available to members of such groups, as well as limit their opportunity for full participation in the governance of our communities, the faculty recognizes a special obligation in its admissions policy to contribute to the solution of the problem.

Qualified minority applicants are therefore admitted under the minority admissions program in such number that the entering class will have a reasonable proportion of minority persons, in view of the obligation stated above and of the overall objective of the law school to provide legal education for qualified persons generally. For the purpose of determining the number to be specially admitted under the program, and not as a ceiling on minority admissions generally, the faculty currently believes that approximately 15 to 20 percent is such a reasonable proportion if there are sufficient qualified applicants available. Under the minority admissions program, admission is offered to those applicants who have a reasonable prospect of academic success at the law school, determined in each case by considering the numerical indicators along with the listed factors in Section 2, above, but without regard to the restriction upon number contained in that section.

No particular internal percentage or proportion among various minority groups in the entering class is specified; rather, the law school strives for a reasonable internal balance given the particular makeup of each year's applicant population.

As to some or all ethnic groups within the scope of the minority admissions program, it may be appropriate to give a preference in some degree to residents of the state; that determination is made each year in view of all the particulars of that year's situation, and the preference is given when necessary to meet some substantial local need for minority representation.

NOTES

1. The grades are calculated on a conventional 4.0 scale, and the LSAT is scored on a scale ranging from 200 to 800. A Writing Test given on the same day as the LSAT and administered with it is also included in the formula; it is scored on a scale of 20 to 80. The Admissions Committee combines these scores into the Average by calculating the sum of 51.3, 3.4751 X the grade-point average, .0159 X LSAT score, and .0456 X the Writing Test score. App. 24. For a brief discussion of the use of the LSAT in combination with undergraduate grades to predict law school success, see Winterbottom, Comments on "A Study of the Criteria for Legal Education and Admission to the Bar," An Article by Dr. Thomas M. Goolsby, Jr., 21 J. Legal Ed. 75 (1968).

2. The only other substantial group admitted at this point were 19 "military" applicants. These were students who had previously been admitted to the school but who had either been unable to come, or forced to leave during their tenure, because of the draft. They were given preferential treatment upon reapplication after completing their military obligation. Since neither party has raised any issue concerning this group of applicants, the remaining consideration of the admissions procedure will not discuss them. Four minority applicants were also admitted at this time, although none apparently had scores above 77. App. 31. Their admission was presumably pursuant to the procedure for minority applicants described below.

3. This was a Council on Legal Education Opportunities program, federally funded by the Office of Economic Opportunity and sponsored by the American Bar Association, the Association of American Law Schools, the National Bar Association, and the Law School Admissions Council.

4. Testimony of the Chairman of the Admissions Committee, Statement of Facts 353.

5. The Guide to Applicants explained:

"We gauged the potential for outstanding performance in law school not only from the existence of high test scores and grade point averages, but also from careful analysis of recommendations, the quality of work in difficult analytical seminars, courses, and writing programs, the academic standards of the school attended by the applicant, the applicant's graduate work (if any), and the nature of the applicant's employment (if any), since graduation.

"An applicant's ability to make significant contributions to law school classes and the community at large was assessed from such factors and his extracurricular and community activities, employment, and general background.

"We gave no preference to, but did not discriminate against, either Washington residents or women in making our determinations. An applicant's racial or ethnic background was considered as one factor in our general attempt to convert formal credentials into realistic predictions." 82 Wash. 2d 11, 18–19, 507 P. 2d 1169, 1174.

6. The respondents provided the following table in response to an interrogatory during the proceedings in the state court:

Predicted First Year Averages	Number of Applications Received	Number Accepted
81	1	1
80	2	2
79	11	11
78	42	42
77	105	93
76	169	53
75	210	22

App. 34.

7. Although there is apparently no evidence in point in the record, respondents suggest that at least some of these eight students were also admitted on a preferential basis. Brief for Respondents 40 n. 27.

8. United States Bureau of the Census, Census of Population: 1970, General Population Characteristics, Washington, Final Report PC (1)—B49, Table 18.

9. For a history of gradual acceptance among law schools of standardized tests as an admission tool, see Ramsey, Law School Admissions: Science, Art, or Hunch?, 12 J. Legal Ed. 503 (1960).

10. For a survey of the use of the LSAT by American law schools as of 1965, see Lunneborg & Radford, The LSAT: A Survey of Actual Practice, 18 J. Legal Ed. 313 (1966).

11. Rock, Motivation, Moderators, and Test Bias, 1970 U. Tol. L. Rev. 527, 535.

12. At the outset the Committee may have chosen only a range, with the precise number to be determined later in the process as the total number of minority applicants, and some tentative assessment of their quality, could be determined. This appears to be the current articulated policy, see Appendix § 6, and we are advised by the respondents that § 6 "represents a more formal statement of the policy which was in effect in 1971 . . . but does not represent any change in policy." Letter to the Court dated March 19, 1974, p. 1. The fact that the Committee did not set a precise number in advance is obviously irrelevant to the legal analysis. Nor does it matter that there is some minimal level of achievement below which the Committee would not reach in order to achieve its stated goal as to the proportion of the class reserved for minority groups, so long as the Committee was willing, in order to achieve that goal, to admit minority applicants who, in the Committee's own judgment, were less qualified than other rejected applicants and who would not otherwise have been admitted.

13. See n. 12, *supra,* and Appendix § 6.

14. Uncommon Controversy, Report Prepared for American Friends Service Committee 29–30 (1970).

15. See C. Fee, Chief Joseph, The Biography of a Great Indian (1936).

16. See F. Brockway, African Socialism (1963); African Socialism (W. Friedland & C. Rosberg ed. 1964).

17. See L. Senghor, On African Socialism (M. Cook ed. 1964).

18. We are not faced here with a situation where barriers are overtly or covertly put in the path of members of one racial group which are not required by others. There was also no showing that the purpose of the school's policy was to eliminate arbitrary and irrelevant barriers to entry by certain racial groups into the legal profession groups. *Griggs* v. *Duke Power Co.,* 401 U.S. 424. In *Swann* v. *Charlotte-Mecklenburg Board of Education,* 402 U.S. 1, 16, we stated that as a matter of educational policy school authorities could, within their broad discretion, specify that each school within its district have a prescribed ratio of Negro to white students reflecting the proportion for the district as a whole, in order to disestablish a dual school system. But there is a crucial difference between the policy suggested in *Swann* and that under consideration here: the *Swann* policy would impinge on no person's constitutional rights, because no one would be excluded from a public school and no one has a right to attend a segregated public school.

19. *Sweatt* held that a State could not justify denying a black admission to its regular law school by creating a new law school for blacks. We held that the new law school did not meet the requirements of "equality" set forth in *Plessy* v. *Ferguson,* 163 U.S. 537.

The student, we said, was entitled to "legal education equivalent to that offered by the State to students of other races. Such education is not available to him in a separate law school as offered by the State." 339 U.S. 629, 635.

20. Those cases involved an exercise of the war power, a great leveler of other rights. Our Navy was sunk at Pearl Harbor and no one knew where the Japanese fleet was. We were advised on oral argument that if the Japanese landed troops on our west coast nothing could stop them west of the Rockies. The military judgment was that, to aid in the prospective defense of the west coast, the enclaves of Americans of Japanese ancestry should be moved inland, lest the invaders by donning civilian clothes would wreak even more serious havoc on our western ports. The decisions were extreme and went to the verge of wartime power; and they have been severely criticized. It is, however, easy in retrospect to denounce what was done, as there actually was no attempted Japanese invasion of our country. While our Joint Chiefs of Staff were worrying about Japanese soldiers landing on the west coast, they actually were landing in Burma and at Kota Bharu in Malaya. But those making plans for defense of the Nation had no such knowledge and were planning for the worst. Moreover, the day we decided *Korematsu* we also decided *Ex parte Endo,* 323 U.S. 283, holding that while evacuation of the Americans of Japanese ancestry was allowable under extreme war conditions, their detention after evacuation was not. We said:

"A citizen who is concededly loyal presents no problem of espionage or sabotage. Loyalty is a matter of the heart and mind, not of race, creed, or color. He who is loyal is by definition not a spy or a saboteur. When the power to detain is derived from the power to protect the war effort against espionage and sabotage, detention which has no relationship to that objective is unauthorized." *Id.,* at 302.

21. See n. 3, *supra.*

22. In *Johnson* v. *Committee on Examinations,* 407 U.S. 915, we denied certiorari in a case presenting a similar issue. There the petitioner claimed that the bar examiners reconsidered the papers submitted by failing minority applicants whose scores were close to the cutoff point, with the result that some minority applicants were admitted to the Bar although they initially had examination scores lower than those of white applicants who failed.

As the Arizona Supreme Court denied Johnson admission summarily, in an original proceeding, there were no judicial findings either sustaining or rejecting his factual claims of racial bias, putting the case in an awkward posture for review here. Johnson subsequently brought a civil rights action in Federal District Court, seeking both damages and injunctive relief. The District Court dismissed the action and the Court of Appeals affirmed, holding that the lower federal courts did not have jurisdiction to review the decisions of the Arizona Supreme Court on admissions to the state bar. Johnson then sought review here and we denied his motion for leave to file a petition for mandamus, prohibition and/or certiorari on February 19, 1974. *Johnson* v. *Wilmer,* 415 U.S. 911. Thus in the entire history of the case no court had ever actually sustained Johnson's factual contentions concerning racial bias in the bar examiners' procedures. *DeFunis* thus appears to be the first case here squarely presenting the problem.

23. Underlying all cultural background tests are potential ideological issues that have plagued bar associations and the courts. *In re Summers,* 325 U.S. 561, involved the denial of the practice of law to a man who could not conscientiously bear arms. The vote against him was five to four. *Konigsberg* v. *State Bar,* 353 U.S. 252, followed, after remand, by *Konigsberg* v. *State Bar,* 366 U.S. 36, resulted in barring one from admission to a state bar because of his refusal to answer questions concerning Communist Party membership. He, too, was excluded five to four. The petitioner in *Schware* v. *Board of Bar Examiners,* 353 U.S. 232, was, however, admitted to

practice even though he had about 10 years earlier been a member of the Communist Party. But in *In re Anastaplo*, 366 U.S. 82, a five-to-four decision, barred a man from admission to a state bar not because he invoked the Fifth Amendment when asked about membership in the Communist Party, but because he asserted that the First Amendment protected him

from that inquiry. *Baird* v. *State Bar of Arizona*, 401 U.S. 1, held by a divided vote that a person could not be kept out of the state bar for refusing to answer whether he had ever been a member of the Communist Party; and see *In re Stolar*, 401 U.S. 23.

24. See *Slaughter House Cases*, 16 Wall. 36, 81.

R O N A L D M . D W O R K I N

The DeFunis Case: The Right to Go to Law School *

I

In 1945 a black man named Sweatt applied to the University of Texas Law School, but was refused admission because state law provided that only whites could attend. The Supreme Court declared that this law violated Sweatt's rights under the Fourteenth Amendment to the United States Constitution, which provides that no state shall deny any man the equal protection of its laws.[1] In 1970 a Jew named DeFunis applied to the University of Washington Law School; he was rejected although his test scores and college grades were such that he would have been admitted if he were black or Filipino or a Chicano or an American Indan. DeFunis asked the Supreme Court to declare that the Washington practice, which offered less exacting standards to minority groups, violated his rights under the Fourteenth Amendment as well.[2]

The Washington admissions procedures were complex. Applications were divided into two groups. The majority—those not from the designated minority groups—were first screened so as to eliminate all applicants whose predicted average, which is a function of college grades and aptitude test scores, fell below a certain level. Majority applicants who survived this initial cut were then placed in categories that received

progressively more careful consideration. Minority group applications, on the other hand, were not screened, but all received the most careful consideration by a special committee consisting of a black law professor and a white professor who had taught in programs to aid black law students. Most of the minority applicants who were accepted in the year in which DeFunis was rejected had predicted averages below the cut-off level, and the law school conceded that any minority applicant with his average would certainly have been accepted.

The DeFunis case split those political action groups that have traditionally supported liberal causes, as Ann Fagan Ginger's useful collection shows. The B'nai B'rith Anti-Defamation League and the AFL-CIO, for example, filed briefs as *amici curiae* in support of DeFunis's claim, while the American Hebrew Women's Council, the UAW, and the UMWA filed briefs against it.

These splits among old allies demonstrate both the practical and the philosophical importance of the case. In the past liberals held, within one set of attitudes, three propositions: that racial classification is an evil in itself; that every person has a right to an educational opportunity commensurate with his abilities; and that affirmative state action is proper to remedy the serious inequalities of American society. In the last decade, however, the opinion has grown that these three liberal propositions are in fact not compatible, because the most effective programs of state action are

* From *The New York Review of Books*, February 5, 1976. Reprinted with permission from *The New York Review of Books*. Copyright © 1968, 1976 Nyrev, Inc. Also by permission of the author.

those that give a competitive advantage to minority racial groups.

That opinion has, of course, been challenged. Some educators argue that benign quotas are ineffective, even self-defeating, because preferential treatment will reinforce the sense of inferiority that many blacks already have. Others make a more general objection. They argue that any racial discrimination, even for the purpose of benefiting minorities, will in fact harm those minorities, because prejudice is fostered whenever racial distinctions are tolerated for any purpose whatever. But these are complex and controversial empirical judgments, and it is far too early, as wise critics concede, to decide whether preferential treatment does more harm or good. Nor is it the business of judges, particularly in constitutional cases, to overthrow decisions of other officials because the judges disagree about the efficiency of social policies. This empirical criticism is therefore reinforced by the moral argument that even if reverse discrimination does benefit minorities, and does reduce prejudice in the long run, it is nevertheless wrong because distinctions of race are inherently unjust. They are unjust because they violate the rights of individual members of groups not so favored, who may thereby lose a place as DeFunis did.

DeFunis presented this moral argument, in the form of a constitutional claim, to the courts. The Supreme Court did not, in the end, decide whether the argument was good or bad. DeFunis had in fact been admitted to the law school after one lower court had decided in his favor, and the law school said that he would be allowed to graduate however the case was finally decided. The Court therefore held that the case was moot and dismissed the appeal on that ground. But Mr. Justice Douglas disagreed with this neutral disposition of the case: he wrote a dissenting opinion in which he argued that the Court should have upheld DeFunis's claim on the merits.

Many universities and colleges have taken Justice Douglas's opinion as handwriting on the wall, and have changed their practices, in anticipation of a later Court decision in which his opinion prevails. In fact, his opinion pointed out that law schools might achieve much the same result as the University of Washington admissions procedures by using a more sophisticated policy. A school might stipulate, for example, that applicants from all races and groups would be considered together, but that certain minority applicants' aptitude tests would be graded differently, or given less weight in overall predicted average, because experience had shown that standard examinations were for different reasons a poorer test of the actual ability of these applicants. But if this technique is used deliberately to achieve the same result, it is devious, and it remains to ask why the candid program the University of Washington used was either unjust or unconstitutional.

II

DeFunis plainly has no constitutional right that the state provide him a legal education of a certain quality. His rights would not be violated if his state did not have a law school at all, or if it had a law school with so few places that he could not win one on intellectual merit. Nor does he have a right to insist that intelligence be the exclusive test of admission. Law schools do rely heavily on intellectual tests for admission. That seems proper, however, not because applicants have a right to be judged in that way, but because it is reasonable to think that the community as a whole is better off if its lawyers are more intelligent. Intellectual standards are justified, that is, not because they reward the clever, but because they seem to serve a useful social policy.

Law schools sometimes serve such policy better, moreover, by supplementing intelligence tests with other sorts of standards: they sometimes prefer industrious applicants, for example, to those who are brighter but lazier. They also serve special policies for which intelligence is not relevant. The University of Washington law school, for example, gave special preference not only to the minority applicants but to veterans who had been at the school before going to war; neither DeFunis, nor any of the briefs submitted in his behalf, complained of that preference.

DeFunis does not have an absolute right to a law school place, or a right that only intelligence be used as a standard for admission. He says he nevertheless has a right that race *not* be used as a standard, no matter how well a racial classification might work to promote the general welfare or to reduce social and economic inequality. He does not claim, however, that he has this right as a distinct and independent political right that is protected by the Constitution specifically, like his right to freedom of speech and religion. The Constitution does not condemn racial classification directly, as it does condemn censorship or the establishment of a religion. DeFunis claims that his right that race not be used as a criterion of admission follows from the more abstract right of equality that is protected by the Fourteenth Amendment, which provides that no state shall deny to any person the equal protection of the law.

But the legal arguments made on both sides show that neither the text of the Constitution nor the prior decisions of the Supreme Court decisively settle the question whether, as a matter of law, the equal protection clause makes all racial classifications unconstitutional. The clause makes the concept of equality a test of legislation, but it does not stipulate any particular conception of that concept.[3] Those who wrote the clause intended to attack certain consequences of slavery and racial prejudice, but it is unlikely that they intended to outlaw all racial classifications, or that they expected that this would be the result of what they wrote. They outlawed whatever policies would violate equality, but left it to others to decide, from time to time, what that means. There cannot be a good legal argument in favor of DeFunis, therefore, unless there is a good moral argument that all racial classifications, even those that make society as a whole more equal, are inherently offensive to an individual's right to equal protection for himself.

There is nothing paradoxical, of course, in the idea that an individual's right to equal protection may sometimes conflict with an otherwise desirable social policy, including the policy of making the community more nearly equal overall. Suppose a law school were to charge a few middle-class students, selected by lot, double tuition in order to increase the scholarship fund for poor students. It would be serving a desirable policy—equality of opportunity—by means that violated the right of the students selected by lot to be treated equally with other students who could also afford the increased fees. It is, in fact, part of the importance of DeFunis's case that it forces us to acknowledge the distinction between equality as a policy and equality as a right, a distinction that political theory has virtually ignored. He

argues that the University of Washington violated his individual right to equality for the sake of a policy of greater equality overall, in the same way that double tuition for arbitrarily chosen students would violate their rights for the same purpose.

We must therefore concentrate our attention on that claim. We must try to define the central concept on which it turns, which is the concept of an individual right to equality made a constitutional right by the equal protection clause. What rights to equality do citizens have as individuals which might defeat programs aimed at important economic and social policies, including the social policy of improving equality overall?

There are two different sorts of rights they may be said to have. The first is the right to *equal treatment,* which is the right to an equal distribution of some opportunity or resource or burden. Every person, for example, has a right to an equal vote in a democracy: that is the nerve of the Supreme Court's decision that one man must have one vote even if a different and more complex arrangement would better secure the collective welfare. The second is the right to *treatment as an equal,* which is the right, not to receive the same distribution of some burden or benefit, but to be treated with the same respect and concern as anyone else. If I have two children, and one is dying from a disease that is making the other uncomfortable, I do not show equal concern if I flip a coin to decide which should have the remaining dose of a drug. This example shows that the right to treatment as an equal is fundamental, and the right to equal treatment derivative. In some circumstances the right to treatment as an equal will entail a right to equal treatment, but not, by any means, in all circumstances.

DeFunis does not have a right to equal treatment in the assignment of law school places; he does not have a right to a place just because others are given places. Individuals may have a right to equal treatment in elementary education, because someone who is denied elementary education is unlikely to lead a useful life. But legal education is not so vital that everyone has an equal right to be admitted.

DeFunis does have the second sort of right, that is, a right to treatment as an equal in the decision over which admissions standards should be used. He has a right that his interests be treated as fully and sympathetically as the interests of any others when the law school decides whether to count race as a pertinent criterion for admission. But we must be careful not to overstate what that means.

Suppose an applicant complains that his right to be treated as an equal is violated by tests that place the less intelligent candidates at a disadvantage against the more intelligent. A law school might properly reply in the following way. *Any* standard will place certain candidates at a disadvantage as against others; but an admissions policy may nevertheless be justified if it seems reasonable to expect that the overall gain to the community exceeds the overall loss, and if no other policy that does not provide a comparable disadvantage would produce even roughly the same gain. An individual's right to be treated as an equal means that his potential loss must be treated as a matter of concern; but that loss may nevertheless be outweighed by the gain to the community as a whole. If it is, then the less intelligent applicant cannot claim that he is cheated of his right to be treated as an equal just because he suffers a disadvantage that others do not.

The University of Washington may make the same reply to DeFunis. Any admissions policy must put some applicants at a disadvantage, and a policy of preference for minority applicants can reasonably be supposed to benefit the community as a whole even when the loss to candidates like DeFunis is taken into account. If there are more black lawyers they will help to provide better legal services to the black community, and so reduce social tensions. It might well improve the quality of legal education for all students, moreover, to have a greater number of blacks taking part in classroom discussions of social problems. If blacks are seen as successful law students, further, this might well encourage other blacks to apply who do meet the ordinary intellectual standards, and that, in turn, would raise the intellectual quality of the bar. In any case, preferential admissions of blacks should decrease the difference in wealth and power that now exists between different racial groups, and so make the community more equal overall.

It is, as I said, controversial whether a preferential admissions program will in fact promote these various policies, but it cannot be said to be implausible that it will. The disadvantage to applicants like DeFunis is, on that hypothesis, a cost that must be paid for a greater gain; it is in that way like the disadvantage to less intelligent students that is the cost of ordinary admissions policies.[4]

We now see the difference between DeFunis's case and the case we imagined, in which a law school charged students selected at random higher fees. The special disadvantage to these students was not necessary to achieve the gain in scholarship funds, because the same gain would have been achieved by a more equal distribution of the cost among all the students who could afford it. That is not true of DeFunis. He did suffer from the Washington policy more than those majority applicants who were accepted. But that discrimination was not arbitrary; it was a consequence of the meritocratic standards he approves. DeFunis's argument therefore fails. The equal protection clause gives constitutional standing to the right to be treated as an equal, but he cannot find, in that right, any support for his claim that the clause makes all racial classifications illegal.

III

If we dismiss DeFunis's claim in this straightforward way, however, we are left with this puzzle. How can so many able lawyers, who supported his claim both in morality and law, have made that mistake? These lawyers all agree that intelligence is a proper criterion for admission to law schools. They do not suppose that anyone's constitutional right to be treated as an equal is compromised by that criterion. Why do they deny that race, in the circumstances of this decade, may also be a proper criterion?

They fear, perhaps, that racial criteria will be misused; that such criteria will serve as an excuse for prejudice against the minorities that are not favored, like Jews. But that cannot explain their opposition. Any criteria may be misused, and in any case they think that racial criteria are wrong in principle, and not simply open to abuse.

Why? The answer lies in their belief that, in theory as well as in practice, DeFunis and Sweatt must stand or fall together. They believe that it is illogical for liberals to condemn Texas for raising a color barrier against Sweatt, and then applaud Washington for raising a color barrier against DeFunis. The difference between these two cases, they suppose, must be only the subjective preference of liberals for certain minorities now in fashion. If there is something wrong with racial classifications, then it must be something that is wrong with racial classifications as such, not just classifications that work against those groups currently in favor. That is the unarticulated premise behind the slogan, relied on by defendants of DeFunis, that the Constitution is color blind. That slogan means, of course, just the opposite of what it says: it means that the Constitution is so sensitive to color that it makes any institutional racial classification invalid as a matter of law.

It is of the greatest importance, therefore, to test the assumption that Sweatt and DeFunis must stand or fall together. If that assumption is sound, then the straightforward argument against DeFunis must be fallacious after all, for no argument could convince us that segregation of the sort practiced against Sweatt is justifiable or constitutional.[5] Superficially, moreover, the arguments against DeFunis do indeed seem available against Sweatt, because we can construct an argument that Texas might have used to show that segregation benefits the collective welfare, so that the special disadvantage to blacks is a cost that must be paid to achieve an overall gain.

Suppose the University of Texas admissions committee, though composed of men and women who themselves held no prejudice, decided that the Texas economy demanded more white lawyers than they could educate, but could find no use for black lawyers at all. That might have been, after all, a realistic assessment of the commercial market for lawyers in Texas just after the war. Corporate law firms needed lawyers to serve booming business, but could not afford to hire black lawyers, however skillful, because the firms' practice would be destroyed if they did. It was no doubt true that the black community in Texas had great need of skillful lawyers, and would have preferred to use black lawyers if these were available. But the committee might well have thought that the commercial needs of the state as a whole outweighed that special need.

Or suppose the committee judged, no doubt accurately, that alumni gifts to the law school would fall off drastically if it admitted a black student. The committee might deplore that fact but nevertheless believe that the consequent collective damage would be greater than the damage to black candidates excluded by the racial restriction.

It may be said that these hypothetical arguments are disingenuous, because any policy of excluding blacks would in fact be supported by a prejudice against blacks as such, and arguments of the sort just described would be rationalization only. But if these arguments are in fact sound, then they might be accepted by men who do not have the prejudices the objection assumes. It therefore does not follow from the fact that the admissions officers were prejudiced, if they were, that they would have rejected these arguments if they had not been.

In any case, arguments like those I describe were in fact used by officials who might have been free from prejudice against those they excluded. Many decades ago, as the late Professor Bickel reminds us in his brief for the B'nai B'rith, President Lowell of Harvard University argued in favor of a quota limiting the number of Jews who might be accepted by his university. He said that if Jews were accepted in numbers larger than their proportion of the population, as they certainly would have been if intelligence were the only test, then Harvard would no longer be able to provide to the world men of the qualities and temperament it aimed to produce, men, that is, who were more well rounded and less exclusively intellectual than Jews tended to be, and who, therefore, were better and more likely leaders of other men, both in and out of government.

It was no doubt true, when Lowell spoke, that Jews were less likely to occupy important places in government or at the heads of large public companies. If Harvard wished to serve the general welfare by improving the intellectual qualities of the nation's leaders, it was rational not to allow its classes to be filled up with Jews, even though the men who reached that conclusion might well prefer the company of Jews to that of the Wasps who were more likely to become senators. (Lowell suggested he did, though perhaps the responsibilities of his office prevented him from frequently indulging his preference.)

It might now be said, however, that discrimination against blacks, even when it does serve some plausible policy, is nevertheless unjustified because it is invidious and insulting. The briefs opposing DeFunis make just that argument to distinguish his claim from Sweatt's. Because blacks were the victims of slavery and legal segregation, they say, any discrimination that excludes blacks will be taken as insulting by them, whatever arguments of general welfare might be made in its support. But it is not true, as a general matter, that any social policy is unjust if those whom it puts at a disadvantage feel insulted. Admission to law school by intelligence is not unjust because those who are less intelligent feel insulted by their exclusion. Everything depends upon whether the feeling of insult is produced by some more objective feature that would disqualify the policy even if the insult were not felt. If segregation does improve the general welfare, even when the disadvantage to blacks is fully taken into account, and if no other reason can be found why segregation is nevertheless unjustified, then the insult blacks feel, while understandable, must be based on misperception.

It would be wrong, in any case, to assume that people in the position of DeFunis will not take *their* exclusion to be insulting. They are very likely to think of themselves as members of some other minority, like Jews or Poles or Italians, whom comfortable and successful liberals are willing to sacrifice in order to delay more violent social change. If we wish to distinguish *DeFunis* from *Sweatt* on some argument that uses the concept of an insult, we must show that the treatment of the one, but not of the other, is in fact unjust.

IV

So these familiar arguments that might distinguish the two cases are unconvincing. That seems to confirm the view that Sweatt and DeFunis must be treated alike, and therefore that racial classification must be outlawed altogether. But fortunately a more successful ground of distinction can be found to support our initial sense that the cases are in fact very different. This distinction does not rely, as these unconvincing arguments do, on features peculiar to issues of race or segregation, or even on features peculiar to issues of educational opportunity. It relies instead on further analysis of the idea, which was central to my argument against DeFunis, that in certain circumstances a policy that puts many individuals at a disadvantage is nevertheless justified because it makes the community as a whole better off.

Any institution that uses that idea to justify a discriminatory policy faces a series of theoretical and practical difficulties. There are, in the first place, two distinct senses in which a community may be said to be better off as a whole in spite of the fact that certain of its members are worse off, and any justification must specify which sense is meant. It may be better off in a *utilitarian* sense, that is, because the average or collective level of welfare in the community is improved even though the welfare of some individuals falls. Or it may be better off in an *ideal* sense, that is, because it is more just, or in some other way closer to an ideal society, whether or not average welfare is improved. The University of Washington might use either utilitarian or ideal arguments to justify its racial classification. It might argue, for example, that increasing the number of black lawyers reduced racial tensions, which improves the welfare of almost everyone in the community. That is a utilitarian argument. Or it might argue that, whatever effect minority preference will have on average welfare, it will make the community more equal and therefore more just. That is an ideal, not a utilitarian, argument.

The University of Texas, on the other hand, cannot make an ideal argument for segregation. It cannot claim that segregation makes the community more just whether it improves the average welfare or not. The arguments it makes to defend segregation must therefore all be utilitarian arguments. The arguments I invented, like the argument that white lawyers could do more than black lawyers to improve commercial efficiency in Texas, are utilitarian, since commercial efficiency makes the community better off only if it improves average welfare.

Utilitarian arguments encounter a special difficulty that ideal arguments do not. What is meant by average or collective welfare? How can the welfare of an individual be measured, even in principle, and how can gains in the welfare of different individuals be added and then compared with losses, so as to justify the claim that gains outweigh losses overall? The utilitarian argument that segregation improves average welfare presupposes that such calculations can be made. But how?

Jeremy Bentham, who believed that only

utilitarian arguments could justify political decisions, gave the following answer. He said that the effect of a policy on an individual's welfare could be determined by discovering the amount of pleasure or pain the policy brought him, and that the effect of the policy on the collective welfare could be calculated by adding together all the pleasure and subtracting all of the pain it brought to everyone. But, as Bentham's critics insisted, it is doubtful whether there exists a simple psychological state of pleasure common to all those who benefit from a policy, or of pain common to all those who lose by it; in any case it would be impossible to identify, measure, and add the different pleasures and pains felt by vast numbers of people.

Philosophers and economists who find utilitarian arguments attractive, but who reject Bentham's psychological utilitarianism, propose a different concept of individual and overall welfare. They suppose that whenever an institution or an official must decide upon a policy, the members of the community will each prefer the consequences of one decision to the consequences of others. DeFunis, for example, prefers the consequences of the standard admissions policy to the policy of minority preference the University of Washington used, while the blacks in some urban ghetto might each prefer the consequences of the latter policy to the former. If it can be discovered what each individual prefers, and how intensely, then it might be shown that a particular policy would satisfy on balance more preferences, taking into account their intensity, than alternative policies. On this concept of welfare, a policy makes the community better off in a utilitarian sense if it satisfies the total collection of preferences better than alternative policies would, even though it does not satisfy the preferences of some.[6]

Of course, a law school does not have available any means of making accurate judgments about the preferences of all those whom its admissions policies will affect. It may nevertheless make judgments which, though speculative, cannot be dismissed as implausible. It is, for example, plausible to think that in postwar Texas the preferences of the people were mostly in favor of the consequences of segregation in law schools, even if the intensity of the competing preference for integration, and not simply the number of those holding that preference, is taken into account.

The officials of the Texas law school might have relied upon voting behavior, newspaper editorials, and simply their own sense of their community in reaching that decision and, though they might have been wrong, we cannot now say, even with the benefit of hindsight, that they were.

So even if Bentham's psychological utilitarianism is rejected, law schools may—and in fact do—appeal to preference utilitarianism to provide at least a rough and speculative justification for admissions policies that put some classes of applicants at a disadvantage. But once it is made clear that these utilitarian arguments are based on judgments about the actual preferences of members of the community, a fresh and much more serious difficulty emerges.

The utilitarian argument, that a policy is justified if it satisfies more preferences overall, seems at first sight to be an egalitarian argument. It seems to observe strict impartiality. If the community has only enough medicine to treat some of those who are sick, the argument seems to recommend that those who are sickest be treated first. If the community can afford a swimming pool or a new theater, but not both, and more people want the pool, then it recommends that the community build the pool, unless those who want the theater can show that their preferences are so much more intense that they have more weight in spite of the numbers. One sick man is not to be preferred to another because he is worthier of official concern; the tastes of the theater audience are not to be preferred because they are more admirable. In Bentham's phrase, "each to count for one and none for more than one."

These simple examples suggest that the utilitarian argument not only respects, but embodies, the right of each citizen to be treated as the equal of any other. The chance each individual's preferences have to succeed, in the competition for different social policies, will depend upon how important his preference is to him, and how many others share it, compared to the intensity and number of competing preferences. His chance will not be affected by the esteem or contempt of either officials or fellow citizens, and he will therefore not be subservient or beholden to them.

But if we examine the range of preferences that individuals in fact have, we shall see that the apparent egalitarian character of a utilitarian argument is often deceptive. Preference utilitarianism asks officials to attempt to satisfy people's preferences so far as this is possible. But the preferences of an individual for the consequences of a particular policy may be seen to reflect, on further analysis, either a *personal* preference for his own enjoyment of some goods or opportunities, or an *external* preference for the assignment of goods and opportunities to others, or both. A white law school candidate might have a personal preference for the consequences of segregation, for example, because the policy improves his own chances of success. But he may also have an external preference for those consequences because he has contempt for blacks, disapproves of social situations in which the races mix.

The distinction between personal and external preferences is of great importance for this reason. If a utilitarian argument counts external preferences along with personal preferences, then the egalitarian character of that argument is corrupted. The chance that anyone's preferences have to succeed will then depend not only on the demands made by the personal preferences of others on scarce resources but on the respect or affection they have for him or for his way of life. If external preferences tip the balance, then the fact that a policy makes the community better off in a utilitarian sense would *not* provide a justification compatible with the right of those it disadvantages to be treated as equals.

This corruption of utilitarianism is plain when some people have external preferences because they hold political theories that are themselves contrary to utilitarianism. Suppose many citizens, who are not themselves sick, are racists in political theory, and therefore prefer that scarce medicine be given to a white man who needs it rather than a black man who needs it more. If officials following a utilitarian theory count these political preferences at face value, then the theory will be, from the standpoint of personal preferences, self-defeating, because the distribution of medicine will not be, from that standpoint, utilitarian at all. It would be utilitarian, from that standpoint, only if the preferences of people concerning their own treatment when sick were counted. In any case, self-defeating or not, the distribution will not be egalitarian in the sense defined. Blacks will suffer, to a degree that depends upon the strength of the racist preference, from the fact that others think them less worthy of respect and concern.

There is a similar corruption when the external preferences that are counted are altruistic or moralistic. Suppose many citizens, who themselves do not swim, prefer a new pool to a new theater because they approve of sports and admire athletes, or because they think that the theater is often immoral and ought to be repressed. If such altruistic preferences are counted, so as to reinforce the personal preferences of swimmers, the result will be a form of double counting: each person who wants to swim in a new pool will have the benefit not only of his own preference but also of the preference of someone else who takes pleasure in his being able to do so. If the moralistic preferences are counted, the effect will be the same: actors and audiences will suffer because their preferences are held in lower respect by citizens whose personal preferences are not themselves engaged.

In these examples, external preferences are independent of personal preferences. But of course political, altruistic, and moralistic preferences are often not independent, but grafted on to the personal preferences they reinforce. If I am white and sick, I may also hold a racist political theory. If I want a swimming pool for my own enjoyment I may also be altruistic in favor of my fellow athlete, or I may also think that the theater is immoral. The consequences of counting these external preferences will be as grave for equality as if they were independent of personal preference, because those against whom the external preferences run might be unable or unwilling to develop reciprocal external preferences that would right the balance.

External preferences therefore present a great difficulty for utilitarianism. That theory owes much of its popularity to the assumption that it embodies the right of citizens to be treated as equals. But if external preferences are counted in overall preferences, then this assumption is jeopardized. That is in itself an important and neglected point in political theory; it bears, for example, on the liberal thesis, first made prominent by Mill, that the government has no right to enforce popular morality at law. It is often said that this liberal thesis is inconsistent with utilitarianism, because if the preferences of the majority that homosexuality should be repressed, for example, are sufficiently strong, utilitarianism must give way to their wishes. But the preference against homosexuality is an external preference, and the present argument provides a general reason why utilitarians should not count external preferences of any form. If utilitarianism is suitably reconstituted so as to count only personal preferences, then the liberal thesis is a consequence, not an enemy, of that theory.

It is not, however, always possible to reconstitute a utilitarian argument so as to count only personal preferences. Sometimes personal and external preferences are so inextricably tied together, and so mutually dependent, that no practical test for measuring preferences will be able to discriminate among the personal and external elements in any individual's overall preference. That is especially true when preferences are affected by prejudice. Consider, for example, the preference of a white law student to associate only with white classmates. This may be said to be a personal preference for an association with one kind of colleague rather than another. But it is a personal preference that tends to be parasitic upon external preferences; a white student often prefers the company of other whites because he has racist social and political convictions or because he has contempt for blacks as a group.

If such associational preferences are counted in a utilitarian argument used to justify segregation, then the egalitarian character of the argument is destroyed just as if the underlying external preferences were counted directly. Blacks would be denied their right to be treated as equals because the chance that their preferences would prevail in the design of admissions policy would be crippled by the low esteem in which others hold them. In any community in which prejudice against a particular minority is strong, then the personal preferences upon which a utilitarian argument must fix will be saturated with that prejudice; it follows that in such a community no utilitarian argument purporting to justify a disadvantage to that minority can be fair.[7]

This final difficulty is therefore fatal to Texas's utilitarian arguments in favor of segregation. The preferences that might support any such argument are either distinctly external, like the preferences of the community at large for racial separation, or are inextricably combined with and dependent upon external preferences, like the

preferences of white students for associating with white classmates and of white lawyers for associating with white colleagues. These external preferences are so widespread that they must corrupt any such argument. Texas's claim that segregation makes the community better off in a utilitarian sense is therefore incompatible with Sweatt's right to treatment as an equal guaranteed by the equal protection clause.

It does not matter to this conclusion whether external preferences figure in the justification of a fundamental policy, or in the justification of derivative policies designed to advance a more fundamental policy. Suppose Texas justifies segregation by pointing to the apparently neutral economic policy of increasing community wealth, which could be said to satisfy the personal preferences of everyone for better homes, food, and recreation. If the argument that segregation will improve community wealth depends upon the fact of external preference; if the argument notices, for example, that because of prejudice industry will run more efficiently if factories are segregated; then the argument has the consequence that the black man's personal preferences are defeated by what others think of him.

Utilitarian arguments that justify a disadvantage to members of a race against whom prejudice runs will always be unfair arguments, unless it can be shown that the same disadvantage would have been justified in the absence of the prejudice. If the prejudice is widespread and pervasive, as in fact it is in the case of blacks, that can never be shown. The preferences on which any economic argument justifying segregation must be based will be so intertwined with prejudice that they cannot be disentangled to the degree necessary to make any such contrary-to-fact hypothesis plausible.

We now have an explanation that shows why any form of segregation that disadvantages blacks is, in the United States, an automatic insult to them, and why such segregation offends their right to be treated as equals. The argument confirms our sense that utilitarian arguments purporting to justify segregation are not simply wrong in detail but misplaced in principle. This objection to utilitarian arguments is not, however, limited to race or even prejudice. There are other cases in which counting external preferences would offend the rights of citizens to be treated as equals and it is worth briefly noticing these, if only to protect the argument against the charge that it is constructed *ad hoc* for the racial case. I might have a moralistic prejudice against professional women, or an altruistic preference for what I take to be "virtuous" men. It would be unfair for any law school to count preferences like these in deciding whom to admit to law schools; unfair because these preferences, like racial prejudices, make the success of the personal preferences of an applicant depend on the esteem and approval, rather than on the competing personal preferences, of others.

The same objection does not hold, however, against a utilitarian argument used to justify admission based on intelligence. That policy need not rely, directly or indirectly, on any community sense that intelligent lawyers are intrinsically more worthy of respect. It relies instead upon the law school's own judgment, right or wrong, that intelligent lawyers are more effective in satisfying personal preferences of others, like the preference for increasing wealth or winning law suits.

V

We therefore have the distinctions in hand necessary to distinguish *DeFunis* from *Sweatt*. The arguments for an admissions program that discriminates against blacks are all utilitarian arguments, and they are all utilitarian arguments that rely upon external preferences in such a way as to offend the constitutional right of blacks to be treated as equals. The arguments for an admissions program that discriminates in favor of blacks are both utilitarian and ideal. Some of the utilitarian arguments do rely, at least indirectly, on external preferences, like the preference of certain blacks for lawyers of their own race; but the utilitarian arguments that do not rely on such preferences are strong and may be sufficient. The ideal arguments do not rely upon preferences at all, but on the independent argument that a more equal society is a better society even if its citizens prefer inequality. That argument does not deny anyone's right himself to be treated as an equal.

We are therefore left, in *DeFunis*, with the simple and straightforward argument with which we began. Racial criteria are not necessarily the right standards for deciding which applicants should be accepted by law schools. But neither are intellectual criteria, or indeed, any other set of criteria. The fairness—and constitutionality—of any admissions program must be tested in the same way. It is justified if it serves a plausible policy that respects the right of all members of the community to be treated as equals, but not otherwise. The criteria used by schools that refused to consider blacks fail that test, but the criteria used by Washington do not.

We are all rightly suspicious of racial classifications. They have been used to deny rather than to respect the right of equality, and we are all conscious of the consequent injustice. But if we misunderstand the nature of that injustice because we do not make the simple distinctions that are necessary to understand it, then we are in danger of more injustice still. It may be that preferential admissions programs will not in fact make a more equal society. They may not have the effects their advocates believe they will. That strategic question should be at the center of debate about these programs. But we must not corrupt the debate by supposing that these programs are unfair even if they do work. We must take care not to use the equal protection clause to cheat ourselves of equality.

NOTES

1. Sweatt v. Painter, 339 US 629, 70 S.Ct. 848.
2. DeFunis v. Odegaard, 94 S.Ct. 1704 (1974).
3. See my "The Jurisprudence of Richard Nixon," *The New York Review of Books,* May 4, 1972.
4. I shall argue later in this essay that there are circumstances in which a policy violates someone's right to be treated as an equal in spite of the fact that the social gains from that policy may be said to outweigh the losses. These circumstances arise when the gains that outweigh the losses include the satisfaction of prejudices and other sorts of preferences that it is improper for officials or institutions to take into account at all. But the hypothetical social gains described in this paragraph do not include gains of that character. Of course, if DeFunis had some other right, beyond the right to be treated as an equal, which the University of Washington's policy violated, then the fact that the policy might achieve an overall social gain would not justify the violation. (See my "Taking Rights Seriously," *The New York Review of Books,* December 17, 1970.) If the Washington admissions procedures included a religious test that violated his right to religious freedom, for example, it would offer no excuse for using such a test that it might make the community more cohesive. But DeFunis does not rely on any distinct right beyond his right to equality protected by the equal protection clause.

5. In the actual *Sweatt* decision, the Supreme Court applied the old rule which held that segregaton was constitutionally permitted if facilities were provided for blacks that were "separate but equal." Texas had provided a separate law school for blacks, but the Court held that that school was by no means the equal of the white school. *Sweatt* was decided before the famous *Brown* case in which the Court finally rejected the "separate but equal" rule, and there is no doubt that an all-white law school would be unconstitutional today even if a separate black school provided facilities that were in a material sense the equal of those provided for whites.

6. Many economists and philosophers challenge the intelligibility of preference utilitarianism as well as psychological utilitarianism. They argue that there is no way, even in principle, to calculate and compare the intensity of individual preferences. Since I wish to establish a different failing in certain utilitarian arguments, I assume, for purposes of this essay, that at least rough and speculative calculations about overall community preferences can be made.

7. The argument of this paragraph is powerful but it is not, in itself, sufficient to disqualify all utilitarian arguments that produce substantial disadvantages to minorities who suffer from prejudice. Suppose the government decides, on a utilitarian argument, to allow unemployment to increase because the loss to those who lose their jobs is outweighed by the gain to those who would otherwise suffer from inflation. The burden of this policy will fall disproportionately on blacks, who will be fired first because prejudice runs against them. But though prejudice in this way affects the consequences of the policy of unemployment, it does not figure, even indirectly, in the utilitarian argument that supports that policy. (It figures, if at all, as a utilitarian argument against it.) We cannot say, therefore, that the special damage blacks suffer from a high unemployment policy is unjust for the reasons described in this essay. It may well be unjust for other reasons; if John Rawls is right, for example, it is unjust because the policy improves the condition of the majority at the expense of those already worse off.

REED v. REED ADMINISTRATOR

United States Supreme Court, 1971*

Mr. Chief Justice Burger delivered the opinion of the Court.

Richard Lynn Reed, a minor, died intestate in Ada County, Idaho, on March 29, 1967. His adoptive parents, who had separated sometime prior to his death, are the parties to this appeal. Approximately seven months after Richard's death, his mother, appellant Sally Reed, filed a petition in the Probate Court of Ada County, seeking appointment as administratrix of her son's estate.[1] Prior to the date set for a hearing on the mother's petition, appellee Cecil Reed, the father of the decedent, filed a competing petition seeking to have himself appointed administrator of the son's estate. The probate court held a joint hearing on the two petitions and thereafter ordered that letters of administration be issued to appellee Cecil Reed upon his taking the oath and filing the bond required by law. The court treated §§ 15–312 and 15–314 of the Idaho Code as the controlling statutes and read those sections as compelling a preference for Cecil Reed because he was a male.

Section 15–312[2] designates the persons who are entitled to administer the estate of one who dies intestate. In making these designations, that section lists 11 classes of persons who are so entitled and provides, in substance, that the order in which those classes are listed in the section shall be determinative of the relative rights of competing applicants for letters of administration. One of the 11 classes so enumerated is "[t]he father or mother" of the person dying intestate. Under this section, then, appellant and appellee, being members of the same entitlement class, would seem to have been equally entitled to administer their son's estate. Section 15–314 provides, however, that

"[o]f several persons claiming and equally entitled [under § 15–312] to administer, males must be preferred to females, and relatives of the whole to those of the half blood."

In issuing its order, the probate court implicitly recognized the equality of entitlement of the two applicants under § 15–312 and noted that neither of the applicants was under any legal disability; the court ruled, however, that appellee, being a male, was to be preferred to the female appellant "by reason of Section

*404 U.S. 71 (1971). Excerpts only.

15–314 of the Idaho Code." In stating this conclusion, the probate judge gave no indication that he had attempted to determine the relative capabilities of the competing applicants to perform the functions incident to the administration of an estate. It seems clear the probate judge considered himself bound by statute to give preference to the male candidate over the female, each being otherwise "equally entitled."

Sally Reed appealed from the probate court order, and her appeal was treated by the District Court of the Fourth Judicial District of Idaho as a constitutional attack on § 15–314. In dealing with the attack, that court held that the challenged section violated the Equal Protection Clause of the Fourteenth Amendment[3] and was, therefore, void; the matter was ordered "returned to the Probate Court for its determination of which of the two parties" was better qualified to administer the estate.

This order was never carried out, however, for Cecil Reed took a further appeal to the Idaho Supreme Court, which reversed the District Court and reinstated the original order naming the father administrator of the estate. In reaching this result, the Idaho Supreme Court first dealt with the governing statutory law and held that under § 15–312 "a father and mother are 'equally entitled' to letters of administration," but the preference given to males by § 15–314 is "mandatory" and leaves no room for the exercise of a probate court's discretion in the appointment of administrators. Having thus definitively and authoritatively interpreted the statutory provisions involved, the Idaho Supreme Court then proceeded to examine, and reject, Sally Reed's contention that § 15–314 violates the Equal Protection Clause by giving a mandatory preference to males over females, without regard to their individual qualifications as potential estate administrators.

Sally Reed thereupon appealed for review by this Court . . ., and we noted probable jurisdiction.* Having examined the record and considered the briefs and oral arguments of the parties, we have concluded that the arbitrary preference established in favor of males by § 15–314 of the Idaho Code cannot stand in the face of the Fourteenth Amendment's command that no State deny the equal protection of the laws to any person within its jurisdiction.[4]

Idaho does not, of course, deny letters of administration to women altogether. Indeed, under § 15–312, a woman whose spouse dies intestate has a preference over a son, father, brother, or any other male relative of the decedent. Moreover, we can judicially notice that in this country, presumably due to the greater longevity of women, a large proportion of estates, both intestate and under wills of decedents, are administered by surviving widows.

Section 15–314 is restricted in its operation to those situations where competing applications for letters of administration have been filed by both male and female members of the same entitlement class established by § 15–312. In such situations, § 15–314 provides that different treatment be accorded to the applicants on the basis of their sex; it thus establishes a classification subject to scrutiny under the Equal Protection Clause.

In applying that clause, this Court has consistently recognized that the Fourteenth Amendment does not deny to States the power to treat different classes of persons in different ways. The Equal Protection Clause of that amendment does, however, deny to States the power to legislate that different treatment be accorded to persons placed by a statute into different classes on the basis of criteria wholly unrelated to the objective of that statute. A classification "must be reasonable, not arbitrary, and must rest upon some ground of difference having a fair and substantial relation to the object of the legislation, so that all persons similarly circumstanced shall be treated alike." *Royster Guano Co.* v. *Virginia,* 253 U.S. 412, 415 (1920). The question presented by this case, then, is whether a difference in the sex of competing applicants for letters of administration bears a rational relationship to a state objective that is sought to be advanced by the operation of §§ 15–312 and 15–314.

In upholding the latter section, the Idaho Supreme Court concluded that its objective was to eliminate one area of controversy when two or more persons, equally entitled under § 15–312, seek letters of administration and thereby present the probate court "with the issue of which one should be named." The court also concluded that where such persons are not of the same sex, the elimination of females from consideration "is neither an illogical nor arbitrary method devised by the legislature to resolve an issue that would otherwise require a hearing as to the relative merits . . . of the two or more petitioning relatives. . . ."*

Clearly the objective of reducing the workload on probate courts by eliminating one class of contests is not without some legitimacy. The crucial question, however, in whether § 15–314 advances that objective in a manner consistent with the command of the Equal Protection Clause. We hold that it does not. To give a mandatory preference to members of either sex over members of the other, merely to accomplish the elimination of hearings on the merits, is to make the very kind of arbitrary legislative choice forbidden by the Equal Protection Clause of the Fourteenth Amendment; and whatever may be said as to the positive values of avoiding intrafamily controversy, the choice in this context may not lawfully be mandated solely on the basis of sex.

We note finally that if § 15–314 is viewed merely as

*Citation omitted [Eds.]

*Citation omitted [Eds.]

a modifying appendage to § 15–312 and as aimed at the same objective, its constitutionality is not thereby saved. The objective of § 15–312 clearly is to establish degrees of entitlement of various classes of persons in accordance with their varying degrees and kinds of relationship to the intestate. Regardless of their sex, persons within any one of the enumerated classes of that section are similarly situated with respect to that objective. By providing dissimilar treatment for men and women who are thus similarly situated, the challenged section violates the Equal Protection Clause.

The judgment of the Idaho Supreme Court is reversed and the case remanded for further proceedings not inconsistent with this opinion.

Reversed and remanded.

NOTES

1. In her petition, Sally Reed alleged that her son's estate, consisting of a few items of personal property and a small savings account, had an aggregate value of less than $1,000.

2. Section 15–312 provides as follows:

"Administration of the estate of a person dying intestate must be granted to some one or more of the persons hereinafter mentioned, and they are respectively entitled thereto in the following order:

"1. The surviving husband or wife or some competent person whom he or she may request to have appointed.
"2. The children.
"3. The father or mother.
"4. The brothers.
"5. The sisters.
"6. The grandchildren.
"7. The next of kin entitled to share in the distribution of the estate.
"8. Any of the kindred.
"9. The public administrator.
"10. The creditors of such person at the time of death.
"11. Any person legally competent.
"If the decedent was a member of a partnership at the time of his decease, the surviving partner must in no case be appointed administrator of his estate."

3. The court also held that the statute violated Art. I, § 1, of the Idaho Constitution.

4. We note that § 15–312, set out in n. 2, *supra,* appears to give a superior entitlement to brothers of an intestate (class 4) than is given to sisters (class 5). The parties now before the Court are not affected by the operation of § 15–312 in this respect, however, and appellant has made no challenge to that section.

We further note that on March 12, 1971, the Idaho Legislature adopted the Uniform Probate Code, effective July 1, 1972. Idaho Laws 1971, c. 111, p. 233. On that date, §§ 15–312 and 15–314 of the present code will, then, be effectively repealed, and there is in the new legislation no mandatory preference for males over females as administrators of estates.

FRONTIERO v. RICHARDSON

United States Supreme Court, 1973*

Mr. Justice Brennan announced the judgment of the Court and an opinion in which Mr. Justice Douglas, Mr. Justice White, and Mr. Justice Marshall join.

The question before us concerns the right of a female member of the uniformed services to claim her spouse as a "dependent" for the purposes of obtaining increased quarters allowances and medical and dental benefits under 37 U. S. C. §§ 401, 403, and 10 U. S. C. §§ 1072, 1076, on an equal footing with male members. Under these statutes, a serviceman may claim his wife as a "dependent" without regard to whether she is in fact dependent upon him for any part of her support.

A servicewoman, on the other hand, may not claim her husband as a "dependent" under these programs unless he is in fact dependent upon her for over one-half of his support. Thus, the question for decision is whether this difference in treatment constitutes an unconstitutional discrimination against servicewomen in violation of the Due Process Clause of the Fifth Amendment. A three-judge District Court for the Middle District of Alabama, one judge dissenting, rejected this contention and sustained the constitutionality of the provisions of the statutes making this distinction.* We reverse.

I

In an effort to attract career personnel through reenlistment, Congress established a scheme for the provi-

*93 *S. Ct.* 1764 (1973). Some footnotes omitted, and the remainder renumbered.

sion of fringe benefits to members of the uniformed services on a competitive basis with business and industry. Thus, under 37 U. S. C. § 403, a member of the uniformed services with dependents is entitled to an increased "basic allowance for quarters" and, under 10 U. S. C. § 1076, a member's dependents are provided comprehensive medical and dental care.

Appellant Sharron Frontiero, a lieutenant in the United States Air Force, sought increased quarters allowances, and housing and medical benefits for her husband, appellant Joseph Frontiero, on the ground that he was her "dependent." Although such benefits would automatically have been granted with respect to the wife of a male member of the uniformed services, appellant's application was denied because she failed to demonstrate that her husband was dependent on her for more than one-half of his support.[1] Appellants then commenced this suit, contending that, by making this distinction, the statutes unreasonably discriminate on the basis of sex in violation of the Due Process Clause of the Fifth Amendment.[2] In essence, appellants asserted that the discriminatory impact of the statutes is two-fold: first, as a procedural matter, a female member is required to demonstrate her spouse's dependency, while no such burden is imposed upon male members; and second, as a substantive matter, a male member who does not provide more than one-half of his wife's support receives benefits, while a similarly situated female member is denied such benefits. Appellants therefore sought a permanent injunction against the continued enforcement of these statutes and an order directing the appellees to provide Lieutenant Frontiero with the same housing and medical benefits that a similarly situated male member would receive.

Although the legislative history of these statutes sheds virtually no light on the purposes underlying the differential treatment accorded male and female members, a majority of the three-judge District Court surmised that Congress might reasonably have concluded that, since the husband in our society is generally the "breadwinner" in the family—and the wife typically the "dependent" partner—"it would be more economical to require married female members claiming husbands to prove actual dependency than to extend the presumption of dependency to such members."* Indeed, given the fact that approximately 99% of all members of the uniformed services are male, the District Court speculated that such differential treatment might conceivably lead to a "considerable saving of administrative expense and manpower."

II

At the outset, appellants contend that classifications based upon sex, like classifications based upon race, alienage, and national origin, are inherently suspect and must therefore be subjected to close judicial scrutiny. We agree and, indeed, find at least implicit support for such an approach in our unanimous decision only last Term in *Reed* v. *Reed,* 404 U. S. 71 (1971).

In *Reed,* the Court considered the constitutionality of an Idaho statute providing that, when two individuals are otherwise equally entitled to appointment as administrator of an estate, the male applicant must be preferred to the female. Appellant, the mother of the deceased, and appellee, the father, filed competing petitions for appointment as administrator of their son's estate. Since the parties, as parents of the deceased, were members of the same entitlement class, the statutory preference was invoked and the father's petition was therefore granted. Appellant claimed that this statute, by giving a mandatory preference to males over females without regard to their individual qualifications, violated the Equal Protection Clause of the Fourteenth Amendment.

The Court noted that the Idaho statute "provides that different treatment be accorded to the applicants on the basis of their sex; it thus establishes a classification subject to scrutiny under the Equal Protection Clause." Under "traditional" equal protection analysis, a legislative classification must be sustained unless it is "patently arbitrary" and bears no rational relationship to a legitimate governmental interest.*

In an effort to meet this standard, appellee contended that the statutory scheme was a reasonable measure designed to reduce the workload on probate courts by eliminating one class of contests. Moreover, appellee argued that the mandatory preference for male applicants was in itself reasonable since "men [are] as a rule more conversant with business affairs than . . . women." Indeed, appellee maintained that "it is a matter of common knowledge that women still are not engaged in politics, the professions, business or industry to the extent that men are." And the Idaho Supreme Court, in upholding the constitutionality of this statute, suggested that the Idaho Legislature might reasonably have "concluded that in general men are better qualified to act as an administrator than are women." [*Reed* v. *Reed*]

Despite these contentions, however, the Court held the statutory preference for male applicants unconstitutional. In reaching this result, the Court implicitly rejected appellee's apparently rational explanation of the statutory scheme, and concluded that, by ignoring the individual qualifications of particular applicants, the challenged statute provided "dissimilar treatment for men and women who are . . . similarly situated." *Reed* v. *Reed, supra,* at 77. The Court therefore held that, even though the State's interest in achieving ad-

*Citations omitted [Eds.]

ministrative efficiency "is not without some legiti-macy," "[t]o give a mandatory preference to members of either sex over members of the other, merely to accomplish the elimination of hearings on the merits, is to make the very kind of arbitrary legislative choice forbidden by the [Constitution]. . . ." *Id.,* at 76. This departure from "traditional" rational basis analysis with respect to sex-based classifications is clearly justi-fied.

There can be no doubt that our Nation has had a long and unfortunate history of sex discrimination.[3] Traditionally, such discrimination was rationalized by an attitude of "romantic paternalism" which, in practi-cal effect, put women not on a pedestal, but in a cage. Indeed, this paternalistic attitude became so firmly rooted in our national consciousness that, exactly 100 years ago, a distinguished member of this Court was able to proclaim:

"Man is, or should be, woman's protector and defender. The natural and proper timidity and delicacy which belongs to the female sex evidently unfits it for many of the occupations of civil life. The constitution of the family organization, which is founded in the divine ordinance, as well as in the nature of things, indicates the domestic sphere as that which properly belongs to the domain and functions of womanhood. The harmony, not to say identity, of interests and views which belong, or should belong, to the family institution is repug-nant to the ideas of a woman adopting a distinct and indepen-dent career from that of her husband. . . .
". . . The paramount destiny and mission of woman are to fulfil the noble and benign offices of wife and mother. This is the law of the Creator." *Bradwell* v. *Illinois,* 83 U. S. [16 Wall.] 130, 141 (1873) (Bradley, J., concurring).

As a result of notions such as these, our statute books gradually became laden with gross, stereotypical distinctions between the sexes and, indeed, throughout much of the 19th century, the position of women in our society was, in many respects, comparable to that of blacks under the pre-Civil War slave codes. Neither slaves nor women could hold office, serve on juries, or bring suit in their own names, and married women traditionally were denied the legal capacity to hold or convey property or to serve as legal guardians of their own children. See generally, L. Kantowitz, Women and the Law: The Unfinished Revolution 5–6 (1969); G. Mydral, An American Dilemma 1073 (2d ed. 1962). And although blacks were guaranteed the right to vote in 1870, women were denied even that right—which is itself "preservative of other basic civil and political rights"[4]—until adoption on the Nineteenth Amend-ment half a century later.

It is true, of course, that the position of women in America has improved markedly in recent decades.[5] Nevertheless, it can hardly be doubted that, in part because of the high visibility of the sex characteristic, women still face pervasive, although at times more subtle, discrimination in our educational institutions, on the job market and, perhaps most conspicuously, in the political arena.[6] See generally, K. Amundsen, The Silenced Majority: Women and American Democracy (1971).

Moreover, since sex, like race and national origin, is an immutable characteristic determined solely by the accident of birth, the imposition of special disabilities upon the members of a particular sex because of their sex would seem to violate "the basic concept of our system that legal burdens should bear some relation-ship to individual responsibility. . . ." *Weber* v. *Aetna Casualty & Surety Co.,* 406 U. S. 164, 175 (1972). And what differentiates sex from such nonsuspect statutes as intelligence or physical disability, and aligns it with the recognized suspect criteria, is that the sex charac-teristic frequently bears no relation to ability to per-form or contribute to society. As a result, statutory distinctions between the sexes often have the effect of invidiously relegating the entire class of females to infe-rior legal status without regard to the actual capabili-ties of its individual members.

We might also note that, over the past decade, Con-gress has itself manifested an increasing sensitivity to sex-based classifications. In Tit. VII of the Civil Rights Act of 1964, for example, Congress expressly declared that no employer, labor union, or other organization subject to the provisions of the Act shall discriminate against any individual on the basis of "race, color, religion, *sex,* or national origin." Similarly, the Equal Pay Act of 1963 provides that no employer covered by the Act "shall discriminate . . . between employees on the basis of *sex.* " And §1 of the Equal Rights Amend-ment, passed by Congress on March 22, 1972, and submitted to the legislatures of the States for ratifica-tion, declares that "[e]quality of rights under the law shall not be denied or abridged by the United States or by any State on account of sex." Thus, Congress has itself concluded that classifications based upon sex are inherently invidious, and this conclusion of a coequal branch of Government is not without significance to the question presently under consideration.*

With these considerations in mind, we can only con-clude that classifications based upon sex, like classifica-tions based upon race, alienage, or national origin, are inherently suspect, and must therefore be subjected to strict judicial scrutiny. Applying the analysis man-dated by that stricter standard of review, it is clear that the statutory scheme now before us is constitutionally invalid.

III

The sole basis of the classification established in the challenged statutes is the sex of the individuals in-

* Citations omitted [Eds.]

volved. Thus, under 37 U. S. C. §§ 401, 403, and 10 U. S. C. §§ 2072, 2076, a female member of the uniformed services seeking to obtain housing and medical benefits for her spouse must prove his dependency in fact, whereas no such burden is imposed upon male members. In addition, the statutes operate so as to deny benefits to a female member, such as appellant Sharron Frontiero, who provides less than one-half of her spouse's support, while at the same time granting such benefits to a male member who likewise provides less than one-half of his spouse's support. Thus, to this extent at least, it may fairly be said that these statutes command "dissimilar treatment for men and women who are . . . similarly situated." *Reed* v. *Reed, supra,* at 77.

Moreover, the Government concedes that the differential treatment accorded men and women under these statutes serves no purpose other than mere "administrative convenience." In essence, the Government maintains that, as an empirical matter, wives in our society frequently are dependent upon their husbands, while husbands rarely are dependent upon their wives. Thus, the Government argues that Congress might reasonably have concluded that it would be both cheaper and easier simply conclusively to presume that wives of male members are financially dependent upon their husbands, while burdening female members with the task of establishing dependency in fact.[7]

The Government offers no concrete evidence, however, tending to support its view that such differential treatment in fact saves the Government any money. In order to satisfy the demands of strict judicial scrutiny, the Government must demonstrate, for example, that it is actually cheaper to grant increased benefits with respect to *all* male members, than it is to determine which male members are in fact entitled to such benefits and to grant increased benefits only to those members whose wives actually meet the dependency requirement. Here, however, there is substantial evidence that, if put to the test, many of the wives of male members would fail to qualify for benefits. And in light of the fact that the dependency determination with respect to the husbands of female members is presently made solely on the basis of affidavits, rather than through the more costly hearing process, the Government's explanation of the statutory scheme is, to say the least, questionable.

In any case, our prior decisions make clear that, although efficacious administration of governmental programs is not without some importance, "the Constitution recognizes higher values than speed and efficiency."* And when we enter the realm of "strict

judicial scrutiny," there can be no doubt that "administrative convenience" is not a shibboleth, the mere recitation of which dictates constitutionality.* On the contrary, any statutory scheme which draws a sharp line between the sexes, *solely* for the purpose of achieving administrative convenience, necessarily commands "dissimilar treatment for men and women who are . . . similarly situated," and therefore involves the "very kind of arbitrary legislative choice forbidden by the [Constitution]. . . ." *Reed* v. *Reed, supra,* at 77, 76. We therefore conclude that, by according differential treatment to male and female members of the uniformed services for the sole purpose of achieving administrative convenience, the challenged statutes violate the Due Process Clause of the Fifth Amendment insofar as they require a female member to prove the dependency of her husband.

Reversed.

Mr. Justice Stewart concurs in the judgment, agreeing that the statutes before us work an invidious discrimination in violation of the Constitution. *Reed* v. *Reed,* 404 U. S. 71.

Mr. Justice Rehnquist dissents for the reasons stated by Judge Rives in his opinion for the District Court, *Frontiero* v. *Laird,* 341 F. Supp. 201 (1972).

Mr. Justice Powell, with whom The Chief Justice and Mr. Justice Blackmun join, concurring in the judgment.

I agree that the challenged statutes constitute an unconstitutional discrimination against service women in violation of the Due Process Clause of the Fifth Amendment, but I cannot join the opinion of Mr. Justice Brennan, which would hold that all classifications based upon sex, "like classifications based upon race, alienage, and national origin," are "inherently suspect and must therefore be subjected to close judicial scrutiny." It is unnecessary for the Court in this case to characterize sex as a suspect classification, with all of the far-reaching implications of such a holding. *Reed* v. *Reed,* 404 U. S. 71 (1971), which abundantly supports our decision today, did not add sex to the narrowly limited group of classifications which are inherently suspect. In my view, we can and should decide this case on the authority of *Reed* and reserve for the future any expansion of its rationale.

There is another, and I find compelling, reason for deferring a general categorizing of sex classifications as invoking the strictest test of judicial scrutiny. The Equal Rights Amendment, which if adopted will resolve the substance of this precise question, has been approved by the Congress and submitted for ratifica-

*Citations omitted [Eds.]

*Citations omitted [Eds.]

tion by the States. If this Amendment is duly adopted, it will represent the will of the people accomplished in the manner prescribed by the Constitution. By acting prematurely and unnecessarily, as I view it, the Court has assumed a decisional responsibility at the very time when state legislatures, functioning within the traditional democratic process, are debating the proposed Amendment. It seems to me that this reaching out to pre-empt by judicial action a major political decision which is currently in process of resolution does not reflect appropriate respect for duly prescribed legislative processes.

There are times when this Court, under our system, cannot avoid a constitutional decision on issues which normally should be resolved by the elected representatives of the people. But democratic institutions are weakened, and confidence in the restraint of the Court is impaired, when we appear unnecessarily to decide sensitive issues of broad social and political importance at the very time they are under consideration within the prescribed constitutional processes.

NOTES

1. Appellant Joseph Frontiero is a full-time student at Huntingdon College in Montgomery, Alabama. According to the agreed stipulation of facts, his living expenses, including his share of the household expenses, total approximately $354 per month. Since he receives $205 per month in veterans' benefits, it is clear that he is not dependent upon appellant Sharron Frontiero for more than one-half of his support.

2. "[W]hile the Fifth Amendment contains no equal protection clause, it does forbid discrimination that is 'so unjustifiable as to be violative of due process.'" *Schneider* v. *Rusk,* 377 U. S. 163, 168 (1964).

3. Indeed, the position of women in this country at its inception is reflected in the view expressed by Thomas Jefferson that women should be neither seen nor heard in society's decisionmaking councils. See M. Gruberg, Women in American Politics 4 (1968). See also A. de Tocqueville, Democracy in America, pt. 2 (Reeves tr. 1840), in World's Classic Series 400 (Galaxy ed. 1947).

4. *Reynolds* v. *Sims,* 377 U. S. 533, 562 (1964).

5. See generally, The President's Task Force on Women's Rights and Responsibilities, A Matter of Simple Justice (1970); L. Kantowitz, Women and the Law: The Unfinished Revolution (1969); A. Montague, Man's Most Dangerous Myth (4th ed. 1964); The President's Commission on the Status of Women, American Women (1963).

6. It is true, of course, that when viewed in the abstract, women do not constitute a small and powerless minority. Nevertheless, in part because of past discrimination, women are vastly underrepresented in this Nation's decisionmaking councils. There has never been a female President, nor a female member of this Court. Not a single woman presently sits in the United States Senate, and only 14 women hold seats in the House of Representatives. And, as appellants point out, this underrepresentation is present throughout all levels of our State and Federal Government. See Joint Reply Brief of Appellants and American Civil Liberties Union (*Amicus Curiae*) 9.

7. It should be noted that these statutes are not in any sense designed to rectify the effects of past discrimination against women. On the contrary, these statutes seize upon a group—women—who have historically suffered discrimination in employment, and rely on the effects of this past discrimination as a justification for heaping on additional economic disadvantages.

HARVARD LAW REVIEW

Patient Selection for Artificial and Transplanted Organs *

I will not permit considerations of race, religion, nationality, party politics or social standing to intervene between my duty and my patient. Physician's Oath.[1]

In recent years scientific and medical research has developed remarkable new curative techniques—among them, artificial organs and organ transplants. Physicians have now successfully transplanted the human kidney, heart, and liver, and replaced the kidney and parts of the heart with man-made devices. As these developments advance beyond the experimental stage, complex ethical and legal problems are presented. Demand exceeds supply because of the scarcity of natural or artificial organs [2] and the financial and logistical problems which limit the number of patients who can be helped.[3] When vital organs are involved, selection of recipients is a determination of life or death; the frequent need for quick decisions if treatment is to be effective serves to compound the problem of fair allocation. The likelihood of continued medical advances indicates that the difficulty will intensify as more people are affected. This Note will survey the scientific developments in artificial organs and transplantation and the current patient selection practices. After examining the competing values which should govern the selection process, it will consider some of the equal protection and due process problems involved. Finally, the Note will suggest substantive and procedural measures for a fair system of allocation.

I. SCIENTIFIC DEVELOPMENTS

The most dramatic achievement in the development of an artificial vital organ has been the artificial kidney (hemodialysis). The patient is connected to a dialysis machine by tubes (cannulae) inserted into an artery and vein in his arm

* From *Harvard Law Review,* Vol. 82 (1969), pp. 1322–1342. Copyright 1969 by the Harvard Law Review Association. Reprinted by permission of the publisher.

or leg. His blood then passes through the machine, where harmful waste products and chemicals are filtered out, the fluid content of the body regulated, and needed substances added to the bloodstream. When dialysis is complete, the machine is disconnected and a shunt is used to allow the blood to pass directly from artery to vein via the cannulae.[4] Since the patient need not constantly be connected to the dialysis machine, in many respects he can lead a normal life.[5] With the development of hemodialysis units which may safely be used in the home, it has been possible in some cases to eliminate the disruption of frequent hospital visits.[6] Unfortunately, only about 800 persons are receiving hemodialysis, whereas an estimated 5,000 to 10,000 new patients each year require such treatment to survive.[7] Perfection of an artificial heart, projected for 1970, is likely to engender a similarly severe supply-demand gap, since an estimated 100,000 people a year need this device.[8] Such problems will continue to recur as artificial replacements for other organs are developed.[9]

In organ transplantation, similar shortages seem unavoidable. Kidney transplants are becoming increasingly successful, and with further development of tissue-typing techniques (histocompatibility), drugs to prevent the body from rejecting the transplant (immunosuppression), and means to control infection,[10] success in a majority of kidney transplants from unrelated living and cadaver donors seems imminent.[11] Yet, approximately 7,700 people died in the United States during 1967 for lack of this operation.[12] Heart transplants, though apparently still in the experimental stages, have been performed since Dr. Barnard's first operation on December 3, 1967,[13] and the feasibility of liver transplants has been clearly established not only by animal experiments, but also by successful transplantation between human patients at the University of Colorado.[14] The impending allocation problems again are immense: the National Institutes of Health estimated that successful heart transplants could have saved 80,000 Americans who died of coronary disease in 1967; [15] and according to the last available study in 1963, there were approximately 4,000 potential liver recipients in the United States. [16]

II. CURRENT PRACTICES IN PATIENT SELECTION

In the period since 1960, [17] when the artificial kidney was first successfully used as a long-term treatment for chronic renal failure, a pattern has emerged with respect to patient selection. Most hospitals narrow the field of selection on the basis of age, physical condition, "cooperativeness" in adhering to the rehabilitation routine, and "rehabilitation potential." [18] Age limits generally exclude children under thirteen, who normally are unable to mature physically under dialysis, and older persons, who are more prone to complicating illnesses and possess shorter life expectancies. [19] Patients are usually required to be in good physical health apart from kidney disability. [20] They must also be able and willing to "cooperate"—that is, to care for themselves, guard against infection at the cannulae sites, follow a strict diet, and withstand the stress of treatment. [21] Consequently, most dialysis centers require the potential patient to be an emotionally mature and stable individual, [22] and some hospitals utilize psychological evaluation to ensure this result. [23] In addition, the degree of emotional support a prospective patient can receive from those around him is frequently considered in evaluating the probable success of treatment. The stability of his home and work life is often examined, [24] and psychological evaluation is sometimes made of his spouse. [25] In judging rehabilitation potential, many doctors evaluate their success in terms of whether the patient can return to society as a "useful" member, rather than in terms of survival. [26] Of course, the market mechanism frequently plays an additional crucial role in narrowing the pool of eligible patients: [27] a recent study has placed the annual cost of hemodialysis at 15,000 dollars. [28] At many hospitals, if the patient cannot afford long-term treatment or make suitable advance arrangements for payment, he is automatically rejected. [29] Furthermore, the demands of continuous treatment favor those who already reside near the center or who can move most easily. [30]

In most hospitals, the standards under which findings of "cooperativeness" and "rehabilitation potential" are made are so broad that patient selection is effectively based wholly on doctors' opinions. [31] At some hospitals, however, such criteria are narrower in scope and do not reduce the ranks of prospective patients to the number for whom treatment is available. Further development of implantable artificial organs not requiring the continuous care and supervision which dialysis entails may diminish the role of "cooperativeness" and "rehabilitation potential" in narrowing the field of eligible patients among whom ultimate choice must be made. In order to make a final selection some dialysis centers undertake a comparative evaluation of the patients' social worth, assessing such factors as occupational status, family relations, and community participation. [32] At the Seattle Artificial Kidney Center, an anonymous lay committee makes these social judgments; [33] patient selection committees composed of "physicians, social workers, rehabilitation workers, and other specialists" have been used in two regional centers established by the California Department of Public Health. [34] Frequently, however, the physicians directly involved in the treatment make this determination. [35] Other hospitals avoid social worth evaluations by using a first come, first served rule or a lottery, and a few of these will eliminate only those clearly unfit for treatment. [36] Selection decisions are made within time limits imposed on one side by the necessity of awaiting a prognosis of complete renal failure, and on the other, by the medical need to initiate pre-dialysis therapy and the possibility that patients will require treatment sooner than expected. [37] Thus, at the Seattle Artificial Kidney Center, for example, patients are selected between three and six months before they are likely to need dialysis. [38]

Although organ transplantation is still sufficiently experimental that formal allocation procedures have not been implemented, it seems likely that patient selection practices will resemble those used by dialysis centers. [39] Age, physical condition, and rehabilitation potential are now used as criteria in patient selection for heart and kidney transplants. But unlike dialysis, there is generally no minimum age requirement; in fact, young children requiring a new heart must rely on transplantation rather than an implanted artificial organ, since the latter cannot grow with the child.[40] An absence of complicating illness is important—for example, patients subject to glomerulonephritis, a disease that tends to attack and destroy the renal transplant, are considered unsuitable; [41] Dr. Barnard's heart team in Capetown has required that the recipient's heart disease be the sole responsible factor in his illness.[42] Rehabilitation potential as a selection criterion for renal transplantation resembles the standard in dialysis. In Boston, an organ bank presently concerned with kidney transplants advises physicians to consider the patient's family support and social setting, his emotional adjustment, and his capacity to understand the implications of transplantation.[43] But except for immediate postoperative care, improvements in transplants may make continuous treatment unnecessary following a successful operation, and therefore, "cooperativeness" may become less significant.[44] This factor may also reduce the importance of the market mechanism, since a single rather than perennial expenditure will be required. However, cost is today a substantial element,[45] and residence near the hospital is necessary in order that the patient be immediately available when a suitable donor dies.[46] Selection for organ transplantation requires an additional stage which is not present in artificial organ programs. When patients have been found otherwise suitable for transplantation, they are tested for blood- and tissue-type. Then, when a donor becomes available, the patient whose blood-type is compatible and whose tissue-type most closely matches the donor's is selected.[47] When time does not permit donor-recipient matching, some hospitals select the patient who will most probably be compatible with a random donor.[48]

III. COMPETING VALUES AND INTERESTS

The constitutional precepts of equal protection and due process seem relevant to the problem of patient selection practices. But the operative demands of these provisions are yet to be determined in the area of organ allocation. As a practical matter, judicial intervention in the patient selection process probably will be limited by insufficient time to secure review and by the judiciary's reluctance to meddle in hospital decisions.[49] When legislatures or administrators try to establish the most rational and least offensive selection procedures, a broad range of factors other than constitutional limitations must be taken into account. It is useful, therefore, to set forth independently the competing interests relevant to patient selection, before considering how they inform constitutional demands and proper legislative response.

A. UNIVERSAL TREATMENT

Unhappily it is a premise of selection in artificial organ and organ transplant programs that some individuals are thereby denied the opportunity to survive. It is difficult to accept the fact that existing methods of prolonging life are inaccessible to large numbers of citizens,[50] and therefore it might be argued that the only fair solution is universal treatment. But even if lack of money were the only barrier to universal distribution,[51] shifting sufficient funds to organ programs might disserve the goal of maximizing total health care. For example, funds for research as to causes of renal failure or for provision of adequate medical attention to large numbers of disadvantaged persons [52] may, in the long run, result in a greater number of lives saved. Since the state must make some such allocation of resources, selection may be unavoidable.

B. EQUAL OPPORTUNITY FOR SURVIVAL

Even more troubling than objections to selection are objections to some of the criteria used. Selection alone does not necessarily deny the principle of equality of human life; individuals could be chosen on a random basis. But where society uses the standards of reward for past accomplishments or likelihood of future achievement, it is making the unwonted normative judgment that one individual's life is more worthy of preservation than another's. In the case of deliberate taking of life, "[t]he governing standard is not the merit or need or value of the victim but equality of worth as a human being." [53] The operation of this principle was illustrated in the famous shipwreck case of *United States v. Holmes*,[54] where some of the occupants of a longboat had to be removed so that the longboat would not sink and drown all; there, the only fair solution the court could suggest for deciding who should live and who should perish was a lottery. A social worth classification, on the other hand, embodies a value judgment of who the "good" people are, and can easily become a manifestation of majoritarian oppression. Deliberate discriminatory motives aside, it is reasonable to presume that the majority's judgment of the preferred people reflects its own values.[55] Social worth classifications appear especially prone to discriminate against the poor and underprivileged.[56] Criteria of occupation and community participation, for example, would exclude the unemployed and the alienated.

C. MAXIMIZING USE OF RESOURCES

Most of the arguments supporting purposeful rather than random selection of patients relate to the goal of maximizing society's use of available resources. An initial selection is exercised by physicians in determining fitness for treatment. A medical judgment that treatment will benefit the patient—through prolonged life, for example—seems necessary in order to justify commitment of resources. But physicians' judgments have extended farther, to consider nonmedical questions of "useful" survival—whether an individual will be able to resume a gainful occupation,[57] for example, or whether an older person has a life expectancy of sufficient length.[58] These decisions are akin to the more explicit social worth criteria which measure an individual's potential contribution to society. The justification generally offered for all such distinctions is that since all cannot be saved, society is entitled to minimize its losses by saving those who can contribute most. This maximization of social utility argument seems problematical at best. While majority agreement may be reached on some standards, quantification and meaningful comparison is almost impossible when several persons with several attributes are involved.[59] From a larger perspective, the benefits to society of preserving more productive individuals in need of organs are marginal; currently, with the small numbers involved, a policy of favoring employed people, for example, will have little influence upon national productivity. The use of some social worth criteria alternatively can be explained as an attempt to reward past performance and to

encourage similar performance in others.[60] Any substantial effect on primary activity, however, seems extremely unlikely, since people normally do not order their lives in contemplation of needing an artificial or transplanted organ. Finally, society's objectives of maximizing productivity and rewarding desirable conduct cannot be viewed in a vacuum. The small return to society from social worth evaluations must be balanced against the infringement of equality of life; both maximizing productivity and rewarding good conduct can no doubt be achieved by alternatives less offensive than denying equal opportunity for survival to some members of the community.

D. ADMINISTRATION OF THE SELECTION PROCESS

After medical decisions have been made, the further costs of administering a first come, first served or lottery system of selection should not be significant. When social worth criteria are used, on the other hand, substantial administrative costs may be expected. Some hospitals, for example, send out trained investigators to compile extensive background data for evaluating potential recipients.[61] Add to this the time spent by decisionmakers in scrutinizing records and comparing applicants, and the total cost in many cases may cancel out the already marginal gain to be derived from selecting the worthiest individual. An even greater problem is the difficulty of establishing fair procedures for administration of social worth criteria. If society's objectives are of such importance that the normal presumption in favor of equality is overcome, standards should be applied carefully and accurately. But to achieve this objective would require extensive checks and procedural safeguards to guarantee the accuracy of information used and careful adherence to establish selection bases. In fact, the time limits imposed on the decisionmaking process may preclude such certainty. Furthermore, the difficulty of establishing explicit and specifically defined criteria of social value may result in delegation of considerable discretion to administrators. Vague standards and wide discretion not only yield less consistency, but may also diminish effective control of selection practices by the political process and conceal arbitrary and discriminatory action.[62]

IV. Sources of Control

A. CONSTITUTIONAL LIMITATIONS

1. State Action. Whether hospital practice in patient selection is subject to the demands of due process and equal protection depends initially upon a finding of state action.[63] State-operated hospitals are certainly subject to such guarantees, and recent decisions indicate that most private hospitals are within the reach of these constitutional restrictions. A case-by-case method to determine state action, by sifting facts and weighing circumstances, was applied by the Fourth Circuit to a private hospital in *Sinkins v. Moses H. Cone Memorial Hospital.*[64] There, receipt of federal and state funds under the Hill-Burton hospital construction program in conjunction with a significant degree of state and federal planning was deemed sufficient state involvement to justify finding state action.[65] *Eaton v. Grubbs*[66] concerned a hospital not receiving Hill-Burton funds, yet the court found that other factors—including state regulation pursuant to North Carolina's participation in that program, a reverter clause, capital construction subsidies, tax exemption, eminent domain power, and original status of the hospital building as a government project—together resulted in state action. Other indicia of state involvement are participation by private hospitals in Medicare and Medicaid programs requiring extensive government planning,[67] and direct state funding and supervision of a specific transplant or artificial organ program. In Illinois, for example, the legislature has appropriated one million dollars for dialysis; the state is playing an active role in establishing and approving centers to receive these funds and in the formulation of patient selection standards.[68] Finally, the public function performed by a private agency has sometimes been regarded as a significant indicium of state action.[69] Although historically hospitals have not been public institutions in this country, today most people do not differentiate between public and private hospitals, and regard hospital care as a state responsibility.[70]

2. Equal Protection. While it has been argued that a state can distribute its largess as it pleases, the right-privilege distinction has been seriously undermined in the equal protection area: a state must avoid arbitrary classifications in disbursing funds or benefits.[71] Judicial willingness to characterize a classification as arbitrary has varied with the importance of the underlying interests involved and the nature of the classification employed. When "suspect" classifications such as race or alienage are used, or when distinctions are set up which affect adversely the fundamental personal interests of a particular class, clear justification of unequal treatment is demanded.[72] The interest in survival seems to require such justification of patient selection practices, particularly when coupled with criteria of selection that have characteristics of suspect classifications.

(a) Ability to Pay. While universal treatment may not be possible because of the limited facilities available, the question of whether ability to pay is a valid operative criterion for selection remains. Wealth has sometimes been regarded as a suspect classification needful of strict scrutiny.[73] In criminal procedure cases, the Court has compelled states to provide certain legal services to an accused indigent which a wealthier person could obtain on his own.[74] However, there are compelling state interests running counter to a requirement that specialized treatments such as artificial organs or transplants be provided without charge, or that the state aid all those who would have been selected had they been able to afford treatment. Free medical assistance for these expensive treatments may interfere with a sound legislative program to maximize health care. Legislative determinations probably should be given greater deference by the courts in the area of medical services than in the area of criminal procedure. The very wisdom of judicial intervention to require free treatment is questionable. It could prompt decreased appropriations for new facilities from a hostile state legislature anticipating the multiplied costs entailed, for even general medical care is not yet viewed as a right to which all are entitled regardless of cost. If the legislature should deny funds to support a free-treatment system, hospitals would be unable to comply with a command to waive costs, and the judiciary would be in the difficult position of attempting to compel legislative disbursements.[75]

(b) Social Worth. Although social worth classifications have not specifically been labelled "suspect," they present a serious danger of discriminatory treatment of minority interests;

when applied with respect to the important interest of survival, compelling justification for their use should be required. Whether such justification exists depends upon the specific state interests involved.

(i) Occupation. Occupational status is a criterion which can be applied with some precision. In most circumstances this criterion presents an easily resolvable factual issue, such as whether an individual is or is not employed, or what the nature of his job is. In addition, the criterion may be directly related to an acute societal need to maximize its resources—for example, ability to contribute to the national defense. An individual engaged in a critical occupation might be given priority when the "proper utilization of our most skilled human resources, especially those in shortest supply" [76] is deemed essential to the nation's existence. In wartime especially, greater deference is due the legislative judgment in national security matters,[77] and congressional power to favor with life-support aids those who will contribute most to the war effort may be necessary. But in peacetime, the relationship between occupation and national security becomes less obvious. When a state cannot justify its occupation-oriented selection practices on the basis of any clear and acute social necessities, the problem of discriminatory treatment becomes more salient. Since blue-collar workers would have more difficulty in resuming their occupations while undergoing hemodialysis than white-collar workers, for example, their chance to receive treatment would correspondingly be reduced.[78] Since means less burdensome to any particular class—such as job training programs —are available to realize this marginal increment to productivity, it is difficult to justify an occupational criterion.

(ii) Family. Society's interest in protecting the family may be asserted as a justification for assigning priority to parents. A standard of selection based on the number of children would be a definite and measurable criterion. In the case of a sole supporter, his death may create a financial burden for the community through increased welfare costs. Although the consideration of minimizing welfare expenses may be unpersuasive since the amount involved is inconsiderable, a parent's death is likely to create more than financial loss for his children. As long as society

accords high priority to the values of the family structure, the injury inflicted on children by reason of a parent's death may overcome the demand for equality.

(iii) Religion and Morality. Churchgoing has been considered significant in patient selection in Seattle,[79] but criteria of religiosity and church attendance appear to violate the establishment clause of the first amendment.[80] It has been held that when a statute's essential purpose has nothing to do with promoting morality, access to the statute's benefits cannot be conditioned upon adherence to norms of moral behavior.[81] Although a state constitutionally can punish immoral conduct,[82] and organs cannot be universally distributed, the justification is weak for the use of morality as a selection criterion where survival is concerned. The state has many alternative ways to encourage or reward morality which do not conflict with equality of access to life-preserving treatment.

3. Due Process. When decisions are made whether a person may have access to important benefits, the procedural safeguards demanded by due process vary with several considerations: the character of the information used, the nature of the questions decided,[83] the interests at stake,[84] and any countervailing factors to full procedural protection—in patient selection, especially, the need for speedy decisions. When selection decisions are arrived at only after extensive examination of background information,[85] the dangers of deciding on the basis of distorted and incomplete data generally necessitate a significant degree of procedural protection.[86] And, when an inquiry is made whether a person fits within a specified class, as in social worth judgments, the individual nature of the question presented ordinarily dictates a full hearing,[87] although the need for rapid adjudication may preclude the confrontation and cross-examination of a complete trial-type hearing.[88]

Anonymous committee decisions, such as those employed by Seattle, are intolerable. Although probably designed to avoid pressure on committee members from potential recipients and to ensure impartially,[89] secret proceedings prevent the check on arbitrary action that publicity and outward responsibility provide.[90] Anonymity might be combined with a full record and written findings, but the resultant sacrifice in public accountability of the decisionmakers does not seem outweighed by the danger of improper influence, to which judges and juries also are subject.[91] Use of secret information in reaching decisions also appears incompatible with due process. The possibility that full disclosure would reduce sources of information is outweighed by the importance of ensuring, as far as possible, that the information received is truthful. Along with full disclosure and decision on the record, the patient is entitled to an opportunity to rebut adverse evidence and to introduce additional information, particularly since he is best situated to explain or refute.[92] But the time factor may limit the hearing's scope: confrontation of the hospital examiner, but not of the people he interviewed, may be all that is possible. Confrontation of the investigator, however, seems essential to fairness because his report may conceal a shallow inquiry; subjecting his findings to close scrutiny at a hearing should prompt careful compilation and analysis of background data.

B. LEGISLATIVE PROPOSALS

Although the medical profession's interest in noninterference from lay personnel can be urged as a reason against legislative involvement in patient selection, that argument assumes that legislative intrusion would be short-sighted and insensitive to medical needs.[93] It is true that during the early experimental stages of new artificial organs or transplant operations, rigid legislation might impose improper medical standards derived from insufficient knowledge, divert innovators from full-time study on improving new treatment methods, or retard medical progress through a misleadingly high failure rate that produces erroneous assessment of medical advances.[94] And when immediate choice is necessary—because of the sudden appearance of a donor, for example—doctors must be able quickly to choose a patient lest the opportunity pass unused.[95] But insofar as nonmedical, social decisions are being made, legislative regulation seems clearly proper.[96] And as treatment becomes increasingly reliable, even the apparently medical requirements that affect selection deserve careful scrutiny.

1. Medical Evaluations. The use of ambiguous criteria like "cooperativeness" and "rehabilitation potential" facilitates consideration by physi-

cians of nonmedical factors. When ascertainable, these factors may significantly determine chances of success,[97] but some doctors and researchers have noted their basic uncertainty and subjectivity; in fact, little consistency of application of these standards among hospitals is apparent.[98] The troublesomeness of "cooperativeness" and "rehabilitation potential" is intensified by their likelihood of excluding minority group members.[99] State, regional or national agencies should be directed to compile hospital data in order to determine the validity of such standards. A broad term like "uncooperativeness" should be broken down into its specific components, such as low intelligence, a life history of "impulsive, irresponsible behavior," self-destructive wishes, and difficulty in relating to authority figures.[100] A demonstrated connection between the favored traits severally considered and ability to survive should be demanded if such criteria are to continue in use.[101] Reliable findings will not be possible until those expected to become failures are also given treatment as "control" groups.[102] Agencies responsible for collecting such data could ultimately provide more definite guidelines for selection and initiate periodic revision of standards in conformity with new knowledge. These guidelines would not preclude experimentation in order to develop superior methods, so long as the regular patient selection standards can be applied as modified to suit the investigator's needs.

Even when physical condition is the sole medical criterion, fairness is enhanced by establishing a board for medical selection, so that the patient will not have to convince the examining physician of error in his diagnosis. Assuming that some aspects of "cooperativeness" and "rehabilitation potential" are proper medical criteria, the committee could also counteract possible subjectivity in individual physicians' diagnoses. If this board is hospital-based, there is a danger that the resident specialists' conclusions would be favored over those of the patient's outside experts whenever disagreement develops; on the other hand, decision outside the hospital entails a sacrifice in the value of peer discipline and may prolong the selection process unduly.

2. Social Evaluations. If a legislature decides to make social worth classifications, the interests at stake—the patient's life and a legislative purpose so important that equality of human life is outweighed—demand a fair and reliable decisionmaking process. For simple factual questions such as number of dependents, a hearing need only be provided when the patient's claim is disputed. But where more complicated criteria such as contribution to the community are involved, opportunity to confront damaging witnesses should be provided where time permits.[103] Perhaps the only feasible means of accommodating the interest in confrontation and the demands of decisionmaking is to leave cross-examination of all except the hospital investigator to the committee's discretion.

Two means of social worth selection are possible: comparative evaluation among applicants or an elimination process that excludes—unless no other suitable recipients are available—patients who do not meet certain standards.[104] In comparative evaluation, although patients will have more incentive to attack the testimony or information supplied by other patients, and allowing them to cross-examine could thus further accurate comparison, an adversary system seems unworkable; in this multiparty context it would probably be chaotic and antithetical to rapid decisions. If an elimination process is utilized, the practicality of allowing patients an opportunity to be heard before reaching tentative decisions should at least be tested. Although rapid disposition of cases will be easier if hearings are provided only following adverse decisions, tentatively rejected patients would be in the difficult position of trying to convince the selection committee of its initial error. Presence of counsel at either type of proceeding would help to secure correct interpretation and application of selection criteria, and exclusion of irrelevant, prejudicial information. Counsel's participation, however, would have to be subject to the decisionmaker's regulation to prevent breakdown of the process by excessive delay.

The panel which makes medical decisions should be separate from the committee entrusted with ultimate selection among the medically qualified, so that information relevant to one stage does not affect the other. A separate panel of physicians may not be possible in light of doctors' work demands; since physicians are not especially qualified to judge social values, lay committees can be used. Legal advice from a city

solicitor or state attorney should be made readily available to facilitate correct application of formulated standards to individual fact situations.

While judicial review generally is useful to secure compliance with selection criteria and procedures, the principal, and perhaps controlling, drawback to judicial review is the time limitation.[105] Perhaps with provision made for advancing cases on the docket, the courts feasibly could hear allegations of unconstitutional or ultra vires action, especially when plain error on the face of the record allows summary judicial action.[106] But even if timely review is possible to determine whether proper factors were considered and whether the decision comports with the weight of the evidence, there may be no time for a hearing on remand to compare the applicants anew.

With the avenue of judicial review necessarily limited, an alternative method of regulating the decisionmaking process is needed. Since an appeal board presents the same problems as judicial review, a supervisory body might be set up to investigate local practices, with power when necessary to seek injunctive and declaratory relief. This agency should report regularly to the legislature not only to ensure its responsibility to the public, but also to facilitate legislative reform of organ allocation practices.

3. Alternatives to Social Worth Classifications.
If prediction could be sufficiently accurate, perhaps those closest to death (but not so ill as to be no longer medically suitable) should be entitled to a transplant, since there is always hope that more donors will appear. This factor is greatly reduced in hemodialysis, however, since the available quantity of machines is readily ascertainable, and access to treatment depends upon expansion of hospital facilities or the death of a current dialysis recipient. Unfortunately, the method of selecting those nearest death also precludes the advance certainty which other means of selection can provide, especially in hemodialysis where final selection by tissue-typing is unnecessary.

The significant procedural obstacles to a system that can reliably measure social worth undercuts a determination that the value of maximizing social productivity or rewarding past performance justifies a disregard of the principle of equality of human life. A first come, first served procedure—traditional hospital practice in the absence of unusual circumstances such as those of hemodialysis [107]—or a lottery provides a more egalitarian and practical alternative for selection among medically qualified patients.[108] The first come, first served system seems salutary in enabling a sick person to estimate immediately his chances of selection, so that he can try to find an opening elsewhere if he probably will not be taken.

NOTES

1. Adopted at Second General Assembly of the World Medical Association, Geneva, Switzerland, Sept. 1948, reprinted in 138 J.A.M.A. 435 (1948).

2. See, e.g., N.Y. Times, Oct. 29, 1968, at I, col. I (scarcity of heart donors).

3. Kidney machines, for example, require extensive supporting personnel, and adequate facilities are unlikely to be available outside the larger cities. Sanders & Dukeminier, "Medical Advance and Legal Lag: Hemodialysis and Kidney Transplantation," 15 *U.C.L.A.L. Rev.* 357, 358 (1968) [hereinafter cited as Sanders & Dukeminier].

4. See Scribner, "The Artificial Kidney," in *Senate Comm. on Gov't Operations, Subcomm. on Gov't Research, 90th Cong., 1st Sess., Research in the Service of Man: Biomedical Knowledge, Development, and Use* 182, 182–85 (Comm. Print 1967) [hereinafter cited as *Research in the Service of Man*].

5. A person with complete kidney failure needs treatments of 6 to 12 hours, 2 or 3 times a week. Sanders & Dukeminier 360.

6. See Eschbach, Barnett, Daly, Cole, & Scribner, "Hemodialysis in the Home," 67 *Annals Internal Med.* 1149 (1967).

7. Sanders & Dukeminier 366. The latter figure varies because of the remaining uncertainty as to when treatment will be effective. In fact, over 100,000 persons in the United States die annually of kidney disease. Proceedings, Conference to Consider the Treatment of Patients with Chronic Kidney Disease With Uremia, New York, June 20–22, 1963, at 15–16.

8. Lederberg, "The Heart Gap Will Cause Soul-Ache," *Washington Post*, July 24, 1966, § E, at 7, cols. 1–2. Electronic pace-makers and plastic heart valves are presently employed where total heart replacement is unnecessary. Since pacemakers are more widely available, the allocation problem is much less serious. By 1967, 25,000 people were alive and functioning with the aid of this device. *Hearings on Biomedical Development, Evaluation of Existing Federal Institutions Before the Subcomm. on Gov't Research of the Senate Comm. on Gov't Operations*, 90th Cong., 1st Sess. 251 (1967) (testimony of Dr. Adrian Kantrowitz).

9. Artificial lungs, liver, pancreas, small intestine, and many other organs are forecast. Schreiner, "Achievements and Possibilities in Artificial Organs," in *Research in the Service of Man* 173, 175–79.

10. See Rubini, Goldman, Agre, Koppel, Kopple, Gral, Shinaberger, & Sokol, "Dialysis and Transplantation: Some Interactions and Comparisons," 14 *Trans. Am. Soc'y Artif. Internal Organs* 355, 356 (1968).

11. The estimated survival rate one year after operation with cadaver donors rose from 39% in 1967, Murray, Barnes, & Atkinson, *Fifth Report of the Human Kidney Transplant Registry*, 5 *Transplantation* 752, 774 (1967), to 45% in 1968.

Committee of the Transplant Registry, *Sixth Report of the Human Kidney Transplant Registry*, 6 *Transplantation* 944, 951 (1968).

12. 114 *Cong. Rec.* S1103 (daily ed. Feb. 8, 1968) (remarks of Sen. Mondale).

13. For a detailed description of the preparation of that operation and post-transplant care see the series of articles contained in 41 *S. Afr. Med. J.* 1260–77 (1967).

14. Starzl, Groth, Brettschneider, Moon, Fulginiti, Cotton, & Porter, "Extended Survival in 3 Cases of Orthotopic Homotransplantation of the Human Liver," 63 *Surgery* 549 (1968).

15. *Hearings on S. J. Res. 145 Before the Subcomm. on Gov't Research of the State Comm. on Gov't Operations*, 90th Cong., 2d Sess. 12 (1968) (remarks of Sen. Mondale) [hereinafter cited as *Hearings on S. J. Res. 145*].

16. See 93 Science News, Mar. 2, 1968, at 214.

17. See Quinton, Dillard, & Scribner, "Cannulation of Blood Vessels for Prolonged Hemodialysis," 6 *Trans. Am. Soc'y Artif. Internal Organs* 104 (1960).

18. Of 11 dialysis centers supported by the Public Health Service Kidney Disease Control Program that replied to a questionnaire, all 11 listed as criteria for selection freedom from other debilitating or systemic illness, 8 mentioned age within the range of 15 to 60 years, 7 used "motivation, cooperativeness, family support," and 6 considered potential for rehabilitation. Abram & Wadlington, "Selection of Patients for Artificial and Transplanted Organs," 69 *Annals Internal Med.* 615, 618 (1968).

19. Sanders & Dukeminier 367–68; de Wardener, "Some Ethical and Economic Problems Associated With Intermittent Haemodialysis," in *CIBA Foundation Symposium, Ethics in Medical Progress* 104, 107–08 (G. Wolstenholme & M. O'Connor eds. 1966) [hereinafter cited as *CIBA Foundation Symposium*].

20. See Schupak & Merrill, "Experience With Long-term Intermittent Hemodialysis," 62 *Annals Internal Med.* 509, 516 (1965).

21. Sanders & Dukeminier 368–69; Scribner, Fergus, Boen, & Thomas, "Some Therapeutic Approaches to Chronic Renal Insufficiency," 16 *Annual Rev. Med.* 285, 291 (1965).

22. E.g., Wadsworth Veterans Administration Hospital in Los Angeles. Rubini & Goldman, "Chronic Renal Disease: Some Sociological Aspects of Dialysis and Transplantation," 108 *Cal. Med.* 90 (1968).

23. E.g., Veterans Administration Hospital in Washington, D.C. Gombos, Lee, Harton, & Cummings, "One Year's Experience with an Intermittent Dialysis Program," 61 *Annals Internal Med.* 462, (1964).

24. Id.; J. Husek, Psychological Aspects of Chronic Hemodialysis: A Summary and Review of the Literature; Suggestions for Further Research, 1966, at 8 (mimeo.) (prepared at School of Public Health, UCLA).

25. E.g., University of Washington Medical School. Sand, Livingston, & Wright, "Psychological Assessment of Candidates for a Hemodialysis Program," 64 *Annals Internal Med.* 602, 602–04 (1966).

26. Schupak & Merril, supra note 20, at 516; Scribner, Fergus, Boen, & Thomas, supra note 21, at 291 (likelihood of maintaining "a full-time gainful occupation").

27. See Proceedings, Conference on the Ethical Aspects of Experimentation on Human Subjects, Boston, Nov. 3 & 4, 1967, at 92 (remarks of Prof. Curran).

28. See *Hearings on S. J. Res. 145*, at 20 (statement of Dr. John S. Najarian).

29. See, e.g., Transcript of WNBC-TV broadcast of *Who Shall Live?* at 7 (Nov. 28, 1965).

30. See Proceedings, Conference on the Ethical Aspects of

Experimentation on Human Subjects, supra note 27, at 93 (remarks of Dr. Louis Lasagna).

31 See de Wardener, "Some Ethical and Economic Problems Associated with Intermittent Haemodialysis," in *CIBA Foundation Symposium* 104, 106–08.

32. For a detailed description of criteria in patient selection and the methods of decisionmaking see S. Goldenfarb, Patient Selection for the Artificial Kidney: A Medico-Legal Case Study, Mar. 10, 1967, at 35–55 (unpublished third-year student paper submitted to Prof. William J. Curran, Harvard Law School).

33. Alexander, "They Decide Who Lives, Who Dies," *Life,* Nov. 9, 1962, at 102.

34. Breslow, "Public Health Report," 107 *Cal. Med.* 360 (1967).

35. Abram & Wadlington, *supra* note 18, at 618–19.

36. E.g., Elmhurst, N.Y. General Hospital. Schupak, Sullivan, & Lee, "Chronic Hemodialysis in 'Unselected' Patients," 67 *Annals Internal Med.* 708 (1967) (using first come, first served).

37. See Proceedings, Conference on Dialysis as a "Practical Workshop," New York, June 26–28, 1966, at 3–4, 11–12.

38. Pendras & Erickson, "Hemodialysis: A Successful Therapy for Chronic Uremia," 64 *Annals Internal Med.* 293, 307 (1966).

39. If the immunological barrier, which severely narrows the number of patients suitable for transplantation from an available donor, is broken, the sphere of medical judgments will contract; this would increase the number medically qualified among whom some further selection must be made. Sanders & Dukeminier 393.

40. *Hearings on S. J. Res.* 145, at 36 (statement of Dr. Adrian Kantrowitz).

41. *Hearings on Biomedical Development, Evaluation of Existing Federal Institutions,* supra note 8, at 100–01 (testimony of Dr. James A. Shannon, Director, National Institutes of Health).

42. Schrire & Beck, "Human Heart Transplantation—The Pre-Operative Assessment," 41 *S. Afr. Med. J.* 1263 (1967).

43. Interhospital Organ Bank, Organ Donation for Transplantation: Information for Physicians, Oct. 26, 1968, at 1.

44. See Eschbach, Barnett, Daly, Cole, & Scribner, supra note 6, at 1161.

45. A recent estimate of the cost of a renal transplant is $15,000. See *Hearings on S. J. Res.* 145, at 20 (statement of Dr. Najarian). Heart transplants with post-operative care cost approximately $75,000, according to National Institutes of Health figures. Id. at 87 (remarks of Sen. Ribicoff).

46. Sanders & Dukeminier 393.

47. See Amos, "Transplantation—Opportunities and Problems," in *Research in the Service of Man* 177, 179.

48. Rubini, Goldman, Agre, Koppel, Kopple, Gral, Shinaberger, & Sokol, supra note 10, at 359.

49. See *Health Law Center, Problems in Hospital Law* 10 (1968). But see Manlove v. Wilmington Gen. Hosp., 53 Del. 338, 169 A.2d 18 (Super. Ct.), aff'd on other grounds, 54 Del. 15, 174 A.2d 135 (1961) (private hospital has duty to render emergency assistance because of its public function).

50. See pp. 1323–24 supra.

51. Other obstacles are the need for doctors and supporting personnel qualified to provide the treatment and, in the case of transplants, sufficient donors. See p. 1322 & note 3 supra.

52. The same amount of funds to support 25,000 persons on dialysis could provide comprehensive ambulatory health care for more than 1,250,000 poor people. 114 *Cong. Rec.* S1103 (daily ed. Feb. 8, 1968) (remarks of Sen. Mondale).

53. Freund, "Ethical Problems in Human Experimentation," 273 *N. Eng. J. Med.* 687, 688 (1965). Although in some sense social worth of convicted criminals may be used as a criterion for clemency from capital punishment, the grant of life to one is not at the expense of another. Sanders & Dukeminier 375–76. Similarly, in wrongful death actions no comparisons are drawn; the damage action seeks to provide appropriate recompense for a death that has already occurred.

54. 26 F. Cas. 360 (No. 15,383) (C.C.E.D. Pa. 1842).

55. See *The Federalist* No. 10 (J. Madison).

56. It is especially difficult to justify such discrimination at this level, since as a practical matter, many members of these groups never request treatment; those on the fringe of society are also likely to be on the fringe of medical care. Letter from Dr. George Schreiner, President, National Kidney Foundation, to the *Harvard Law Review,* Dec. 31, 1968.

57. See note 26 supra.

58. See p. 1325 supra.

59. See Sanders & Dukeminier 376–78.

60. See generally Developments in the Law—Equal Protection, 82 *Harv. L. Rev.* 1065, 1166–67 (1969).

61. Letter from Dr. Laurence R. Tancredi, Social Analysis and Evaluation Program, Dep't of Health, Educ., & Welfare, to the *Harvard Law Review,* Dec. 9, 1968; see Husek, supra note 24, at 8; Transcript of WNBC-TV broadcast of *Who Shall Live?,* at 6 (Nov. 28, 1965).

62. See Cahn & Cahn, "The New Sovereign Immunity," 81 *Harv. L. Rev.* 929, 944–48 (1968).

63. See, e.g., Civil Rights Cases, 109 U.S. 3, 10–19 (1883).

64. 323 F.2d 959 (4th Cir. 1963), cert. denied, 376 U.S. 938 (1964), citing Burton v. Wilmington Parking Authority, 365 U.S. 715 (1961); see Sams v. Ohio Valley Gen. Hosp. Ass'n, 257 F. Supp. 369, 371 (N.D.W. Va. 1966).

65. When state or municipal funding provides virtually the sole support for a private institution, state action has been found, see Kerr v. Enoch Pratt Free Library, 149 F.2d 212 (4th Cir.), cert denied, 326 U.S. 721 (1945), but less significant appropriations to aid a private group, without other indicia of state involvement, have generally been considered insufficient. See Developments in the Law—Academic Freedom, 81 *Harv. L. Rev.* 1045, 1056–57 & n.7 (1968).

66. 329 F.2d 710 (4th Cir. 1964).

67. 42 U.S.C. §§ 1395, 1396 (Supp. III, 1968).

68. Ill. Ann. Stat. ch. 111½, §§ 22.31–.33 (Smith-Hurd Supp. 1969); Act of Aug. 17, 1967, § 4, [1967] Ill. Laws 3080 (uncodified appropriation). See also *Hearings on Biomedical Development, Evaluation of Existing Federal Institutions,* supra note 8, at 94 (testimony of Dr. James Shannon, Director, National Institutes of Health) (NIH closely involved in development of artificial kidney and heart); id. at 105–15 (regional medical programs for heart disease).

69. See Terry v. Adams, 345 U.S. 461, 484 (1953) (Clark, J., concurring) (four Justices, in plurality opinion, found private political organization to have taken on "those attributes of government which draw the Constitution's safeguards into play"); cf. Food Employees Local 590 v. Logan Valley Plaza, Inc., 391 U.S. 308 (1968) (picketing on property of privately owned shopping center protected by first amendment).

70. *Hearings on S. J. Res.* 145, at 274–75 (statement of Chief Judge Bazelon, D.C. Cir.). The "public character" of a park, see Evans v. Newton, 382 U.S. 296, 302 (1966), and the importance of an orphanage to the general welfare, see Pennsylvania v. Brown, 270 F. Supp. 782, 791–92 (E.D. Pa. 1967), aff'd 392 F.2d 120 (3d Cir. 1968), cert. denied, 391 U.S. 921 (1968), have been considered significant in finding state action.

71. See 1 K. Davis, *Administrative Law Treatise* § 7.12, at 455–57 (1958) [hereinafter cited as Davis]; Van Alstyne, "The Demise of the Right-Privilege Distinction in Constitutional

Law," 81 *Harv. L. Rev.* 1439, 1454–57 (1968).

72. See generally Developments in the Law—Equal Protection, 82 *Harv. L. Rev.* 1065, 1087–1132 (1969).

73. See Harper v. Virginia Bd. of Elections, 383 U.S. 663 (1966) (poll tax); Griffin v. Illinois, 351 U.S. 12 (1956) (transcripts on appeal). See also Foote, "The Coming Constitutional Crisis in Bail: II," 113 *U. Pa. L. Rev.* 1125 (1965).

74. See Douglas v. California, 372 U.S. 353 (1963) (counsel on appeal); Griffin v. Illinois, 351 U.S. 12 (1956). See generally Note, Discriminations Against the Poor and the Fourteenth Amendment, 81 *Harv. L. Rev.* 435 (1967). A possible distinction between the criminal appeals cases and patient selection is that in patient selection illness, not the state, threatens the individual. The distinction is difficult to maintain, however, for Griffin asserted that a right of appellate review is not constitutionally required. 351 U.S. at 18. If that is the case, the state's threat had ended with the prior determination of guilt, and the appeals in both Douglas and Griffin offered an escape from punishment.

75. But cf. Griffin v. County School Bd., 377 U.S. 218, 233–34 (1964) (county supervisors may be compelled to raise funds to reopen schools). A similar problem arose from the cases providing free counsel and transcripts, see Cox, "The Supreme Court, 1965 Term, Foreward: Constitutional Adjudication and the Promotion of Human Rights," 80 *Harv. L. Rev.* 91, 93 (1966), but in criminal cases courts have the power to order that prisoners who have been discriminated against be released. A court can do nothing to discharge an unfairly treated patient from the burden of his illness.

76. *Civilian Advisory Panel on Military Manpower Procurement, 90th Cong., 1st Sess., Report to the House Comm. on Armed Services* 13 (Comm. Print 1967) (occupational deferments in selective service).

77. Cf. Korematsu v. United States, 323 U.S. 214, 223–24 (1944); Hirabayashi v. United States, 320 U.S. 81, 93 (1943).

78. See Proceedings, Conference on Dialysis as a "Practical Workshop," New York, June 26–28, 1966, at 41–42 (statement of Dr. Milton Rubini, Wadsworth Veterans Administration Hospital, Los Angeles). But since heavy physical activity is subsequently restricted, preference of heavy laborers over unemployed could not be so explained.

79. Schreiner, "Problems of Ethics in Relation to Haemodialysis and Transplantation," in *CIBA Foundation Symposium* 126, 128.

80. See, e.g., Everson v. Board of Educ., 330 U.S. 1, 15–16 (1947) (dictum).

81. See Glona v. American Guar. & Liab. Ins. Co., 391 U.S. 73 (1968) (wrongful death action by mother for loss of illegitimate son).

82. King v. Smith, 392 U.S. 309, 334 (1968) (dictum).

83. See I *Davis* § 7.01, at 407–11.

84. The right-privilege distinction, which has served in the past as a shield for arbitrariness, breaks down in practice as the importance of the underlying interests are recognized. See Dixon v. Alabama Bd. of Educ., 294 F.2d 150 (5th Cir.), cert. denied, 368 U.S. 930 (1961); 1 *Davis* §§ 7.11–.13, at 452–73.

85. Such data is compiled to evaluate "cooperativeness" and "rehabilitation potential" as well as social worth. See sources cited at note 61 supra.

86. See Willner v. Committee on Character & Fitness, 373 U.S. 96 (1963) (confrontation and cross-examination required by due process for bar admissions). In child custody cases, for example, where trained investigators are frequently used by the courts, full disclosure and decision on the record is generally held required by due process. E.g., Williams v. Williams, 8 Ill. App. 2d 1, 130 N.E.2d 291 (1955); see Foster & Freed, "Child Custody (Part II)," 39 *N.Y.U.L. Rev.* 615, 618, 622 (1964). The inadequacies and unfairness of post-conviction sentencing procedure, a prominent exception to the general rule in favor of full disclosure, are discussed in Note, "Procedural Due Process at Judicial Sentencing for Felony," 81 *Harv. L. Rev.* 821, 826–46 (1968).

87. 1 *Davis* § 7.07, at 420–22; compare Londoner v. Denver, 210 U.S. 373 (1908), with Bi-Metallic Inv. Co. v. State Bd. of Equalization, 239 U.S. 441 (1915).

88. See 1 *Davis* § 7.02, at 412.

89. Murray, Tu, Albers, Burnell, & Scribner, "A Community Hemodialysis Center for the Treatment of Chronic Uremia," 8 *Trans. Am. Soc'y Artif. Internal Organs* 315, 316 (1962).

90. See Joint Anti-Fascist Refugee Comm. v. McGrath, 341 U.S. 123, 170–72 (1951) (Frankfurter, J., concurring) (listing charitable organizations as Communist); In re Oliver, 333 U.S. 257, 266–73 (1948) (secret summary conviction for contempt). To the extent deliberations are secret, the moral authority and acceptability of the results also may be undermined. The partial invisibility of selective service determinations has been a strong factor in reducing public confidence in that system. See *Civilian Advisory Panel on Military Manpower Procurement*, supra note 76, at 14–15.

91. In patient selection, however, since individuals who have not offended society would otherwise be subjected to public scrutiny, perhaps the patients' names should be withheld from the public.

92. Cf. 1 *Davis* § 7.02, at 412–13.

93. Considerable apprehension on these grounds has been expressed to a proposed commission to evaluate the implications of biomedical advances. E.g., *Hearings on S.J. Res.* 145, at 84–87 (testimony of Dr. Christiaan Barnard).

94. de Wardener, "Some Ethical and Economic Problems Associated with Intermittent Haemodialysis," in *CIBA Foundation Symposium* 104, 108. In fact, guaranteeing fairness in patient selection is not the matter of central concern when an unproven medical technique is used; rather, it is ensuring that human experimentation is confined within ethically acceptable limits. See, e.g., *Boston University Law-Medicine Research Institute, Clinical Investigation in Medicine: Legal, Ethical, and Moral Aspects* 1–309 (I. Ladimer & R. Newman eds. 1963).

95. In practice, situations demanding immediate decision without time for rational deliberation may be rare in hemodialysis, see p. 1327 supra, and will arise less frequently in transplantation as organ preservation techniques are improved; but in the latter case present capability is still rudimentary, and final selection is a matter of hours. See Robertson & Jacob, "The Significance and Future of Organ Banking," 74 *Case & Com.* 17, 17–19, 21–23 (1969).

96. See Munn v. Illinois, 94 U.S. 113, 123–30 (1877).

97. Compare Sand, Livingston, & Wright, supra note 25, at 608, with Retan & Lewis, "Repeated Dialysis of Indigent Patients for Chronic Renal Failure," 64 *Annals Internal Med.* 284, 292 (1966). But see Schupak, Sullivan, & Lee, supra note 36, at 716.

98. See Husek, supra note 24, at 8.

99. Some tests for rehabilitation potential, for example, might work to exclude Negroes from consideration, even those who may appear to meet white middle-class standards. Compare Sand, Livingston, & Wright, supra note 25, at 603 (dangers of accepting for dialysis persons with low self-esteem and lacking firm identifications with family, friends, or job), with A. Kardiner & L. Ovesey, *The Mark of Oppression: Explorations in the Personality of the American Negro* 301–17, 359–67 (Meridian ed. 1962) (Negroes found to have low self-esteem and poor relations to family, friends, and job).

100. Sand, Livingston, & Wright, supra note 25, at 602–03.

101. The value of both psychological testing and examina-

tion in prediction of patient response under dialysis is uncertain. See Husek, supra note 24, at 8–16; M. Meldrum, J. Wolfram, & M. Rubini, Chronic Hemodialysis: Socio-Economic Impact on a Veteran Patient Group, 1966, at 11–12 (mimeo.) (prepared at Veterans Administration Center, Los Angeles, and UCLA Dep't of Med.); Sanders & Dukeminier 369–70. The doctor who first successfully used a dialysis machine deplores psychological evaluations: "To have seen a psychiatrist once in one's life jeopardizes one's employment with many companies. Are we from now on also going to exclude the same people from the treatment of uremia?" Kolff, "Letter to the Editor," 61 *Annals Internal Med.* 359, 360 (1964).

102. Such studies are not generally undertaken. Husek, supra note 24, at 29.

103. See Willner v. Committee on Character & Fitness, 373 U.S. 906, 107–08 (1963) (Goldberg, J., concurring).

104. For example, residency, parenthood, and employment requirements could be established as standards. Since these would not automatically equate the number of eligible recipients with the number for whom treatment is available, the process probably would be completed on a first come, first served basis. The practicality of elimination in transplantation presently is doubtful because of tissue-typing problems.

105. Cf. Falbo v. United States, 320 U.S. 549 (1944) (speed necessary for military mobilization precludes pre-induction review). The right to review even of alleged unconstitutional agency action may be contingent upon a balancing process. See Saferstein, "Nonreviewability: A Functional Analysis of 'Committed to Agency Discretion,'" 82 *Harv. L. Rev.* 367, 373 n.31 (1968).

106. The Court has shown great reluctance, even when faced with a reasonably apparent legislative intention to exclude review, to deny redress where manifest abuse of authority occurs. Compare Clark v. Gabriel, 393 U.S. 256 (1968), with Oestereich v. Selective Service System Local Bd. No. 11, 393 U.S. 233 (1968).

107. See G. Schreiner, Ethics of Chronic Dialysis, 1968, at 10–13 (mimeo.), to be published in *Chronic Maintenance Dialysis* (M. Rubini ed. 1969).

108. Until development of more effective immunosuppression treatment reduces the need for sophisticated tissue-typing, the patient highest on the waiting list or first selected in the lottery would not necessarily be chosen for transplantation. These methods, like social worth selection, could only establish an order of preference; the first *compatible* recipient would be chosen.

PAUL FREUND

Organ Transplants: Ethical and Legal Problems *

Until we secure an adequate supply of organs— natural or artificial—to meet the needs, there will be problems of allocation of these resources: from whom they should come and to whom they should be transferred. By what criteria should these decisions be made? The question implicates moral, legal, and medical considerations, which differ in the cases of removal after death and removal during life.

The moral and legal problems attending the taking of an organ from a cadaver appear to be well on the way to resolution. Although objection to the mutilation of a corpse has been traditional in Orthodox Judaism, as the life-saving potential of transplants has become clearer the resistance

on religious grounds has weakened.[1] Legal obstacles have been more widespread. Under the principles of the common law a person could not in his lifetime determine by will or agreement how his bodily organs should be treated after death; and the authority of the next of kin was essentially limited to providing a decent burial. While more recent legal precedents could be construed to authorize the next of kin to donate organs, the authority was not beyond peradventure clear, and since the next of kin might be unknown, or unavailable or hostile, the procedure for securing approval was at best unsatisfactory especially in situations where the utmost promptness in removal was essential for the viability of the organ.[2]

The problem of obtaining the necessary consent has now been resolved from another direction. The Uniform Anatomical Gift Act, which has been adopted in forty-eight states authorizes

* From *Proceedings of the American Philosophical Society,* Vol. 115 (1971), pp. 276–281. Reprinted by permission of the author and publisher, the American Philosophical Society. (Footnotes renumbered.)

an individual to donate his body, or certain organs or tissues for purpose of transplantation or other scientific use, by means of a relatively simple witnessed document, and there is a growing practice of using a card to signify his authorization. Many persons are now card-carrying potential donors of organs. Alternatively, the Act authorizes the next of kin (in order of priority, beginning with a surviving spouse) to grant authorization. The most serious problems that remain in the field of transplants from cadavers are thus the biological ones: the medical requirement that certain organs, notably the heart, be utilized in an oxygenated condition, precluding storage or even appreciable delay, and so necessitating early typing and matching of tissues.

Turning from the donation of organs after death to their donation for live transplants, we have to differentiate between paired and unpaired organs.

In the case of paired organs, like kidneys, the law is permissive, where the loss and the risk of further injury to the donor are moderate in relation to the anticipated benefit to the recipient. Indeed, a renal transplant has been authorized by a Massachusetts court even between minors who were twins, despite the rule that a child may not be made the subject of harm unless for his own benefit; the court reasoned, after interviewing the healthy twin, that he would suffer lasting psychic trauma if he were not allowed to contribute an organ to his brother so that they could continue to enjoy the blessings of life together.

From the ground of permitting the donation of a paired organ to save a life, should the law move to the position of requiring such contributions through a process of random selection? In Kantian terms, would we will a universal rule imposing an obligation on others to save us, and in return accept an obligation to save others in the same way? Compulsory vaccination is of course a different matter, since an unvaccinated person may be a positive menace. The law has hesitated to equate a duty to come to the aid of another with a duty to refrain from doing harm. Why should this reluctance persist? Three possible reasons can be suggested. First, there is a practical calculus. Compulsory giving may range along a spectrum from taxation to enforced martyrdom. There is an intuitively felt difference between the taking of one's substance and of one's

selfhood. In a situation of catastrophe one can imagine a conscription of blood, which is self-replenishing, more readily than a conscription of organs. The disproportion between risk to the donor and expected benefit to the donee would have to be greater and surer to warrant compulsion than to support a voluntary sacrifice; otherwise we might be in the position of the traveler in the desert, carrying a canister of water sufficient for one person, who is obliged to share it with another and thereby causes two deaths. Secondly, there would be practical problems of selection among all possible donors, since randomness is not a self-defining concept. And finally, enforced giving would diminish the moral quality of the act, though this consideration would be less relevant if scope were also left for voluntary donations. . . .

Coming now to the transplanting of an unpaired organ like the heart or liver, we confront the medical-moral-legal problem of how to obtain the organ early enough to make it viable and yet not secure it by performing a lethal operation on a living person. For a lethal operation, regardless of the consent of the subject, would be in violation of the criminal law. Why should this be so? Why should the law not recognize a right to dispose of one's life as one pleases? It is a question that has engaged philosophers from Socrates to Camus. There are, of course, many limitations in law and morals on an individual's freedom to do with himself as he will even though his action causes no particular harm to others. He may, for example, sell his services but may not sell himself into slavery. A secular explanation might take this form: since freedom of the will is the ground asserted for the legal privilege, an act that would irretrievably destroy this freedom forfeits the claim to immunity within its own terms. A similar rationale can be advanced for the law's protective intervention against self-destruction. But it would be disingenuous not to take account of the religious background of the law's concern.[3]

Although the Old Testament does not specifically denounce suicide, the Talmudists, building on the Sixth Commandment and other more remote Biblical texts, condemned the act. Plato, in the *Laws* (Book IX), justifies self-destruction when (as in Socrates' case) it is visibly ordained by an authoritative judgment, and he would bow also to the direction of Destiny, but in other cases it would be improper to take one's life without the approval of divine authority. The Christian disapproval derives from Augustine, who, it has been suggested, was disturbed by the excesses of a sect whose members, intent on the life hereafter, destroyed themselves in hordes when they believed themselves to be in a state of grace. Aquinas reasoned that suicide was an act contrary to man's nature, that it diminished society, and that it usurped the divine function. Again an exception was recognized for divine direction, apprehended mainly by saints.

English law, reflecting this religious heritage doubtless reinforced by the king's interest in conserving the manpower of the realm, dishonored the body of a suicide and visited forfeiture of property upon his heirs. (Roman law, with impeccable logic, had decreed forfeiture only in cases where the suicide was committed in order to avoid conviction of an offense that itself would have entailed such forfeiture.) The practice of burying a suicide at a crossroads, with a stake driven into the ground (to prevent the evil spirits from rising and doing mischief) was formally abolished in England in 1823, and forfeiture continued until as late as 1870. There were, to be sure, escape valves in the law. A finding that the act was committed while the mind was unbalanced was one; and there might be a question whether the event was due to a positive self-destructive act or to a passive exposure to deadly forces (did the water come to Ophelia, or did she go to the water, in the quibble of the gravedigger?)

In America, the states have taken different positions on the criminality of an act of suicide, a question not wholly academic, since it determines whether an unsuccessful attempt is punishable and since it affects the question whether one who aids and abets a suicide is himself guilty of a crime. In a substantial but decreasing number of states, suicide is still classified as a crime. And even if it were not a crime, it would not follow inevitably that inducing or aiding and abetting would likewise be innocent. Innocence would logically follow if the reason for immunity of the suicide itself were a policy to encourage it: but if the policy is simply to tolerate it, or to recognize that a potential suicide is not deterred by a legal rule, there is no logical entailment that an accessory must likewise be granted a privilege.

The bearing of this point on the performance by a surgeon of a consented to lethal operation is evident.

There have been, to be sure, powerful dissenting voices amid the chorus of condemnation. The Stoics and Epicureans admired a rational decision to end one's life. When Horatio reaches for the poisoned cup in Hamlet's hands he exclaims, "I am more an antique Roman than a Dane"(that is, than an Englishman, as is generally to be understood in Shakespeare). In England, John Donne wryly ascribed the official rejection of suicide to a desire to conserve the supply of members of a depressed working class, and David Hume could see nothing more "unnatural" in hastening one's death than in averting it by dodging a dangerous falling stone. But these were voices of nonconformity.

Should there be a special rule in any event, however, for altruistic suicide? Certainly the sentiment of society does not condemn, but in fact extols, certain forms, at least, of self-willed death in the service of fellow men. The soldier who falls on a grenade to save the lives of his comrades, the firefighter who exposes himself to the flames to rescue another, the man who throws himself in front of a train to toss out of danger a fallen child—these are heroic figures to be celebrated, not dishonored.

In comparing these examples of self-sacrifice with the willing of one's death for purposes of transplant, one should notice certain features of those instances. In each of them one or more of the following characteristics is present: the diversion of a deadly force; a vocation calling for disregard of self, upon which others may be relying; a sudden impulse, an almost reflexive act that would not in any event be amenable to the encouragement or deterrence of law.

These may be distinctions without a difference. Perhaps the time has come to face straightforwardly the question whether a dying patient should not be allowed to consent to surgical intervention for the sake of saving another's life. Such an approach would at least have the merit of focusing on the ethical and social issues involved. Considerations of this kind would then be afforded and weighed in opposition. It would be argued that to confer this discretion on a patient would put him in a psychologically intolerable position: he would be under great pressure to follow the noble course: if he did not a stigma might attach to his name, and if he did he would, by setting an example, make the decision even more intolerable for others in a similar position.[4] That the question cannot arise because of legal constraints may be a salutary shield for those who wish to take leave of life in peace and gentleness. But the most telling argument is that which concerns the physician. To take on the role of an active intervenor to end a life—an executioner, as it might be made to appear—would introduce a confusion of functions that could be unsettling to a practitioner of medicine and could erode the absolute trust that ought to prevail on the part of patients toward their physician. The judgment whether to use extraordinary supportive measures to prolong the life of a hopelessly ill patient, and whether to withdraw such measures in order not to prolong the process of dying, is agonizing enough. At least in making those decisions the physician can reflect that he is allowing natural forces to prevail and is not becoming an active destroyer. Even this discretion, which received the approval of Pope Pius XII in 1957, has not unfailingly seemed manifestly right. We quote today the lines of Arthur Hugh Clough as if they were a forthright prescription of the moral course:

Thou shalt not kill, yet need not strive
Officiously to keep alive.

Actually the lines were highly ironic, part of a satirical poem called "The Latest Decalogue," containing such companion couplets as

Thou shalt not covet; but tradition
Approves all forms of competition.

It is a striking example of the ethical heresy of one generation becoming the moral dogma of another.

Perhaps, despite the cogent objections that have been offered, we shall one day reach a consensus that will accept the self-sacrifice of a living person through the intervention of a surgeon. But at present the approach has taken a different turn—a redefinition of death that will in fact, if not in primary purpose, facilitate the removal of viable organs for transplantation. The problem, in short, is defined as a scientific one. It is pointed out that death is a process, in which various organs cease to function at various times. Tradi-

tionally the crucial time has been taken to be the cessation of the natural heartbeat. But aside from the convenience of the test and the figurative view of the heart as the vital center, there is no compelling reason for making that organ the decisive one in determining death. The proposed new definition focuses on brain death, evidenced by an irreversible coma, which in turn is identified by absence of reflexes, lack of response to intense stimuli, cessation of natural breathing, and a flat electroencephalogram, recorded over a period of twenty-four hours. All of these signs can be consistent with a continuing natural heartbeat, reinforced by artificial respiration. A finding of death according to these criteria would justify both the withdrawal of supportive measures and the availability of the heart and other organs for transplant. As explained by Dr. Henry K. Beecher, the chairman of the group at Harvard which has proposed the new definition, "Death is to be declared and *then* the respirator turned off." [5]

A number of practical questions are raised by this proposal.[6] How infallible is it as a prognosticator that neural activity in the brain will not revive? The sponsors are confident of its reliability provided the patient has not been in a state of hypothermia or of narcotic toxicity. Should it be adopted in some quarters even though in others the traditional definition is retained, and if so may there not be awkward problems of determining priority of death among the victims of a common disaster, where priority may determine succession to property? [7] How will the new definition affect the physician's discretion regarding the use or continuance of extraordinary measures? Must the physician in all cases wait for a find of brain death before the respirator is turned off, and if so may not the new definition produce the paradoxical result in some cases of actually extending the period of dying? What will be the logistical and legal problems of transporting a person declared dead but with a heartbeat supported by artificial respiration, who is moved to another state as a source of material for a transplant? Since, under the new definition, the body is a cadaver, what obstacles are presented by state laws that require special permission and embalming as a condition of transporting a body out of the state?

Beyond these practical problems there are deeper philosophical issues. Is the new definition a scientific tactic that obscures and diverts attention from the moral and social issues presented by extraordinary supportive measures and by the procedures for organ transplantation? Is it a convenient and plausible fiction—the tribute that change pays to continuity—which enables us to achieve new results without altering but merely by redefining the words of the old rules? Is it in effect an effort to answer some vexing, specific, diverse questions by a definitional generality, as if the way to consider the problems of abortion were to work out a definition of "life"? One is reminded of the cautionary words of I. A. Richards:

The temptation to introduce premature ultimates— Beauty in Aesthetics, the Mind and its faculties in psychology, Life in physiology, are representative examples—is especially great for believers in Abstract Entities. The objection to such Ultimates is that they bring an investigation to a dead end too suddenly.[8]

It is not essential that these questions be answered; it is only important, perhaps, that they shall have been asked—important lest the scientists be taken to have resolved through their special competence what are searching moral questions—lest, in short, the complex inquiry be brought to an end too suddenly.

There is one further question that ought to be raised in connection with the selection of donors: should a person be encouraged or permitted to sell his organs for purposes of transplant? In the case of donations of blood, where the risk to the donor is negligible, the question is relatively unimportant. We would not object on moral grounds to paying someone to stand in line for us at a ticket counter, though we would have the most serious moral qualms about paying for someone to take our place in a conscript army.[9] To save oneself by putting another in mortal danger through trading on his poverty strikes one as an immoral bargain. Is the case different if the bargain is struck not by the more affluent beneficiary but more impersonally by the state or a philanthropic institution? The question is analogous to that raised by a so-called volunteer army, using the inducement of higher pay for service, and the answer is equally debatable. The Uniform Anatomical Gift Act takes no position on the issue, leaving it to state law, although it can be said that the acceptability of compensation is strongest where the donation is to be made after death. In the case of an *inter vivos* transplant of serious nature, the allowance of a pecuniary motive is repugnant, as if society had a vested interest in maintaining an impoverished class of citizens to serve as risk-takers for others. If the need for organs is felt to be crucial, and if both payment and conscription are ruled out, a possibility remains of liberalizing the law concerning bodies at death, by enacting that post-mortem removal of organs may be effected unless the decedent or next of kin have affirmatively interposed an objection.[10] This is a step whose consideration ought to await evidence on the adequacy of the Uniform Act.

It is time to turn from the selection of donors to that of donees. Few decisions can be as harrowing as the choice of who shall live and who shall die, as any judge or governor can attest; and yet in those cases the law is dealing with persons whose guilt, at least in a legal sense, has been found, and where there is no constraint on sparing the lives of all. In our problem we are dealing with the constraints of scarcity and the consequent necessity of preferences for secular salvation and doom of innocent persons.

In 1943, when penicillin was in short supply for our forces in North Africa, two groups of soldiers could have benefited from its use: those who had contracted venereal disease, and those who suffered from infected battle wounds. The consulting surgeon advised, on moral grounds, that the wounded be given priority, but the medical officer in charge ruled that preference be given to the other group. The latter, he reasoned, could be restored to active duty more quickly, and immediate manpower was needed; moreover, if untreated they could be a threat to others. For good or ill, life's values are seldom so one-dimensional as they are on the front lines in wartime. Nevertheless efforts have been made to assess the comparative worth of patients to society in the rationing of scarce medical resources, notably renal dialysis equipment. At the center in Seattle, after a medical and psychiatric screening to identify those patients who could benefit substantially from the treatment, they are evaluated by an anonymous but predominantly lay committee, operating under no more definite criteria than social worth, which in practice has been judged by such factors as the number and need of dependents and civic service performed, such as scout leadership, religious-social teaching, and Red Cross activities.[11] One less confident that one's middle-class values represent eternal verities or even the clear hope of the future might well find it impossible to serve on such a committee. More pointedly, where the facilities are operated by a public agency there is a real question whether some more articulated and warrantable standards must be formulated to satisfy the demands of the constitutional guarantees of due process of law and equal protection of the laws.[12] When mortals are called on to make ultimate choice for life or death among their innocent fellows, the only tolerable criterion may be equality of worth as a human being. Translated into practical terms this means a procedure for selection based on randomness within a group, or on objective factors like age or priority of application.

Scarcity of resources presents not only a problem of selection of donors and donees but of allocation of medical facilities and personnel between transplant and other undertakings. At a large teaching hospital in Boston the decision was made not to engage in heart transplant surgery at the present time. To have done so would have required a material inroad on the program of open-heart surgery, where the operative results have been favorable in eighty to ninety per cent of the cases. Meanwhile basic work on the biological aspects of transplantation continued. Not every institution that has undertaken heart transplants, it can be said, was ideally suited for the mission. Should the decision to engage or not to engage in this form of surgery be left to the individual institution, or should not an effort be made to ration this enterprise in order to achieve a minimum of dislocation and a maximum of scientific progress in the experimental stage of a promising therapeutic procedure?

The upshot of our whole discussion is that the choices enforced by a scarcity of resources, and the awesome moral questions raised by deliberate programs to increase the number of donors of viable organs, point to a search for a solution that would by-pass these issues, so uncomfortable for human decision. It may not be thought an evasion, one hopes, to suggest that what is urgently needed is a program for the development of artificial organs, like teeth and limbs, to supersede the transplant of natural organs. The physical obstacles are admittedly formidable: how, for example, to provide a lasting and safe power supply for an implanted mechanical heart, and how to overcome the problem of clotting presented by a large foreign surface at the site of the heart. Yet the eventuality of biologists and engineers supplanting moralists and lawyers in the collaborative quest for bodily renewal is a consummation devoutly to be wished.

NOTES

1. D. Daube, "Limitations on Self-Sacrifice in Jewish Law and Tradition." *Theology* 72 (1969): pp. 291, 299; Carroll, "The Ethics of Transplantation," *Amer. Bar Assn. Jour.* 56 (1970): pp. 137, 138. (The Chief Rabbi of Israel hailed the first heart transplant in that country; the rabbinate, at the same time, asserted that post-mortem operations are prohibited by the Torah.)

2. ". . . in the light of current medical advances . . . existing 'anatomical' statutes, such as [the law providing for surrender of unclaimed bodies for the advance of medical science] are inadequate, and the need for appropriate statutory provision to implement the desires of the dying to aid the living is increasingly urgent," *Holland v. Metalious,* 105 N. H. 290, 293. 198 Atl.2d 654, 656 (1964).

3. The religious and historical background is described in Glanville Williams, *The Sanctity of Life and the Criminal Law* (Farber, London, 1958), c. 7, and N. St. John-Stevas, *Life, Death and the Law* (Indiana, Bloomington, 1961), c. 6, on which the following paragraphs draw.

4. Daube, *supra* note 1.

5. H. K. Beecher, "Scarce Resources and Medical Advancement," in *Experimentation with Human Subjects* (P. A. Freund, ed., Braziller, N.Y., 1970), pp. 67, 84.

6. See D. Rutstein, "The Ethical Design of Human Experiments," *op. cit. supra* note 7: pp. 383, 386–387. See also Paul Ramsey, *The Patient as Person* (Yale, New Haven, 1970), c. 2. This book, which came to my attention after this paper was prepared, is of great value for the whole discussion. Similarly valuable on the entire subject of transplants is the recent volume, David W. Meyers, *The Human Body and the Law* (Aldine, Chicago, 1970).

7. See e.g., *Smith v. Smith,* 229 Ark. 579, 317 S. W. 2d 275 (1958), pointing out that the Uniform Simultaneous Death Act, prescribing a rule of succession where deaths occur in a common disaster, applies only where there is no sufficient evidence to determine which party died first. The court rejected the "unusual and unique allegation" that a victim who remained unconscious for seventeen days had in fact, according to "modern medical science," died at the time of the accident.

8. I. A. Richards, *Principles of Literary Criticism* (Harcourt, Brace, New York, 1948), p. 40.

9. Nevertheless it is to be recalled that in our early history it was customary to condition the exemption of conscientious objectors from military service on their providing a substitute or the money necessary to engage one. See J. Cardozo, in *Hamilton v. Regents,* 293 U.S. 245, 266–277 (1934).

10. D. Sanders and J. Dukeminier, "Medical Advance and Legal Lag: Hemodialysis and Kidney Transplantation," *U. C. L. A. Law Rev.* 15 (1968): pp. 357, 410–413.

11. *Idem* at pp. 366–380.

12. See Note, "Patient Selection for Artificial and Transplant Organs," *Harv. Law Rev.* 82 (1969): pp. 1322, 1331–1337.

NICHOLAS RESCHER

The Allocation of Exotic Medical Lifesaving Therapy *

I. THE PROBLEM

Technological progress has in recent years transformed the limits of the possible in medical therapy. However, the elevated state of sophistication of modern medical technology has brought the economists' classic problem of scarcity in its wake as an unfortunate side product. The enormously sophisticated and complex equipment and the highly trained teams of experts requisite for its utilization are scarce resources in relation to potential demand. The administrators of the great medical institutions that preside over these scarce resources thus come to be faced increasingly with the awesome choice: *Whose life to save?*

A (somewhat hypothetical) paradigm example of this problem may be sketched within the following set of definitive assumptions: We suppose that persons in some particular medically morbid condition are "mortally afflicted": It is virtually certain that they will die within a short time period (say ninety days). We assume that some very complex course of treatment (e.g., a heart transplant) represents a substantial probability of life prolongation for persons in this mortally afflicted condition. We assume that the facilities available in terms of human resources, mechanical instrumentalities, and requisite materials (e.g., hearts in the case of a heart transplant) make it possible to give a certain treatment—this "exotic (medical) lifesaving therapy," or ELT for short—to a certain, relatively small number of people. And finally we assume that a substantially greater pool of people in the mortally afflicted condition is at hand. The problem then may be formulated as follows: How is one to select within the pool of afflicted patients the ones to be given the ELT treatment in question; how to select those "whose lives are to be saved"?

* From *Ethics,* Vol. 79 (1969), pp. 173–186. Copyright 1969 by The University of Chicago Press. Reprinted by permission of the author, Nicholas Rescher, and the publisher, The University Of Chicago Press.

Faced with many candidates for an ELT process that can be made available to only a few, doctors and medical administrators confront the decision of who is to be given a chance at survival and who is, in effect, to be condemned to die.

As has already been implied, the "heroic" variety of spare-part surgery can pretty well be assimilated to this paradigm. One can foresee the time when heart transplantation, for example, will have become pretty much a routine medical procedure, albeit on a very limited basis, since a cardiac surgeon with the technical competence to transplant hearts can operate at best a rather small number of times each week and the elaborate facilities for such operations will most probably exist on a modest scale. Moreover, in "spare-part" surgery there is always the problem of availability of the "spare parts" themselves. A report in one British newspaper gives the following picture: "Of the 150,000 who die of heart disease each year [in the U.K.], Mr. Donald Longmore, research surgeon at the National Heart Hospital [in London] estimates that 22,000 might be eligible for heart surgery. Another 30,000 would need heart and lung transplants. But there are probably only between 7,000 and 14,000 potential donors a year." [1] Envisaging this situation in which at the very most something like one in four heart-malfunction victims can be saved, we clearly confront a problem in ELT allocation.

A perhaps even more drastic case in point is afforded by long-term haemodialysis, an ongoing process by which a complex device—an "artificial kidney machine"—is used periodically in cases of chronic renal failure to substitute for a non-functional kidney in "cleaning" potential poisons from the blood. Only a few major institutions have chronic haemodialysis units, whose complex operation is an extremely expensive proposition. For the present and the foreseeable future the situation is that "the number of places available for chronic haemodialysis is hopelessly inadequate." [2]

The traditional medical ethos has insulated the physician against facing the very existence of this problem. When swearing the Hippocratic Oath, he commits himself to work for the benefit of the sick in "whatsoever house I enter." [3] In taking this stance, the physician substantially renounces the explicit choice of saving certain lives rather than others. Of course, doctors have always in fact had to face such choices on the battlefield or in times of disaster, but there the issue had to be resolved hurriedly, under pressure, and in circumstances in which the very nature of the case effectively precluded calm deliberation by the decision maker as well as criticism by others. In sharp contrast, however, cases of the type we have postulated in the present discussion arise predictably, and represent choices to be made deliberately and "in cold blood."

It is, to begin with, appropriate to remark that this problem is not fundamentally a medical problem. For when there are sufficiently many afflicted candidates for ELT then—so we may assume—there will also be more than enough for whom the purely medical grounds for ELT allocation are decisively strong in any individual case, and just about equally strong throughout the group. But in this circumstance a selection of some afflicted patients over and against others cannot *ex hypothesi* be made on the basis of purely medical considerations.

The selection problem, as we have said, is in substantial measure not a medical one. It is a problem *for* medical men, which must somehow be solved by them, but that does not make it a medical issue—any more than the problem of hospital building is a medical issue. As a problem it belongs to the category of philosophical problems—specifically a problem of moral philosophy or ethics. Structurally, it bears a substantial kinship with those issues in this field that revolve about the notorious whom-to-save-on-the-lifeboat and whom-to-throw-to-the-wolves-pursuing-the-sled questions. But whereas questions of this just-indicated sort are artificial, hypothetical, and far-fetched, the ELT issue poses a *genuine* policy question for the responsible administrators in medical institutions, indeed a question that threatens to become commonplace in the foreseeable future.

Now what the medical administrator needs to have, and what the philosopher is presumably *ex officio* in a position to help in providing, is a body of *rational guidelines* for making choices in these literally life-or-death situations. This is an issue in which many interested parties have a substantial stake, including the responsible decision maker who wants to satisfy his conscience that he is acting in a reasonable way. Moreover, the family and associates of the man who is turned away—to say nothing of the man himself—have the right to an acceptable explanation. And indeed even the general public wants to know that what is being done is fitting and proper. All of these interested parties are entitled to insist that a reasonable code of operating principles provides a defensible rationale for making the life-and-death choices involved in ELT.

II. THE TWO TYPES OF CRITERIA

Two distinguishable types of criteria are bound up in the issue of making ELT choices. We shall call these *Criteria of Inclusion* and *Criteria of Comparison*, respectively. The distinction at issue here requires some explanation. We can think of the selection as being made by a two-stage process: (1) the selection from among all possible candidates (by a suitable screening process) of a group to be taken under serious consideration as candidates for therapy, and then (2) the actual singling out, within this group, of the particular individuals to whom therapy is to be given. Thus the first process narrows down the range of comparative choice by eliminating *en bloc* whole categories of potential candidates. The second process calls for a more refined, case-by-case comparison of those candidates that remain. By means of the first set of criteria one forms a selection group; by means of the second set, an actual selection is made within this group.

Thus what we shall call a "selection system" for the choice of patients to receive therapy of the ELT type will consist of criteria of these two kinds. Such a system will be acceptable only when the reasonableness of its component criteria can be established.

III. ESSENTIAL FEATURES OF AN ACCEPTABLE ELT SELECTION SYSTEM

To qualify as reasonable, an ELT selection must meet two important "regulative" requirements: it must be *simple* enough to be readily intelligible, and it must be *plausible,* that is, patently reasonable in a way that can be apprehended easily and without involving ramified subtleties. Those medical administrators responsible for ELT choices must follow a modus operandi that virtually all the people involved can readily understand to be acceptable (at a reasonable level of generality, at any rate). Appearances are critically important here. It is not enough that the choice be made in a *justifiable* way; it must be possible for people—*plain* people—to "see" (i.e., understand without elaborate teaching or indoctrination) that *it is justified,* insofar as any mode of procedure can be justified in cases of this sort.

One "constitutive" requirement is obviously an essential feature of a reasonable selection system: all of its component criteria—those of inclusion and those of comparison alike—must be reasonable in the sense of being *rationally defensible.* The ramifications of this requirement call for detailed consideration. But one of its aspects should be noted without further ado: it must be *fair*—it must treat relevantly like cases alike, leaving no room for "influence" or favoritism, etc.

IV. THE BASIC SCREENING STAGE: CRITERIA OF INCLUSION (AND EXCLUSION)

Three sorts of considerations are prominent among the plausible criteria of inclusion/exclusion at the basic screening stage: the constituency factor, the progress-of-science factor, and the prospect-of-success factor.

A. THE CONSTITUENCY FACTOR

It is a "fact of life" that ELT can be available only in the institutional setting of a hospital or medical institute or the like. Such institutions generally have normal clientele boundaries. A veterans' hospital will not concern itself primarily with treating nonveterans, a children's hospital cannot be expected to accommodate the "senior citizen," an army hospital can regard college professors as outside its sphere. Sometimes the boundaries are geographic—a state hospital may admit only residents of a certain state. (There are, of course, indefensible constituency principles— say race or religion, party membership, or ability to pay; and there are cases of borderline legitimacy, e.g., sex.[4]) A medical institution is justified in considering for ELT only persons within its own constituency, provided this constituency is constituted upon a defensible basis. Thus the haemodialysis selection committee in Seattle "agreed to consider only those applications who were residents of the state of Washington. . . . They justified this stand on the grounds that since the basic research . . . had been done at . . . a state-supported institution—the people whose taxes had paid for the research should be its first beneficiaries." [5]

While thus insisting that constituency considerations represent a valid and legitimate factor in ELT selection, I do feel there is much to be said for minimizing their role in life-or-death cases. Indeed a refusal to recognize them at all is a significant part of medical tradition, going back to the very oath of Hippocrates. They represent a departure from the ideal arising with the institutionalization of medicine, moving it away from its original status as an art practiced by an individual practitioner.

B. THE PROGRESS-OF-SCIENCE FACTOR

The needs of medical research can provide a second valid principle of inclusion. The research interests of the medical staff in relation to the specific nature of the cases at issue is a significant consideration. It may be important for the progress of medical science—and thus of potential benefit to many persons in the future—to determine how effective the ELT at issue is with diabetics or persons over sixty or with a negative RH factor. Considerations of this sort represent another type of legitimate factor in ELT selection.

A very definitely *borderline* case under this head would revolve around the question of a patient's willingness to pay, not in monetary terms, but in offering himself as an experimental subject, say by contracting to return at designated times for a series of tests substantially unrelated to his own health, but yielding data of importance to medical knowledge in general.

C. THE PROSPECT-OF-SUCCESS FACTOR

It may be that while the ELT at issue is not without *some* effectiveness in general, it has been established to be highly effective only with patients in certain specific categories (e.g., females under forty of a specific blood type). This difference in effectiveness—in the absolute or in the probability of success—is (we assume) so marked as to constitute virtually a difference in kind rather than in degree. In this case, it would be perfectly legitimate to adopt the general rule of making the ELT at issue available only or primarily to persons in this substantial-promise-of-success category. (It is on grounds of this sort that young children and persons over fifty are generally ruled out as candidates for haemodialysis.)

We have maintained that the three factors of constituency, progress of science, and prospect of success represent legitimate criteria of inclusion for ELT selection. But it remains to examine the considerations which legitimate them. The legitimating factors are in the final analysis practical or pragmatic in nature. From the practical angle it is advantageous—indeed to some extent necessary—that the arrangements governing medical institutions should embody certain constituency principles. It makes good pragmatic and utilitarian sense that progress-of-science considerations should be operative here. And, finally, the practical aspect is reinforced by a whole host of other considerations—including moral ones —in supporting the prospect-of-success criterion. The workings of each of these factors are of course conditioned by the ever-present element of limited availability. They are operative only in this context, that is, prospect of success is a legitimate consideration at all only because we are dealing with a situation of scarcity.

V. THE FINAL SELECTION STAGE: CRITERIA OF SELECTION

Five sorts of elements must, as we see it, figure primarily among the plausible criteria of selection that are to be brought to bear in further screening the group constituted after application of the criteria of inclusion: the relative-likelihood-of success factor, the life-expectancy factor, the family role factor, the potential-contributions factor, and the services-rendered factor. The first two represent the *biomedical* aspect, the second three the *social* aspect.

A. THE RELATIVE-LIKELIHOOD-OF-SUCCESS FACTOR

It is clear that the relative likelihood of success is a legitimate and appropriate factor in making a selection within the group of qualified patients that are to receive ELT. This is obviously one of the considerations that must count very significantly in a reasonable selection procedure.

The present criterion is of course closely related to item *C* of the preceding section. There we were concerned with prospect-of-success considerations categorically and *en bloc*. Here at present they come into play in a particularized case-by-case comparison among individuals. If the therapy at issue is not a once-and-for-all proposition and requires ongoing treatment, cognate considerations must be brought in. Thus, for example, in the case of a chronic ELT procedure such as haemodialysis it would clearly make sense to give priority to patients with a potentially reversible condition (who would thus need treatment for only a fraction of their remaining lives).

B. THE LIFE-EXPECTANCY FACTOR

Even if the ELT is "successful" in the patient's case he may, considering his age and/or other aspects of his general medical condition, look forward to only a very short probable future life. This is obviously another factor that must be taken into account.

C. THE FAMILY ROLE FACTOR

A person's life is a thing of importance not only to himself but to others—friends, associates, neighbors, colleagues, etc. But his (or her) relationship to his immediate family is a thing of unique intimacy and significance. The nature of his relationship to his wife, children, and parents, and the issue of their financial and psychological dependence upon him, are obviously matters that deserve to be given weight in the ELT selection process. Other things being anything like equal, the mother of minor children must take priority over the middle-age bachelor.

D. THE POTENTIAL FUTURE-CONTRIBUTIONS FACTOR (PROSPECTIVE SERVICE)

In "choosing to save" one life rather than another, "the society," through the mediation of the particular medical institution in question—which should certainly look upon itself as a trustee for the social interest—is clearly warranted in considering the likely pattern of future *services to be rendered* by the patient (adequate recovery assumed), considering his age, talent, training, and past record of performance. In its allocations of ELT, society "invests" a scarce resource in one person as against another and is thus entitled to look to the probable prospective "return" on its investment.

It may well be that a thoroughly egalitarian society is reluctant to put someone's social contribution into the scale in situations of the sort at issue. One popular article states that "the most difficult standard would be the candidate's value to society," and goes on to quote someone who said: "You can't just pick a brilliant painter over a laborer. The average citizen would be quickly eliminated." [6] But what if it were not a brilliant painter but a brilliant surgeon or medical researcher that was at issue? One wonders if the author of the *obiter dictum* that one "can't just pick" would still feel equally sure of his ground. In any case, the fact that the standard is difficult to apply is certainly no reason for not attempting to apply it. The problem of ELT selection is inevitably burdened with difficult standards.

Some might feel that in assessing a patient's value to society one should ask not only who if permitted to continue living can make the greatest contribution to society in some creative or constructive way, but also who by dying would leave behind the greatest burden on society in assuming the discharge of their residual responsibilities.[7] Certainly the philosophical utilitarian would give equal weight to both these considerations. Just here is where I would part ways with orthodox utilitarianism. For—though this is not the place to do so—I should be prepared to argue that a civilized society has an obligation to promote the furtherance of positive achievements in cultural and related areas even if this means the assumption of certain added burdens.[8]

E. THE PAST SERVICES-RENDERED FACTOR (RETROSPECTIVE SERVICE)

A person's services to another person or group have always been taken to constitute a valid basis for a claim upon this person or group—of course a moral and not necessarily a legal claim. Society's obligation for the recognition and reward of services rendered—an obligation whose discharge is also very possibly conducive to self-interest in the long run—is thus another factor to be taken into account. This should be viewed as a morally necessary correlative of the previously considered factor of *prospective* service. It would be morally indefensible of society in effect to say: "Never mind about services you rendered yesterday—it is only the services to be rendered tomorrow that will count with us today." We live in very future-oriented times, constantly preoccupied in a distinctly utilitarian way with future satisfactions. And this disinclines us to give much recognition to past services. But parity considerations of the sort just adduced indicate that such recognition should be given *on grounds of equity.* No doubt a justification for given weight to services rendered can also be attempted along utilitarian lines. ("The reward of past services rendered spurs people on to greater future efforts and is thus socially advantageous in the long-run future.") In saying that past services should be counted "on grounds of equity"—rather than "on grounds of utility"—I take the view that even if this utilitarian defense could somehow be shown to be fallacious, I should still be prepared to maintain the propriety of taking services rendered into account. The position does not rest on a utilitarian basis and so would not collapse with the removal of such a basis.[9]

As we have said, these five factors fall into three groups: the biomedical factors A and B, the familial factor C, and the social factors D and E. With items A and B the need for a detailed analysis of the medical considerations comes to the fore. The age of the patient, his medical history, his physical and psychological condition, his specific disease, etc., will all need to be taken into exact account. These biomedical factors represent technical issues: they call for the physicians' expert judgment and the medical statisticians' hard data. And they are ethically uncontroversial factors—their legitimacy and appropriateness are evident from the very nature of the case.

Greater problems arise with the familial and social factors. They involve intangibles that are difficult to judge. How is one to develop subcriteria for weighing the relative social contributions of (say) an architect or a librarian or a mother of young children? And they involve highly problematic issues. (For example, should good moral character be rated a plus and bad a minus in judging services rendered?) And there is something strikingly unpleasant in grappling with issues of this sort for people brought up in times greatly inclined towards maxims of the type "Judge not!" and "Live and let live!" All the same, in the situation that concerns us here such distasteful problems must be faced, since a failure to choose to save some is tantamount to sentencing all. Unpleasant choices are intrinsic to the problem of ELT selection; they are of the very essence of the matter.[10]

But is reference to all these factors indeed inevitable? The justification for taking account of the medical factors is pretty obvious. But why should the social aspect of services rendered and to be rendered be taken into account at all? The answer is that they must be taken into account not from the *medical* but from the *ethical* point of view. Despite disagreement on many fundamental issues, moral philosophers of the present day are pretty well in consensus that the justification of human actions is to be sought largely and primarily—if not exclusively—in the principles of utility and of justice.[11] But utility requires reference of services to be rendered and justice calls for a recognition of services that have been rendered. Moral considerations would thus demand recognition of these two factors. (This, of course, still leaves open the question of whether the point of view provides a valid basis of action: Why base one's actions upon moral principles?—or, to put it bluntly—Why be moral? The present paper is, however, hardly the place to grapple with so fundamental an issue, which has been canvassed in the literature of philosophical ethics since Plato.)

VI. MORE THAN MEDICAL ISSUES ARE INVOLVED

An active controversy has of late sprung up in medical circles over the question of whether non-physician laymen should be given a role in ELT selection (in the specific context of chronic haemodialysis). One physician writes: "I think that the assessment of the candidates should be made by a senior doctor on the [dialysis] unit, but I am sure that it would be helpful to him—both in sharing responsibility and in avoiding personal pressure—if a small unnamed group of people [presumably including laymen] officially made the final decision. I visualize the doctor bringing the data to the group, explaining the points in relation to each case, and obtaining their approval of his order of priority.[12]

Essentially this procedure of a selection committee of laymen has for some years been in use

in one of the most publicized chronic dialysis units, that of the Swedish Hospital of Seattle, Washington.[13] Many physicians are apparently reluctant to see the choice of allocation of medical therapy pass out of strictly medical hands. Thus in a recent symposium on the "Selection of Patients for Haemodialysis," [14] Dr. Ralph Shakman writes: "Who is to implement the selection? In my opinion it must ultimately be the responsibility of the consultants in charge of the renal units . . . I can see no reason for delegating this responsibility to lay persons. Surely the latter would be better employed if they could be persuaded to devote their time and energy to raise more and more money for us to spend on our patients." [15] Other contributors to this symposium strike much the same note. Dr. F. M. Parsons writes: "In an attempt to overcome . . . difficulties in selection some have advocated introducing certain specified lay people into the discussions. Is it wise? I doubt whether a committee of this type can adjudicate as satisfactorily as two medical colleagues, particularly as successful therapy involves close cooperation between doctor and patient." [16] And Dr. M. A. Wilson writes in the same symposium: "The suggestion has been made that lay panels should select individuals for dialysis from among a group who are medically suitable. Though this would relieve the doctor-in-charge of a heavy load of responsibility, it would place the burden on those who have no personal knowledge and have to base their judgments on medical or social reports. I do not believe this would result in better decisions for the group or improve the doctor-patient relationship in individual cases." [17]

But no amount of flag waving about the doctor's facing up to his responsibility—or prostrations before the idol of the doctor-patient relationship and reluctance to admit laymen into the sacred precincts of the conference chambers of medical consultations—can obscure the essential fact that ELT selection is not a wholly medical problem. When there are more than enough places in an ELT program to accommodate all who need it, then it will clearly be a medical question to decide who does have the need and which among these would successfully respond. But when an admitted gross insufficiency of places exists, when there are ten or fifty or one hundred highly eligible candidates for each place in the program, then it is unrealistic to take the view that purely medical criteria can furnish a sufficient basis for selection. The question of ELT selection becomes serious as a phenomenon of scale—because, as more candidates present themselves, strictly medical factors are increasingly less adequate as a selection criterion precisely because by numerical category-crowding there will be more and more cases whose "status is much the same" so far as purely medical considerations go.

The ELT selection problem clearly poses issues that transcend the medical sphere because—in the nature of the case—many residual issues remain to be dealt with once *all* of the medical questions have been faced. Because of this there is good reason why laymen as well as physicians should be involved in the selection process. Once the medical considerations have been brought to bear, fundamental social issues remain to be resolved. The instrumentalities of ELT have been created through the social investment of scarce resources, and the interests of the society deserve to play a role in their utilization. As representatives of their social interests, lay opinions should function to complement and supplement medical views once the proper arena of medical considerations is left behind.[18] Those physicians who have urged the presence of lay members on selection panels can, from this point of view, be recognized as having seen the issue in proper perspective.

One physician has argued against lay representation on selection panels for haemodialysis as follows: "If the doctor advises dialysis and the lay panel refuses, the patient will regard this as a death sentence passed by an anonymous court from which he has no right of appeal."[19] But this drawback is not specific to the use of a lay panel. Rather, it is a feature inherent in every *selection* procedure, regardless of whether the selection is done by the head doctor of the unit, by a panel of physicians, etc. No matter who does the selecting among patients recommended for dialysis, the feelings of the patient who has been rejected (and knows it) can be expected to be much the same, provided that he recognizes the actual nature of the choice (and is not deceived by the possibly convenient but ultimately poisonous fiction that because the selection was made by physicians it was made entirely on medical grounds).

In summary, then, the question of ELT selection would appear to be one that is in its very nature heavily laden with issues of medical research, practice, and administration. But it will not be a question that can be resolved on solely medical grounds. Strictly social issues of justice and utility will invariably arise in this area —questions going outside the medical area in whose resolution medical laymen can and should play a substantial role.

VII. THE INHERENT IMPERFECTION (NON-OPTIMALITY) OF ANY SELECTION SYSTEM

Our discussion to this point of the design of a selection system for ELT has left a gap that is a very fundamental and serious omission. We have argued that five factors must be taken into substantial and explicit account:

A. *Relative likelihood of success.*—Is the chance of the treatment's being "successful" to be rated as high, good, average, etc.?[20]

B. *Expectancy of future life.*—Assuming the "success" of the treatment, how much longer does the patient stand a good chance (75 per cent or better) of living—considering his age and general condition?

C. *Family role.*—To what extent does the patient have responsibilities to others in his immediate family?

D. *Social contributions rendered.*—Are the patient's past services to his society outstanding, substantial, average, etc.?

E. *Social contributions to be rendered.*—Considering his age, talents, training, and past record of performance, is there a substantial probability that the patient will—*adequate recovery being assumed*—render in the future services to his society that can be characterized as outstanding, substantial, average, etc.?

This list is clearly insufficient for the construction of a reasonable selection system, since that would require not only *that these factors be taken into account* (somehow or other), but—going beyond this—would specify *a specific set of procedures for taking account of them.* The specific procedures that would constitute such a system would have to take account of the interrelationship of these factors (e.g., *B* and *E*), and to set out exact guidelines as to the relevant weight that is to be given to each of them. This is something our discussion has not as yet considered.

In fact, I should want to maintain that there is no such thing here as a single rationally superior selection system. The position of affairs seems to me to be something like this: (1) It is necessary (for reasons already canvassed) to *have* a system, and to have a system that is rationally defensible, and (2) to be rationally defensible, this system must take the factors *A–E* into substantial and explicit account. But (3) the exact manner in which a rationally defensible system takes account of these factors cannot be fixed in any one specific way on the basis of general considerations. Any of the variety of ways that give *A–E* "their due" will be acceptable and viable. One cannot hope to find within this range of workable systems some one that is *optimal* in relation to the alternatives. There is no one system that does "the (uniquely) best"—only a variety of systems that do "as well as one can expect to do" in cases of this sort.

The situation is structurally very much akin to that of rules of partition of an estate among the relations of a decedent. It is important *that there be* such rules. And it is reasonable that spouse, children, parents, siblings, etc., be taken account of in these rules. But the question of the exact method of division—say that when the decedent has neither living spouse nor living children then his estate is to be divided, dividing 60 per cent between parents, 40 per cent between siblings versus dividing 90 per cent between parents, 10 per cent between siblings—cannot be settled on the basis of any general abstract considerations of reasonableness. Within broad limits, a *variety* of resolutions are all perfectly acceptable—so that no one procedure can justifiably be regarded as "the (uniquely) best" because it is superior to all others.[21]

VIII. A POSSIBLE BASIS FOR A REASONABLE SELECTION SYSTEM

Having said that there is no such thing as *the optimal* selection system for ELT, I want now to sketch out the broad features of what I would regard as *one acceptable* system.

The basis for the system would be a point rating. The scoring here at issue would give roughly equal weight to the medical considerations (*A* and *B*) in comparison with the extramedical considerations (*C* = family role, *D* = services rendered, and *E* = services to be rendered), also giving roughly equal weight to the three items involved here (*C, D,* and *E*). The result of such a scoring procedure would provide the essential *starting point* of our ELT selection mechanism. I deliberately say "starting point" because it seems to me that one should not follow the results of this scoring in an *automatic* way. I would propose that the actual selection should only be guided but not actually be dictated by this scoring procedure, along lines now to be explained.

IX. THE DESIRABILITY OF INTRODUCING AN ELEMENT OF CHANCE

The detailed procedure I would propose—not of course as optimal (for reasons we have seen), but as eminently acceptable—would combine the scoring procedure just discussed with an element of chance. The resulting selection system would function as follows:

1. First the criteria of inclusion of Section IV above would be applied to constitute a *first phase selection group*—which (we shall suppose) is substantially larger than the number *n* of persons who can actually be accommodated with ELT.

2. Next the criteria of selection of Section V are brought to bear via a scoring procedure of the type described in Section VIII. On this basis a *second phase selection group* is constituted which is only *somewhat* larger—say by a third or a half—than the critical number *n* at issue.

3. If this second phase selection group is relatively homogeneous as regards rating by the scoring procedure—that is, if there are no really major disparities within this group (as would be likely if the initial group was significantly larger than *n*)—then the final selection is made by *random* selection of *n* persons from within this group.

This introduction of the element of chance—in what could be dramatized as a "lottery of life and death"—must be justified. The fact is that such a procedure would bring with it three substantial advantages.

First, as we have argued above (in Section VII), any acceptable selection system is inherently nonoptimal. The introduction of the element of chance prevents the results that life-and-death choices are made by the automatic appliction of an admittedly imperfect selection method.

Second, a recourse to chance would doubtless make matters easier for the rejected patient and those who have a specific interest in him. It would surely be quite hard for them to accept his exclusion by relatively mechanical application of objective criteria in whose implementation subjective judgment is involved. But the circumstances of life have conditioned us to accept the workings of chance and to tolerate the element of luck (good or bad): human life is an inherently contingent process. Nobody, after all, has an absolute right to ELT—but most of us would feel that we have "every bit as much right" to it as anyone else in significantly similar circumstances. The introduction of the element of chance assures a like handling of like cases over the widest possible area that seems reasonable in the circumstances.

Third (and perhaps least), such a recourse to random selection does much to relieve the administrators of the selection system of the awesome burden of ultimate and absolute responsibility.

These three considerations would seem to build up a substantial case for introducing the element of chance into the mechanism of the system for ELT selection in a way limited and circumscribed by other weightier considerations, along some such lines as those set forth above.[22]

It should be recognized that this injection of *man-made* chance supplements the element of *natural* chance that is present inevitably and in any case (apart from the role of change in singling out certain persons as victims for the affliction at issue). As F. M. Parsons has observed: "any vacancies [in an ELT program—specifically haemodialysis] will be filled immediately by the first suitable patients, even though their claims for therapy may subsequently prove less than those of other patients refused later."[23] Life is a chancy business and even the most rational of human arrangements can cover this over to a very limited extent at best.

NOTES

1. Christine Doyle, "Spare-Part Heart Surgeons Worried by Their Success," *Observer,* May 12, 1968.

2. J. D. N. Nabarro, "Selection of Patients for Haemodialysis," *British Medical Journal* (March 11, 1967), p. 623. Although several thousand patients die in the U.K. each year from renal failure—there are about thirty new cases per million of population—only 10 per cent of these can for the foreseeable future be accommodated with chronic haemodialysis. Kidney transplantation—itself a very tricky procedure—

cannot make a more than minor contribution here. As this article goes to press, I learn that patients can be maintained in home dialysis at an operating cost about half that of maintaining them in a hospital dialysis unit (roughly an $8,000 minimum). In the United States, around 7,000 patients with terminal uremia who could benefit from haemodialysis evolve yearly. As of mid-1968, some 1,000 of these can be accommodated in existing hospital units. By June 1967, a world-wide total of some 120 patients were in treatment by home dialysis. (Data from a forthcoming paper, "Home Dialysis," by C. M. Conty and H. V. Murdaugh. See also R. A. Baillod *et. al.,* "Overnight Haemodialysis in the Home," *Proceedings of the European Dialysis and Transplant Association,* VI [1965], 99 ff).

3. For the Hippocratic Oath see *Hippocrates: Works* (Loeb ed.; London, 1959), I, p. 298.

4. Another example of borderline legitimacy is posed by an endowment "with strings attached," e.g., "In accepting this legacy the hospital agrees to admit and provide all needed treatment for any direct descendent of myself, its founder."

5. Shana Alexander, "They Decide Who Lives, Who Dies," *Life,* LIII (November 9, 1962), 102–25 (see p. 107).

6. Lawrence Lader, "Who Has the Right To Live?" *Good Housekeeping* (January 1968), p. 144.

7. This approach could thus be continued to embrace the previous factor, that of family role, the preceding item *(C).*

8. Moreover a doctrinaire utilitarian would presumably be willing to withdraw a continuing mode of ELT such as haemodialysis from a patient to make room for a more promising candidate who came to view at a later stage and who could not otherwise be accommodated. I should be unwilling to adopt this course, partly on grounds of utility (with a view to the demoralization of insecurity), partly on the nonutilitarian ground that a "moral commitment" has been made and must be honored.

9. Of course the difficult question remains of the relative weight that should be given to prospective and retrospective service in cases where these factors conflict. There is good reason to treat them on a par.

10. This in the symposium on "Selection of Patients for Haemodialysis," *British Medical Journal* (March 11, 1967), pp. 622–24. F. M. Parsons writes: "But other forms of selecting patients [distinct from first come, first served] are suspect in my view if they imply evaluation of man by man. What criteria could be used? Who could justify a claim that the life of a mayor would be more valuable than that of the humblest citizen of his borough? Whatever we may think as individuals none of us is indispensable." But having just set out this hard-line view he immediately backs away from it: "On the other hand, to assume that there was little to choose between Alexander Fleming and Adolf Hitler . . . would be nonsense, and we should be naive if we were to pretend that we could not be influenced by their achievements and characters if we had to choose between the two of them. Whether we like it or not we cannot escape the fact that this kind of selection for long-term haemodialysis will be required until very large sums of money become available for equipment and services [so that *everyone* who needs treatment can be accommodated]."

11. The relative fundamentality of these principles is, however, a substantially disputed issue.

12. J. D. N. Nabarro, *op. cit.,* p. 622.

13. See Shana Alexander, *op. cit.*

14. *British Medical Journal* (March 11, 1967), pp. 622–24.

15. *Ibid.,* p. 624. Another contributor writes in the same symposium, "The selection of the few [to receive haemodialysis] is proving very difficult—a true 'Doctor's Dilemma'—for almost everybody would agree that this must be a medical

decision, preferably reached by consultation among colleagues" (Dr. F. M. Parsons, *ibid.,* p. 623).

16. "The Selection of Patients for Haemodialysis," *op. cit.* (n. 10 above), p. 623.

17. Dr. Wilson's article concludes with the perplexing suggestion—wildly beside the point given the structure of the situation at issue—that "the final decision will be made by the patient." But this contention is only marginally more ludicrous than Parson's contention that in selecting patients for haemodialysis "gainful employment in a well chosen occupation is necessary to achieve the best results" since "only the minority wish to live on charity" *(ibid.).*

18. To say this is of course not to deny that such questions of applied medical ethics will invariably involve a host of medical considerations—it is only to insist that extramedical considerations will also invariably be at issue.

19. M. A. Wilson, "Selection of Patients for Haemodialysis," *op. cit.,* p. 624.

20. In the case of an ongoing treatment involving complex procedure and dietary and other mode-of-life restrictions —and chronic haemodialysis definitely falls into this category—the patient's psychological makeup, his willpower to "stick with it" in the face of substantial discouragements— will obviously also be a substantial factor here. The man who gives up, takes not his life alone, but (figuratively speaking) also that of the person he replaced in the treatment schedule.

21. To say that acceptable solutions can range over broad limits is *not* to say that there are no limits at all. It is an obviously intriguing and fundamental problem to raise the question of the factors that set these limits. This complex issue cannot be dealt with adequately here. Suffice it to say that considerations regarding precedent and people's expectations,

factors of social utility, and matters of fairness and sense of justice all come into play.

22. One writer has mooted the suggestion that: "Perhaps the right thing to do, difficult as it may be to accept, is to select [for haemodialysis] from among the medical and psychologically qualified patients on a strictly random basis" (S. Gorovitz,"Ethics and the Allocation of Medical Resources," *Medical Research Engineering,* V [1966], p. 7). Outright random selection would, however, seem indefensible because of its refusal to give weight to considerations which, under the circumstances, *deserve* to be given weight. The proposed procedure of superimposing a certain degree of randomness upon the rational-choice criteria would seem to combine the advantages of the two without importing the worst defects of either.

23. "Selection of Patients for Haemodialysis," *op. cit.,* p. 623. The question of whether a patient for chronic treatment should ever be terminated from the program (say if he contracts cancer) poses a variety of difficult ethical problems with which we need not at present concern ourselves. But it does seem plausible to take the (somewhat antiutilitarian) view that a patient should not be terminated simply because a "better qualified" patient comes along later on. It would seem that a quasi-contractual relationship has been created through established expectations and reciprocal understandings, and that the situation is in this regard akin to that of the man who, having undertaken to sell his house to one buyer, cannot afterward unilaterally undo this arrangement to sell it to a higher bidder who "needs it worse" (thus maximizing the over-all utility).

24. I acknowledge with thanks the help of Miss Hazel Johnson, Reference Librarian at the University of Pittsburgh Library, in connection with the bibliography.

Suggestions for Further Reading

Ake, C., "Justice as Equality," *Philosophy and Public Affairs,* Vol. 5 (1975), pp. 69–89.

Baldwin, R. W., *Social Justice* (1966).

Barry, Brian, *The Liberal Theory of Justice: A Critical Examination of the Principal Doctrines in 'A Theory of Justice' by John Rawls* (1973).

Bayles, Michael, "Compensatory Reverse Discrimination in Hiring," in *Social Theory and Practice,* Vol. 2 (1973), pp. 301–12.

Bayles, Michael, "Reparation to Wronged Groups," *Analysis,* Vol. 33 (1973).

Bedau, Hugo A., ed. *Justice and Equality* (1971).

Benn, S. I. and R. S. Peters, *Social Principles and the Democratic State* (1958), Chaps. 5, 6.

Bergler, E. and Meerloo, J. A. M., *Justice and Injustice* (1963).

Blackstone, W. T., "Reverse Discrimination and Compensatory Justice," *Social Theory and Practice,* Vol. 77 (1967).

Blackstone, W. T., "On the Meaning and Justification of the Equality Principle," *Ethics,* Vol. 3 (1975), pp. 253–288.

Bowie, Norman E., *Towards a New Theory of Distributive Justice* (1971).

Brandt, Richard B., *Ethical Theory* (1959), Chap. 16.

Brandt, Richard B., ed., *Social Justice* (1962).

Brown, Emerson, Falk, Freedman, "The Equal Rights Amendment: A Constitutional Basis for Equal Rights for Women," 80 *Yale L.J.* 871, (1971).

Buchanan, A., "Distributive Justice and Legitimate Expectations," *Philosophical Studies,* Vol. 28 (1975), pp. 419–25.

Cahn, Edmond, *The Sense of Injustice* (1949).

Childress, James F., "Who Shall Live When Not All Can Live?," *Soundings,* Vol. 53 (1970).

Cohen, M., Nagel, T., and Scanlon, T. (eds.), *Equality and Preferential Treatment* (1976).

Coleman, Jules, "Justice and Preferential Hiring," *The*

Journal of Critical Analysis, Vol. 5 (1973), pp. 27–30.

Daniels, Norman (ed.), *Reading Rawls* (1975).

DeFunis Symposium, 75 *Columbia Law Review* 483 (1975).

Ely, J. H., "Reverse Racial Discrimination," 41 *Univ. of Chicago Law Review* 723 (1974).

Feinberg, Joel, "Justice and Personal Desert," reprinted in *Doing and Deserving* (1970), pp. 55–94.

Feinberg, Joel, "Noncomparative Justice," *Philosophical Review,* Vol. LXXXIII (1974), pp. 297–338.

Feinberg, Joel, *Social Philosophy* (1973), Chap. 7.

Fiss, O. M., "Groups and the Equal Protection Clause," *Philosophy and Public Affairs,* Vol. 5 (1976), pp. 107–177.

Frankel, Charles, "The New Egalitarianism and the Old," *Commentary,* Vol. 56 (1973).

Freund, Paul A., "The Equal Rights Amendment is Not the Way," 6 *Harv. Civ. Rights—Civ. Lib. L. Rev.* 234 (1971).

Friedrich, C. J. and J. W. Chapman, eds., *Nomos VI: Justice* (1963).

Getman, J. G., "Emerging Constitutional Principle of Sexual Equality," 1972 *Supreme Court Review* 157.

Ginger, A. F. (ed.), *DeFunis vs. Odegaard and the University of Washington* (1974).

Ginsberg, Morris, *On Justice in Society* (1965).

Glazer, H., *Affirmative Discrimination* (1975).

Godwin, William, *Political Justice* (1890).

Gorovitz, Samuel *et al* (eds.), *Moral Problems in Medicine* (1976).

Greenawalt, K., "Judicial Scrutiny of 'Benign' Racial Preference in Law School Admissions," 75 *Columbia Law Review* 483 (1975).

Hardie, W. F., *Aristotle's Ethical Theory* (1968), Chap. X.

Hart, H. L. A., *The Concept of Law* (1961), Chaps. 5, 6.

Hart, H. L. A., "Rawls on Liberty and its Priority," 40 *Univ. of Chicago Law Review* (1973).

Held, Virginia, "John Locke on Robert Nozick." *Social Research* (1976).

Hobhouse, L. T., *Elements of Social Justice* (1922), Chaps. 5, 6.

Honoré, A. M., "Ownership," in Guest, A. G. (ed.), *Oxford Essays in Jurisprudence* (1971).

Honoré, A. M., "Social Justice," 8 *McGill L.J.* 78, (1962).

Hume, David, *An Enquiry Concerning the Principles of Morals* (1777), Chap. III.

Jencks, Christopher, *Inequality* (1972).

Kamenka, Eugene, *The Ethical Foundations of Marxism* (1962).

Katzner, Louis, "Presumptivist and Nonpresumptivist Principles of Formal Justice," *Ethics,* Vol. LXXXI (1971), pp. 253–58.

Kaufman, Walter, *Without Guilt and Justice* (1973), Chaps. 1–3.

Kelsen, Hans, *What is Justice?* (1957).

Kurland, Philip B., "The Equal Rights Amendment: Some Problems of Construction," 6 *Harv. Civ. Rights—Civ. Lib. L. Rev.* 243 (1971).

Lamont, W. D., *The Problems of Moral Judgment* (1946), Chap. 5.

Lewis, Anthony, *Gideon's Trumpet* (1964).

Lucas, J. R., *The Principles of Politics* (1966), Chaps. 28–9, 55–60.

Lyons, D., "On Formal Justice," 58 *Cornell Law Review* 833 (1973).

Lyons, David, *The Forms and Limits of Utilitarianism* (1965), Chap. 5.

Lyons, David, "Rights Against Humanity," *Philosophical Review,* Vol. 85 (1976). Review of Nozick.

Lyons, David, "The Nature of the Contract Argument," 59 *Cornell Law Review* (1974), 1064.

Macleod, A. M., "Rawls's Theory of Justice" (1973) 1021.

Macpherson, C. B., *The Political Theory of Possessive Individualism: Hobbes to Locke* (1962).

Nagel, Thomas, "Equal Treatment and Compensatory Discrimination," *Philosophy and Public Affairs,* Vol. 2 (1973), pp. 348–63.

Nagel, Thomas, "Libertarianism Without Foundations" (Review of Nozick) 85 *Yale Law Journal* (1975) 136.

Nagel, Thomas, "Rawls on Justice," *Philosophical Review,* Vol. 82 (1973).

Narveson, Jan, *Morality and Utility* (1967), Chaps. 6, 7.

Nell, Onora, "Lifeboat Earth," *Philosophy and Public Affairs,* Vol. 4 (1975), pp. 273–292.

Newton, Lisa H., "Reverse Discrimination as Unjustified," *Ethics,* Vol. 83 (1973), pp. 308–312.

Nickel, J. W., "Preferential Policies in Hiring and Admissions: A Jurisprudential Approach," 75 *Columbia Law Review* 534 (1975).

Note, "Are Sex-Based Classifications Constitutionally Suspect?" 66 *Northwestern U.L. Rev.* 581 (1971).

Note, "Decline and Fall of the New Equal Protection: A Polemical Approach," 58 *Va. L. Rev.* 1489 (1972).

Note, "Legality of Homosexual Marriage," 82 *Yale L. J.* 573 (1973).

Note, "Pregnancy Discharges in the Military: The Air Force Experience," 86 *Harv. L. Rev.* 568 (1973).

Note, "Reverse Discrimination," 41 *U. Cincinnati L. Rev.* 250 (1972).

Note, "Scarce Resources," 69 *Columbia Law Review* 620 (1969).

Olafson, Frederick, A., ed., *Justice and Social Policy* (1961).

O'Neil, R. M., "Preferential Admissions," 80 *Yale Law Journal* 699 (1971).

Oppenheim, Felix E., "Egalitarianism as a Descriptive Concept," *American Philosophical Quarterly,* Vol. 7 (1970).

Outka, Gene, "Social Justice and Equal Access to Health Care," *Perspectives in Biology and Medicine* (1975), pp. 185–203.

Pennock, J. R. and Chapman, J. W., eds., Nomos IX: *Equality* (1967).

Perelman, Chaim, *The Idea of Justice and the Problem of Argument* (1963).

Perelman, Chaim, *Justice* (1967).

Piaget, Jean, *The Moral Judgment of the Child* (1932).

Posner, R. A., "De Funis Case and Constitutionality of Preferential Treatment of Minorities," 1974 *Supreme Court Review* 1.

Pritchard, Michael S., "Human Dignity and Justice," *Ethics,* Vol. 82 (1972).

Ramsey, Paul, *The Patient as Person* (1970), Chap. 7, "Choosing How to Choose: Patients and Spare Medical Resources."

Raphael, D. D., *Problems of Political Philosophy* (1970), Chap. 7.

Rashdall, Hastings, *Theory of Good and Evil* (1924), Vol. I, Chap. 8.

Rawls, John, *A Theory of Justice* (1972).

Rescher, Nicholas, *Distributive Justice* (1966).

Sandalow, Terrance, "Racial Preferences in Higher Education," 42 *Univ. of Chicago Law Review* 653 (1975).

Sartorius, Rolf E., *Individual Conduct and Social Norms* (1975).

Scanlon, Thomas M., Jr., "Nozick on Rights, Liberty, and Property," *Philosophy and Public Affairs,* Vol. 6 (1976), pp. 3–25.

Scanlon, Thomas M., Jr., "Rawls' Theory of Justice," 121 *Univ. of Pa. Law Review* (1973).

Sidgwick, Henry, *Elements of Politics,* Chap. 8, "Remedies for Wrongs."

Sidgwick, Henry, *The Methods of Ethics,* 7th Ed. (1874), Book I, Chap. V.

Simon, R., "Preferential Hiring," *Philosophy and Public Affairs,* Vol. 3 (1974), pp. 312–330.

Singer, P., "Famine, Affluence, and Morality," *Philosophy and Public Affairs,* Vol. I (1972), pp. 229–243.

Singer, Peter, "The Right to be Rich or Poor," *New York Review of Books,* (1975).

Slote, M. A., "Desert, Consent, and Justice," *Philosophy and Public Affairs,* Vol. 2 (1973).

Spiegelberg, Herbert, "'Accident of Birth': A Non-Utilitarian Motif in Mill's Philosophy," *Journal of the History of Ideas,* Vol. 22 (1961), pp. 475–92.

Spiegelberg, Herbert, "Good Fortune Obligates: Albert Schweitzer's Second Ethical Principle," *Ethics,* Vol. 85 (1975), pp. 227–34.

Spiegelberg, Herbert, "Human Dignity: A Challenge to Contemporary Philosophy," *Philosophy Forum,* Vol. 9 (1971).

Symposium, "De Funis: The Road Not Taken," 60 *Virginia Law Review* 917 (1974).

Symposium, "Equal Rights for Women: A Symposium on the Proposed Constitutional Amendment," 6 *Harv. Civ. Rights—Civ. Lib. L. Rev.* 215 (1971).

Tawney, R. H. *Equality* (1929).

Taylor, Paul W., "Reverse Discrimination and Compensatory Justice," *Analysis,* Vol. 33 (1973), pp. 177–182.

Thalberg, Irving, "Reverse Discrimination and the Future," *Philosophical Forum,* Vol. 5 (1973), pp. 294–308.

Thibaut, J., and Walder, L., "Procedural Justice as Fairness," 26 *Stanford Law Review* 1271 (1974).

Thomson, Judith J., "Preferential Hiring," *Philosophy and Public Affairs,* Vol. 2 (1973), pp. 364–84.

Varian, H., "Distributive Justice, Welfare Economics, and the Theory of Fairness," *Philosophy and Public Affairs,* Vol. 4 (1975), pp. 223–247.

Von Wright, G. H., *The Varieties of Goodness* (1963), Chap. X.

Williams, Bernard, "The Idea of Equality," in *Philosophy, Politics and Society,* 2nd series, ed. P. Laslett and W. G. Runciman (1962).

Wilson, John, *Equality* (1966).

Wolff, Robert Paul, *Understanding Rawls* (1976).

Woozley, A. D., "Injustice," *American Philosophical Quarterly,* Monograph No. 7 (1973), pp. 109–22.

Young, Michael, *The Rise of the Meritocracy* (1958).